# AWS

## Certified SysOps Adm̲...

### Study Guide

### Second Edition

# AWS
## Certified SysOps Administrator
### Study Guide
#### Second Edition

Sara Perrott

Brett McLaughlin

SYBEX®
A Wiley Brand

*I dedicate this book to my husband for his patience and encouragement throughout the writing process. Getting this book finished meant many missed nights in Azeroth; it's a labor of love for sure!*
*—Sara Perrott*

*This one is for Addie, who has literally grown up before my eyes while I've been working on this book. Addie, I'm so proud of you, and love you tons, even though you won't understand a word of what's in this giant tome.*
*—Brett McLaughlin*

# Acknowledgments

While a book may be a labor of love for an author, there is a fantastic team of people behind the author or authors that makes the book a reality. First off, a shout-out to our team at Wiley, who put in a lot of hard work to take the book from a manuscript to the finished book in front of you now. My gratitude to our editor, Adaobi Obi Tulton, who kept us on task and helped to polish the text. Another shout-out to our technical editor, John Mueller, whose guidance and keen eye helped to make this book better.

My personal thanks also to my agent, Carole Jelen, and to my coworkers, who put up with my need to take extra personal days to finish the book.

—Sara Perrott

Sara speaks the truth when she says that it's rarely clear to anyone but the authors just how much help is needed to pull off a book. In this case, Sara is both a great author and someone who came in to help when I was frankly drowning! She's made this book tremendously more valuable and you wouldn't have it in your hands without her saving the day.

Adaobi also deserves more praise than can fit into a short paragraph. From helpful comments to gentle nudges to (at times) much-needed, "Look, I really need that chapter, Brett," every email I received from Adaobi was right on time and just what was needed.

The rest of my thanks to the entire Wiley team, our technical editor, John, and my own agent (and Sara's), Carole. Until next time, when we can all do it again!

—Brett McLaughlin

# About the Authors

**Sara Perrott** is an information security professional with a systems and network engineering background. She shares her passion for all things information technology by teaching classes related to Windows Server, Amazon Web Services, networking, and virtualization, as well as other classes when needed at a local community college. She enjoys speaking at public events and presented most recently at the RSA Conference in 2019. Sara also enjoys technical editing and technical proofreading and has had the pleasure to work on a few projects doing this type of work.

When Sara is not working or writing, she enjoys spending time with her husband playing World of Warcraft, building robots, and playing with her ham radio. She also loves playing with her two pugs. Sara has a website where you can see some of the things she has been up to at www.saraperrott.com. You can also follow her on Twitter (@PerrottSara) and Facebook (@PerrottSara).

**Brett McLaughlin** has been working and writing in the technology space for over 20 years. Today, Brett's focus is squarely on cloud and enterprise computing. He has quickly become a trusted name in helping companies execute a migration to the cloud—and, in particular, Amazon Web Services—by translating confusing cloud concepts into a clear, executive-level vision. He is the chief technical officer (CTO) of Volusion, an e-commerce platform company based in Austin, Texas. Prior to Volusion, Brett has led large-scale cloud migrations for NASA's Earth Science program and the RockCreek Group's financial platform.

In addition to his work with technology, Brett is a gifted and in-demand author and video educator. In addition to numerous AWS-specific projects for Wiley, he has recently completed over 12 hours of certification training, also for Wiley, and is in preproduction on two cloud-based introductory courses for LinkedIn Learning. He is an AWS Certified Solutions Architect, Business Professional, and has managed the advancement of small businesses to AWS Partners, at both the standard and advanced tiers. You can find Brett online most easily at www.brettdmclaughlin.com.

# About the Technical Editor

**John Mueller** is a freelance author and technical editor. He has writing in his blood, having produced 114 books and more than 600 articles to date. The topics range from networking to artificial intelligence and from database management to heads-down programming. Some of his current books include discussions of data science, machine learning, and algorithms. His technical editing skills have helped more than 70 authors refine the content of their manuscripts. John has provided technical editing services to various magazines, performed various kinds of consulting, and writes certification exams. Be sure to read John's blog at http://blog.johnmuellerbooks.com/. You can reach John on the Internet at John@JohnMuellerBooks.com. John also has a website at www.johnmuellerbooks.com/.

# Contents at a Glance

# Contents

# Table of Exercises

# Introduction

Anyone who has taken an AWS certification exam can tell you that the exams are not easy. The right study materials can make all the difference when taking the AWS Certified SysOps Administrator – Associate exam.

To pass the exam, you must understand the various services across the AWS ecosystem that enable you to do system administration work. This book is an excellent resource for your certification journey. In addition to this book, Sybex offers *AWS Certified SysOps Administrator – Associate Exam Practice Tests*, which gives you a variety of questions related to the material in this book and beyond to ensure that you are well prepared to take the exam. Other materials that I recommend would be the AWS documentation (typically available as HTML and PDF) and the FAQs.

You should have hands-on experience with AWS before taking this exam. The exercises in this book will help you build on that experience. When you first sign up for an AWS account, you get 12 months of free-tier access. This means that as long as you stick to free tier–eligible items, and you don't exceed the hours or usage specified, you can practice building your infrastructure in AWS. Practice with the console, but also practice with the AWS command-line interface (CLI). You don't have to be an AWS CLI expert to pass the exam, but you should be familiar enough with it to know the format of common AWS CLI commands.

I highly recommend reading the book cover to cover. At the end of each chapter, pause and take a moment to go through the review questions to test your knowledge of the material you have covered. Once you have finished the book, take advantage of the practice tests and flashcards available to you online after registering your book. These study aides will ensure that you have the knowledge necessary to pass the exam.

When you register for the exam, you have your choice of either PSI or Pearson Vue for your testing center. As of this writing, the cost for the associate exam is $150 USD. The questions will be in either a multiple-choice or a multiple-answer format. You have a total of 130 minutes to finish the exam.

Now that you know the basics and the recommended resources, let's review how this book is laid out.

## Part I, "AWS Fundamentals"

The first part of the book starts with the foundational topics that you need to know and understand before you dig into the rest of the book content. These topics include the Shared Responsibility Model and various methods to access resources in AWS.

## Part II, "Monitoring and Reporting"

The second part of the book focuses entirely on monitoring and reporting tools that are available within AWS. You will learn more about Amazon CloudWatch, AWS CloudTrail,

AWS Config, and AWS Organizations. Each chapter in this part provides coverage on these topics in detail.

## Part III, "High Availability"

In the third part of this book, the focus shifts to highly available services and creating highly available architectures. AWS' managed service for databases, Amazon Relational Database Service (RDS), is discussed along with Auto Scaling.

## Part IV, "Deployment and Provisioning"

In the fourth part of the book, we look at virtual private cloud (VPC) peering and bastion hosts. We also cover AWS Systems Manager, as well as all of its components that make it a valuable deployment and provisioning utility.

## Part V, "Storage and Data Management"

In the fifth part of the book, we look at storage with a focus on Simple Storage Service (S3), Glacier, and Elastic Block Store (EBS). We also examine data security and encryption as well as data life-cycle management.

## Part VI, "Security and Compliance"

In the sixth part of the book, the focus changes to security and compliance topics. We first cover identity and access management (IAM), and then reporting and logging from a security and compliance perspective. We end this part with a chapter on additional security tools that you need to know and understand for the exam.

## Part VII, "Networking"

In the seventh part of the book, we cover networking topics. We start with networking basics, virtual private cloud, and network address translation (NAT), and we end with DNS services and Route 53.

## Part VIII, "Automation and Optimization"

In the eighth and final section, we shift to automation and optimization. Infrastructure as a Service is discussed, and AWS CloudFormation is covered in detail. Elastic Beanstalk is also covered, which is AWS' platform as a service (PaaS).

# What Does This Book Cover?

This book covers the topics that you will need to understand to prepare you to take the AWS Certified SysOps Administrator – Associate exam. The topics that we cover in this book include the following:

- **Chapter 1: "Introduction to Systems Operations on AWS":** This chapter is an overview of what AWS is and the services it provides. In addition, it discusses system operations and the various ways to interact with AWS and its resources.

- **Chapter 2: "Amazon CloudWatch":** This chapter discusses monitoring in AWS using Amazon CloudWatch. It discusses types of monitoring and metrics and explains how Amazon CloudWatch works.

- **Chapter 3: "AWS Organizations":** This chapter discusses AWS Organizations and how you can use this feature to centralize various aspects of AWS account management, including centralized billing for multiple AWS accounts.

- **Chapter 4: "AWS Config":** This chapter discusses using AWS Config to manage changes to your resources within your AWS account.

- **Chapter 5: "AWS CloudTrail":** This chapter explores AWS' CloudTrail and explains how it is used to monitor API calls within your AWS account.

- **Chapter 6: "Amazon Relational Database Service":** This chapter discusses AWS managed database service. Achieving scalability and high availability are discussed in addition to supported database engines.

- **Chapter 7: "Auto Scaling":** This chapter covers everything you need to know about Auto Scaling, including how to specify capacity, and services other than EC2, which can take advantage of Auto Scaling.

- **Chapter 8: "Hubs, Spokes, and Bastion Hosts":** In this chapter, you learn all about VPC peering, including using hub-and-spoke architecture. You will also learn about bastion hosts, including what they are and why you might want to use them.

- **Chapter 9: "AWS Systems Manager":** This chapter covers AWS Systems Manager and the components of Systems Manager that make it such a useful tool in your arsenal. The Run command, Patch Manager, Parameter Store, Session Manager, and State Manager are all covered.

- **Chapter 10: "Simple Storage Service (S3)":** This chapter covers S3 and Glacier, lifecycle management, encryption, and versioning. We also discuss storage gateways and why you would use them.

- **Chapter 11: "Elastic Block Store (EBS)":** This chapter explains what EBS is and what types of EBS are available to use. Encryption of EBS volumes is also covered.

- **Chapter 12: "Amazon Machine Image (AMI)":** This chapter discusses AMIs, AMI permissions, AMI storage. and common administrative tasks related to AMIs.

- **Chapter 13: "IAM":** This chapter covers the administration of users, groups, roles, and polices within AWS. Other identity services are also discussed.

- **Chapter 14: "Reporting and Logging":** This chapter covers the various reporting, monitoring, and logging tools available in AWS. This includes more on CloudWatch, CloudTrail, and AWS Config.

- **Chapter 15: "Additional Security Tools":** This chapter covers the other security tools that are likely to show up on the exam, including Amazon Inspector and Amazon GuardDuty.

- **Chapter 16: "Virtual Private Cloud (VPC)":** This chapter includes a refresher on networking basics and then discusses networking and routing in AWS.

- **Chapter 17: "Route 53":** This chapter discusses DNS, Route 53, and the various routing policies available to you through Route 53.

- **Chapter 18: "CloudFormation":** In this chapter, automation through infrastructure as a service is discussed and how AWS uses CloudFormation to automate infrastructure using templates and stacks.

- **Chapter 19: "Elastic Beanstalk":** In this chapter, you learn about Elastic Beanstalk and how it can enable you to run your web applications without having to concern yourself with the networking and configuration of instances to run your applications on.

# Interactive Online Learning Environment and Test Bank

Tools have been developed to aid you in studying for the Amazon Certified SysOps Administrator – Associate exam. These tools are all available for no additional charge here:

www.wiley.com/go/sybextestprep

Just register your book to gain access to the electronic resources that are listed here.

- **Practice Exams:** Two 50-question practice exams are available to test your knowledge. These questions are different from the review questions at the end of each chapter.

- **Flashcards:** One-hundred flashcards are available for you to test your knowledge of AWS terms and concepts. If you don't get them correct the first time through, try again! These are designed to reinforce the concepts you have learned throughout the book.

- **Glossary:** Throughout the book, you'll see italicized words that are important key terms. A glossary of these key terms with their definitions is provided. The best part about the glossary is that it's searchable!

# Exam Objectives

The AWS Certified SysOps Administrator – Associate exam is designed with system administrators who have been working with AWS in an operational capacity for at least one year in mind. The exam candidate will ideally have experience in deploying resources and managing existing resources, as well as performing basic operational tasks like troubleshooting issues and monitoring and reporting.

As a general rule, before you take this exam, you should:

- Have at least one year of experience in systems administration in AWS.

- Have hands-on experience with AWS management including the AWS Management Console, AWS CLI, and AWS SDK.

- Understand networking concepts and methodologies in relation to AWS networking infrastructure.

- Know how to monitor systems for performance and availability.

- Understand basic security and compliance requirements, as well as the tools within AWS that can help with auditing and monitoring.

- Have the ability to translate an architectural document in a functional AWS environment.

# Objective Map

This table provides you with a listing of each domain on the exam, the weights assigned to each domain, and a listing of the chapters where content in the domains is addressed.

| Domain | Exam Percentage | Chapters |
|---|---|---|
| **Domain 1: Monitoring and Reporting** | **22%** | |
| 1.1 Create and maintain metrics and alarms utilizing AWS monitoring services | | 2, 3, 4, 5, 14 |
| 1.2 Recognize and differentiate performance and availability metrics | | 2, 14, 16 |
| 1.3 Perform the steps necessary to remediate based on performance and availability metrics | | 2, 5, 14 |

| Domain | Exam Percentage | Chapters |
|---|---|---|
| **Domain 2: High Availability** | 8% | |
| 2.1 Implement scalability and elasticity based on use case | | 1, 6, 7, 12, 16, 17, 18, 19 |
| 2.2 Recognize and differentiate highly available and resilient environments on AWS | | 1, 6, 7, 10, 11, 12, 13, 15, 16, 17, 18, 19 |
| **Domain 3: Deployment and Provisioning** | 14% | |
| 3.1 Identify and execute steps required to provision cloud resources | | 1, 6, 7, 8, 9, 10, 11, 12, 13, 16, 17, 18, 19 |
| 3.2 Identify and remediate deployment issues | | 4, 5, 6, 9, 11, 12, 14, 16, 17, 18, 19 |
| **Domain 4: Storage and Data Management** | 12% | |
| 4.1 Create and manage data retention | | 10, 11 |
| 4.2 Identify and implement data protection, encryption, and capacity planning needs | | 10, 11, 12 |
| **Domain 5: Security and Compliance** | 18% | |
| 5.1 Implement and manage security policies on AWS | | 1, 4, 9, 13, 15 |
| 5.2 Implement access controls when using AWS | | 1, 3, 4, 9, 10, 12, 13, 15 |
| 5.3 Differentiate between the roles and responsibility within the shared responsibility model | | 1, 13, 15 |
| **Domain 6: Networking** | 14% | |
| 6.1 Apply AWS networking features | | 1, 16, 17 |
| 6.2 Implement connectivity services of AWS | | 16, 17 |
| 6.3 Gather and interpret relevant information for network troubleshooting | | 5, 14, 16 |

| Domain | Exam Percentage | Chapters |
|---|---|---|
| **Domain 7: Automation and Optimization** | **12%** | |
| 7.1 Use AWS services and features to manage and assess resource utilization | | 1, 2, 7, 8, 14, 19 |
| 7.2 Employ cost optimization strategies for efficient resource utilization | | 3, 7, 11, 19 |
| 7.3 Automate manual or repeatable process to minimize management overhead | | 2, 4, 5, 7, 8, 9, 12, 18, 19 |

# Assessment Test

1. True or False: An availability zone is the largest geographic area within the AWS environment.

   **A.** True

   **B.** False

2. Which of these is not a valid region within AWS?

   **A.** us-west-2

   **B.** cn-north-1

   **C.** ap-northeast-2

   **D.** eu-northeast-1

3. Which of the below options best describes what a CloudWatch alarm is?

   **A.** An alarm is raised when an event is reported that is outside of the threshold that was defined.

   **B.** An alarm is raised when a metric is reported that is outside of the threshold that was defined.

   **C.** An alarm is raised when an application is down.

   **D.** An alarm is raised when there are issues with AWS services.

4. Which of these is not a component of CloudWatch Events?

   **A.** Events

   **B.** Rules

   **C.** Metrics

   **D.** Targets

5. What is the term used to describe a container that is used to collect related metrics in CloudWatch?

   **A.** Namespace

   **B.** Bucket

   **C.** Metrics container

   **D.** Container host

6. Which of these is not a benefit provided by AWS Organizations?

   **A.** Consolidate and deploy security policies.

   **B.** Consolidate user management.

   **C.** Consolidate billing.

   **D.** Consolidate Amazon EC2 instances.

**7.** What is the best description of an organization in relation to AWS and AWS Organizations?

    **A.** A collection of IAM user accounts

    **B.** A collection of inter-related networks

    **C.** A collection of businesses

    **D.** A collection of AWS accounts

**8.** In IAM, you group user accounts into a group. What do you group your AWS accounts into in AWS Organizations?

    **A.** Container

    **B.** Organizational Unit

    **C.** Security group

    **D.** Distribution group

**9.** Which AWS service provides configuration management for systems in AWS and systems on-premises?

    **A.** Amazon Inspector

    **B.** AWS Config

    **C.** AWS Organizations

    **D.** AWS Systems Manager

**10.** True or False: Rules in AWS Config are used to tell AWS Config what to do if a configuration is not correct.

    **A.** True

    **B.** False

**11.** How many custom rules can you create in a single AWS account for AWS Config?

    **A.** 25

    **B.** 50

    **C.** 75

    **D.** 100

**12.** What does a trail do in AWS CloudTrail?

    **A.** Tells AWS CloudTrail which events you want to record but does not address where to put the logs for those events

    **B.** Tells AWS CloudTrail which events you want to record and where to put the logs for those events

    **C.** Tells AWS CloudTrail you want to record all events

    **D.** Tells AWS CloudTrail where you want to store logs

13. You want to ensure that new regions will automatically have AWS CloudTrail enabled for them, and that you are monitoring both management and data events. What is the best way to accomplish this?

    **A.**  Use the default option which is all-region trails and select which events you want to log.

    **B.**  Enable all-region trails rather than the default single region trail.

    **C.**  Use the default option which is all-region trails and all events logged.

    **D.**  You can't set AWS CloudTrail at a regional level.

14. Which permissions do you need to give your users or admins to work with AWS CloudTrail? (Choose two.)

    **A.**  AWSCloudTrailUser

    **B.**  AWSCloudTrailFullAccess

    **C.**  AWSCloudTrailAdmin

    **D.**  AWSCloudTrailReadOnlyAccess

15. True or False: The default settings in Amazon RDS are cost efficient.

    **A.**  True

    **B.**  False

16. You need to ensure that your databases can survive the failure of an availability zone. What is the best solution for this requirement?

    **A.**  Amazon RDS provides this feature by default, you just need to select the availability zone you want for the standby instance.

    **B.**  Amazon RDS provides this feature by default; you don't need to do anything extra.

    **C.**  Install your DBMS on EC2 instances and enable Multi-AZ configuration.

    **D.**  Use Amazon RDS with Multi-AZ configuration.

17. True or False: Multi-AZ is for disaster recovery, and read replicas are for performance.

    **A.**  True

    **B.**  False

18. When do health checks occur on the instances in an Auto Scaling group?

    **A.**  When the instances are in a Running state

    **B.**  When the instances are in a Standby state

    **C.**  When the instances are in an InService state

    **D.**  When the instances are in a Pending state

19. Which of these is something that would not be included in a launch configuration?

    **A.**  ID of the AMI

    **B.**  Hostname

    **C.**  Instance type

    **D.**  One or more security groups

**20.** True/False: VPC peering uses transitive trusts.

   **A.** True

   **B.** False

**21.** Where must a bastion host be located?

   **A.** Public subnet

   **B.** Private subnet

   **C.** A separate subnet from everything else

   **D.** Behind a VPN connection

**22.** In order for AWS Systems Manager to monitor, install software and configure systems, which of these is true?

   **A.** The systems must be Linux.

   **B.** The systems must be Windows.

   **C.** The systems have to be in AWS.

   **D.** The SSM agent must be installed on the system.

**23.** Which of these are not a valid document type in AWS Systems Manager?

   **A.** Command

   **B.** Policy

   **C.** Security

   **D.** Automation

**24.** Which storage products are classified as object storage? (Choose two.)

   **A.** Amazon EFS

   **B.** Amazon Glacier

   **C.** Amazon S3

   **D.** Amazon EBS

**25.** What is the largest size permitted for an object in S3?

   **A.** 500 GB

   **B.** 1 TB

   **C.** 5 TB

   **D.** Unlimited

**26.** Which region does s3.amazonaws.com belong to?

   **A.** us-east-1

   **B.** us-east-2

   **C.** us-west-1

   **D.** us-west-2

**27.** Which of these products is a block storage solution?

    **A.** Amazon EFS

    **B.** Amazon Glacier

    **C.** Amazon S3

    **D.** Amazon EBS

**28.** When you terminate an EC2 instance, how do you ensure that the root volume is not deleted?

    **A.** Set the "delete on termination" flag to false for the volume in question.

    **B.** Set the "delete on termination" flag to true for the volume in question.

    **C.** You don't need to take any action as root volumes are not deleted when an EC2 instance is terminated.

    **D.** There is no way to keep the root volume from being deleted.

**29.** Of the different types of EBS volumes, which type offers the highest number of IOPS?

    **A.** General Purpose SSD

    **B.** Provisioned IOPS SSD

    **C.** Throughput Optimized HDD

    **D.** Cold HDD

**30.** Which of these is not an accessibility type of AMI?

    **A.** Public

    **B.** Shared

    **C.** Private

    **D.** Isolated

**31.** True or False: Instance-backed AMIs are a great solution for when you need to ensure data will persist after an instance has been terminated.

    **A.** True

    **B.** False

**32.** Which type of policy is recommended by AWS in most cases when setting permissions within IAM?

    **A.** Security

    **B.** Managed

    **C.** Inline

    **D.** Network

**33.** To create an access key which will allow a user to securely connect with the AWS CLI and AWS API, what command would you use within the AWS CLI?

    **A.** `aws iam create-security-key`

    **B.** `aws ec2 create-access-key`

    **C.** `aws iam create-access-key`

    **D.** `aws ec2 create-security-key`

**34.** Which product can you use to monitor for the invocation of AWS Lambda functions?

    **A.** AWS CloudTrail

    **B.** Amazon CloudWatch

    **C.** AWS Systems Manager

    **D.** Amazon GuardDuty

**35.** Which of these is not a valid alarm state for Amazon CloudWatch?

    **A.** ALARM

    **B.** OK

    **C.** STANDBY

    **D.** INSUFFICIENT_DATA

**36.** If you have missing datapoints in Amazon CloudWatch, and you want to ensure that Amazon CloudWatch does not consider the datapoints that were not captured, which setting should you choose?

    **A.** NotBreaching

    **B.** Breaching

    **C.** Ignore

    **D.** Missing

**37.** Which of the following are assessments available in AWS Inspector? (Choose two.)

    **A.** Security assessments

    **B.** Network assessments

    **C.** Vulnerability assessments

    **D.** Host assessments

**38.** Which of these is not a type of activity that Amazon GuardDuty monitors for?

    **A.** Malicious insider

    **B.** Reconnaissance

    **C.** Instance compromise

    **D.** Account compromise

**39.** What is the largest and most basic component in AWS networking?

    **A.** Network Access Control List (NACL)

    **B.** Subnet

    **C.** Virtual Private Cloud (VPC)

    **D.** Security Group

**40.** Which of these is valid CIDR notation for an IPv4 VPC in AWS?

    **A.** /26

    **B.** /8

    **C.** /12

    **D.** /29

**41.** Which of these is valid CIDR notation for an IPv6 VPC in AWS?

    **A.** /64

    **B.** /32

    **C.** /28

    **D.** /56

**42.** Which network port does DNS use for queries?

    **A.** 123

    **B.** 389

    **C.** 53

    **D.** 88

**43.** Which DNS record type is used to resolve IP addresses to hostnames?

    **A.** A

    **B.** PTR

    **C.** CNAME

    **D.** NS

**44.** Which type of record is used to route traffic to AWS resources such as Amazon S3 buckets?

    **A.** Alias

    **B.** CNAME

    **C.** A

    **D.** PTR

**45.** Which languages are used in CloudFormation templates? (Choose two.)

    **A.** XML

    **B.** Javascript

    **C.** JSON

    **D.** YAML

**46.** Which component is the only required component in a CloudFormation template?

   **A.** Description

   **B.** Resources

   **C.** Metadata

   **D.** Parameters

**47.** Which built-in function is required if you want to pass user data into a CloudFormation template?

   **A.** Fn::Cidr

   **B.** Fn::GetAtt

   **C.** Fn::ImportValue

   **D.** Fn::Base64

**48.** Which of these is not one of the three architectural models used with Elastic Beanstalk?

   **A.** Dual instance deployment

   **B.** Single instance deployment

   **C.** Load balancer and Auto Scaling group

   **D.** Auto Scaling group only

**49.** What is the name of the zip file that contains all of the configuration files and scripts you need to build a platform in Elastic Beanstalk?

   **A.** Platform definition file

   **B.** Platform archive

   **C.** Platform configuration file

   **D.** platform.yaml

**50.** True/False: The platform definition file is named packer.yaml.

   **A.** True

   **B.** False

# Answers to Assessment Test

1.  **B.** A region is the largest geographic area within AWS. Regions may contain two or more availability zones.

2.  **D.** eu-northeast-1 is not a valid region. European regions will only contain central and west. While you don't need to memorize all the regions for the exam, you should have an idea of what the valid names are. us-west-2 is US West (Oregon), cn-north-1 is China (Beijing), and ap-northeast-2 is Asia Pacific (Sydney).

3.  **B.** An alarm is raised when a metric is reported that is outside of the threshold that was defined. Alarms aren't necessarily something bad, in fact they may be used to trigger good events, such as an Auto Scaling event when a CPU is over 90 percent utilized.

4.  **C.** Events, rules, and targets are all components of CloudWatch Events. Metrics are used to measure statistics in CloudWatch, however CloudWatch Events is a separate offering from CloudWatch.

5.  **A.** A namespace is a container that is used to collect related metrics in CloudWatch. There are many offered by AWS, and you can create custom namespaces. Buckets are used in Amazon S3, not Amazon CloudWatch. Metrics container is not an actual thing in AWS. A container host is used to support containers using software like Docker.

6.  **D.** AWS Organizations does many things. The most commonly used features are consolidated user management, billing, and a central place to store and deploy security policies. It does not help in consolidating Amazon EC2 instances.

7.  **D.** An organization inside of AWS Organizations is a collection of AWS accounts. IAM user accounts are still managed in IAM. An organization in this context is not a collection of inter-related networks or businesses.

8.  **B.** AWS accounts are grouped into organizational units in AWS Organizations. These organizational units are normally used to group like resources such as a Production OU and a Development OU.

9.  **B.** AWS Config provides configuration management for both AWS systems and on-prem systems. Amazon Inspector is used for performing vulnerability assessments. AWS Organizations is used to consolidate billing, accounts, and policies. AWS Systems Manager does not perform configuration management, though it does have tie-ins to AWS Config.

10. **B.** Rules in AWS Config are used to decide what the desired or allowed configuration is. If a rule is broken, then something is not configured properly. The rule does not specify an action to be taken.

11. **B.** In a single AWS account, you can create up to 50 custom rules in AWS Config.

12. **B.** In AWS CloudTrail, a trail is what indicates which events you want to record and where to store them. Logs are typically stored in an Amazon S3 bucket.

**13.** A. By default, all-region trails are enabled. You can make changes to what you want AWS CloudTrail to keep track of and those settings will apply across all regions. By default, only management events are logged, so you would need to choose to log data events as well.

**14.** B, D. Administrators who need to create trails will need AWSCloudTrailFullAccess, and AWSCloudTrailReadOnlyAccess is needed for users who need to view trails and the S3 buckets where log data is stored.

**15.** B. The default settings for Amazon RDS are not necessarily cost efficient. It is best to tweak the settings to meet your use case.

**16.** D. Amazon RDS has a configuration option for Multi-AZ support. This creates a standby instance in another availability zone that can take over should the primary instance fail. You must select it when you create your database.

**17.** A. Multi-AZ is meant for disaster recovery as the standby instance does not take any traffic unless something happens to the primary instance. Read replicas are used to improve read performance.

**18.** C. Health checks occur on instances in an Auto Scaling group when those instances are in an InService state.

**19.** B. Hostname is not something that is set by the launch configuration. The launch configuration will typically contain the AMI ID to use for the instance, the instance type, the key pair needed to connect to the instance, the security groups for the instance, and any storage drives that should be connected.

**20.** B. VPC peering uses non-transitive trusts. Trust must be set explicitly between VPCs.

**21.** A. A bastion host must be accessible from the Internet, so it must be located in a public subnet.

**22.** D. For AWS Systems Manager to monitor, install software, or configure systems, the SSM agent must be installed on the system. Windows and Linux are both supported, as are on-premises systems in addition to AWS systems.

**23.** C. AWS Systems Manager has three valid document types: command, policy, and automation documents.

**24.** B, C. Amazon S3 and Amazon Glacier are both types of object storage. Object storage stores items as objects, and those objects are all accessible by APIs.

**25.** C. Objects stored in S3 can be up to 5 TB in size.

**26.** A. US East (N. Virginia) known as us-east-1 is the region that uses s3.amazonaws.com. All of the other regions are identified specifically in the s3 URL. For example, us-east-2 uses the URL s3.us-east-2.amazonaws.com.

**27.** D. Amazon EBS is the block storage solution offered by AWS.

**28.** A. To keep the root volume from being deleted when an EC2 instance is terminated (default behavior), you must set the "delete on termination" flag to false.

**29.** B. Provisioned IOPS SSD offers the highest number of IOPS of all the EBS storage options.

**30.** D. There are three accessibility types for AMIs: public, shared, and private. Public is available to all, shared is available to other AWS accounts that have been granted access, and private is only available to the AWS account where the AMI was made.

**31.** B. Instance-backed AMIs are good for short-lived workloads. The storage is destroyed when the instance is terminated. EBS-backed AMIs are used when you need the storage to persist after instance termination.

**32.** B. AWS recommends using managed policies which can be applied to multiple users, groups, and/or roles.

**33.** C. In the AWS CLI, you would use the command aws iam create-access-key to create the access key for a user.

**34.** A. AWS CloudTrail can be used to monitor for AWS Lambda events including the invocation of functions.

**35.** C. Amazon CloudWatch has three valid alarm states. Those are ALARM, OK, and INSUFFICIENT_DATA.

**36.** D. If you use "missing" Amazon CloudWatch does not consider missing data points when deciding if an alarm state should change.

**37.** B, D. AWS Inspector offers network assessments and host assessments. Network assessments don't require the installation of an agent; however, host assessments do require the Amazon Inspector agent be installed.

**38.** A. Amazon GuardDuty does not monitor for malicious insiders, although specific suspicious activity like the installation of a virus would be identified. Amazon GuardDuty monitors for reconnaissance activities, instance compromise, and account compromise.

**39.** C. The Virtual Private Cloud or VPC is the largest and most basic component of AWS networking. Within it you will find subnets, NACLs, and security groups.

**40.** A. IPv4 VPCs can have anything between /16 and /28.

**41.** D. While IPv4 VPCs can use a range of different network sizes, IPv6 VPCs only use /56.

**42.** C. Normal DNS queries use UDP/53, while IPv6 or DNSSEC signed queries use TCP/53. 123 is NTP, 389 is LDAP, and 88 is Kerberos.

**43.** B. PTR records are used to resolve IP addresses to hostnames.

**44.** A. In AWS, alias records are used to route traffic to AWS resources. It is easy to confuse CNAME records with alias records, but in AWS they perform two separate functions.

**45.** C, D. CloudFormation templates can be written in either JSON or YAML.

**46.** B.  While there are multiple components that can be used in a CloudFormation template, resources is the only required component.

**47.** D.  When user data is passed into a CloudFormation template, it must be encoded in Base64. So you would want to use the Fn::Base64 function.

**48.** A.  Dual instance deployment is not an architectural model used with Elastic Beanstalk.

**49.** B.  The platform archive is a zip file that contains all of the configuration files and scripts you need to build a platform in Elastic Beanstalk.

**50.** B.  The platform definition file is named `platform.yaml`.

# AWS Fundamentals

# Chapter 1

# Introduction to Systems Operations on AWS

**THE AWS CERTIFIED SYSOPS ADMINISTRATOR – ASSOCIATE EXAM TOPICS COVERED IN THIS CHAPTER MAY INCLUDE, BUT ARE NOT LIMITED TO, THE FOLLOWING:**

**Domain 2.0: High Availability**

✓ 2.1 Implement scalability and elasticity based on use case.

✓ 2.2 Recognize and differentiate highly available and resilient environments on AWS.

✓ Content may include the following:

- Selecting AWS services and best practices for building highly available and scalable architectures
- Identifying which services scale automatically and which require administrator intervention

**Domain 3.0: Deployment and Provisioning**

✓ 3.1 Identify and execute steps required to provision cloud resources.

✓ Content may include the following:

- Familiarity with multi-tier architectures
- Where you can go for documentation and help with your AWS deployments

**Domain 5.0: Security and Compliance**

✓ 5.1 Implement and manage security policies on AWS.

✓ 5.2 Implement access controls when using AWS.

✓ **5.3 Differentiate between the roles and responsibility within the shared responsibility model.**

✓ **Content may include the following:**

- Advantages of a cloud model for security and access control
- How AWS clearly delineates the role of you, the SysOps Administrator, and AWS as maintainers of the cloud

**Domain 6.0: Networking**

✓ **6.1 Apply AWS networking features.**

✓ **Content may include the following:**

- What AWS provides in terms of networking and troubleshooting services
- The basics of Amazon Virtual Private Cloud (Amazon VPC)

**Domain 7.0: Automation and Optimization**

✓ **7.1 Use AWS services and features to manage and assess resource utilization.**

✓ **Content may include the following:**

- How AWS defines the cloud and provides a complete ecosystem for application hosting and operations
- What AWS provides in terms of managed services, and the basics of those managed services

You simply cannot claim to be a competent systems administrator without a working knowledge of the cloud. As the biggest cloud provider, learning the inner workings of the Amazon Web Services (AWS) cloud infrastructure and how to manage its resources and services is a competitive advantage. This book will advance your skills with AWS and ensure that you are prepared to both understand how AWS works and pass the AWS Certified SysOps Administrator – Associate exam.

In this chapter, you will learn about AWS and its associated services, including:

The available regions within AWS and their corresponding API endpoints

Services available with the Amazon platform broken out by category of service

What systems operations (SysOps) entail and how SysOps questions will appear on the exam

The Shared Responsibility Model, which defines the responsibilities of AWS and of its customers

The AWS Service Level Agreement and what you need to know about it for the exam

How to interact with AWS and the services available to you

What to do when you need support or additional resources with AWS

# The AWS Ecosystem

AWS, at its heart, is a virtualization platform. Figure 1.1 shows a simple look at the AWS stack of resources, from the physical servers that AWS maintains to actual "servers in the cloud."

**FIGURE 1.1** AWS as a virtualization platform

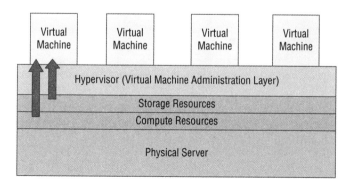

Although there is value in seeing AWS and the cloud, in general, as a translation of on-premises or physical hardware into a virtual model, that metaphor is incomplete. Many times, the cloud introduces new paradigms (such as spot instances) and supplements familiar concepts with new ones (network access control lists behave somewhat like firewalls, while not being a direct replacement). It is helpful to think of certain key resources as virtualized physical devices, but to hold that thought loosely and adapt it when needed to take advantage of cloud models.

## The AWS Services Model

AWS does not merely provide computational power. This same *virtualization* takes place for storage, databases, analytics, networking, mobile and developer tools, administration of management of those services, and more. It is the sum of all of these services that comprise the AWS ecosystem. Figure 1.2 shows just the *categories* of services that AWS provides.

**FIGURE 1.2**    AWS provides a huge array of services, organized into categories.

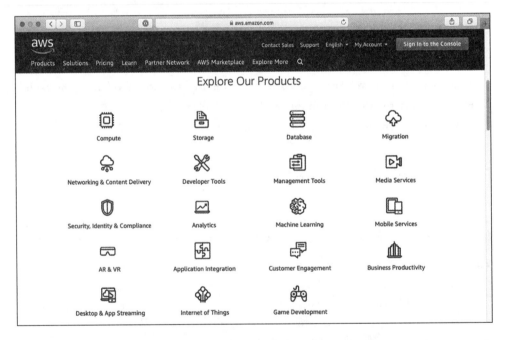

Your job as a SysOps administrator will be to manage deployments of combinations of these services. That means you need to understand the core services and how they inter-relate, as well as how they are deployed and how they run, scale, and eventually shut down (and possibly start up all over again). You're also responsible for more than just "getting things working," but to employ best practices in your decisions.

The core services will all be covered in the following chapters, particularly as they each relate to system administration and operation. However, AWS is always adding more services, and you'll often be tested on what these services do at a high level. It's a good idea to browse this list before taking an exam and at least read through descriptions of any services that are new to you.

## The AWS Global Presence

AWS also maintains datacenters around the world. These datacenters are not directly available to you, but abstractions over them are via availability zones and regions. An *availability zone* (or AZ for short) is an AWS abstraction over a specific area, a sort of pseudo–datacenter. Availability zones are grouped into larger geographical *regions*.

There are always more regions than availability zones, and the number of both is constantly growing. You will want to carefully consider the regions and AZs you launch your instances into, as they are priced differently and also will affect latency from your customers based on their location. Table 1.1 shows a list of all current (nongovernment) regions, along with each region's name and endpoint addresses.

**TABLE 1.1**   Current publicly accessible AWS regions

| Region name | Region | Endpoint |
| --- | --- | --- |
| US East (Ohio) | us-east-2 | apigateway.us-east-2.amazonaws.com |
| US East (N. Virginia) | us-east-1 | apigateway.us-east-1.amazonaws.com |
| US West (N. California) | us-west-1 | apigateway.us-west-1.amazonaws.com |
| US West (Oregon) | us-west-2 | apigateway.us-west-2.amazonaws.com |
| Asia Pacific (Mumbai) | ap-south-1 | apigateway.ap-south-1.amazonaws.com |
| Asia Pacific (Seoul) | ap-northeast-2 | apigateway.ap-northeast-2.amazonaws.com |
| Asia Pacific (Osaka-Local) | ap-northeast-3 | apigateway.ap-northeast-3.amazonaws.com |
| Asia Pacific (Singapore) | ap-southeast-1 | apigateway.ap-southeast-1.amazonaws.com |
| Asia Pacific (Sydney) | ap-southeast-2 | apigateway.ap-southeast-2.amazonaws.com |
| Asia Pacific (Tokyo) | ap-northeast-1 | apigateway.ap-northeast-1.amazonaws.com |

**TABLE 1.1**   Current publicly accessible AWS regions *(continued)*

| Region name | Region | Endpoint |
| --- | --- | --- |
| Canada (Central) | ca-central-1 | apigateway.ca-central-1.amazonaws.com |
| China (Beijing) | cn-north-1 | apigateway.cn-north-1.amazonaws.com.cn |
| China (Ningxia) | cn-northwest-1 | apigateway.cn-northwest-1.amazonaws.com.cn |
| EU (Frankfurt) | eu-central-1 | apigateway.eu-central-1.amazonaws.com |
| EU (Ireland) | eu-west-1 | apigateway.eu-west-1.amazonaws.com |
| EU (London) | eu-west-2 | apigateway.eu-west-2.amazonaws.com |
| EU (Paris) | eu-west-3 | apigateway.eu-west-3.amazonaws.com |
| South America (São Paulo) | sa-east-1 | apigateway.sa-east-1.amazonaws.com |

There might be a half a dozen availability zones within each of these regions, identified by using names like us-east-1a (a number and letter suffix appended to each region name).

Many AWS services have specific details regarding how they function (and *if* they function) across availability zones and regions. An important role of the SysOps administrator is to provision resources correctly so that they are highly available and redundant. You should pay special attention whenever you come across instructions or details about setting up a service across AZs or regions.

Additionally, this is one of the more popular areas for the AWS exam to question you. You'll be asked multiple times about setting up the Amazon Relational Database Service (Amazon RDS) and Amazon Simple Storage Service (Amazon S3) across regions, DynamoDB across availability zones, and how Amazon Virtual Private Clouds (VPCs) are allocated within a region. Pay special attention to these topics!

# AWS Managed Services

AWS is as much a service provider as it is a cloud provider. In addition to the infrastructure it provides, AWS offers a number of managed services. These services are a core part of the job of the SysOps admin to understand, configure, operate, and optimize. Table 1.2 offers a quick overview look at the various AWS service categories, and Table 1.3 shows the (current) managed services within those categories.

**TABLE 1.2**   AWS service categories

| Category | Function |
| --- | --- |
| Compute | Compute services are, essentially, the computers in the cloud. Anything that is primarily aimed at providing CPU cycles to your application is a compute service: instances, containers, and all other services that provide processing power. You'll find Amazon Elastic Compute Cloud (Amazon EC2) instances, Amazon Elastic Container Service (Amazon ECS) containers, and Lambda here, among others. |
| Networking & Content Delivery | This should be self-evident: networking services such as Amazon VPC and Route 53 (for DNS) are in this category. |
| Storage | AWS provides a variety of storage services with numerous subcategories. Probably most notable here are S3 for object storage and Amazon Elastic File System (Amazon EFS) for network-attached storage (NAS)-style storage. Note that storage does *not* include database services. |
| Database | AWS provides data solutions in a variety of flavors: DynamoDB (the AWS NoSQL engine), and RDS, the AWS relational database service, are the most popular. |
| Migration | This is a new but growing category. It includes tools for moving from on-premises environments to AWS. |
| Management Tools | This is an ever-growing category and includes monitoring, logging, scaling, configuration, and anything else you might use to manage your applications and AWS account. |
| Security, Identity, & Compliance | This category contains services for managing authentication and authorization, encrypting data, and handling interactions between services. |
| Developer Tools | AWS is increasing their efforts to provide AWS-centric developer tools, including editors, version control, and deployment. |
| Media Services | This category is the AWS home for anything you might use to process media and serve it to clients on various platforms, including transcoding and format conversion. |
| Analytics | Analytics is the AWS response to the growing data sets on their platform. This category contains tools for business intelligence, offline processing, and search. |
| And more... | The list of categories is growing just as the services themselves are growing. There are a number of additional small categories that are often being reshuffled: media services, game development, Internet of Things, etc. |

Within each of these categories are a number of services, as shown in Table 1.3. Note that this table is *not* exhaustive, and even if it were, it would be outdated in the months between this writing and your reading!

Don't worry too much about the categories themselves. AWS sometimes changes or adds categories, and services often move from one category to another as that service's usage and purpose slightly shifts.

**TABLE 1.3** Core AWS services (by category)

| Category | Service | Function |
|---|---|---|
| Compute | Elastic Compute Cloud (EC2) | EC2 is the basic building block of most applications. EC2 instances are virtual servers that have CPU, memory, storage, and network interfaces, in a variety of sizes. You'll run your web servers and application processes on EC2 instances. |
| | Elastic Container Service (ECS) | ECS is the AWS solution to the management and servicing of containers, and in particular, Docker. Containers can be created and uploaded, run at scale, set to grow and shrink, and generally are more optimized than full EC2 instances. |
| | Lambda | Lambda is the serverless architecture at AWS that has become one of the core components of modern web applications. Lambda can run code without you having to provision servers or compute power, and can be attached to events generated by services like CloudWatch. |
| | Elastic Load Balancing | Incoming network traffic can be directed between multiple web servers to ensure that a single web server isn't overwhelmed while other servers are underused or that traffic isn't directed to failed servers. |
| | Elastic Beanstalk | Beanstalk is a managed service that abstracts the provisioning of AWS compute and networking infrastructure. You are required to do nothing more than push your application code, and Beanstalk automatically launches and manages all the necessary services in the background. |
| Networking & Content Delivery | Virtual Private Cloud (VPC) | VPC is another core component of AWS. As you build out your own AWS environment, your VPCs contain your subnets, have Internet gateways attached, provide a layer of security through network ACLs (NACLs), and are key to understanding how AWS handles networking. |

| Category | Service | Function |
| --- | --- | --- |
| | CloudFront | CloudFront is Amazon's distributed global content delivery network (CDN). CloudFront provides edge locations around the world that store cached content and serve that content without requiring trips all the way back to the servers that originated that content. |
| | Route 53 | AWS now provides a complete DNS service, which also acts as a domain registrar. Route 53 offers a number of routing policies that can control how traffic flows from the Internet to your AWS resources. |
| | Direct Connect | You can use Direct Connect to establish a direct tunnel between your on-premises datacenter and your AWS-based VPCs. You'll need special hardware, but the benefits are significant. |
| Storage | Simple Storage Service (S3) | S3 is one of the most basic AWS services, along with EC2. S3 provides object storage in a variety of flavors, focusing on durability and availability. You can customize S3 with lifecycle policies to handle hot, warm, and cold data, and make that data available to the Internet easily and securely. You can also host static websites on S3. |
| | Glacier | Glacier is a pseudo-category of S3 and is focused on archival storage. Glacier retrieval times are slower, but the overall cost of Glacier is very low, making it an ideal long-term storage solution. |
| | Elastic Block Store (EBS) | EBS is a virtual hard drive. EBS volumes are attached to your EC2 instances and provide storage. This storage is not intended to be long-lived or to replace S3, but it does allow for quick reading and writing of data that does not need to be stored in S3 or a database. |
| | Storage Gateway | Storage Gateway is a fairly complex service that provides a variety of hybrid storage solutions, typically aimed at migration of data to the cloud over time. Storage Gateways have devices on-premises and can be configured to emulate tape libraries and NAS systems, and can locally store and/or cache data that is also copied into S3. |
| Database | Relational Database Service (RDS) | RDS is the AWS service for managing your relational databases. You can run a number of SQL database engines on RDS: MySQL, Microsoft SQL Server, Oracle, Amazon's own Aurora, PostgreSQL, and MariaDB. Although you can still install a database on EC2 instances, RDS is a better choice when possible. |

**TABLE 1.3**   Core AWS services (by category) *(continued)*

| Category | Service | Function |
| --- | --- | --- |
| | DynamoDB | DynamoDB is the AWS offering for NoSQL, and it is fast, entirely scalable without user configuration, and ideal for storing JavaScript Object Notation (JSON) files, object metadata, or anything that does not require table joins or relationships. |
| | ElastiCache | ElastiCache provides data caching and is typically positioned in front of databases to improve performance. With support for both redis and memcached as caching engines, ElastiCache is also highly configurable. |
| | Redshift | Amazon Redshift is a solution for online analytical processing (OLAP). It's also ideal for business intelligence and queries against large data sets, ideally run without a user waiting on results. |
| Migration | Snowball | The most notable migration tool is Snowball. Snowball is a physical device that allows no-hassle transfer of very large data (anything over 5–10 TB, generally) into S3. Amazon sends you the device, you load data onto it and send it back, and that data is loaded into your S3 buckets. |
| | Database/Server Migration Service | These two services allow for relatively straightforward migration of existing databases or virtual machines into AWS-managed resources. |
| Management Tools | CloudWatch | CloudWatch provides a fully functional and integrated monitoring solution for AWS services. You can easily group your resources and monitor them from a single dashboard, as well as trigger events when certain thresholds are met. |
| | CloudFormation | CloudFormation is one of the most important but underused tools in AWS. It allows for templated deployments of a full stack of AWS resources, easily repeatable and stored in version control. |
| | CloudTrail | CloudTrail is an API tracking service. It logs events and API calls for easy analysis, in real time or after the fact. |
| | Config | AWS Config adds change management into your environment. This is the AWS analog to services like Puppet or Chef, and it ensures that nothing changes without you knowing about it. |

| Category | Service | Function |
|---|---|---|
| | Auto Scaling | EC2 instances can easily be grouped and set to increase in number (or *scaled up*) when demand can't be met by currently running instances. As requests decrease, unused instances can be terminated (or *scaled down*). |
| | Trusted Advisor | Trusted Advisor is a service that provides recommendations of basic but key improvements to make to your AWS environment. It often catches security holes and best practices that should be implemented. |
| Security, Identity, & Compliance | Identity and Access Management (IAM) | If EC2 and S3 are the basic building blocks of your applications, IAM is the building block for your account itself. IAM provides for user, group, permission, and role definitions that your developers, admins, managers, financial auditors, and even AWS resources will all use. |
| | Cognito | Cognito is a relatively new but very popular service for providing single sign-on (SSO) to your AWS applications Through user pools and identity pools, you can group and manage millions of users. |
| | AWS Organizations | Another recent addition to AWS, Organizations provides multi-account management and offers a number of consolidated billing features. |
| Media Services | Elastic Transcoder | Elastic Transcoder offers easy transcoding of media files so that they are appropriately played on a variety of media players across the ever-growing number of user devices. |
| | Kinesis | Kinesis provides managed processing and capture of streaming data. Still a new discipline, Kinesis can take in data from smartphones, security cameras, and anything else that is "always on" and providing high data volumes through streaming. |
| Analytics | Athena | Athena is a tool that is focused solely on fast querying of data, typically in large data sets. Because of its singular focus, it's almost always faster and cheaper than broader-functioned tools like relational databases. |
| | Elastic MapReduce (EMR) | EMR is a web service that makes processing huge data sources possible through sharding, clustering, and careful configuration. |

Let's face it: you probably just skipped that entire table. It's a lot of information, it's pretty boring to read, and it's something you can always look up... except on the AWS certification exams. AWS is infamous for asking a few questions in each exam on services that aren't core to the topic (for example, a question about Kinesis on the SysOps exam or a question on SageMaker on the Solutions Architect exam). These questions aren't deep, but they do require a familiarity with the AWS services. Read over the list in the hopes that you'll recognize these services when they come up.

# What Is Systems Operations?

SysOps is simply an abbreviation for systems operations, and SysOps administrator is basically an operator of cloud services, at least in AWS parlance. This means that you'll need to understand and be able to answer in-depth questions on getting an application from a codebase into AWS, turning that code into a running application across various custom and AWS-provided services, managing the running application at scale, and then cleaning the whole thing up when needed.

The key principles that the AWS exam focuses on include the following:

- Deploying services, especially using AWS-provided tools such as CloudFormation.
- Building in scalability, high availability, and redundancy. This will differ from service to service, and you'll need to understand these differences and know how to scale a cluster of EC2 instances just as much as how to properly use an auto scaling group and a multi-AZ RDS configuration. (Don't worry if that doesn't make sense yet; it will soon.)
- Selecting the right service for a particular use case, including factoring in reliability, functionality, and especially cost.
- Migrating existing on-premises installations of resources and applications into the cloud.

Nearly a full 75 percent of the SysOps Administrator – Associate exam will likely be scenario-driven, rather than selecting a term's definition or choosing an AWS limit or policy name. This mirrors reality: Your most important job as a practicing SysOps administrator will be to understand a particular situation and identify the correct AWS tools and technologies for scalability, high availability, and cost.

Because of the scenario-driven nature of the exam, your best preparation for taking the exam is practical experience. Often, you'll be unfamiliar with a specific scenario but able to reason through the solutions using what you've learned on the job. Studying this book and taking practice exams is essential, but so is actually working in AWS as much as possible.

Two helpful mechanisms in understanding your responsibilities as a SysOps administrator are the AWS Shared Responsibility Model and the AWS Service Level Agreement.

## The AWS Shared Responsibility Model

If you were truly responsible for 100 percent of the cloud, you'd have a real problem. AWS doesn't make a lot of things available to its customers. For instance, while you can upgrade the operating system on an EC2 instance, you can't upgrade the operating system of DynamoDB instances. You can't directly rip out pieces of a VPC and replace them, although a bad route is absolutely your problem to fix.

The *AWS Shared Responsibility Model* is how AWS delineates what is your issue, and what is AWS' issue. Obviously, many problems will span AWS and your domain, but knowing where the lines are is essential to effective troubleshooting.

At its simplest, the shared responsibility model states that AWS guarantees the secure and uninterrupted operation of the cloud itself. Physical hardware, storage, networking, and managed services are necessary for AWS to keep running and for you to use. What you put into that cloud, though, is your responsibility. This means operating systems that you install, data, movement of that data across networks, and security of that data is all for you to figure out. Figure 1.3 summarizes the model, the numbers represent availability zones in each region.

**FIGURE 1.3**    The AWS Shared Responsibility Model

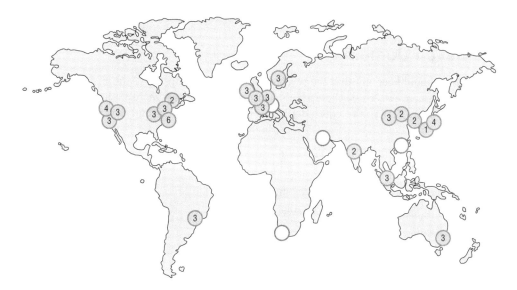

One way to remember this—and a common exam question—is to memorize that AWS is responsible for operation and security *of* the cloud, whereas you are responsible for operation and security *in* the cloud.

## The AWS Service Level Agreement

AWS provides *service level agreements* (SLAs) for most of their services. These SLAs are generally available at https://aws.amazon.com/[*servicename*]/sla/, so for example, the S3 SLA is at https://aws.amazon.com/s3/sla/ and the Lambda SLA is at https://aws.amazon.com/lambda/sla/.

More important than memorizing the details of the various SLAs, you should familiarize yourself with the idea put forth in the Shared Responsibility Model: AWS guarantees that services act in a certain way and that they act that way some percentage of time. It is your job as a SysOps administrator to know when a problem resides with you and the application, and when AWS should be called because the problem falls under the SLA for the affected services.

The only SLA that you should take time to memorize is the SLA for S3. There are routinely exam questions on the various S3 storage classes related to durability and availability. S3 is discussed in a lot more detail in Chapter 10, "Amazon Simple Storage Service (S3)."

## The Seven Domains

Finally, you should keep in mind the seven domains that the SysOps Administrator – Associate exam covers. While these are an exam construct, they're also a helpful checklist when ensuring that you've covered all your bases in preparing and operating cloud applications.

- Domain 1: Monitoring and Reporting
- Domain 2: High Availability
- Domain 3: Deployment and Provisioning
- Domain 4: Storage and Data Management
- Domain 5: Security and Compliance
- Domain 6: Networking
- Domain 7: Automation and Optimization

This book is organized along these lines via parts, where each part aside from Part I (which contains this chapter) corresponds to a domain, and the chapters in that part relate to that domain.

# Working with AWS

Fortunately, AWS takes great pride in backstopping their systems. This means that you will always have multiple tools and layers of support for both managing running AWS systems and troubleshooting when problems aren't immediately apparent in their causes. You'll need to be familiar with all available resources, as there is simply no "one size fits all" tool in working with AWS environments.

## The AWS Management Console

Your best friend when it comes to working with AWS will always be your web browser. AWS provides a command-line interface and programmatic access and several support channels, but much of your time will be spent in the *AWS Management Console*, a web-accessible interface for doing nearly everything there is to do within AWS. Figure 1.4 shows the basic console at initial sign-in.

**FIGURE 1.4**    AWS provides web access to all its services.

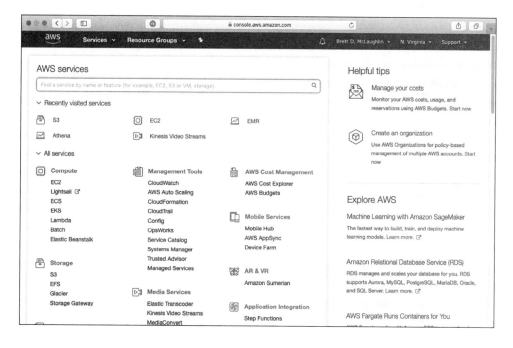

**WARNING**  Be careful with the term "console," as it's overloaded (has multiple meanings) among programmers and AWS developers. The AWS Management Console is actually a web-based application; that makes it almost the exact opposite of the usual meaning of "console" for developers: a command-line interface such as a UNIX shell or macOS or Windows terminal. There's no reason to not use the term console, but just be aware that its meaning can sometimes be confusing without context (such as "AWS console" or "AWS Management Console").

You can drill down into each service; for example, Figure 1.5 shows the S3 section with a few already-created S3 buckets. (Note that a production example would likely have many, many more S3 buckets than this.)

**FIGURE 1.5**  You can create, delete, and view S3 buckets from the service screen of the AWS console.

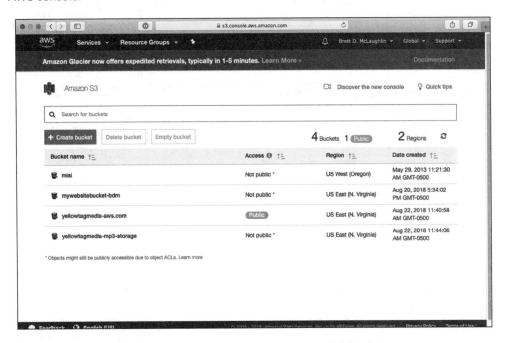

Eventually, you'll build up a suite of your own bookmarked dashboard on CloudWatch and frequently used commands and scripts. For the majority of things, though, nothing beats web-based console access.

# The AWS CLI

As your applications are deployed, you'll often want to interact with them quickly. You'll also eventually have a common set of tasks you perform outside of what tools like CloudWatch give you. This is where the *AWS CLI* (command-line interface) comes into play.

You should take a few moments now and install the AWS CLI on your system. Visit https://docs.aws.amazon.com/cli/latest/userguide/installing.html for current instructions. Link this with your AWS account, and you'll be ready to follow along with the frequent examples throughout this book.

It may come as a surprise, but AWS does not ask a lot of questions regarding the CLI on its various exams, particularly at the Associate level. In fact, there's not as much specific "How would you do this particular thing in the console or on the command line?" as you might think. The questions are a little more theoretical, ensuring that you have a correct understanding of how AWS works. The assumption seems to be that if you know *what* you want to do, using a search engine to find the exact command to execute that "what" is relatively simple.

You should still work through the examples using the CLI, though, as the understanding of how to interact with various AWS services will very much help your overall AWS knowledge base.

# AWS SDKs

Although much of the work you'll do with the console and CLI is operational management, there are times you or your developers may need to interact with AWS programmatically. This is where the *AWS SDK* (software development kit) comes in. AWS offers an SDK in nine languages, from Java to .NET to Python, among others. You can get access to this and other AWS developer tools at https://aws.amazon.com/tools/.

# Technical Support and Online Resources

AWS is ultimately a service organization. For both the exam and real AWS experiences, you should know how to reach AWS and what to expect as a response. AWS clearly defines what happens to various customers when they access support and how long they may wait for a reply.

AWS' first line of defense is their set of support plans. However, for customers who don't have high monthly budgets for support plans, a wealth of information is available online.

## Support Plans

AWS provides four different support plans, and you'll often be asked about these plans on the exam, so this is more than just supplemental information.

Every account is enrolled in the Basic plan. This plan gives you access to customer service primarily through documentation, whitepapers, and the AWS support form. You can also submit tickets for billing and support issues.

One step up from Basic is the Developer plan, which is $29/month to get started. One account holder gets access (limited access, mind you) to a Cloud Support associate. In addition to the Basic plan, this gives you some help troubleshooting, although response times aren't blazing fast.

From Developer, you can spend $100/month (or a lot more!) and get into the Business plan. This plan gives you faster response times, unlimited users, personal help and troubleshooting, and a support API. For any nontrivial production system, this plan should be considered the minimal acceptable support level.

Last is the big plan, the Enterprise support plan. These are custom-bid and aren't useful for smaller companies. However, for large organizations you'll get very fast response times and access to AWS architects, a technical account manager (TAM), and a support concierge. You'll pay for it, though; this plan costs around $15,000 a month and grows from there.

You can read more about AWS support plans at `https://aws.amazon.com/premiumsupport/compare-plans/`.

## Other Support Resources

You can find literally thousands of pages of resources online for AWS; here are a few:

- AWS provides forums and a community to its users, and you can often find great discussions (`https://forums.aws.amazon.com`).
- The home of all of AWS' documentation starts online at `https://aws.amazon.com/documentation/`.
- The FAQ pages for AWS products and services are available when an AWS product or service is selected. For example, S3 FAQs are located at `https://aws.amazon.com/s3/faqs`.

## Key Exam Resources

You'll also want to bookmark a few important pages that will be critical to you passing the AWS SysOps Administrator – Associate exam.

- All things related to AWS and its Operations path is online at `https://aws.amazon.com/training/path-operations/`.
- You'll need to begin your certification journey (if you haven't already) by signing up for a free account at the AWS Certification page: `www.aws.training/certification?src=certification`.
- The main page for the AWS SysOps Administrator – Associate exam is housed online at `https://aws.amazon.com/certification/certified-sysops-admin-associate/`.

# Summary

Hopefully you're starting to realize the scope of AWS if you weren't already aware, and you see that a good SysOps administrator has a *lot* of responsibility. You'll have plenty of management tools, support channels, and even AWS' SLAs, but you need to learn how to use all these resources in concert—and intelligently. People tend to be at their least patient when a system isn't operating correctly, and more often than not, that's the situation in which you'll be the most needed. Take your time through each chapter, though, and you'll quickly gain a handle for the various AWS services.

# Exam Essentials

**Recognize and define AWS managed services.**   AWS offers a dizzying number of managed services and facilities. You will be asked about these, so be familiar with the services and their basic functionality. It is best to review them often as well, because AWS is constantly adding new services to their library.

**Be familiar with the AWS Shared Responsibility Model.**   AWS provides clear guidelines about who is responsible for what in the cloud. You will likely be asked about this, and in particular, which aspects of security are yours as the customer and which are up to AWS.

**Differentiate between the various AWS support plans.**   You will be asked about the four support plans. You don't need to know the details as much as recognize those four support plan names and their basic use.

---

**EXERCISE 1.1**

### Use the AWS CLI

Install and configure the AWS CLI on your local system using the instructions at https://docs.aws.amazon.com/cli/latest/userguide/cli-chap-install.html. You should verify that the CLI is working with the version option:

```
$ aws --version
aws-cli/1.16.78 Python/3.6.5 Darwin/18.2.0 botocore/1.12.68
```

Your response will likely vary slightly depending on the version of the CLI and your version of Python. The only requirement here is that you have Python 3.x installed. Although the CLI will work with Pythion 2.x, that version of Python is headed for deprecation. Your version of the CLI likely will be newer than the one shown, but AWS is pretty good about not removing earlier version features.

As long as you don't get an error from running this command, though, you're ready to use the CLI.

---

### Configure the AWS CLI for Your AWS Account

You need to supply your API key, secret key, and a region to the CLI to make use of it with actual AWS services. You'll need to log into the AWS console, click your username, and then choose My Security Credentials to retrieve or generate these. You can begin this process with the CLI using the configure command:

```
$ aws configure
AWS Access Key ID [None]: YOUR KEY HERE
AWS Secret Access Key [None]: YOUR SECRET KEY HERE
Default region name [None]: us-east-1
Default output format [None]:
```

You can leave the output format blank if you're unsure.

After configuration, you can list your choices:

```
$ aws configure list
      Name                    Value             Type    Location
      ----                    -----             ----    --------
   profile                <not set>             None    None
access_key         ****************QEBQ shared-credentials-file
secret_key         ****************TSxN shared-credentials-file
    region                us-east-1     config-file    ~/.aws/config
```

### List S3 Buckets Using the CLI

As a quick test of the CLI, you can list all your current S3 buckets using the s3 command with ls:

```
$ aws s3 ls
2013-05-29 12:21:30 misi
2018-11-15 10:23:54 my-cloudtrial-account-logs
2018-08-20 18:34:02 mywebsitebucket-bdm
2018-11-14 10:33:02 yellowtagmedia-access
2018-11-12 10:19:30 yellowtagmedia-aws.com
2018-08-22 12:44:06 yellowtagmedia-mp3-storage
```

Your output will obviously vary with your own AWS environment.

---

**EXERCISE 1.4**

### Create a New S3 Bucket Using the CLI

Finally, make sure you can create an S3 bucket using the s3api command and the create-bucket subcommand:

```
$ aws s3api create-bucket --bucket created-with-cli
{
    "Location": "/created-with-cli"
}
```

You'll need to use your own bucket name, as S3 bucket names are global. However, you can verify that the bucket was created now using the s3 command with the ls subcommand:

```
$ aws s3 ls
2018-12-19 10:46:21 created-with-cli
2013-05-29 12:21:30 misi
2018-11-15 10:23:54 my-cloudtrial-account-logs
2018-08-20 18:34:02 mywebsitebucket-bdm
2018-11-14 10:33:02 yellowtagmedia-access
2018-11-12 10:19:30 yellowtagmedia-aws.com
2018-08-22 12:44:06 yellowtagmedia-mp3-storage
```

# Review Questions

You can find the answers in the Appendix.

1. You are tasked with managing multiple AWS accounts for a large organization. What AWS service provides bulk account management and consolidated billing?

   **A.** AWS Identity and Access Management (IAM)

   **B.** AWS Organizations

   **C.** AWS Trusted Advisor

   **D.** AWS Billing Manager

2. Which AWS service should you use to monitor applications and how they interact with your APIs?

   **A.** CloudTrail

   **B.** APIWatch

   **C.** CloudWatch

   **D.** APITrail

3. You are a new hire at a company with several cloud applications. They currently have no monitoring in place for their applications. What is the first service you'd look into adding to their cloud setup?

   **A.** CloudTrail

   **B.** CloudWatch

   **C.** Trusted Advisor

   **D.** System Monitor

4. Which of the following AWS facilities allows an application's resources to grow and shrink with demand?

   **A.** Elastic Load Balancing

   **B.** Elastic Compute

   **C.** Auto Scaling

   **D.** Route53

5. Which of the following AWS facilities are part of a scalable cluster of EC2 instances? (Choose two.)

   **A.** Elastic load balancer

   **B.** CloudFront

   **C.** Auto Scaling groups

   **D.** Lambda

**6.** Which of the following are AWS storage services? (Choose two.)

   **A.** EBS

   **B.** EC2

   **C.** RDS

   **D.** VPC

**7.** What AWS service provides users, groups, roles, and policies?

   **A.** Identity and Authorization Management

   **B.** Identity and Access Management

   **C.** Information and Authorization Management

   **D.** Identity and Authentication Management

**8.** Which of the following statements are true? (Choose all that apply.)

   **A.** AWS is responsible for the security of the cloud.

   **B.** AWS is responsible for security in the cloud.

   **C.** You (the customer) are responsible for the security of the cloud.

   **D.** You (the customer) are responsible for security in the cloud.

**9.** Who is responsible for the security of regions and availability zones?

   **A.** AWS

   **B.** The customer

   **C.** The account owner

   **D.** Responsibility is shared between the customer and AWS.

**10.** Which of the following is the basic networking component of AWS that contains subnets and instances?

   **A.** VPC

   **B.** VPN

   **C.** CLI

   **D.** Elastic Beanstalk

**11.** You are tasked with creating a uniform set of deployment scripts. What AWS facility would you use to standardize your application deployment and provisioning?

   **A.** CloudFront

   **B.** CloudFormation

   **C.** JSON

   **D.** CloudLaunch

**12.** Which of the following is not an AWS support plan?

   **A.** Free

   **B.** Basic

   **C.** Developer

   **D.** Enterprise

**13.** What AWS component acts as an analog to firewalls in on-premises applications?

   **A.** Network ACLs

   **B.** Internet Gateway

   **C.** Amazon VPC

   **D.** CloudFormation templates

**14.** What tool would you use to manage and interact with your AWS resources from a terminal or command prompt?

   **A.** AWS console

   **B.** AWS CLI

   **C.** AWS TLI

   **D.** AWS CloudFormation

**15.** You are tasked with creating a network environment for a company that is moving their web applications into AWS. Which of the following AWS services are most important to creating this environment? (Choose two.)

   **A.** AWS CloudFormation

   **B.** Amazon EC2

   **C.** Amazon VPC

   **D.** Amazon RDS

**16.** You are tasked with preparing a report on the advantages of AWS as compared to on-premises systems. As part of the report, you need to explain the responsiveness of AWS in dealing with services in the event of an outage. What would you need to consult to provide statistics and response times?

   **A.** Amazon VPC

   **B.** AWS Shared Responsibility Model

   **C.** AWS CloudFormation

   **D.** AWS Service Level Agreement

**17.** You are tasked with preparing a report on the advantages of AWS as compared to on-premises systems. As part of the report, you need to explain which parts of the current architecture will no longer be the responsibility of your company to maintain. What would you need to consult to provide statistics and response times?

  **A.** Amazon VPC

  **B.** AWS Shared Responsibility Model

  **C.** AWS CloudFormation

  **D.** AWS Service Level Agreement

**18.** Which of the following represents a separate geographic region in which AWS services run?

  **A.** Availability zone

  **B.** Region

  **C.** Edge location

  **D.** Compute center

**19.** How many availability zones does each AWS region have?

  **A.** 2

  **B.** 3

  **C.** 5

  **D.** It varies based on the region and AWS resource requirements.

**20.** Which of the following acts as a virtual datacenter within AWS?

  **A.** Compute center

  **B.** Region

  **C.** Availability zone

  **D.** Edge location

# Monitoring and Reporting

# Chapter

# 2

# Amazon CloudWatch

**THE AWS CERTIFIED SYSOPS
ADMINISTRATOR – ASSOCIATE EXAM
TOPICS COVERED IN THIS CHAPTER MAY
INCLUDE, BUT ARE NOT LIMITED TO, THE
FOLLOWING:**

**Domain 1.0: Monitoring and Reporting**

✓ **1.1   Create and maintain metrics and alarms utilizing
AWS monitoring services.**

✓ **1.2   Recognize and differentiate performance and availability metrics.**

✓ **1.3   Perform the steps necessary to remediate based on
performance and availability metrics.**

**Domain 7.0: Automation and Optimization**

✓ **7.1   Use AWS services and features to manage and assess
resource utilization.**

✓ **7.3   Automate manual or repeatable process to minimize
management overhead.**

In this chapter, you'll see how *Amazon CloudWatch* works and learn about its three key components: events, targets, and rules. You'll also learn how these relate to the fourth piece of the puzzle: CloudWatch alarms. Put all those together and you've got a robust monitoring solution for your AWS resources.

The chapter starts with an overview of AWS monitoring, but quickly moves into specifics of CloudWatch and how it relates to monitoring key AWS resources:

How AWS defines "monitoring" and how AWS virtualization helps—and at times limits—what can and cannot be monitored

What structures AWS offers through CloudWatch: events, alarms, and the wiring between these two powerful mechanisms

How to monitor compute resources like EC2 instances

How to monitor storage, from S3 to RDS to DynamoDB, and what AWS provides beyond simplistic "how full is my disk?" metrics

What AWS provides to make reporting, grouping, and interpreting the responses from these monitoring metrics an integrated part of your job (and workspace)

The ever-present links to key AWS documentation when you forget a particular metric's name or how to create a custom alarm

Amazon CloudWatch is easily one of the most important tools you'll use as a SysOps administrator. Whether you're ensuring things are not going wrong, or responding when they inevitably do, CloudWatch gives you a window into the applications for which you're responsible. From basics like CPU usage and network latency to carefully crafted application-specific metrics, CloudWatch is your friend. In fact, it's your application physician: CloudWatch should be your first stop in seeing whether your application is healthy.

# Monitoring on AWS

AWS is a cloud platform based on virtualized resources. That has a ton of advantages, as discussed in Chapter 1, "Introduction to Systems Operations on AWS"—and throughout this book—but it comes with some drawbacks. With no accessibility to a datacenter, physical hardware, or racks of storage and networking equipment, there is nothing to "check" to see whether things are behaving. You have a web-based console, a command line, some APIs…but where are the blinking lights? Where are the packet sniffers and patch panels?

In short, they're in CloudWatch. Now, like the rest of AWS, CloudWatch doesn't provide a direct analog for physical devices and on-premises datacenter activities. It does, however, give you a robust system for managing *metrics*. Ultimately, the AWS premise is that as a SysOps admin, you don't care about all those lights and cables as much as you care about metrics: what is the objective number that tells you how something is performing, and what is the acceptable threshold for that number?

Almost every single AWS service and resource provides metrics to CloudWatch, and CloudWatch becomes a sort of repository for all those collected metrics. It gives you tools to wade through the huge amount of collected data and to see those "everything is okay" thresholds for your particular application.

 Be careful in practical situations when you hear the term CloudWatch. Although AWS and exams use the term specifically as a reference to the service—distinguishing it from other managed services and tools that report to it—it often refers to more in practical usage. You'll often hear CloudWatch as a general term meaning "CloudWatch (the service), the data it collects, the reports within it, and the application of those reports." It can often become a catchall term. This is something you'll need to be aware of.

## Monitoring Is Event-Driven

All your monitoring in AWS is event-driven. An *event* (which as you'll later see becomes a CloudWatch event, a more formal idea around this same concept) is simply "something that happens in AWS and is captured." You don't have to do anything with every event, and you certainly won't want to. There are more events than you could ever memorize—and many only make sense to pay attention to in certain contexts.

But when something happens in AWS, it creates an event. For example, when a new EBS volume is created, the createVolume event is triggered, and it can either have a result of available or failed. This event and its result are sent to CloudWatch, the AWS repository. Figure 2.1 shows the flow of this event in a running system.

**FIGURE 2.1** Events are triggered in response to actions within an AWS environment, often with a result reported as well.

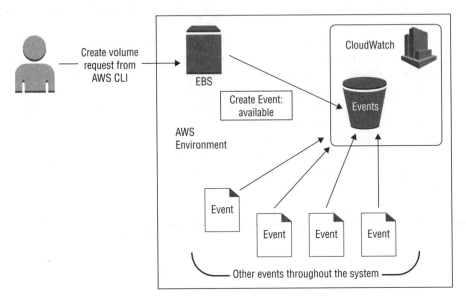

## Monitoring Is Customizable

Now, despite there being an almost innumerable set of events predefined by AWS, there are still times you may need something customized. For instance, perhaps you want to know when the number of queries to a particular queue reaches a certain threshold because there is business logic that should be applied at that stage. You can define these custom metrics easily.

Additionally, once defined, a custom metric behaves just like a predefined one. These custom metrics are added to the event repository alongside standardized metrics and can then be analyzed and interpreted.

You can even build metrics that report on on-premises applications and systems in a hybrid environment, resulting in a complete picture of all your connected systems, rather than just those in the cloud. You end up with a picture like that in Figure 2.2: CloudWatch integrated into your overall system at a very deep layer, providing monitoring that bends to your needs, rather than you bending to it.

**FIGURE 2.2** CloudWatch aggregates predefined and custom metrics on cloud and on-premises systems into a unified vision of your running systems.

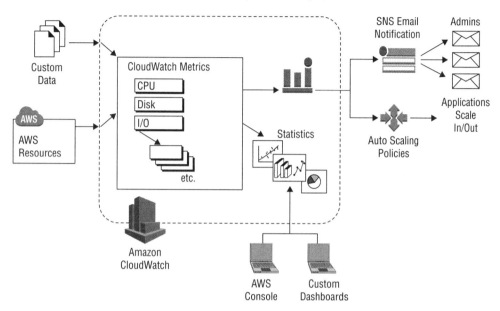

One important limitation of CloudWatch bears mentioning: it functions below the AWS Hypervisor, which means that it functions below (and sometimes at) the virtualization layer of AWS. This means that it can report on things like CPU usage and disk I/O...but it cannot see what is happening above that layer.

This means that CloudWatch cannot tell you what tasks or application processes are affecting performance. It can only report on the information it can directly see at the Hypervisor layer, or things that are reported to it. That's why it cannot (for example) tell you about disk usage, *unless* you write code that checks disk usage and send that metric to CloudWatch.

This is an important topic, and it sometimes shows up on the exam. You might be asked if CloudWatch can report on memory or disk usage by default; it cannot.

## Monitoring Drives Action

The final piece of the AWS monitoring puzzle is what occurs *after* a metric has reported a value or result outside of a predefined "everything is okay" threshold. When this happens, an *alarm* is triggered. An alarm is not necessarily the same as "something is wrong"; instead, think of an alarm as indicating that something needs to happen. That something might be running a piece of code in Lambda, or sending a message to an Auto Scaling group to scale in, or sending out an email via the AWS SNS service.

In short, monitoring in AWS is not just for the purpose of you, the SysOps administrator, actually looking at a dashboard and making a real-time decision. Rather, monitoring is set up in a way that triggers action when you're *not* looking at that dashboard. As you'll see further along in this chapter and then again in later chapters, part of your role is to define these actions. What should happen when CPU usage goes beyond 75 percent? Or when the request queue for your DynamoDB instances really pile up? Monitoring drives these actions.

# Basic CloudWatch Terms and Concepts

AWS introduces a number of terms that mean specific things in CloudWatch. You've already seen a few of these, such as alarm and metric. You'll need to understand these terms to make much sense of CloudWatch or the exam questions about it.

## CloudWatch Is Metric- and Event-Based

CloudWatch collects metrics. A metric is anything that can be tracked and is usually discrete: a number or percentage or value. Formally, AWS says a metric is a time-ordered set of data points, which gets at the notion that metrics are reported repeatedly over time. AWS defines a number of metrics, and you can also define custom metrics.

> Try to keep a metric and an event discrete in your understanding of AWS. An event is predefined and is something that happens, like bytes being received by a network interface. A metric is a measure of that event, or some facet of that event, like how many bytes are received in a given period of time. Events and metric are related, but not synonymous.

## Alarms Indicate Notifiable Change

In addition to metrics, there are alarms. A CloudWatch alarm initiates action. You can set an alarm to respond when a metric is reported with a result value outside of a threshold or result set. For example, an alarm could be set when CPU utilization on your EC2 instances reaches 80 percent. You can also set alarms on lower bounds, such as when that same CPU utilization returns to less than 50 percent.

# Events and CloudWatch Events Are Lower Level

CloudWatch also relies heavily on events. An event is something that happens, usually related to a metric changing or reporting in to CloudWatch, but at a system level. An event can then trigger further action, just as an alarm can.

Events are typically streamed to CloudWatch; they are reported almost constantly from various low-level AWS resources. Additionally—perhaps just to add a little confusion—CloudWatch Events (CWE) is a specific name for this stream of system events. So CloudWatch Events is the formal mechanism through which events (lowercase "e" this time) get to the CloudWatch system.

# CloudWatch Events Has Three Components

Within CloudWatch Events are three key components: events, rules, and targets. An event is the thing that is being reported and is a proxy for that thing happening. A rule is an expression that matches incoming events. If there's a match to an event, the event is routed to a target for processing. A target is another AWS component, typically a piece of code in Lambda or an Auto Scaling group, or perhaps an email that should be sent out.

# Choosing Between Alarms and Events

If you've been following along, you may rightfully be a little confused. Metrics make sense, but how is an event related to an alarm? Which is which? And when do you use alarms versus when do you use events?

In short, alarms are for monitoring any metric reported on your account, related to your application. These typically deal with request latency on your ELBs or perhaps the throughput of an important query that uses your RDS instances. Alarms are for your specific application needs.

Events describe change in your AWS resources. Think of these as logs, reporting on the general health of your application.

Put another way: an alarm might indicate that a professional football player's fatigue level is increasing and therefore he is running more slowly. It's specific to his function in a performance context. An event might indicate that same player's blood pressure is high when he's walking down the street. It's a *general* indication of health unrelated to his function.

Both alarms and events are important, and you'll need to monitor both.

# What's in a Namespace?

Another key concept in CloudWatch is that of the namespace. A *namespace* is just a container for a collection of related CloudWatch metrics. Because so many metrics might share a general purpose—CPU utilization on an EC2 instance, an RDS instance, and a DynamoDB instance, for example—AWS provides namespaces to distinguish these from one another.

AWS provides a number of predefined namespaces, all beginning with AWS/[service]. So AWS/EC2/CPUUtilization is CPU utilization for an EC2 instance, while AWS/DynamoDB/CPUUtilization is the same metric but for DynamoDB. There is a *long* list of namespaces, and it grows as services are added. For the most up-to-date list, check out https://docs.aws.amazon.com/AmazonCloudWatch/latest/monitoring/aws-services-cloudwatch-metrics.html.

You'll also need to work with namespaces yourself. When you create a custom metric, you can place that metric in an AWS namespace or create one of your own. For example, you might create the Media/photos namespace to report on usage of photos in your media suite of applications.

> Keep your namespaces specific, useful, and succinct. YourCompany/
> PerformanceMetrics/Network is a namespace that is easily understood and
> doesn't require 30 seconds of typing or 14 mouse clicks to navigate in the con-
> sole. YourCompany/Mercury/TPIO is a namespace that is obscure, uses code
> names (presumably "Mercury" refers to a system or application), and acronyms
> (what does TPIO stand for?). The former is a good namespace; the latter is not.

## To the 10th Dimension

You can also provide up to 10 dimensions for your metrics. A *dimension* is a name/value pair that helps identify a metric. For a metric reported on an EC2 instance, you might have an InstanceId=1-234567 dimension and an InstanceType=m1.large dimension. These pairs provide additional information about the metric that help separate it from other similar metrics, perhaps on different instances or of different classes.

## Statistics Aggregate Metrics

Add the term *statistic* to your growing CloudWatch vocabulary. A statistic is just what it sounds like: a value that gives you some sense of a particular metric (or metrics) over time. CloudWatch gives you several helpful default statistics, shown in Table 2.1.

**TABLE 2.1**  AWS-provided statistics for CloudWatch metrics

| Metric Name | Description |
| --- | --- |
| Minimum | Over a period, this is the lowest reported value. |
| Maximum | Over a period, this is the highest reported value. |
| Sum | This provides the sum of all reported metric values over a period of time. |
| Average | This is the mean, which is Sum/SampleCount, for a period of time. |
| SampleCount | The total number of reported data points for this statistic set |
| pNN.NN | This gives you the value of a specified percentile, such as p99.99 or p50. |

Statistics are reported over time, so you'll need to specify that time period (more on that later). You can also select a subset of all metrics based on a dimension (or several dimensions). For example, you might want the average for all metrics reported on instances with the dimensions `Domain=Rockville` and `Environment=Prod`.

# Monitoring Compute

EC2 provides some of the easiest-to-interpret and useful metrics of all of AWS' predefined metrics. Instance metrics are recorded for 15 months to give you easy access to historical data as well.

> All instance metrics are provided to CloudWatch in five-minute increments. You can increase this frequency to one-minute increments by turning on detailed monitoring.
>
> Activating detailed monitoring is possible through the console. Select your instance and choose Actions ➢ CloudWatch Monitoring ➢ Enable Detailed Monitoring.

## EC2 Instance Metrics

First, you should realize that there would be pages upon pages of tables if you wanted a list of every single available EC2-related metric. There are metrics for CPU credits, on instances themselves for CPU and disk I/O, status checks, and much, much more. You can view all available EC2 metrics at `https://docs.aws.amazon.com/AWSEC2/latest/UserGuide/viewing_metrics_with_cloudwatch.html`.

Fortunately, many of these are things you can simply look up. There are only a large handful of metrics that you will use over and over and that you should be familiar with for the certification exam. For a start, you *should* be comfortable with the usage of instance metrics, shown in Table 2.2.

**TABLE 2.2**   Predefined instance metrics for EC2 instances

| Metric name | Description |
| --- | --- |
| CPUUtilization | This is one of the fundamental EC2 instance metrics. It tells you the percentage of allocated compute units that are currently in use. |
| DiskReadOps | This reports a count of completed read operations from all instance store volumes available. |
| DiskWriteOps | The counterpart to DiskReadOps, this reports a count of completed read operations from all instance store volumes available. |

**TABLE 2.2**   Predefined instance metrics for EC2 instances *(continued)*

| Metric name | Description |
| --- | --- |
| DiskReadBytes | This reports the bytes read from all available instance store volumes. |
| DiskWriteBytes | This reports the total of all bytes written to instance store volumes available. |
| NetworkIn | The total bytes received on all network interfaces |
| NetworkOut | The total bytes sent out across all network interfaces on the instance |
| NetworkPacketsIn | The number of packets received by *all* network interfaces on the instance. This is available only for basic monitoring. |
| NetworkPacketsOut | The number of packets sent out across *all* network interfaces on the instance. This is also available only for basic monitoring. |

# EC2 EBS Metrics

There are additional compute metrics that are associated with EBS volumes. That may seem a little odd; aren't EBS volumes storage? They certainly are, but many times, metrics for EBS volumes straddle the line between being compute metrics versus storage metrics. The metrics in Table 2.3 are EBS-related and report on storage volumes, but do that reporting in light of the instance to which the EBS volumes are attached.

**TABLE 2.3**   Predefined instance metrics for EBS (note instance class requirements)

| Metric name | Description |
| --- | --- |
| EBSReadOps | A count of the completed read operations from all EBS volumes attached to an instance |
| EBSWriteOps | A count of completed write operations to a specific instance in a specified period of time |
| EBSReadBytes | A count of bytes read from all volumes attached to the reporting instance. Note that this is the byte count, rather than the total number of read operations (that's in EBSReadOps). |
| EBSWriteBytes | A count of all bytes read from EBS volumes in a specific time period |
| EBSIOBalance% | This provides the percentage of I/O credits remaining in the burst bucket and is available only for basic monitoring. |
| EBSByteBalance% | This is the percentage of throughput credits remaining and, like EBSIOBalance%, is available only for basic monitoring. |

> These EBS metrics are specifically available for the following instance types: C5, C5d, M5, M5a, M5d, R5, R5a, R5d, T3, and z1d.

## ECS Metrics

With the addition of containers via ECS, the Elastic Container Service, there is a whole new set of metrics that are now relevant to you as the SysOps administrator. These metrics are all available in the AWS/ECS namespace, and they give you information about a running cluster rather than a specific container. Several key metrics are shown in this namespace in Table 2.4

**TABLE 2.4**   Container-based metrics reported to CloudWatch

| Metric name | Description |
| --- | --- |
| CPUReservation | The percentage of CPU units that are reserved for a running cluster, related to the overall CPU units for all container instances in the cluster. This helps determine what EC2 launch type is used. |
| CPUUtilization | The percentage of CPU units used by the cluster, compared to all CPU units in use by ECS. Note this is *usage*, as opposed to *reservation*. |
| MemoryReservation | The percentage of memory reserved by currently running ECS tasks |
| MemoryUtilization | The percentage of memory in use by ECS tasks. Like CPUUtilization, this is actual *usage*, as opposed to *reservation*. |

# Monitoring Storage

When you move from compute into storage, the world of CloudWatch metrics expands even more rapidly. Whereas in compute you essentially have instances and containers, in compute you have S3, DynamoDB, and RDS as central pillars of a storage solution. You could also add to that RedShift and Elastic MapReduce (EMR), and then you start to touch on CloudFront and ElastiCache, which aren't quite storage but are closely associated.

Here, the Internet is your friend: it's always trivial to look up a metric or set of metrics by service. Simply typing **AWS CloudWatch ElastiCache** will get you what you need quickly. However, there are some metrics that you should know off the top of your head, for both your own use and, of course, the AWS exam.

# S3 Metrics

There are a *lot* of S3 metrics—more than makes sense to repeat on the page. Table 2.5 gives you the most common. These all exist within the AWS/S3 namespace.

**TABLE 2.5**   S3 metrics for daily storage and requests

| Metric name | Description |
| --- | --- |
| BucketSizeBytes | A metric related to the daily storage of your buckets. BucketSizeBytes gives you the amount of data, as bytes, stored in a particular bucket. |
| NumberOfObjects | The total number of objects stored in a bucket, for all storage classes |
| AllRequests | This and the following metrics are related to requests made to our buckets. AllRequests is the total number of HTTP requests, regardless of type, made to a bucket. |
| GetRequests | Total number of GET requests to a bucket. There are similar metrics for other requests: PutRequests, DeleteRequests, HeadRequests, PostRequests, and SelectRequests, each corresponding to a different request type. |
| BytesDownloaded | Total bytes downloaded for requests to a bucket |
| BytesUploaded | Total bytes uploaded to a bucket. These are the bytes that contain a request body, specifically. |
| FirstByteLatency | The per-request time for a completed request, on a first-byte millisecond basis |
| TotalRequestLatency | Elapsed time, in milliseconds, from the first to the last byte of a request |

# RDS Metrics

Like S3, there are more metrics for RDS than is reasonable to memorize. Table 2.6 provides a few key ones, and they are worth at least recognizing and understanding for your certification exam.

**TABLE 2.6**   RDS metrics provided to CloudWatch

| Metric name | Description |
| --- | --- |
| DatabaseConnections | Number of in-use database connections |
| DiskQueueDepth | Number of I/O requests waiting to access the disk |
| FreeStorageSpace | The number of available bytes for storage |
| ReadIOPS | The average number of disk reads per second. There is a corresponding WriteIOPS. |
| ReadLatency | The average time taken for disk read/write operations. The write counterpart is WriteLatency. |
| ReplicaLag | This is a useful one. It reports on the amount of time read replicas of the primary database instance lag behind the source instance. |

There are some differences when working with RDS compared to other metrics, though. RDS is a managed service, so you can't set the frequency of the metrics or switch between basic and detailed metrics. As a result, RDS sends metrics to CloudWatch every minute, and that's not configurable.

## DynamoDB2 Metrics

You should be sensing a theme with storage metrics: there are a *lot* of them in AWS. This makes sense, though. Most storage in AWS is managed, and you have less direct access. AWS recognizes this and sends you a lot of information so that you can keep up with what's happening in those managed services.

DynamoDB metrics are in the AWS/DynamoDB namespace. Similar to most other managed services, they are reported every minute, and that's not configurable. There's one other wrinkle with these metrics: they are reported to CloudWatch only when they are non-zero. That can skew your averages if you're not careful.

Table 2.7 lists a nonexhaustive list of DynamoDB metrics you should familiarize yourself with.

**TABLE 2.7**   DynamoDB metrics reported to CloudWatch

| Metric name | Description |
| --- | --- |
| ConsumedReadCapacityUnits | The number of read capacity units consumed. This helps you track how much throughput you've used, as that is typically what you provision when you set up the database. |
| ConsumedWriteCapacityUnits | This is the companion metric to ConsumedReadCapacityUnits. It gives you consumed write units. |
| ProvisionedReadCapacityUnits | This is the number of units provisioned for reading for a table or index. |
| ProvisionedWriteCapacityUnits | This gives you the number of provisioned unites for writing to a table or index. |
| ReplicationLatency | This gives you the time elapsed between an item appearing in a DynamoDB stream for one replica table and then appearing in another replica. |
| SystemErrors | These are the number of HTTP 500 errors reported by DynamoDB over a period of time. |

Table 2.7 could be much larger and longer. However, the metrics shown are important, and you'll do well to at least recognize them.

> The best thing to do in terms of exam preparation is to ensure you understand the terminology used, rather than memorizing specifics of DynamoDB or S3 or RDS metric names. Understand "latency" and "throughput" and "provisioned," and you can generally reason your way through the exam questions.

# CloudWatch Alarms

So you've got your metrics, and they're all pouring into CloudWatch. So what? What do you do with all this data? Generally, you want to be alerted and then take action. Of course, one of the key best practices—whether in or out of the cloud—is to automate everything you can. It's much better to build a system that does what you want than to do something manually.

Alarms give you the framework to do just that when it comes to monitoring. You create a set of "okay" values, attach an alarm, and then respond to that alarm.

## Create an Alarm Threshold

An alarm is intended to go off when a metric is outside of a set of values you consider "okay." You can set a specific value as a high or low value, or a range of acceptable values. For instance, suppose you want to add instances to an Auto Scaling group when any single instance reports that it is using more than 85 percent of its CPU, and then scale back in when all instances are reporting less than 60 percent CPU utilization.

EC2 instances report a metric for this: CPUUtilization in the AWS/EC2 namespace. You can watch this metric and set an alarm threshold for the metric at 85. You also should specify how many periods the metric must be above that threshold; you might want to scale out only if CPU is above 85 percent for more than four periods.

> You'll need to keep up with your monitoring frequency to set good alarms. Basic monitoring reports every five minutes, so two successive metrics above a threshold might be enough, perhaps three at most. If you're using detailed monitoring, though, you'll get reports every minute, and then you may want five or six consecutive reports.
>
> It's worth noting that CloudWatch always wants two successive values above/below/in a threshold. It's not intended to trigger an alarm after a single value is reported.

## Set Off an Alarm

Once you've set a threshold, CloudWatch takes care of the rest. The new alarm can be in one of three states at any given time: OK, ALARM, and INSUFFICIENT_DATA. These are pretty self-explanatory. When an alarm goes into the ALARM state, you can set off an action.

But that's not the only time you can create an action. You could actually set additional actions for when the alarm returns to the OK state (perhaps scaling back in that Auto Scaling group in the example mentioned earlier).

## Respond to an Alarm

When the alarm initiates an action, you can do something. That something can be a whole range of things: send off an email or provision a new instance or update an ELB. Basically, anything you can do in AWS, you can do in response to an alarm.

Often, you'll invoke code. Part of the beauty of AWS Lambda is that this code can run without a lot of overhead, making the entire CloudWatch alarm framework even more useful.

# CloudWatch Events

So far, the focus has been on metrics reported from AWS managed services and your own resources using EC2 instances, EBS volumes, and the like. These metrics will tell you how resources are serving your application, as well as how the things your application is doing in turn affects your overall provisioning and costs. But that's only part of the picture of your AWS environment.

You also need to know how your system is doing, without regard to your application. If certain resources are unhealthy or not performing at capacity, or if the state of a resource is changing, you have to know that. You may also need to make a change in your use of those or related resources.

This is where CloudWatch Events come in. Now, keep clear that *Amazon CloudWatch Events* (capitalized, and sometimes abbreviated as CWE) is distinct from the metrics that are sent to CloudWatch. CloudWatch Events has its own set of constructs, and it operates a little differently than CloudWatch. But it's key to managing your environment, so it can't be discounted.

## Events

An event is a change in your AWS environment. Now, as mentioned earlier, an event is part of the overall CloudWatch Events structure. You'll must be careful to make this distinction; this means that CloudWatch Events has events, which can be pretty confusing.

An event can be generated in one of four different ways:

- An AWS resource changes state. For example, an EC2 instance moves from pending to running, or a database instance moves from running to terminated.

- API calls and console sign-ins occur. These are reported via CloudTrail (which focuses on logging and API calls) but come across as events.

- You generate an event in your code. This is a bit of a melding of two worlds, but your application code can push events to CloudWatch Events for processing.

- A schedule triggers. You can trigger events with cron-style scheduling on a repeated basis.

All of these are simply tools—hooks that allow you to attach behavior when something happens. And that's where rules come into the picture.

## Rules

A *rule* is the connective tissue between events and targets. A rule matches incoming events, and if there's a match, sends the event to the specified target. A target can then kick off processing, evaluate the event, send an email, or do anything else you like. (You'll soon see this is similar to an alarm for a metric in CloudWatch.)

A rule can also filter parts of an event or send additional bits of information along with the event. It uses JavaScript Object Notation (JSON) to do this. In fact, JSON is the language used for all of this connectivity, so a rule can simply add or filter the JSON that's passed to a target.

## Targets

A *target* processes the JSON data it is sent by a rule, resulting from a match on one or more events. The result is often a stream of JSON to several targets of your choosing.

Typical targets include EC2 instances, Lambda functions (this is a popular one), ECS tasks, step functions, Simple Queue Service (SQS) queues, and Simple Notification Service (SNS) topics. What these targets do with the JSON is really then up to you. You could send off messages via email, scale in or scale out an Auto Scaling group, or provision more instances.

At the point that a target is reached, you can begin to think of further processing as the same as when you've received a CloudWatch alarm, discussed earlier. Although application metrics raising alarms is a different mechanism than events matching rules and being forwarded to targets, once action is taken the system handles things the same way. In fact, there's no reason you couldn't have the same Lambda function triggered by an alarm and function as a target.

# Summary

CloudWatch is a far-reaching tool. Although it's simple enough to say, "CloudWatch is the AWS solution for monitoring," there's much more than that to learn and ultimately master. You need a working knowledge of the various functionality that CloudWatch provides, as well as an understanding of the metrics that AWS provides by default. Much of your work with CloudWatch will involve assembling and interpreting these defaults.

That's not enough on its own, though. As your applications become more complex, so will your uses of CloudWatch. Custom metrics will often be required to solve monitoring that is tuned for your specific application. You'll also find that CloudWatch is one of your key tools for troubleshooting problems. Not sure why an instance is nonresponsive? Throw up a couple of CPU- and network-related metrics and see what's going on at peak and low load times.

Finally, all of this comes together in dashboards and reporting. AWS makes this work easy, but you should be familiar with grouping resources through resource groups and then building out dashboards for easy review. A metric that takes more than a few seconds to locate and understand probably isn't that valuable a metric.

# Resources to Review

Amazon CloudWatch:

https://aws.amazon.com/cloudwatch/

Amazon CloudWatch Events:

https://docs.aws.amazon.com/AmazonCloudWatch/latest/events/
WhatIsCloudWatchEvents.html

Amazon CloudWatch Logs:

https://docs.aws.amazon.com/AmazonCloudWatch/latest/logs/
WhatIsCloudWatchLogs.html

CloudWatch Custom Dashboards:

https://aws.amazon.com/blogs/aws/
cloudwatch-dashboards-create-use-customized-metrics-views/

AWS Services That Publish CloudWatch Metrics:

https://docs.aws.amazon.com/AmazonCloudWatch/latest/monitoring/
aws-services-cloudwatch-metrics.html

# Exam Essentials

**Recognize use cases for which CloudWatch is well suited.** CloudWatch is a monitoring service, and it's going to be your first line of defense in troubleshooting. You'll collect and track metrics and set alarms, from simple metrics such as CPU usage to application-tuned custom ones that you define.

**Recite the core components of a CloudWatch event.** An event in CloudWatch has the event itself, a target, and a rule. Events indicate changes in your environment, targets process events, and rules match events and route them to targets. Get these three concepts straight and you'll be set to handle the more conceptual exam questions.

**Recognize names of CloudWatch metrics.** You will be asked about default AWS monitoring—CPU, status, disk, network, but *not* memory—and about the various metric names. Although memorizing all of them is tough, you should review AWS-defined metric names before taking the exam.

**Explain how a CloudWatch alarm works.** An alarm is a construct that watches a metric and is triggered at certain thresholds. This alarm can then itself trigger actions, such as an Auto Scaling group scaling out or perhaps a Lambda function running. You should be able to describe this process and recognize its usefulness.

**List and explain the three CloudWatch alarm states.**   An alarm can be in three states: OK, ALARM, and INSUFFICIENT_DATA. OK means the metric is within the defined threshold; ALARM means the alarm is "going off" because the metric is outside or has crossed the defined threshold. INSUFFICIENT_DATA should be obvious: there's not enough to report yet.

**Create custom metrics for anything above the Hypervisor.**   It's subtle, but important: CloudWatch knows nothing about specific tasks that are affecting performance, because applications all live above the AWS virtualization layer. This is why CloudWatch doesn't provide a memory metric that lives above the Hypervisor. You can create custom metrics, but they'll require an agent, and they will be more limited than metrics that can interact below that virtualization layer.

# Exercises

Once you have metrics—both predefined and custom—and events flowing into CloudWatch, you're going to quickly find that keeping up with them all is a huge hassle. Each metric sits in a different place, and that means you can spend a whole lot of time hopping from screen to screen, or running tons of CLI commands.

The best way to handle this is to create a dashboard that has your essential metrics all in one place. In this section, you'll do just that.

 This lab assumes that you have some resources up and running in your AWS environment. Otherwise, you'll have very little on which to report. If you don't have any resources, you may want to come back to this lab later in the book.

Another idea would be to take this as an opportunity to create some new EC2 instances and S3 buckets, and play around with moving data back and forth between buckets. Consider connecting to your instances and updating them. Anything that causes interaction, network I/O, or CPU usage is perfect for this section's metrics.

**EXERCISE 2.1**

### Create a Custom CloudWatch Dashboard

**1.**  Log into the AWS management console.

**2.**  On the Services page, choose the Dashboards link along the left. You should see an empty set of dashboards, as shown in Figure 2.3.

**FIGURE 2.3** You can easily create dashboards in CloudWatch through the AWS management console.

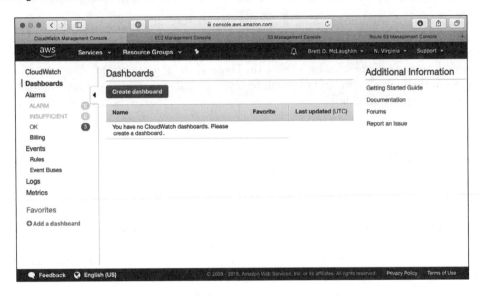

3. Click the Create Dashboard button, and then select a name for your dashboard. That will create the dashboard in CloudWatch.

4. Next up, you'll have to select a metric to add to the dashboard. You have several options, shown in Figure 2.4.

**FIGURE 2.4** CloudWatch dashboards can contain a number of metrics and formats for viewing those metrics.

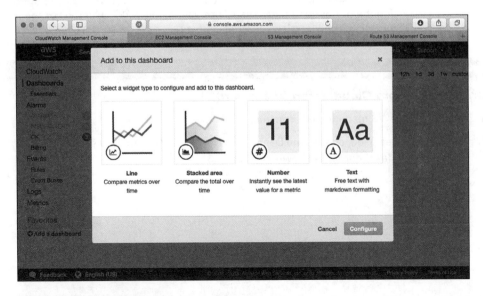

For now, click Cancel.

5. You should be able to click the Dashboards link again and see your new dashboard in the list (which may be a list of just one for you at this point), as shown in Figure 2.5.

**FIGURE 2.5**    Your complete list of dashboards will show up, and you can always add and remove from this list.

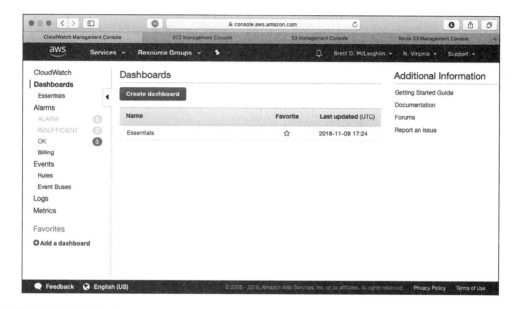

---

### Add EC2 Line Metrics

1. Click on your custom dashboard, and then click the Create Widget button. Select the Line option and click Configure.

2. You'll see an empty graph and some options at the bottom for metrics, all organized by AWS resource. Figure 2.6 shows a simple AWS account that has a few EC2 instances and S3 buckets, and not much else.

3. Select the EC2 option, and then choose Per-Instance Metrics. You can filter metrics here, as there are a lot to choose from. In this case, assuming you have a few EC2 instances, enter **CPU** in the search box, press Enter/Return, and choose CPUUtilization for all your available instances. This is shown for two instances in Figure 2.7.

**FIGURE 2.6** Your screen may look a little different. You'll see options only for resources in your account.

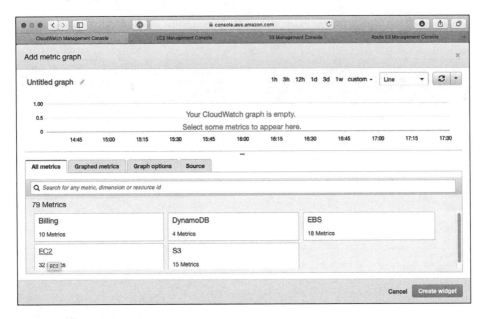

**FIGURE 2.7** As you select metrics, the screen will auto-update with graphics for the selected metrics.

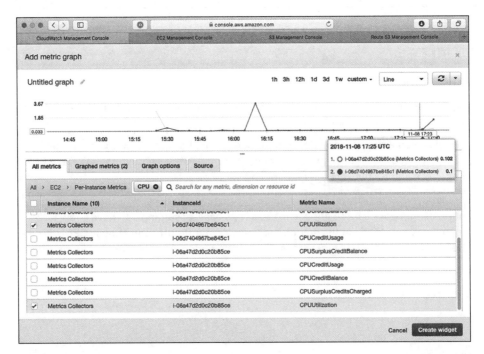

**4.** Now click Create Widget and you'll see the new widget added to your dashboard (as shown in Figure 2.8). Note that even here, the graph is showing you metrics in real time on your new dashboard.

**FIGURE 2.8** You can add as many widgets to your dashboard as you like.

**5.** Finally, click Save Dashboard. This is an important step and often missed! If you don't click Save Dashboard, you'll lose your updates to the dashboard.

---

## EXERCISE 2.3

### Name Your Widgets

Looking back at previous figures, the titles of the widgets really aren't that helpful: "NetworkIn, NetworkOut" isn't great if you have no idea what it's reporting on. It's a good idea to name your widgets in a helpful way.

**1.** At your main dashboard screen, select the widget you want to rename, and look for the three vertical dots next to the current title of a widget. Figure 2.9 shows a widget with this highlighted.

**FIGURE 2.9** The three vertical dots are for widget actions.

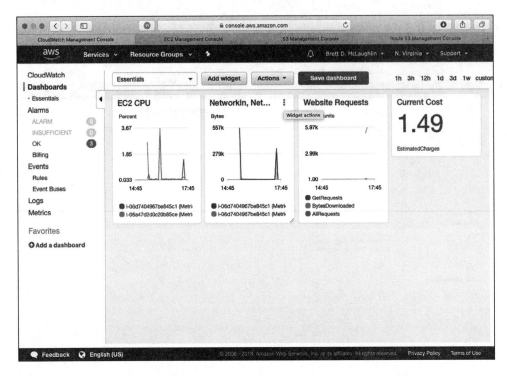

2. Click Edit in the submenu.

3. When the graph appears, click the name of the widget, type a new name, and press Enter/Return.

   Your widget will now have a much more human-readable—and therefore helpful—title.

**EXERCISE 2.4**

## Create a Text Widget

1. You can easily add labels and explanatory text to your dashboard. Click Add Widget again and select the Text widget, then click Configure.

2. You can use markdown text to fill out the widget with custom text-based content. There are formatting examples to make this simple.

3. Save the widget. Figure 2.10 shows a simple example that explains how three metric widgets are related.

**FIGURE 2.10**    Text widgets help turn dashboards into user-friendly mechanisms for monitoring.

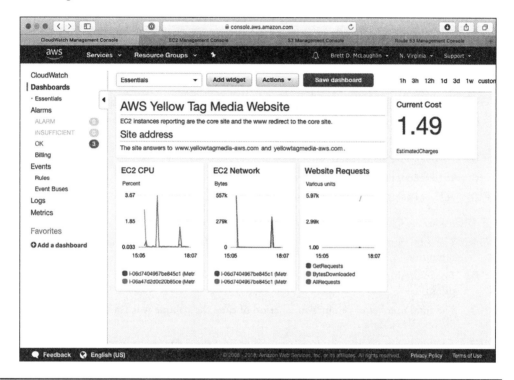

# Review Questions

You can find the answers in the Appendix.

1. What is the default frequency at which CloudWatch collects metrics?

   A. 30 seconds

   B. 1 minute

   C. 5 minutes

   D. 10 minutes

2. Which CloudWatch metric should you look at to determine how many of available input/output operations per second (IOPS) have been delivered on an EBS volume?

   A. ReadWriteThroughputPercentage

   B. ThroughputPercentage

   C. VolumeConsumedReadWriteOps

   D. VolumeThroughputPercentage

3. What does the CloudWatch metric VolumeIdleTime report?

   A. The total number of minutes in a period of time when no read or write operations were submitted

   B. The total number of seconds in a period of time when no read or write operations were submitted

   C. The total number of minutes in a period of time the volume was waiting on an instance to complete a data transfer

   D. The total number of seconds in a period of time the volume was waiting on an instance to complete a data transfer

4. Which CloudWatch metric would you use to see how much of available CPU is being used by a stalled EC2 instance?

   A. CPUUsage

   B. ComputeUtilization

   C. CPUUtilization

   D. ReadWriteUtilization

5. Why might you use a resource group in CloudWatch?

   A. You need to monitor EC2 instances that are in multiple regions.

   B. You need to monitor EC2 instances that are in multiple availability zones.

   C. You need to monitor EC2 instances, S3 buckets, and an ECS cluster through a single dashboard.

   D. You need to monitor nondefault metrics on a set of EC2 instances and S3 buckets.

**6.** You want to enable detailed monitoring on an EC2 instance. What steps should you follow?

   **A.** Stop the instance, select Enable Detailed Monitoring, and restart the instance.

   **B.** Select the instance and select Enable Detailed Monitoring.

   **C.** Stop the instance, terminate the instance, create a new instance, select Enable Detailed Monitoring, and start the new instance.

   **D.** Snapshot the instance, create a new instance from the snapshot, select Enable Detailed Monitoring on the new instance, and then start the new instance.

**7.** What mechanism in AWS is used to group resources into a resource group?

   **A.** The user-defined tags on the resources

   **B.** The user-defined IAM role on the resources

   **C.** Shared characteristics in the resource names

   **D.** Ownership of the resources

**8.** Which of the following is not supplied as a default metric in CloudWatch?

   **A.** Memory Usage

   **B.** CPU Usage

   **C.** Disk Usage

   **D.** Network IO

**9.** What is the most frequent granularity that CloudWatch performs for updating the status of a standard metric?

   **A.** 30 seconds

   **B.** 1 minute

   **C.** 90 seconds

   **D.** 5 minutes

**10.** What different levels of monitoring does CloudWatch offer? (Choose two.)

   **A.** Free

   **B.** Basic

   **C.** Frequent

   **D.** Detailed

**11.** Which of the following are monitored on your EC2 instances by default CloudWatch metrics? (Choose two.)

   **A.** CPU

   **B.** Memory

   **C.** Throughput

   **D.** Status

12. Which of the following statements is true regarding how CloudWatch monitors an Auto Scaling group created in the AWS management console versus one created via the CLI?

    A. An Auto Scaling group created using the CLI will use basic monitoring, but one created using the console will use detailed monitoring.

    B. An Auto Scaling group created using the CLI will use detailed monitoring, but one created using the console will use basic monitoring.

    C. Regardless of the creation method, Auto Scaling groups use basic monitoring by default.

    D. Regardless of the creation method, Auto Scaling groups use detailed monitoring by default.

13. Which of the following is not possible using a custom CloudWatch metric?

    A. Scaling in an Auto Scaling group based on a concurrent connections metric

    B. Scaling out an Auto Scaling group based on number of requests received by the group

    C. Scaling out an Auto Scaling group based on number of active threads in the group

    D. Scaling in an Auto Scaling group when CPU usage gets low

14. You have a custom CloudWatch metric that is monitoring network spikes on requests coming into your DynamoDB instances. You are seeing recurring spikes every third, fourth, and fifth minute of the hour. One of your developers believes the culprit is a long-running process triggered from an EC2 instance. How can you best validate your developer's hypothesis without affecting system performance?

    A. Increase the frequency of the metric collection to every 10 seconds and see if the spikes are persistent or they happen only at certain times within the third, fourth, and fifth minutes.

    B. Increase the frequency of the metric collection to every 10 seconds and add an additional metric to monitor bytes out from the EC2 instance's network interface.

    C. Add additional metrics to monitor bytes out from the EC2 instance running the process and see if there is a correspondence between the bytes out of the instance and the bytes into the DynamoDB instances.

    D. Turn the process on the instance off and see if the network spikes still occur on the DynamoDB instances.

15. You have enabled detailed monitoring for CloudWatch on all standard metrics. How often will metrics be reported?

    A. 30 seconds

    B. 1 minute

    C. 5 minutes

    D. 10 minutes

**16.** How often can a high-resolution metric be reported?

   **A.** 30 seconds

   **B.** 1 minute

   **C.** 1 second

   **D.** 1 millisecond

**17.** Which of the following is not a cause for a CloudWatch Event being triggered?

   **A.** A preset schedule causes the triggering of the event.

   **B.** An EC2 instance starts up.

   **C.** A user logs into the AWS console.

   **D.** Code on an EC2 instance makes a request to a REST API.

**18.** Which of the following is the prefix to predefined AWS events?

   **A.** AMZ

   **B.** AWS

   **C.** Amazon

   **D.** AMZN

**19.** Which of the following would require custom programming—beyond easily defined CloudWatch alarms—to monitor?

   **A.** Network usage increasing to 80 percent or more of allocated capacity

   **B.** Network latency increasing to over 10 ms

   **C.** Network output dropping to 0 bytes

   **D.** Network usage dropping by more than 50 percent in a given hour

**20.** Which of the following connects CloudWatch Events to targets?

   **A.** Rules

   **B.** Triggers

   **C.** Metrics

   **D.** Outputs

# Chapter 3

# AWS Organizations

THE AWS CERTIFIED SYSOPS ADMINISTRATOR – ASSOCIATE EXAM TOPICS COVERED IN THIS CHAPTER MAY INCLUDE, BUT ARE NOT LIMITED TO, THE FOLLOWING:

**Domain 1.0: Monitoring and Reporting**

✓ 1.1   Create and maintain alarms utilizing AWS monitoring services.

**Domain 5.0: Security and Compliance**

✓ 5.2   Implement access controls when using AWS.

**Domain 7.0: Automation and Optimization**

✓ 7.2   Employ cost-optimization strategies for efficient resource utilization.

*AWS Organizations* is a monitoring solution that provides for monitoring of actual AWS accounts. In Chapter 1, "Amazon CloudWatch", you saw how CloudWatch provided monitoring of the resources in a single account: your instances and buckets and load balancers. But in the modern cloud era, most medium and large organizations have multiple AWS accounts. This presents a different type of monitoring challenge.

While Identity and Access Management (IAM) offers groups, roles, permissions, and users, and provides tools to manage those constructs, management of users across accounts has been a longstanding AWS issue. The same is true of managing billing across multiple accounts. AWS Organizations is the recent AWS offering to address these common issues.

This chapter explains the role of AWS Organizations, and then goes into the following details:

The core concepts of AWS Organizations: organizational units, service control policies, and consolidated billing

Benefits of AWS Organizations, especially related to cross-account budgeting and discounts

Relationship to IAM and user management across accounts

Why AWS Organizations is a better solution for resource management than tagging

Managing permissions at a cross-account level with service control policies

# Managing Multiple Accounts

In the early days of AWS and cloud providers, most organizations had a single account, or at most one account per office. This made cross-account management at best a minor concern. Applications were deployed to single accounts, and with AWS IAM (Identity and Access Management), multiple users could access the single account.

However, with the near-standardization of the cloud as a fixture in technical organizations, and now a major force in nontechnical ones, multiple accounts are common. It's not unusual for a single organization's office to have multiple accounts, and for large organizations to have 10, 20, or even more individual AWS accounts. But this is where management headaches abound.

Every account has its own set of IAM users, each with various resource permissions. On top of that, each account has EC2 instances and S3 buckets and DynamoDB instances and Auto Scaling groups...and the list goes on. Keeping up with these for one account is not trivial; keeping up with them across multiple accounts is very difficult.

AWS Organizations is aimed squarely at these problems. It provides a native AWS solution for managing policies across accounts. These policies can be applied to accounts themselves, adding cross-account permissions and management through a centralized tool and interface.

## AWS Organizations Consolidates User Management

The AWS Organizations tool provides an API for user creation and management. You can create users and accounts with this API, and then add those accounts to groups. That in itself is nothing revolutionary, but those new users and groups can have policies attached that define their permissions.

These policies are important; they provide a mechanism to indicate what a user or group can do—across accounts. This means that you can ensure that developers across an organization have access to the services they need, without having to tweak or create policies on a per-account basis. It also means that changes to the policy will affect all (in this case) developers, rather than needing to take those steps on each of the organization's accounts.

Even though AWS Organizations is largely described as a multi-account management tool, it's often the ability to standardize user groups and permissions across accounts that is its most powerful feature. This is especially true for medium or small organizations that aren't managing more than 10 accounts.

Creating groups and using those groups and their associated permissions in a uniform manner across multiple accounts is hugely beneficial. You will quickly find that tracking down access issues and troubleshooting permission-related problems is faster and less cumbersome than without AWS Organizations.

## AWS Organizations Consolidates Billing

You also get consolidated billing through AWS Organizations. While policy and permission management is probably most satisfying for the AWS SysOps administrator, financial managers have long asked for help with billing concerns across accounts. Setting up a single payment method for multiple accounts is incredibly helpful.

Another key benefit here, though, is that charges across accounts are aggregated. The result is that higher spends—considering all accounts combined—can result in more significant discounts from AWS. These volume discounts might not apply if 10 accounts were taken individually but *could* apply if those accounts are aggregated.

You'll almost certainly be asked something along these lines on the exam. AWS uses the exams in part for marketing their services, and every exam, practice exam, and study guide you'll find on both the Certified Solutions Architect and the Certified SysOps Administrator – Associate exams have questions related to AWS Organizations consolidating billing. It's a big deal for AWS and their customers, which means it's a big deal for you on the exam.

# Core AWS Organizations Concepts

Like most AWS services, AWS Organizations introduces some core concepts into the vernacular. The SysOps administrator exam doesn't focus much on the internals of AWS Organizations, so you'll likely be asked something about consolidated billing, and then perhaps a few questions on these key concepts.

## An Organization Is a Collection of Accounts

AWS Organizations is the name of the tool itself. But within that, an *organization* is a collection of AWS accounts. You can manage these accounts as a unit, group them, apply permissions to those groups, and generally treat accounts almost as you'd treat users in IAM.

It is extremely rare for a single company to have multiple organizations, and for the purposes of the exam, you should consider that an organization in AWS Organizations maps to an organization in the "real world." So an organization is a collection of all the accounts associated with a company. Each account has its own resources, services, bills, and so forth.

It's also extremely important to recognize that even though accounts can share an organization, each individual account's resources are *not* mixed in any way. Services, instances, resources, and applications are all kept separate through account boundaries, even when those accounts are within the same organization.

## Organizations Have a Master Account

There is one consideration in working with AWS Organizations you'll need to take into account: an organization requires a master account. This account is the owner of the organization and has the ability to create other accounts, move accounts that exist into and out of the organization, and attach policies to accounts (more on that shortly).

The master account also should be the account from which payment flows. It's sometimes called a "payer account" by AWS and has payment responsibility. It's also inflexible; you can't change the master account within an organization.

As a best practice, the master account should not have its own AWS resources and services beyond managing billing and permissions. It should be a sort of "management account" that is empty and handles only payment, permissions management, and the generation of bills for the organization.

> AWS calls accounts in an organization other than the master account *member accounts*. So for any organization, you have a single master account and then as many member accounts as there are additional accounts within the organization.

## Manage Organizational Units Across Accounts

One of the things that AWS Organizations does well is avoid mixing terminology with IAM. So rather than call a set of accounts a "group," a term that already has meaning in IAM, AWS Organizations calls that set of accounts an *organizational unit*.

An organizational unit—or more typically, OU—is just a categorization. You might have a production OU with all your accounts serving production resources. You might also have your research and development accounts in an R&D OU. These OUs give you logical organization of your member accounts.

> You may recognize the term *organizational unit* from directory servers, especially from the days of the Lightweight Directory Access Protocol (LDAP). The concept is the same: a group of accounts that share a common purpose or role within a larger organization.

You can nest OUs as well. So you might have an OU for your East Coast accounts and, within that, a testing and production OU. Figure 3.1 shows an example hierarchy of accounts.

**FIGURE 3.1**   Hierarchies should serve the overall organization and don't have to be consistent in naming or approach.

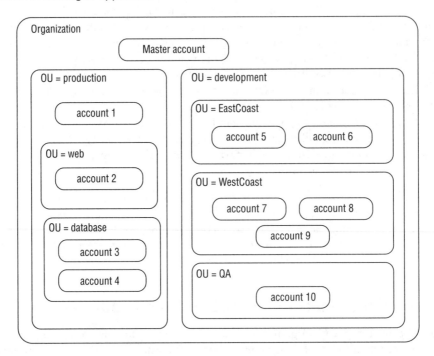

Notice in Figure 3.1 that the OUs are not always representing the same thing. There are groupings by environment (production and development), function (web and database), and location (EastCoast and WestCoast). These OUs should be whatever is appropriate, and there's no best practice that should be followed.

## Apply Service Control Policies

You should already be familiar with the IAM use of policies. Policies control permissions. For example, here is a policy in IAM that allows reading and writing to an S3 bucket called myPhotoStorage:

```
{
    "Version": "2012-10-17",
    "Statement": [
        {
            "Effect": "Allow",
            "Action": ["s3:ListBucket"],
            "Resource": ["arn:aws:s3:::myPhotoStorage"]
        },
        {
            "Effect": "Allow",
```

```
        "Action": [
            "s3:PutObject",
            "s3:GetObject"
        ],
        "Resource": ["arn:aws:s3:::myPhotoStorage/*"]
    }
  ]
}
```

AWS Organizations provides a similar concept called a *service control policy*. Like a policy, a service control policy (SCP) controls permissions. However, SCPs can be applied to an entire account or, more commonly, to an organizational unit. It's easiest to relate this to what you already know about IAM users and groups and policies, as shown in Figure 3.2.

**FIGURE 3.2**   AWS Organizations concepts map almost directly to IAM users, groups, and permissions.

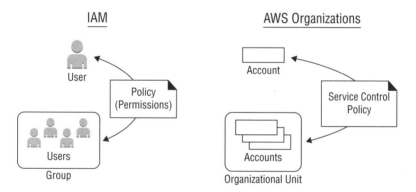

## Creating Useful SCPs for Accounts

There are some significant differences between permissions via IAM policies and AWS Organizations service control policies. An IAM policy typically is built to allow one user or service to access another service or perhaps some subset of that service's functionality; for example, the IAM policy shown previously allows access to a particular S3 bucket.

A service control policy builds account-wide—and ideally, multi-account-wide—permissions. Here's an example from AWS' own documentation that restricts VPCs from having Internet gateways attached to them. The result is that VPCs can't be changed to public-facing:

```
{
  "Version": "2012-10-17",
  "Statement": [
    {
      "Effect": "Deny",
```

```
    "Action": [
      "ec2:AttachInternetGateway",
      "ec2:CreateInternetGateway",
      "ec2:AttachEgressOnlyInternetGateway",
      "ec2:CreateVpcPeeringConnection",
      "ec2:AcceptVpcPeeringConnection"
    ],
    "Resource": "*"
  }
 ]
}
```

This is a great organization-wide policy, because it might be applied to a development organizational unit, ensuring that all accounts focused on development, and not production, are kept private.

## Avoid Overlapping with IAM (When Possible)

It's easy to fall into the trap of doing everything in AWS Organizations…including things that belong in IAM. If a permission is an organization-wide concern, it should exist as an SCP in AWS Organizations. If a permission applies to specific users or instances in one account, keep that as an IAM policy. You'll find that this separation will help you find things when the pressure is on (and perhaps your servers are unintentionally offline).

Another way to think about this is to say "Does this new permission apply to a specific account or to a *class* of accounts?" If you need to ensure that no production instances can turn off detailed monitoring, that might be a good candidate for an SCP; it applies to a class of accounts. If you need to ensure that the testing group in Boston can read instance logs in your testing environment, that might *seem* like an organizational issue, but it's actually not. It's a permission that should be applied to a specific account's users—and not all users in that account, either!

 Just as AWS Organizations is extremely helpful for consistency of groups and permissions across accounts, its potential overlap with IAM is extremely difficult to curb if you're not careful. You know you're doing things correctly when you're using *both* AWS Organizations and IAM in concert.

# AWS Organizations and Consolidated Billing

Consolidated billing isn't new to AWS Organizations; it's always been an AWS offering. However, consolidated billing features have now been moved into the AWS Organizations structure and service. You assign payment options to a master account, and that account then handles payment for all member accounts within the organization.

## Compliance Benefits

There are also potential compliance benefits here. You can ensure payment meets any regulatory concerns through a master account, rather than treating each member account separately. Organizational units can help here as well by grouping accounts that may have different compliance or regulatory concerns.

## Prefer AWS Organizations over Tagging

It's worth noting that prior to AWS Organizations—and even as AWS Organizations was just rolling out—the primary mechanism for handling accounting over multiple accounts was tagging. Resources such as instances or buckets would be assigned tags, and then billing reports would be generated based on those tags. In this way, account and financial managers received a sort of "pseudo OU."

The problem with tagging is that it's almost never comprehensive. Even if you get all the instances and buckets and top-line resources tagged, there are many services and processes that AWS bills for that aren't obvious. It becomes a game of chasing down untagged resources, tagging them, and then finding more untagged resources—and it's not a fun game at all. Using AWS Organizations is a significantly easier solution.

AWS Organizations doesn't cost anything, so there is only upside. AWS typically offers discounts based on overall spending as well, so combining member accounts bills up through AWS Organizations may save you money.

Be aware that your AWS bill will take payment through an AWS Organizations master account, but it will *not* reflect your organizational structure. You won't see bills except via accounts and tags, at least as of this writing.

# Summary

AWS Organizations moves management of services, resources, and AWS constructs up a level of abstraction from IAM. Where IAM offers management within an account, AWS Organizations offers management of an account and across multiple accounts.

With organizations, organizational units, and service control policies, you can emulate IAM users, groups, and policies (or permissions). Organize member accounts into an organization controlled by a master account, and then group those accounts into organizational units (the analog to groups) and assign service control policies to those OUs. That's all AWS Organizations is about...plus billing.

With consolidated billing, you get the benefit of the combined spending of all your accounts. The upside here is you can consolidate payments into a single master account and gain volume discounts from AWS at increased spending levels.

# Exam Essentials

**Explain how AWS Organizations simplifies multi-account management.**   AWS Organizations replaces clumsier solutions such as tagging your resources. It provides consolidated billing and centralized payment.

**Recognize the benefits of consolidated billing.**   By combining multiple accounts' costs, your organization may become eligible for volume discounts not otherwise obtainable. You also reduce the number of payments in many cases through a centralized payment via the master account.

**Define key AWS Organizations terms: master account, organizational unit, and service control policy.**   Every organization has a single master account, ideally that handles only policies, account management, and payment. All other accounts are member accounts. Member accounts can be grouped into organizational units, which can in turn be hierarchical. One organizational unit can contain other organizational units, and a single member account can be in multiple organizational units at one time. Service control policies are permissions applied to organizational units.

**Explain how permissions are applied across accounts.**   A service control policy applied to an organizational units affects all accounts within that organizational unit. These policies can grant or restrict access to AWS services or resources. Best practice is to use service control policies only for cross-account permissions and use IAM policies for permissions within an account.

# Exercises

To complete the two exercises that follow, you will need two separate AWS accounts. One account will be the master account and the other will be a member account. The directions that follow assume that you have access to two accounts in AWS.

---
**EXERCISE 3.1**
---

### Create an AWS Organization

In this exercise, you will create an AWS Organization with two AWS accounts.

1. Log into the AWS Management Console.

2. Scroll down to Management & Governance and choose AWS Organizations.

3. Click Create Organization, and then Create Organization in the dialog box that pops up.

4. Navigate to the verification email that is sent to the email address on file for the master account. Once you verify the email address, you can proceed.

5. Click the blue Add Account button.

6. Choose Invite Account.

7. Enter the email address of the root user for the second AWS account, and click Invite. The status will say Open.

8. Log in as the root user of the second AWS account.

9. Click Services, scroll down to Management & Governance, and choose AWS Organizations.

10. Click the link that says "Invitations 1" on the left side of the screen.

11. Click Accept, and then Confirm.

The second account is now linked to the first account through AWS Organizations.

You may proceed to Exercise 3.2.

---

**EXERCISE 3.2**

## Define and Apply an SCP

In this exercise, you will create an SCP that will prevent an account from being given access to AWS Lambda and you will apply it to the second AWS account.

1. From within the AWS Organizations console, click Policies.

2. Click the blue Create Policy button.

3. Enter the policy name, in this case **No Lambda Access**.

4. In the Policy section, scroll down and select Lambda.

5. Select the All Actions check box.

6. Select Add Resource. For the following options, make these selections:

> **AWS Service:** Lambda
>
> **Resource Type:** All Resources
>
> **Resource ARN:** *

7. Click Add Resource.

8. Click Create Policy.

**EXERCISE 3.2** *(continued)*

9.  Navigate to Organize Accounts.

10. Click Enable in the Enable/Disable Policy Types area.

11. Select the check box next to the second account.

12. Click the arrow next to Service Control Policies.

13. Click Attach next to the No Lambda Access SCP.

The SCP is now applied.

# Review Questions

You can find the answers in the Appendix.

1.  You are responsible for 12 different AWS accounts. You have been tasked with monitoring reducing costs across these accounts and want to recommend AWS Organizations and its consolidated billing features. Which of the following could you use to support your argument that AWS Organizations should be used? (Choose two.)

    **A.**  Traffic between accounts will not be subject to data transfer charges if those accounts are all in AWS Organizations.

    **B.**  Multiple accounts can be combined and, through that combination, receive discounts that may reduce the total cost of all the accounts.

    **C.**  All accounts can be tracked individually and through a single tool.

    **D.**  All accounts in AWS Organizations will receive a 5 percent billing reduction in consolidated billing.

2.  Which of the following are not components of IAM? (Choose two.)

    **A.**  Users

    **B.**  Roles

    **C.**  Organizational units

    **D.**  Service control policies

3.  What is an AWS Organization OU?

    **A.**  Orchestration unit

    **B.**  Organizational unit

    **C.**  Operational unit

    **D.**  Offer of urgency

4.  What is an AWS Organization SCP?

    **A.**  Service control policy

    **B.**  Service control permissions

    **C.**  Standard controlling permissions

    **D.**  Service conversion policy

5.  To which of the following constructs is an AWS Organization SCP applied?

    **A.**  To a service control policy

    **B.**  To an IAM role

    **C.**  To an organizational unit

    **D.**  To a SAML user store

6. Which of the following most closely mirrors an IAM permission document?

   **A.** A service control policy

   **B.** A service component policy

   **C.** An organizational unit

   **D.** An organizational policy

7. To which of the following constructs can a service control policy be applied? (Choose two.)

   **A.** A user

   **B.** An organizational unit

   **C.** An account

   **D.** A group

8. Which of the following is not a feature of AWS Organizations?

   **A.** Multi-account management

   **B.** Batch account creation

   **C.** Consolidated billing

   **D.** Multi-account permissions

9. Which tool would you use to reduce or eliminate SSH access to a development account's EC2 instances?

   **A.** IAM

   **B.** CloudTrail

   **C.** AWS Organizations

   **D.** Trusted Advisor

10. Which tool would you use to reduce or eliminate SSH access to all EC2 instances as a security policy in your company?

    **A.** IAM

    **B.** CloudTrail

    **C.** AWS Organizations

    **D.** Trusted Advisor

11. What is the best reason to use AWS Organizations as the primary mechanism for billing management as opposed to resource tagging?

    **A.** You can tag only 100 resources in a single AWS account.

    **B.** You can tag only compute resources in an AWS account.

    **C.** Resource tags are ephemeral and are lost when a resource restarts.

    **D.** Tagging is generally not comprehensive due to low-level AWS system services.

**12.** Which of the following is not an advantage of using AWS Organizations for consolidated billing?

    **A.** You'll receive a single bill for all of your accounts.

    **B.** You'll receive combined usage reports for resources across all of your accounts.

    **C.** You'll receive a discount on data movement between regions across all your accounts.

    **D.** You'll receive volume discounts based on usage across all your accounts.

**13.** Your organization has 14 different accounts, all recently moved to management via AWS Organizations. Three accounts use reserved instances, each purchased at different price points. After moving these accounts into AWS Organizations, at what price are these reserved instances charged?

    **A.** Each account will continue to use its existing reserved instance hourly price.

    **B.** All accounts will use the lowest hourly price for all accounts.

    **C.** All accounts will use the average hourly price for all accounts.

    **D.** Hourly price for the instances will need to be recalculated by the AWS account Technical Account Manager (TAM).

**14.** Which of the following might you use in setting up standardized development, test, and production accounts for your organization? (Choose two.)

    **A.** Organizational units

    **B.** Service control policies

    **C.** Consolidated billing

    **D.** Resource tagging

**15.** Which of the following might you use in centralizing billing management of development, test, and production accounts for your organization? (Choose two.)

    **A.** Organizational units

    **B.** Service control policies

    **C.** Consolidated billing

    **D.** Resource tagging

**16.** How many master accounts should an organization have?

    **A.** At least one

    **B.** Exactly one

    **C.** Two or more

    **D.** One for every region in the organization

**17.** How many member accounts should an organization have?

   **A.** At least one

   **B.** Exactly one

   **C.** Two or more

   **D.** One for every region in the organization

**18.** To how many organizational units can an account belong?

   **A.** Exactly one

   **B.** One or more

   **C.** One for every region in which the account has resources

   **D.** One for every account in the organization

**19.** To how many OUs can another organizational unit belong?

   **A.** Zero, since nesting OUs is disallowed

   **B.** Exactly 0ne

   **C.** One or more

   **D.** One for every account in the organization

**20.** You have taken responsibility for a company's multiple AWS accounts. They currently have eight accounts and receive a bill for each account monthly. They would like to receive a single bill each month. Which of the following steps are required to implement this change? (Choose two.)

   **A.** Set up AWS Organizations.

   **B.** Turn on consolidated billing.

   **C.** Create a service control policy and apply it to all of the organization's accounts.

   **D.** Choose your master account from your available accounts, or create a new master account.

# Chapter 4

# AWS Config

**THE AWS CERTIFIED SYSOPS ADMINISTRATOR — ASSOCIATE EXAM TOPICS COVERED IN THIS CHAPTER MAY INCLUDE, BUT ARE NOT LIMITED TO, THE FOLLOWING:**

**Domain 1.0: Monitoring and Reporting**

✓ 1.1 Create and maintain alarms utilizing AWS monitoring services

**Domain 3.0: Deployment and Provisioning**

✓ 3.2 Identify and remediate deployment issues

**Domain 5.0: Security and Compliance**

✓ 5.1 Implement and manage security policies on AWS

✓ 5.2 Implement access controls when using AWS

**Domain 7.0: Automation and Optimization**

✓ 7.3 Automate manual or repeatable process to minimize management overhead

*AWS Config*, like AWS Organizations, doesn't provide functionality that is unique or novel to the cloud. Instead, it addresses a common need of the SysOps administrator: configuration management. Configuration management is a process—and in this case, a tool-based one—for managing the resources and services in place within an environment. In the AWS context, those resources and services are the instances, containers, databases, queues, and other pieces of your applications.

There are some best-of-breed options for configuration management in on-premises enterprise applications, and this chapter begins addressing those tools and their role in a system. Then, you'll learn how those tools translate to AWS and how the terms about which they're concerned slightly change meaning in a cloud environment. Finally, you'll see how rules and configuration items are the key components of AWS Config and the AWS approach to configuration management.

This chapter covers:

The role of configuration management in an enterprise application

The differences in on-premises configuration management and cloud configuration management

The use cases for which AWS Config was created and how each is handled by AWS Config

Rules and triggers within AWS Config

Configuration items and their relationship to the resources to which they refer

# Managing Configuration Changes

Believe it or not, there was once a time where an "application" was a single server, with software providing web, business logic, and database services. High availability meant having *two* of those servers, networked together. And in *really* large enterprises, there might be a load balancer (or even two!) tying things together.

Of course, that sounds like the dark ages of computing now. It's commonplace to find multiple web servers (each with dedicated hardware, or at least large virtualized machines), application servers, database servers, sharding and caching on additional virtualized hardware, load balancers, logging, and monitoring. Each component is often redundant, meaning duplicate hardware—physical or virtual—and each component has complex configuration. Rarely is anything run "out of the box" anymore.

If some of the terms you just read aren't familiar to you, it's okay. This book goes into detail about how AWS provides each of those components to your applications and, in many cases (like sharding and searching), exactly how those services operate.

The result? A lot of setup and configuration going into a running application. Worse, this configuration needs to be kept in sync, if one web server changes configuration to deal with a new security patch or subnet, all the web servers need the same changes. The same is true of database servers, load balancers, SMS gateways...and the list goes on.

For you, the SysOps administrator, this is quite literally a worst-case situation. In addition to all the running machines, you now have a configuration problem. You have to keep all these systems in sync, updated with the latest software (within whatever margin your organization deems acceptable), and running in accordance with your security, network, compliance, and usage policies.

This is the world of configuration management, the process for establishing and maintaining consistency in the systems you manage. You've got to keep these systems performing well and patched, and you have to make sure that web server A looks the same as web servers B and C (except in the case where you explicitly want two servers to be distinct from each other).

## Continuous Everything

Part of the difficulty for any configuration management solution is the movement toward continuous everything. For developers, there's a move toward *continuous integration*, where tests are run against every code commit, and *continuous deployment*, where deployments are made either every code commit or at least many times a day.

You may want to begin thinking of "continuous" as a synonym for "ongoing." It's not accurate that anything—deployment, testing, and so forth—is "continuous" in a literal sense. The term continuous in these contexts means that it's a recurring process with relatively small periods of inactivity between the current deployment (or test, assessment, or monitoring) and the next one.

In these continuous environments, it's possible that software and hardware can be changed hundreds of times a day. On top of that, those changes can't be allowed to affect running applications, often serving very large user loads.

For you, the SysOps administrator, you should add a couple more continuous terms: continuous monitoring and continuous assessment. *Continuous monitoring* is simply an ongoing process by which you watch what's going on with your systems, especially as it relates to their configuration. How much memory is allocated to that virtual machine? What does the routing table look like between your web servers and your database servers?

Add to that *continuous assessment*, which takes the information from your continuous monitoring and determines if it's correct—keeping in mind that every organization may define "correct" differently.

A good configuration management solution, then, will employ both continuous monitoring and continuous assessment. Further, it should enable continuous integration and especially continuous deployment for your development teams, as it ensures that the systems on which they depend are running and are properly configured.

## On-Premises Solutions

Although it's not always useful to talk about on-premises solutions and compare them to cloud offerings, in the case of configuration management it is. Two products have become synonymous with configuration management in enterprise applications: Puppet (www.puppet.com) and Chef (www.chef.io). These bear mentioning not just because they're useful tools, but because many organizations have them woven into the fabric of their applications and don't want to simply "move off of them" in a cloud transition.

Both tools offer agents that reside on physical or virtual machines and report back to a management server on configuration. The management server can then easily alert an administrator (that's you!) when changes are made. Additionally, both tools offer the ability to undo unauthorized changes automatically. They can do the same for authorized changes that fall outside of predefined parameters.

These tools offer a look at solid configuration management. They also reveal that configuration management is hard. Thousands of hours are often spent getting allowed configurations defined correctly for an organization's security and compliance policies.

Fortunately, both products can be launched into an AWS environment. Although there are some serious licensing concerns—remember, the cloud is elastic and can start as many instances on demand as your billing can handle, and then some—you can still largely move a Puppet or Chef setup directly into AWS. For both tools, *AWS OpsWorks* offers a specific AWS-integrated tool for working with Chef and Puppet.

AWS OpsWorks rarely appears on the certification exam. All you need to know for the test is that if you have existing Chef or Puppet code, OpsWorks gives you a direct path to using that code largely unchanged on AWS.

## Configuration in the Cloud

If you don't have an existing configuration management solution, or you're building in the cloud as your initial platform, you're going to need a configuration management solution, and there's no good reason to use Puppet or Chef in these cases. This is where AWS Config comes in; it provides an AWS-native option that doesn't require a lot of previous configuration management experience.

AWS Config gives you continuous monitoring and continuous assessment, as well as all the change management and troubleshooting that comes with these facilities. AWS Config also provides this functionality across accounts and regions, which is a nice tool to go with your organizational setup (see Chapter 3: AWS Organizations for more on why you should be using AWS Organizations if you're not already).

AWS Config is available globally but is enabled on a per-region basis. This allows you to manage costs associated with resource configuration management more granularly.

# AWS Config Use Cases

So far, configuration management has been treated as a sort of cluster of functionality: maintaining valid configuration, ensuring compliance, providing a level of security, and more. However, in your role as a SysOps administrator, and in some cases on the exam, you should be able to differentiate between these various pieces of configuration management and understand how each is part of AWS Config's capabilities.

## Centralized Configuration Management

First and foremost, AWS Config provides configuration management of all your AWS resources in a single place. This is true across accounts as well. Consider Figure 4.1, an organization with multiple accounts, each with multiple resources, where each resource has configuration data.

**FIGURE 4.1**    In a large enterprise organization, you're likely to have many resources across multiple accounts.

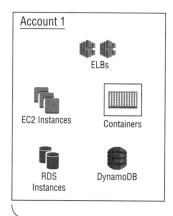
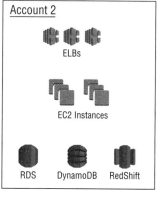
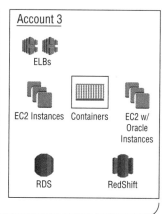

Entire Organization

Even with a decent configuration management tool in each account, you'll have to reconcile configuration across accounts. AWS Config addresses this problem by aggregating configuration across accounts into a single account, as shown in Figure 4.2.

**FIGURE 4.2** AWS Config centralizes configuration management across accounts.

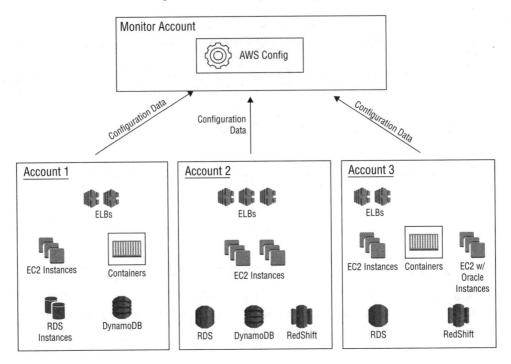

 Some SysOps administrators will use the master account for an organization in AWS Organizations as the account to which configuration data is aggregated. This approach typically isn't a great idea, though, because this monitoring account will grow. You could easily end up with AWS Config, CloudWatch, CloudTrail, and more. Consider creating an account specifically for your monitoring needs and locking that account down via IAM to yourself and other SysOps administrators.

This is a huge boon to the SysOps administrator. It's common to have instances in multiple accounts serving, for example, web content. You want to ensure that all those instances—regardless of account—are consistent in configuration. AWS Config provides for just that.

## Audit Trails

AWS Config also provides help with auditing needs. Though it's typical to think of auditing in the same breath as AWS CloudTrail (more on that in the section "AWS Config or AWS CloudTrail?" later), AWS Config is also a help here. Because AWS treats configuration as code and stores historical configuration data, you have the full resource configuration history of your environment. You can even correlate these changes with the logs that AWS CloudTrail provides to show a complete event-driven history of your resources and their configuration changes.

Not only do you then know when a resource was changed, but you also have a history of who made the change, from where was the change made, and more. This is essential for any government organization or ITIL reporting. Add to this that you get all this information as part of setting up AWS Config, and it makes a lot of sense to add AWS Config to your baseline AWS environment monitoring setup.

## Configuration as Security

As we've already mentioned in the "Audit Trails" section earlier, configuration history provides a layer of security that goes beyond the real-time access to your systems. IAM users and roles tend to provide the broadest access to a privileged set of users. Those users are going to be your most experienced operators as well. Unfortunately, that means that if something goes wrong, it's typical that your best engineers are the ones who are most likely to be blamed.

However, things go a lot better if you're able to provide an IP address from which a change was made, a time, exactly what the change was, and to how many resources. That sort of clarity in dealing with an unauthorized change can help you isolate a breach—or perhaps an inadvertent change—and remediate quickly.

# AWS Config Rules and Responses

Once you understand how AWS Config is used, you must get a handle on how to put rules in place, evaluate those rules, and potentially take remediation action. Fortunately, AWS Config is extremely straightforward, and the rules it provides will cover the majority of your needs.

## Rules Are Desired Configurations

A rule in AWS Config is simply a desired configuration for a resource. It can describe a specific value, or a set of values, that a property can take. You should think of a rule not as a desired state, but as an allowed state. In other words, a rule being broken meaning something is wrong or incorrect, not just suboptimal.

**WARNING**    It is possible to define allowed values for configuration items very narrowly. In essence, you can collapse "values that are allowed" and "values that are optimal" into a single "perfect value." However, this approach often has negative consequences. Remember that the goal of AWS Config is not to give you performance metrics or ensure your system is running optimally; that's more the domain of CloudWatch.

AWS Config is ensuring that your system complies with the policies and security posture of your organization. Make sure that a broken rule tells you that something is out of this compliance, and not merely that you might want to check a configuration item.

## A Configuration Item Represents a Specific Configuration

A rule evaluates a resource's configuration at a given point in time. The resource itself provides configuration information through configuration items. A *configuration item* (CI) is an attribute and value (or values) for that attribute, reported against a specific resource.

A configuration item includes several key pieces of information, listed in Table 4.1.

**TABLE 4.1**    Components of a configuration item

| Component | Purpose | Included information |
| --- | --- | --- |
| Metadata | Information about the configuration item itself (*not* the reported resource) | Version ID, when the CI was captured, status of the CI (whether it was captured without a problem), and a state ID that indicates ordering of the CIs for a specific resource |
| Resource attributes | Describe the various configurable items on the reported resource | The ID of the resource, key:value pairs for the resource, the type of resource, the resource's ARN (Amazon Resource Name), the AZ in which the resource resides, and the time the resource was created |
| Relationships | Detail how this resource relates to other resources | Relationships, such as the ID of an EBS volume attached to the reported EC2 instance |
| Current configuration of the resource | The actual configuration at the given time | Data returned from a call to the DescribeVolumes API for the resource. This information varies widely based on resource type. |

# Rules Are Evaluated

When you write a rule, AWS Config evaluates the values reported in configuration item attributes against the rule. If the value doesn't match, then the rule is considered broken and the configuration is reported as noncompliant. A notification is then sent, and your AWS Config dashboard will report the noncompliant item.

## AWS Provides Prebuilt Rules

AWS supplies you with hundreds of prebuilt rules that can be applied to your resources. For example, Figure 4.3 shows the variety of rules that were available from starting up AWS Config in a very simple account with only a few instances, S3 buckets, static website hosting, and DNS entries.

**FIGURE 4.3**   AWS Config comes with a number of prebuilt rules. Notice that in this sample, 49 managed rules are available, just as a starting point!

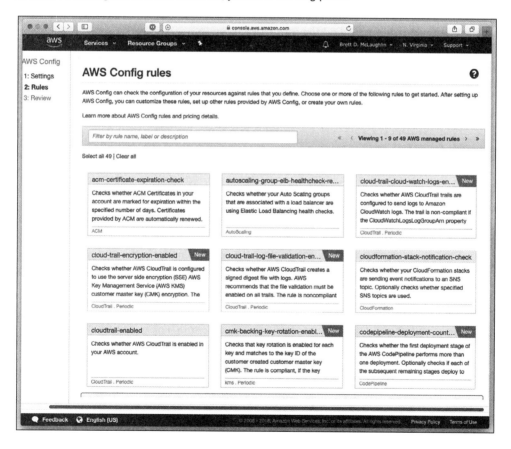

Of course, many of these rules are for "always on" AWS services like CloudWatch and CloudTrail, as well as the various AWS developer tools like CodeDeploy and CodePipeline. Still, this should get you started quickly, and you can avoid having to write custom code just to get basic configuration management in place.

## You Can Write Your Own Rules

In the event that AWS' rules don't meet your needs, you can write your own. You define a rule in AWS Config and then relate that rule to an AWS Lambda function that you write. This function needs to evaluate a configuration item—which AWS Config will pass to the function—and report as to whether the configuration is compliant.

You can create 150 rules in a single AWS account by default. You can get this limit raised by contacting AWS if needed.

For example, here is a fragment of a Java function that checks for Multi-Factor Authentication (MFA) enabled on the root IAM account:

```
// Evaluates whether the AWS Account published in the event has an MFA device assigned.
private ComplianceType getCompliance(AmazonIdentityManagement iamClient) {
    GetAccountSummaryResult result = iamClient.getAccountSummary();
    Integer mfaEnabledCount = result.getSummaryMap().get(MFA_ENABLED_PROPERTY);
    if (mfaEnabledCount != null && mfaEnabledCount > 0) {
        return ComplianceType.COMPLIANT; // The account has an MFA device assigned.
    } else {
        return ComplianceType.NON_COMPLIANT; // The account does not have an MFA device assigned.
    }
}
```

Note that the function receives a configuration item from AWS Config, and then reports back, with either a COMPLIANT or a NON_COMPLIANT result. That's the essence of all rules, custom or otherwise: to evaluate and respond with one of those two states.

Some custom rules are defined in an AWS-supported repository at https://github.com/awslabs/aws-config-rules. In fact, the previous rule is from that repository.

## Trigger Evaluation in Two Ways

So you have a rule and AWS Config is reporting via configuration items. What triggers the evaluation? You have two choices:

- **Periodic triggers:** Set AWS Config to evaluate rules on a specific frequency. You can set this frequency to 1 hour, 3 hours, 6 hours, 12 hours, or 24 hours.
- **Change triggers:** Set AWS Config to evaluate rules any time a configuration change on a resource is reported.

For change triggers specifically, you can narrow the resources to which this trigger applies through a tag, resource type, or resource ID(s). This allows you to ensure you're not overwhelmed with change notifications across your environment.

You may want to use a combination of both of these approaches. It's common to have change triggers and then add to that a periodic check for compliance and reporting.

# AWS Config or AWS CloudTrail?

It's easy at a high level to confuse AWS Config and AWS CloudTrail, especially since both perform auditing functions. However, keeping the two separate isn't that difficult if you just pay attention to the names:

- **AWS Config:** Configuration
- **AWS CloudTrail:** API trails

AWS Config deals with configuration of your resources. Yes, this provides an audit trail, but the trail is specific to those configurations. AWS CloudTrail has nothing to do with configuration; it logs the trail of API calls to your resources. Again, this provides audit information, but that information relates to API calls and logs, *not* to the configuration of what provides those API calls with a response.

On the certification exam, you will almost always see the word "configuration" related to AWS Config, and "logging" or "API" related to AWS CloudTrail. Keep those key words in mind, and you'll remember how each service is different from the other.

# Summary

AWS does take a lot of configuration management out of the realm of "impossible to manage" and into "click a few buttons on a management console." (Or, if you prefer, "type a few commands into the CLI.") As a result, it's easy to think that configuration management is a solved problem in the cloud. That's just not true, though. Even with dashboards and easy management interfaces, a medium-sized AWS environment can easily have hundreds of instances; more than 10 Auto Scaling groups; multiple RDS, DynamoDB, and RedShift configurations; 50 or more S3 buckets; and VPCs all over the world. No web console is going to make that degree of configuration management easy.

AWS Config doesn't solve all these problems, but it does provide a simple, useful framework for ensuring that things don't change unless you *intend* for them to change. If all AWS Config did was provide you with triggers for notification when an instance changes, it would be a helpful service.

Add to that rules, periodic triggers, configuration instances, and the ability to monitor managed services like RDS as well as more change-prone ones like EC2, and you've got a pretty powerful tool. While it's true that AWS Config likely will appear on only a few questions on your certification exam, it's still well worth learning to be an effective SysOps administrator.

# Resources to Review

AWS Config:

```
https://aws.amazon.com/config/
```

AWS Config Developer Guide:

```
https://docs.aws.amazon.com/config/latest/developerguide/WhatIsConfig.html
```

AWS Config Rules Repository on GitHub:

```
https://github.com/awslabs/aws-config-rules
```

# Exam Essentials

**Explain the use of AWS Config in monitoring, especially as compared to CloudWatch and CloudTrail.**   CloudWatch monitors the status of running applications. CloudTrail logs and provides audit trails, especially for API calls. AWS Config is distinct from both of these as it is concerned with the configuration of resources, rather than their runtime state. Anything that affects the setup of a resource and its interaction with other AWS resources is largely under this umbrella.

**List the benefits of AWS Config.**   AWS Config provides centralized configuration management without requiring third-party tools. It also provides configuration audit trails, a sort of configuration equivalent to the API audit trails provided by CloudTrail. And through both of these AWS Config adds a layer of security and compliance to your application by ensuring changes to your environments are always surfaced and evaluated.

**Explain AWS Config rules.**   A rule simply states that a certain configuration—or more often, a certain part of a configuration—should be within a set of values. That rule is broken when a change moves configuration outside of allowed thresholds for those values.

**Explain how AWS Config rules are evaluated.**   There is typically code associated with a rule defining how that rule is evaluated. If you define a custom rule, you'll write your own code to evaluate configuration and report back as to whether the configuration follows or breaks the custom rule. This code is then attached to the rule as a Lambda function.

**Describe the two ways rule evaluation can be triggered.**   Two triggers cause AWS Config rules to evaluate: change-based triggers and periodic triggers. A change-based trigger causes a rule to evaluate a configuration when there's a change in the environment. A periodic trigger evaluates a configuration at a predefined frequency.

# Exercises

### Create a New S3 Bucket for Storing Configuration Information

Setting up AWS Config using the CLI is pretty easy. First, though, there are a few prereq-uisites. You're going to need a place to put configuration information. Use the CLI (set up in Chapter 1: Introduction to Systems Operations on AWS) to create an S3 bucket for this purpose:

```
$ aws s3api create-bucket --bucket yellowtagmedia-configuration
{
    "Location": "/yellowtagmedia-configuration"
}
```

Remember that S3 bucket names are global and must be unique, so make sure you're using your own bucket name.

### Create a New SNS Topic for Notifications of Configuration Changes

You'll also need a new SNS (Amazon Simple Notification Service) topic for AWS Config. This hasn't been covered yet, but you can create a topic using the CLI and the sns com-mand with the create-topic subcommand:

```
$ aws sns create-topic --name yellowtagmedia-configuration-notice
{
    "TopicArn": "arn:aws:sns:us-east-1:XXXXXXXXXX:yellowtagmedia-configuration-notice"
}
```

Make a note of the full Amazon Resource Name (ARN) for this topic; you'll need it shortly.

You can verify this topic exists by logging into the AWS console with a web browser. Go to the SNS section and select Topics from the left menu. Your new topic should appear. You can create a subscription to this topic by clicking Create Subscription, choosing Email as the protocol. and entering in a valid email address.

### Create a New IAM Role for the AWS Config Service to Use

Finally, you'll need an IAM role with appropriate permissions for the AWS Config service. While you can do this with the AWS CLI, it gets a little complicated; in this case, the console is a much better choice.

Open up the AWS console in your web browser, log in, and go to the IAM section. Select Roles from the left menu and then click the Create Role button. The default value of AWS service as the type of trusted identity is fine. Then select Config as the service that will use this role. This screen is shown in Figure 4.4.

**FIGURE 4.4**   You should see all available AWS services. You want to choose Config here, select the Config use case, and then click Next.

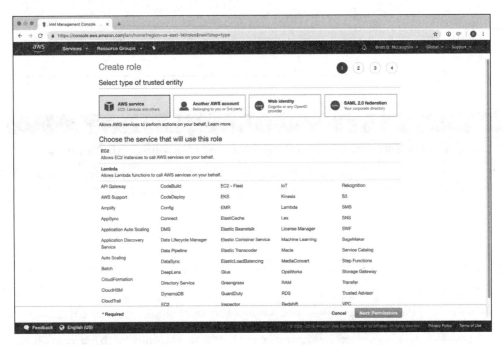

You'll need to select the basic Config – Customizable use case, and then click Next: Permissions. (The basic Config use case will *not* work with this setup.) Note the option for working with AWS Config in conjunction with AWS Organizations in the event you are using that service.

You can click through the next several screens. You'll see that you need to attach the pre-created `AWSConfigServiceRolePolicy`, and you can optionally add tags to the role. Review these options, name the role as shown in Figure 4.5, and then create the role.

**FIGURE 4.5**    Your new role is ready for use by AWS Config at this point.

---

**EXERCISE 4.4**

## Give Your New Role Permission to Access Your S3 Bucket

You have a role, but it needs permissions to access the configuration bucket you created earlier. That can also be done through the console, since you're already there working with IAM.

On the main IAM screen in the console, select Roles and then choose the role you just created. On the Permissions tab, click the Add Inline Policy button on the far right. Choose the JSON tab and then you can enter the following policy:

```
{
  "Version": "2012-10-17",
  "Statement":
  [
    {
      "Effect": "Allow",
      "Action": ["s3:PutObject"],
      "Resource": ["arn:aws:s3:::yellowtagmedia-configuration/AWSLogs/YOUR_AWS_ACCOUNT_ID/*"],
      "Condition":
```

```
        {
          "StringLike":
            {
              "s3:x-amz-acl": "bucket-owner-full-control"
            }
        }
    },
    {
      "Effect": "Allow",
      "Action": ["s3:GetBucketAcl"],
      "Resource": "arn:aws:s3:::yellowtagmedia-configuration"
    }
  ]
}
```

This is the standard AWS IAM role policy for accessing S3 buckets, and you'll need to make a few changes. Replace the bolded text with the name of your own S3 bucket in two places, and update the account ID with your own AWS account ID. Then click the Review Policy button.

Now you can name the policy (as shown in Figure 4.6) and create it.

**FIGURE 4.6** Creating this custom policy will attach it to your custom IAM role as well.

Unfortunately, this isn't your only step. Now you need a similar policy to allow this role to use your newly created SNS topic. This is a similar process, though.

Add another inline policy to your IAM role:

```
{
  "Version": "2012-10-17",
  "Statement":
  [
    {
      "Effect":"Allow",
      "Action":"sns:Publish",
      "Resource":"arn:aws:sns:us-east-1:XXXXXXXXXXXX:yellowtagmedia-configuration-notice"
    }
  ]
}
```

Update this to use the ARN of the SNS topic you created earlier, and then create the new policy.

Finally, you should see something similar to Figure 4.7: a role ready for use by AWS Config.

**FIGURE 4.7**    You should now have an IAM role with custom policies for accessing your S3 bucket, your SNS topic, and monitoring configuration across all your AWS resources.

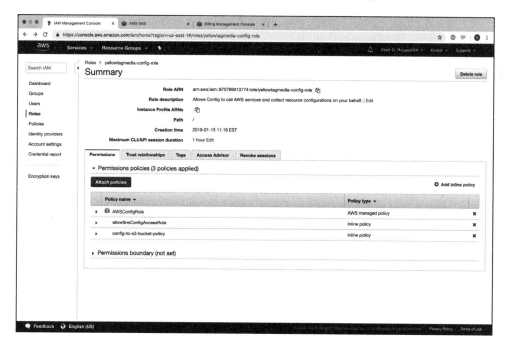

## Turn On AWS Config and Direct It to the Created Resources

Now you can finally go back to the console. Here's where everything is tied together. Use the `configservice` command with the `subscribe` subcommand, and then provide the S3 target bucket, the SNS topic, and the IAM role you created:

```
$ aws configservice subscribe --s3-bucket yellowtagmedia-configuration
--sns-topic arn:aws:sns:us-east-1:XXXXXXXXXXX:yellowtagmedia-configuration-notice
--iam-role arn:aws:iam::XXXXXXXXXXXXX:role/yellowtagmedia-config-role
{
    "Location": "/yellowtagmedia-configuration"
}
```

Make sure you get those ARNs correct or you'll get an error. You're looking for a response like this:

```
Using existing S3 bucket: yellowtagmedia-configuration
Using existing SNS topic: arn:aws:sns:us-east-1:XXXXXXXXXX:yellowtagmedia-configuration-notice
Subscribe succeeded:

Configuration Recorders: [
    {
        "name": "default",
        "roleARN": "arn:aws:iam::XXXXXXXX:role/yellowtagmedia-config-role",
        "recordingGroup": {
            "allSupported": true,
            "includeGlobalResourceTypes": false,
            "resourceTypes": []
        }
    }
]

Delivery Channels: [
    {
        "name": "default",
        "s3BucketName": "yellowtagmedia-configuration",
        "snsTopicARN": "arn:aws:sns:us-east-1:XXXXXXXX:yellowtagmedia-configuration-notice"
    }
]
```

You'll know this is working almost immediately if you've subscribed to your SNS topic via email; a flood of emails will pour in. In the time it took to write this single paragraph, over 51 emails flooded into my own account.

Now, AWS Config will report all changes to the environment to the S3 bucket and the SNS topic, and anyone subscribed to the topic will get those notifications.

**EXERCISE 4.6**

## Turn Off AWS Config

AWS Config is a paid service. If you let it run continuously, you'll almost certainly crash through AWS' free account limits. To stop recording events, use the `stop-configuration-recorder` subcommand:

```
$ aws configservice stop-configuration-recorder --configuration-recorder-name default
```

You can get a little more extreme and delete the recorder as well:

```
$ aws configservice delete-configuration-recorder --configuration-recorder-name default
```

This will ensure you're not paying for the service in a test capacity.

# Review Questions

You can find the answers in the Appendix.

1. Which of the following does AWS Config provide? (Choose two.)
   A. Continuous deployment
   B. Continuous integration
   C. Continuous monitoring
   D. Continuous assessment

2. You have set up AWS Config and want to notify your systems administrators if a change has been made. To what service should you connect AWS Config?
   A. AWS CloudTrail
   B. AWS CloudWatch.
   C. SNS.
   D. S

3. Where does AWS Config store configuration for the various services it monitors?
   A. RDS
   B. S3
   C. DynamoDB
   D. EFS

4. Which of the following are not parts of a configuration item for a resource in the cloud? (Choose two.)
   A. A map of relationships between the resource and other resources
   B. AWS CloudWatch event IDs related to the resource
   C. Configuration data specific to the resource
   D. Metadata about connected resources

5. You have a configuration item for an EC2 instance. Which of the following might be part of a configuration item for this instance? (Choose two.)
   A. The user who created the EC2 instance
   B. The instance type of the EC2 instance
   C. The time that the configuration item was captured
   D. How long the EC2 instance has been running

**6.** You have created a custom rule and want to add it to AWS Config. What do you need to do to ensure evaluation of the rule?

   **A.** Create an EC2 instance and upload code to evaluate the rule to that instance.

   **B.** Create a Lambda function and upload code to evaluate the rule to the function.

   **C.** Paste code to evaluate the rule into the Add Evaluation Rule box in the AWS management console for the rule.

   **D.** Create a CloudFormation template and add code to evaluate the rule to the template.

**7.** Which of the following are types of triggers for AWS Config rules? (Choose two.)

   **A.** Configuration changes

   **B.** Cyclic

   **C.** Periodic

   **D.** Recurring

**8.** Which of the following are part of the resource configuration history that AWS Config provides? (Choose two.)

   **A.** A record of who made a change to a resource

   **B.** The source IP address of an API call to a REST API

   **C.** The source IP address of a change made to the size of an EBS volume

   **D.** The number of AWS console logins on a given day

**9.** How can you configure AWS Config to prevent noncompliant changes to resources?

   **A.** Turn on Ensure Compliancy in the AWS management console under the AWS Config section.

   **B.** Use the AWS CLI to enable the Ensure Compliance option in AWS Config.

   **C.** Write AWS Config rules to prevent changes from being made.

   **D.** You cannot prevent changes with AWS Config.

**10.** How is AWS Config enabled on an AWS account?

   **A.** Once for the entire account

   **B.** Once for every region in the account

   **C.** AWS Config can be turned on or off multiple times but is configured on a per-region basis.

   **D.** AWS Config can be turned on or off multiple times, but that enabling applies to the entire account.

**11.** To what does the term continuous integration refer?

    **A.** The ongoing integration of code into a version repository, typically with automatic testing ensuring no regressions are introduced by the new code

    **B.** The ongoing integration of configuration changes into AWS, typically with automated testing to ensure no regressions are introduced by the new configuration

    **C.** The ongoing integration of new development practices into a team, especially related to testing and deployment

    **D.** The ongoing integration of new releases into a particular environment, typically with automated testing of the deployment after it completes

**12.** How many rules can you create by default in a single AWS account?

    **A.** 25

    **B.** 50

    **C.** 100

    **D.** 150

**13.** Which of the following are required to create a new rule in AWS Config? (Choose two.)

    **A.** Whether the rule is change-triggered or periodic

    **B.** The ID or type of the resource to monitor

    **C.** A tag key to match on a resource

    **D.** The target to send the rule notification to

**14.** Which of the following are allowed frequencies for periodic rules? (Choose two.)

    **A.** 5 minutes

    **B.** 1 hour

    **C.** 12 hours

    **D.** 48 hours

**15.** You have recently added a number of AWS Config rules to ensure your resources are compliant. However, despite adding these rules, you are still receiving notices from your compliance team that resources are not correctly configured. What could be the source of this problem?

    **A.** Your config rules are likely inactive. Once you create a rule, you must set that rule to active to ensure resources are kept compliant.

    **B.** Your compliance rules do not match the compliance requirements from your organization's compliance team. Ensure that the rules are a match for requirements.

**C.** Reduce the time between compliance checks in AWS Config. This will ensure less non-compliant time for resources that fall out of compliance.

**D.** AWS Config rules do not prevent resources from falling out of compliance. They only notify when that has occurred. You would need to write code in a Lambda or other method to restore a resource back into compliance.

**16.** You have created three rules in AWS Config related to CloudTrail. This rule checks to see if CloudTrail is enabled in your AWS account, if CloudTrail is configured to use server-side encryption keys, and if file validation is turned on for all trails. In your environment, CloudTrail is currently enabled and using server-side encryption but is not doing file validation on all trails. What would you expect the evaluation of this ruleset to return?

**A.** Compliant

**B.** Partially Compliant

**C.** Noncompliant

**D.** You will receive two Compliant evaluations and one Noncompliant evaluation.

**17.** Which of the following questions does AWS Config not provide you with a means of answering?

**A.** "What did my AWS resource look like yesterday at 8:00 p.m.?"

**B.** "What should my AWS resource look like to be in compliance with my organization's policies?"

**C.** "Who made an API call to modify this resource?"

**D.** "Which of my AWS resources are out of compliance with my preset organizational policies?"

**18.** Which of the following services should you use to monitor all of your resources via AWS Config across multiple accounts and regions? (Choose two.)

**A.** Consolidated Billing

**B.** AWS Organizations

**C.** Multi-Account Multi-Region Data Aggregation

**D.** Multi-Account Authorization and Aggregation

**19.** Which of the following steps are required to aggregate configuration data across multiple AWS accounts? (Choose two.)

**A.** Create an S3 bucket for storing the information.

**B.** Apply IAM policies to the bucket to allow writing to it from the other AWS accounts AWS Config service.

**C.** Use the AWS Log Aggregator service to aggregate logs across the different accounts.

**D.** Set up an SNS topic for notifications.

**20.** Recently, your AWS costs have risen significantly and are attached to the AWS Config service. When you open up AWS Config, you find a huge number of rules and configuration items that are unfamiliar to you. How can you determine who added these rules to AWS Config?

    **A.** You can't; because only administrators can access AWS Config, all access is considered valid and not logged.

    **B.** You need to check S3 for the automatically generated AWS Config logs.

    **C.** You need to check CloudTrail, as API access to AWS Config is logged just as it is to any other resource with an API.

    **D.** The AWS Console shows a history of who created all rules.

# AWS CloudTrail

**THE AWS CERTIFIED SYSOPS ADMINISTRATOR — ASSOCIATE EXAM TOPICS COVERED IN THIS CHAPTER MAY INCLUDE, BUT ARE NOT LIMITED TO, THE FOLLOWING:**

**Domain 1.0: Monitoring and Reporting**

✓ 1.1   Create and maintain alarms utilizing AWS monitoring services

✓ 1.3   Perform the steps necessary to remediate based on performance and availability metrics

**Domain 3.0: Deployment and Provisioning**

✓ 3.2   Identify and remediate deployment issues

**Domain 6.0: Networking**

✓ 6.3   Gather and interpret relevant information for network troubleshooting

**Domain 7.0: Automation and Optimization**

✓ 7.3   Automate manual or repeatable process to minimize management overhead

At this point, you should have application monitoring via CloudWatch, account management through AWS Organizations, and configuration management across accounts with AWS Config. So what's left in the management and monitoring space? Well, it turns out there's still a big piece to tackle: logging of API calls.

In a typical multi-tier application—which is to say, in a typical modern application—most communication between tiers and with application clients takes place over what amounts to API calls. A key part of monitoring is logging those API calls and making sense of them. In the same way that CloudWatch monitors the health of your resources, CloudTrail monitors the use and appropriate behavior of your resources' communication.

CloudTrail is a straightforward managed AWS service. This chapter explains:

What an API means in an AWS context

The role of APIs in good application design

How CloudTrail uses a trail to represent account activity and provide traceability of that activity

The types of AWS CloudTrail trails, including all-region and single-region trails

Using CloudTrail for monitoring and, in particular, as a source for SNS notifications

# API Logs Are Trails of Data

The cloud strongly favors decoupled and distributed architectures. This means that you don't want your web servers, business logic, and database servers all existing on a single piece of hardware (even if that hardware is purely virtual, as in AWS). It's far more typical—and a better idea for scaling and performance—to separate these components and have them communicate over internal networks. So whether or not you realize it, good application design is all about a set of components that communicate via APIs.

Just as your custom applications can publish APIs, almost all of AWS' managed services provide APIs. RDS publishes an API. EC2 instances publish metadata through an API, and the Elastic Container Service (ECS) is API-based, just to name a few. That means that even in simpler applications, a significant amount of communication is happening between your code and AWS services.

This communication is what *AWS CloudTrail* is all about. If you can get a handle on this communication, you'll be able to monitor and react to your application's real-time health and activity.

# What Exactly Is a Trail?

Everything in CloudTrail is based on the concept of trails. A *trail* is just a specific configuration that indicates what events (API calls, inter-resource communication, and so forth) you want to record and where you want to put the logs of those events.

> If you haven't already noticed, AWS is somewhat infamous for doubling up on terms. There are CloudTrail trails, CloudWatch Event events, and several more doubled terms of this flavor. It's easy to get tripped up by them when they appear on exam questions, but there's no reason to. Just recall that this is how AWS handles their naming and you'll be fine.

So think of CloudTrail as having trails and each trail logging–specific event to a specific location. Typically that location is an S3 bucket. Figure 5.1 shows a simple trail that will log access to a specific S3 bucket (yellowtagmedia-aws.com, which is hosting a static website) and store the logged access in a new S3 bucket, yellowtagmedia-access.

**FIGURE 5.1**   Trails record a certain type of activity and store that activity as log files in a specific S3 bucket.

## Trails Can Work Across Regions

There are two types of trails. The first is a trail that applies to all regions. You specify a trail, and then CloudTrail applies that trail to all regions. The logs still go to an S3 bucket you choose.

Trails apply across all regions by default.

All-region trails are ideal because you get a single configuration that is applied across all your regions consistently. You also get all your logs from all regions in a single S3 bucket.

If you launch resources in a new region, trails that apply to all regions automatically are applied to the new region. You don't have to do anything to get the trail configuration, which is another benefit to trails across all regions.

## Trails Can Work Within a Region

You can also create a trail that applies to only one region. There's not as often a good reason to take this approach, because typically if you want to log a certain type of activity in one region, you would want to log it in all regions. The primary use case here would be that you are troubleshooting something very specific—perhaps a certain set of instances are receiving unusual traffic or there has been a breach. In those cases, you might want to log—and log with a lot of verbosity—actions, events, and API calls in a specific region only.

In the single-region case, things work almost identically to cross-region trails. All activity is logged to an S3 bucket. You can then examine the logs and see the trail on your CloudTrail dashboard.

With both cross-region and single-region trails, you can output logs to any S3 bucket, regardless of the region within which the bucket exists.

## One Region, Multiple Trails

You can have a trail across all regions, and a trail that tracks events within a single region. Then, you can have more than one trail for both of these trail types (cross-region and single-region). In fact, that's typical, you might want one trail to track S3 access and another to track Lambda function access.

   You also might want multiple trails to report similar things and create variants of the same logs. This is common if you need a trail for developers that logs high-level API usage—for their own performance and improvement tasks—and another more detailed trail tracking the same API usage for security or compliance reasons. AWS allows you to create up to five trails per region, although you can often get this limit raised by contacting AWS support.

 A trail that works across regions counts as one of the five allowed trails in every region. For example, you could have three cross-region trails and two single-region trails in one region before you hit your limit.

## The CloudTrail Process

Once you've set up a trail, CloudTrail begins a two-step process of capturing and storing logs. Figure 5.2 illustrates this process.

**FIGURE 5.2**   CloudTrail consistently captures activity and stores the logs of that activity in S3 buckets.

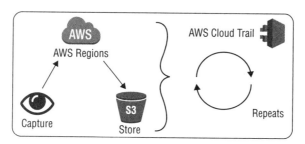

   Although that's helpful, AWS intends you to then add to this process, via CloudWatch alarms and review. Figure 5.3 shows the additional steps of action and review that AWS recommends once logs have been deposited to S3.

**FIGURE 5.3**   You should build your own pipeline out from the storage that CloudTrail provides to ongoing action and analysis.

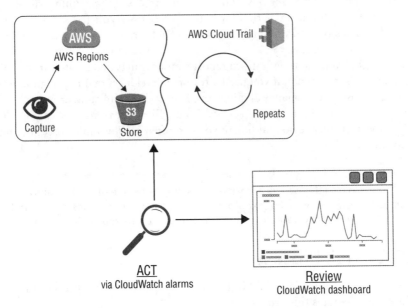

# CloudTrail as a Monitoring Tool

Now that you've seen the capturing portion of CloudTrail, it's time to get into actually doing something with the logs it produces. Once you have logs, you can view them, analyze them with a tool like *Amazon Athena*, as well as interpret them and even sound alarms in CloudWatch.

## Viewing CloudTrail Logs

CloudTrail places logs in the S3 bucket you specify and does a lot of path-based organization for you. You'll have your bucket name, any prefix you indicated when you set the trail up, and then a folder called AWSLogs. Under this directory, you'll have your AWS account number, then a folder called CloudTrail. From there, logs are organized into further folders: the region, then the year, then the month, and then the date. Within that final folder you'll find actual logs.

For example, a full path to a log might looks like yellowtagmedia-access/AWSLogs/ 860645612347/CloudTrail/us-east-1/2019/01/04. This is a *lot* of navigation, but it makes locating exactly what you want easy (for humans and AWS tools). Individual files have names like 860645612347_CloudTrail_us-east-1_20181114T1530Z_B8HMwFSVHtT5dEYn.json.gz, which is another mouthful. Logs are GZipped to reduce space; you can unzip them using any standard decompression tool (and most operating systems will handle this automatically as well).

Finally, you can crack open this file and see...a lot of information. Here's just a small sample of representative content:

```
{"Records":[{"eventVersion":"1.05","userIdentity":{"type":"AWSAccount","
principalId":"","accountId":"ANONYMOUS_PRINCIPAL"},"eventTime":"2018-11-
15T08:06:52Z","eventSource":"s3.amazonaws.com","eventName":"HeadObject",
"awsRegion":"us-east-1","sourceIPAddress":"109.86.212.239","userAgent":"[Go-
http-client/1.1]","requestParameters":{"bucketName":"yellowtagmedia-aws
.com","key":"index.html"},"responseElements":null,"additionalEventData":{"x-
amz-id-2":"q1ANAIW7skRD/aYAGS927dfjA/27SBRm0fD3WfRHX1YUZgXIaiHmwF6vxpl4RTE09
6+o+8="},"requestID":"C56525332834B6C6","eventID":"16a423d1-a9a3-482c-a981-
754dd81edc9a","readOnly":true,"resources":[{"type":"AWS::S3::Object","ARN":"arn
:aws:s3:::yellowtagmedia-aws.com/index.html"},{"accountId":"860645612347","type
":"AWS::S3::Bucket","ARN":"arn:aws:s3:::yellowtagmedia-aws.com"}],"eventType":"
AwsApiCall","recipientAccountId":"860645612347","sharedEventID":"25429b5f-ec72-
4b3d-9908-709f31232cb9"}]}
```

> **NOTE** In case you were concerned about my sanity, these are not actual AWS account IDs.

If you're not at all sure what you're looking at, that's okay. There is a lot of useful information here, but for now, just know that every single access of an API generates information like this. The time of the event, information about the event (in this case, access to a static file hosted on an S3 bucket), details about the owner AWS account, and more. However, all this information is tremendously powerful and useful for monitoring and responding to specific events.

## Connect a CloudTrail Trail to SNS

One easy first step in adding some automated monitoring to CloudTrail is to set a trail to notify you via *Amazon SNS* when a trail writes a new log to S3. This is pretty simple, as when you create a trail, you'll have this option available. Just tell CloudTrail to fire off the notification and you're done.

However, keep in mind that with many trails, logs are going to be written to S3 a *lot*—and recall from the previous section how much is captured for every single access. If you're trailing all read access to S3 buckets, for example, and you have buckets that are accessed often, an SNS notification doesn't make sense. You need to be selective about when to send notifications; it can be expensive, and it can create "noise" for administrators and eventually get ignored.

Consider a trail that sends out a notification for a security or compliance management event. You would want to be notified only if something abnormal or disallowed occurred.

## CloudTrail Handles Permissions...Sometimes

If you use CloudTrail's trail creation tool to handle creating an S3 bucket and an SNS topic, everything just "magically" happens. Although CloudTrail needs IAM permissions to write to S3 and permissions to create new notifications in SNS, these are all taken care of for you by the CloudTrail tool.

However, if you set up S3 or SNS access after the fact, you will likely need to set some or even all of these permissions yourself. This is especially true for SNS; you can find several example IAM policies online in AWS' documentation at `https://docs.aws.amazon.com/sns/latest/dg/AccessPolicyLanguage_UseCases_Sns.html`.

You'll also need to set up IAM permissions for users who want to work with CloudTrail. Two key policies are already set up for just this:

- `AWSCloudTrailFullAccess` should be given to users who need to create trails. These are typically your SysOps administrators.

- `AWSCloudTrailReadOnlyAccess` must be given to anyone who should be able to view trails and the S3 buckets with log data.

# Summary

Like AWS Organizations and AWS Config, AWS CloudTrail isn't particularly complicated. Once you get the basics of how terminology is used and a handle on how trails are processed, it's pretty straightforward. The power in CloudTrail isn't its complexity, though. It's that it—especially along CloudWatch, AWS Organizations, and AWS Config—gives you a more complete picture of your AWS environment and the applications running within that environment.

For the exam, just make sure you understand the basics of trails, that CloudTrail is usually the right tool when it comes to API calls or resource-to-resource communication, and the difference between CloudTrail's log and other system logging. Get those down and you should have no issues.

# Resources to Review

AWS CloudTrail:

`https://aws.amazon.com/cloudtrail/`

API Reference (yes, CloudTrail itself has an API):

`https://docs.aws.amazon.com/awscloudtrail/latest/APIReference/Welcome.html`

A good AWS re:INVENT talk on using CloudTrail for governance from 2017:

`www.youtube.com/watch?time_continue=2&v=mbdC6IhOROk`

# Exam Essentials

**Differentiate between CloudWatch, CloudTrail, and AWS Config.** In a nutshell, CloudWatch is for real-time performance and health monitoring of your environment. CloudTrail monitors API logs and events within your AWS environment. AWS Config monitors the configuration of your environment. All three provide compliance, auditing, and security.

**Describe the two types of trails: cross-region and single-region.** A cross-region trail functions in all regions of your account. All logs are then placed in a single S3 bucket. A single-region trail applies to one region only and can place logs in any S3 bucket, regardless of that bucket's region.

**Explain how cross-region trails automatically function in new regions.** A cross-region trail will automatically begin capturing activity in any new region that is stood up in an environment without any user intervention. Logs for new activity are placed in the same S3 bucket as logs for existing regions and aggregated in seamlessly.

**Describe the best practices for acting on and reviewing CloudTrail logs.** It is not enough to simply turn on CloudTrail and create a few trails. You should set up CloudWatch alarms related to those trails and potentially send events out via SNS. You should also be continually reviewing logs via a CloudWatch (not CloudTrail!) dashboard that has alarms connected to your CloudTrail logs in S3. Further, you may want to consider using a tool like Amazon Athena for deeper analysis of large log file stores.

# Exercises

A lot of the CloudTrail concepts are a bit esoteric until you start using the tool. Then, you'll find that they're quite simple. In this lab, you'll create a trail to monitor S3 buckets and then look at the created logs.

### EXERCISE 5.1

### Create a New Cross-Region Trail for Logging S3 Write Access

In this exercise, you will create a cross-region trail in AWS CloudTrail. It will be configured to log write events for Amazon S3 buckets.

1. Log into the AWS management console.

2. On the Services page, choose CloudTrail under the Management Tools heading.

3. Select Trails from the left-hand menu.

4. Click the Create Trail button.

5.  Enter a name for the trail, like `All_S3_Write_Access`.

6.  Make sure you leave the default selection of Apply Trail To All Regions. That will ensure this trail captures S3 write activity in all buckets in all regions.

7.  For Read/Write events, select Write Only. This will capture just the writes to S3, which is the point here. At this stage, your setup should look similar to Figure 5.4.

**FIGURE 5.4**    Create a new CloudTrail trail across all regions to capture write events to all your S3 buckets.

8.  Scroll down and check the Select All S3 Buckets In Your Account option.

9.  Create a new S3 bucket for your logs and give the new bucket a name.

10. Open the Advanced options and type **logs** as a prefix for your logs. Your console should look similar to Figure 5.5 at this point.

11. Leave the rest of the options at their defaults and click Create Trail. Figure 5.6 shows the CloudTrail Trails section with the created trail active.

**FIGURE 5.5** Creating a trail is pretty simple. You provide a few names and CloudTrail does most of the work.

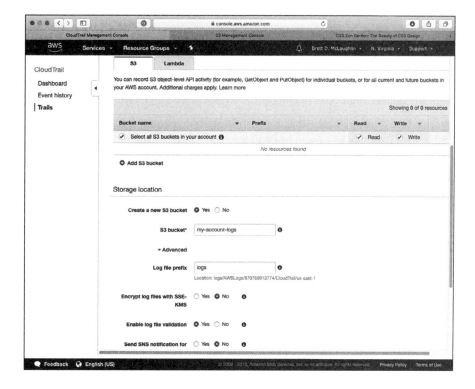

**FIGURE 5.6** All of your active trails appear in the CloudTrail Trails section of the console.

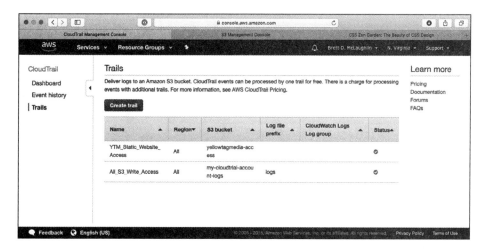

**EXERCISE 5.2**

### View a CloudTrail log

In this exercise, you will see how easy it is to view an AWS CloudTrail log.

1. Wait at least 15 minutes; it typically takes that long for a new trail to begin writing logs to S3. Then go to the S3 section of the AWS management console.

2. Select the bucket you chose in creating your trail (Step 9 of Exercise 5.1).

3. Navigate to the logs/ folder (this may be different if you entered a different prefix in Step 10 of Exercise 5.1). From here, you'll have limited options: an AWSLogs folder, then an account, and then a year, month, and date.

4. You can then select any of the logs; the number you have will vary based on your trail and how long it's been up and active. You should see something similar to Figure 5.7.

**FIGURE 5.7**    CloudTrail writes a new file every time it adds to the trail. Each is available in your S3 bucket.

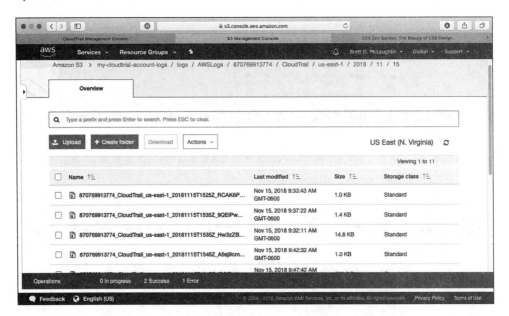

5. You can download any of these logs. You can also click on each log to get metadata for the file, as shown in Figure 5.8.

**FIGURE 5.8**  The metadata for files gives you basic information, as well as when the file was written and the encryption of the file.

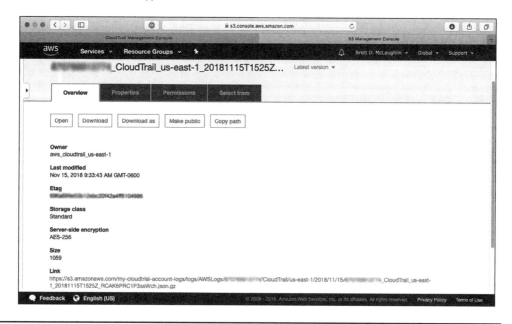

---

## Set Up Automatic Notifications When a Trail Writes a Log

In this exercise, you will set up Amazon SNS to send a notification anytime an AWS CloudTrail trail writes to a log.

1. Go back to your CloudTrail dashboard, and then select the Trails section. Click on your trail, find the Storage Location section, and click the Edit icon.

2. Select the Yes option next to Send SNS Notification.

3. Select Yes to create a new SNS topic and then name it.

4. Make sure you save your changes to the trail.

5. Now go to the SNS section in the console and select the Topics option on the left. You should now see your new topic, as shown in Figure 5.9.

**FIGURE 5.9** All your topics are listed here. Most of them in this example are defaults, but you should also see a topic named whatever you entered in Step 3—in this case, mine is named every_single_access-trail.

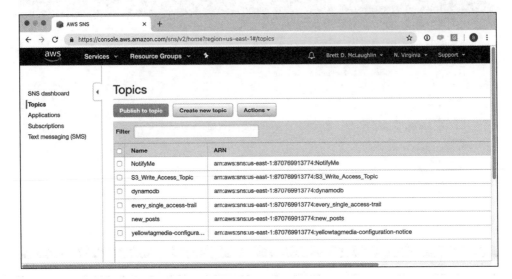

6. At this point, you can subscribe to this topic using a variety of options: an application, Apple's Push Notification service, or Google's Cloud Messaging service. For more on setting up these services, consult https://aws.amazon.com/blogs/aws/push-notifications-to-mobile-devices-using-amazon-sns/ or https://docs.aws.amazon.com/sns/latest/dg/sns-mobile-application-as-subscriber.html.

# Review Questions

You can find the answers in the Appendix.

1.  Which AWS tool would you use to monitor performance of your application?
    A.  CloudWatch
    B.  CloudTrail
    C.  AWS Config
    D.  AWS Organizations

2.  Which AWS tool would you use to audit API usage of your application?
    A.  CloudWatch
    B.  CloudTrail
    C.  AWS Config
    D.  AWS Organizations

3.  Which AWS tool would you use to audit configuration changes to your AWS environment?
    A.  CloudWatch
    B.  CloudTrail
    C.  AWS Config
    D.  AWS Organizations

4.  Your management is concerned that too many people are using the AWS Config tool, potentially violating security protocols. What tool would you use to audit the usage of the AWS Config tool?
    A.  CloudWatch
    B.  CloudTrail
    C.  AWS Config
    D.  AWS Organizations

5.  You have created a trail with the default settings to log access to Lambda functions. You currently have functions in US East 2 and US West 1. You're launching a new Lambda function in US East 1 and want to ensure that CloudTrail logs access to this function as well. What do you need to do?
    A.  Update the trail configuration and add US East 1 as a region to monitor.
    B.  Update the trail configuration and provide an S3 bucket for logged events in US East 1.
    C.  Restart the trail in CloudTrail.
    D.  Nothing. Access to the new Lambda function in the new region will automatically be handled by the existing trail.

**6.** How many trails can you create in a single region?

   **A.** 3

   **B.** 5

   **C.** 20

   **D.** There is no preset limit on the number of trails you can have in a region.

**7.** You have eight trails in your AWS CloudTrail configuration. Three apply to all regions and deposit logs in an S3 bucket in EU West 1. Two trails are single region, in EU West 2, depositing logs in an S3 bucket in EU West 2. One is in EU West 1 and uses the same EU West 1 bucket as the cross-region trails. Finally, you have a trail in US West 2. In what region must you locate the S3 bucket for the US West 2 trail to deposit logs?

   **A.** US West 2

   **B.** EU West 1

   **C.** EU West 2

   **D.** Any region you like

**8.** You have eight trails in your AWS CloudTrail configuration. Three apply to all regions and deposit logs in an S3 bucket in EU West 1. Two trails are single region, in EU West 2, depositing logs in an S3 bucket in EU West 2. One is in EU West 1 and uses the same EU West 1 bucket as the cross-region trails. Finally, you have a trail in US West 2 writing logs to an S3 bucket in US West 2. How many more trails can you create in EU West 2 if those trails are intended to work across all regions?

   **A.** 0

   **B.** 1

   **C.** 2

   **D.** 3

**9.** You have eight trails in your AWS CloudTrail configuration. Three apply to all regions and deposit logs in an S3 bucket in EU West 1. Two trails are single region, in EU West 2, depositing logs in an S3 bucket in EU West 2. One is in EU West 1 and uses the same EU West 1 bucket as the cross-region trails. Finally, you have a trail in US West 2 writing logs to an S3 bucket in US West 2. You are trying to create a new trail to function across all regions but are getting an error. What is preventing you from creating this trail?

   **A.** You have already created the maximum number of cross-region trails (three).

   **B.** You have already created the maximum number of trails for a single account (seven).

   **C.** You have already created the maximum number of trails in EU West 1 (five).

   **D.** You have already created the maximum number of trails in EU West 2 (five).

**10.** What is AWS' system for sending out alerts and alarms based on specific events in an environment?

   **A.** SQS

   **B.** SNS

**C.** SWF

**D.** CloudTrail

**11.** Which services listed here might be used as part of a solution to monitor potentially inse-cure interactions between an AWS application's API layer and non-AWS services? (Choose two.)

**A.** SNS

**B.** SWF

**C.** CloudWatch

**D.** CloudTrail

**12.** Which of the following services might be used to detect a potential security breach of your applications running in AWS? (Choose two.)

**A.** CloudWatch

**B.** CloudTrail

**C.** Trusted Advisor

**D.** SWF

**13.** You are in charge of a cloud migration from an on-premises datacenter to AWS. The system currently has a number of custom scripts that process system and application logs for audit-ing purposes. What AWS managed service could you use to replace these scripts and reduce the need for instances to run these custom processes?

**A.** CloudWatch

**B.** CloudTrail

**C.** Trusted Advisor

**D.** SWF

**14.** You have just started working at a new organization with existing AWS accounts. What do you need to do in order to set up CloudTrail on these accounts?

**A.** Turn on the CloudTrail service.

**B.** Create a new trail for the CloudTrail service.

**C.** Nothing; CloudTrail is automatically on and already logging activity.

**D.** Enable AWS Organizations and set up a service control policy that allows CloudTrail access.

**15.** Which of the following services is not supported by CloudTrail?

**A.** Amazon Athena

**B.** Amazon CloudFront

**C.** AWS Elastic Beanstalk

**D.** All of the above services are supported by CloudTrail.

**16.** When applying a trail to all regions, how many actual trails are created?

    **A.** A single trail is used across all the regions.

    **B.** Trails that are configured like Auto Scaling groups will automatically grow and collapse based on total volume across all the regions.

    **C.** One trail is created for each region, and a master trail is created in the default region.

    **D.** One trail is created for each region.

**17.** Which of the following is not an option for encrypting and securing log files created by CloudTrail?

    **A.** S3 Server-side Encryption (SSE)

    **B.** S3 KMS-Managed Keys (KMS)

    **C.** S3 MFA Delete

    **D.** Customer-Managed Keys

**18.** Which of the following is not included as part of an event associated with an activity logged by CloudTrail?

    **A.** Who made the request

    **B.** The parameters for the action requested

    **C.** The username of the requestor

    **D.** The response returned by the requested service

**19.** You have turned on SSE-KMS encryption for your CloudTrail log files. What additional step do you need to make for processing those log files in another application?

    **A.** Set up a decryption pipeline using Lambda.

    **B.** Turn on Automatic Decryption in AWS CloudTrail.

    **C.** Upload your KMS key to AWS CloudTrail.

    **D.** You do not need to take any steps because logs are automatically decrypted.

**20.** You want to ensure that no changes are made to your security groups and network access control lists (NACLs) across your account. What services would you use to create an alarm if someone tried to use the CLI to modify or delete a security group or NACL? (Choose two.)

    **A.** SNS

    **B.** AWS Config

    **C.** AWS CloudTrail

    **D.** AWS CloudWatch

# High Availability

# Chapter

# 6

# Amazon Relational Database Service

THE AWS CERTIFIED SYSOPS
ADMINISTRATOR – ASSOCIATE EXAM
TOPICS COVERED IN THIS CHAPTER MAY
INCLUDE, BUT ARE NOT LIMITED TO, THE
FOLLOWING:

Domain 2.0: High Availability

✓ 2.1  Implement scalability and elasticity based on
   use case

✓ 2.2  Recognize and differentiate highly available and
   resilient environments on AWS

Domain 3.0: Deployment and Provisioning

✓ 3.1  Identify and execute steps required to provision
   cloud resources

✓ 3.2  Identify and remediate deployment issues

Amazon Relational Database Service—more commonly referred to as Amazon RDS (or even just RDS)—is a scalable managed service for providing applications with a relational database in the cloud. While the managed nature of the service dramatically improves ease of operation, the real strength of Amazon RDS is its scalability. Databases are notoriously difficult to monitor, back up, scale up and down (in and out, in AWS terminology), and optimize for changing usage. Amazon RDS provides the majority of this functionality "out of the box."

Savvy AWS SysOps administrators are not only experienced working with Amazon RDS, but are also actively maintaining at least one RDS instance. And because AWS offers a number of databases and options under the Amazon RDS umbrella, you'll need to understand the common configurations and use cases to properly use Amazon RDS in your own environment.

This chapter covers:

The role of Amazon RDS in a scalable application architecture

Setting up a Multi-AZ (availability zone) configuration in Amazon RDS

Configuring read replicas for Amazon RDS

Distinguishing between high availability and disaster recovery in your Amazon RDS configuration

# Creating Databases with Amazon RDS

The primary service that Amazon RDS offers is scalability. With RDS, it is relatively easy to increase your database footprint. (There's more to say on the "relatively" modifier shortly.) That scalability comes in a few categories:

- The ability to grow your RDS storage without massive pain

- The ability to manage additional RDS storage without massive hiring

- The ability to integrate features that enhance your RDS' performance and usability without massive infrastructure

It's important to keep in mind here that "scalability" doesn't *just* apply to the sheer number of tables or columns or schemas. It applies to the role of your databases in your overall application architecture, and specifically to how easy it is to grow these databases as your organization's needs grow.

# Amazon RDS vs. Your Own Instances

There's absolutely nothing preventing you from spinning up your own EC2 instance, SSHing into the instance, and installing your database manually on that instance. In fact, you can get quite a close configuration to an Amazon RDS instance if you know what you're doing.

Then, when things get busy, it's up to you to maintain that database. You'll need to monitor the database. You'll need to manage table space. You'll need to keep up with upgrades to the database and upgrades to the instance itself. Basically, you "own" that instance and everything on it. In other words, unless you have the unusual ambition of being an early-2000s database administrator, you're going to spend a lot of time doing things you probably don't want to do.

This is where Amazon RDS comes in. Although it does not completely remove an administration and operation burden, it dramatically reduces it. You can spin up an Amazon RDS instance in minutes and have an application connecting to it shortly thereafter. You'll configure the most basic options—the use case, the instance class, how much storage and I/O you want to provision—and then AWS does the rest. You'll even get an estimate cost breakdown before you confirm your settings (see Figure 6.1 and Figure 6.2).

**FIGURE 6.1**    Setting up RDS—in this case, to use PostgreSQL—takes less than 5 minutes.

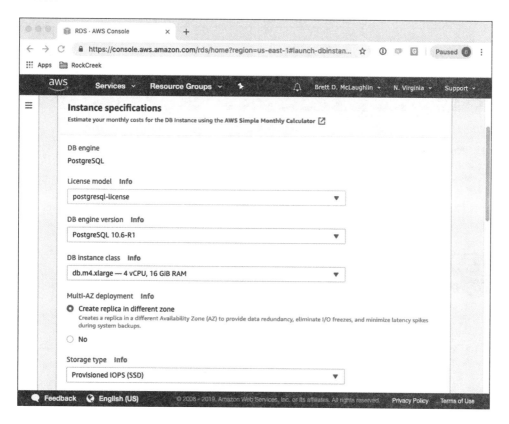

**FIGURE 6.2**    Before you lock your choices in, AWS gives you an estimated monthly cost for your selections.

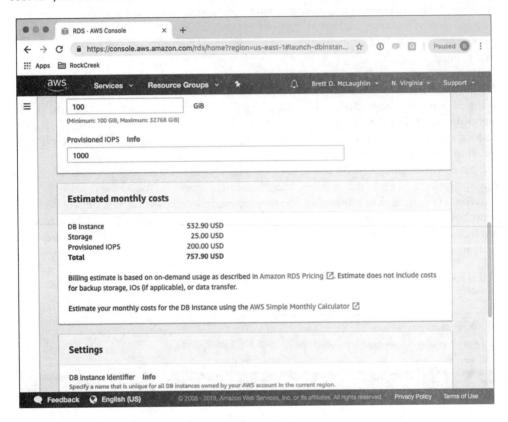

 It's important to realize that even when using Amazon RDS, you are in fact using AWS instances. Unlike a service like DynamoDB, you're going to have to interact with instance sizing and a few other instance configuration parameters, even within the context of the Amazon RDS managed service.

 While AWS often provides pretty reasonable defaults, this is not always the case with Amazon RDS. The default production use case for PostgreSQL typically costs nearly $800 a month, and the dev/test is still a notable $400. You'll want to tweak settings quite a bit to bring costs inline with your budget and expected usage.

Still, even with the pricier options and larger instance sizes, Amazon RDS gives you a very fast path to a database (or database cluster) with minimal fuss. And of course you can scale these costs as you scale your databases.

## Supported Database Engines

Amazon RDS supports most of the common database engines you'd use in a relational context:

- Amazon Aurora
- PostgreSQL
- MySQL
- MariaDB
- Oracle
- Microsoft SQL Server

For the most part, these engines all function as they do in their hosted versions. Further, setup with each engine is more or less the same; the primary differences relate to parameters key to the vendor.

However, you'll see that not all Amazon RDS features are available for all database engines. As a general rule, Amazon RDS offers the *largest* feature set with Amazon Aurora, followed closely by MySQL and PostgreSQL.

## Database Configuration and Parameter Groups

Amazon RDS uses a database parameter group to store the configuration values used for your instances. When you create a new instance, a default parameter group is used. This group contains default values that AWS supplies, and these values are generally optimized for the instance size and engine you're using.

You can also create your own database parameter group and set your own configuration values. That can be helpful if you need to set up a lot of instances with a set of standard values that don't match the AWS defaults. You can choose the Placement Groups option on the RDS page in the Amazon console, and Figure 6.3 shows the list of existing default groups you'll get. Figure 6.4 shows the options you can set once you create your own parameter group.

**FIGURE 6.3**    AWS builds default groups for your existing RDS setups, and you can create additional parameter groups as well.

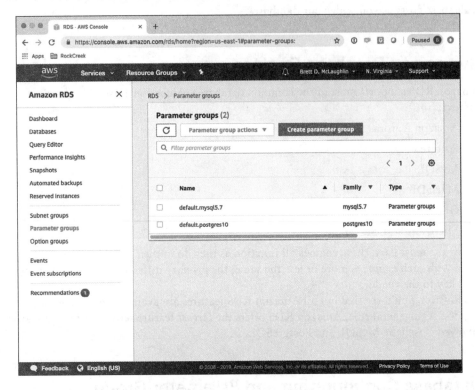

**FIGURE 6.4**    Virtually any options you can choose when you create an instance are available when you set up your parameter group.

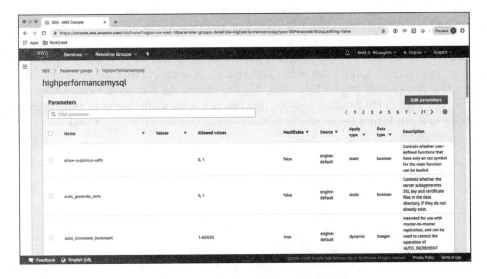

# Scalability with Amazon RDS

Scalability in the case of Amazon RDS doesn't mean that AWS just takes care of everything. While there are options in that vein—DynamoDB is the obvious one—AWS instead gives you the ability to upsize your database instances quickly and easily. You can literally select a database and change its instance size in a few clicks. Figure 6.5 shows this in the Amazon web console.

**FIGURE 6.5**    AWS will handle all the work in sizing up your database instance.

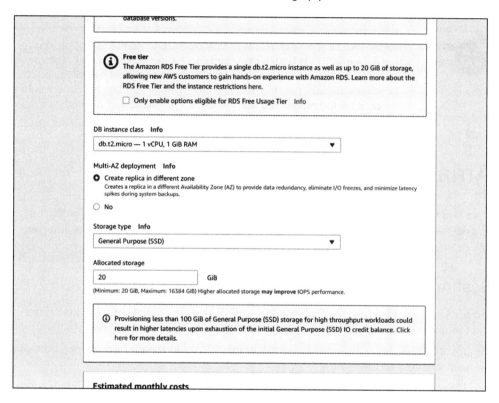

Just know that this requires your intervention—AWS will happily let your database hit 100 percent of its provisioned storage and I/O if you aren't paying attention, and it won't do a thing to reduce the load or increase the database capacity. However, you have the ability to address those sorts of issues with a few button clicks in the console.

> You can also set up read replicas, which improve performance as your application needs grow; that's covered a bit later in this chapter.

Because AWS requires your intervention to scale, it's best to think about Amazon RDS's scalability as supporting long-term growth. If you size and provision your database in a manner that requires growing it every day—or even every week—you're going to quickly become frustrated. In those instances, you'd be better using an option like DynamoDB, which does scale seamlessly and without user intervention (although at a cost).

Ultimately, Amazon RDS as a managed service sits somewhere between managing your own EC2 instances with database servers installed and a managed service like DynamoDB. You will have to administer the instances, but configuration and upsizing is dramatically easier than manually managing the process yourself.

> For the certification exam, it is *critical* that you understand and recognize that Amazon RDS is both a managed service and a service that requires you to understand and size instances. You can expect to be asked about databases via RDS running on a certain instance size and how you would increase performance. You need to know that increasing the instance size is a possible option, just as is adding read replicas.

# Amazon RDS Key Features

Once you have a database (or databases) set up using Amazon RDS, you get a number of immediate features and benefits. These are all things that would require manual intervention or setup if you were not using Amazon RDS.

## Scaling Amazon RDS Instances

In addition to the ease of scaling already mentioned, you get a couple of other key advantages to instance scaling:

- You can scale your instances memory, storage, CPU, and Input/Output Operations per second (IOPs) independently.

- These scaling options incur minimal downtime, even more so if you are using a multi-AZ setup.

- Amazon RDS will handle the patching and failure detection on new RDS instances as well as continuing this for any scaled database instances.

## Backing Up Amazon RDS Instances

Amazon RDS gives you two different options for backing up and restoration of your databases:

- You can turn on automated backups. This will allow you to do point-in-time recovery of your instance. Amazon RDS will do full daily snapshots of your database and capture transaction logs, with a default retention period of seven days.

- You can also perform manual snapshots of your database at any time and save those snapshots as long as you like.

In both cases, you can restore your database from snapshot through the AWS CLI or web console.

## Securing Amazon RDS Instances

Part of the Amazon RDS advantage is the increased security you get "for free" when using the service.

- Instances are automatically patched when security or reliability updates are available, ensuring a more secure database instance without manual intervention.

- You can control access to the database instances via IAM quite easily.

- Amazon RDS instances can be launched into private VPCs and set to use SSL, all as a standard part of setting up the instances.

# Multi-AZ Configuration

One of the key features of Amazon RDS is its multi-AZ configuration. This is exactly what it sounds like: a configuration for an Amazon RDS database that spans multiple availability zones. This option provides disaster recovery support for Amazon RDS in a very simple manner.

## Creating a Multi-AZ Deployment

It is incredibly simple to set up a multi-AZ configuration. When you're creating an RDS instance, you simply click Yes next to Create Replica In Different Zone. This is shown in Figure 6.6. That's it…Amazon RDS takes care of the rest.

Enabling multi-AZ does a number of things for you:

- Creates an additional database instance in an availability zone separate from your primary database instance

- Sets up synchronous replication from your primary database instance to the additional database instance

- Provides automatic failover from the primary instance to the secondary instance in the case of a primary instance problem

It's very, very, very important to recognize that all of these features are designed for disaster recovery. The secondary database instance is *never* active or accessible unless the primary instance has failed. If you are looking for performance improvements, consider resizing your database instance or creating read replicas.

**FIGURE 6.6**   Amazon RDS needs nothing more than a radio button click to set up your multi-AZ configuration.

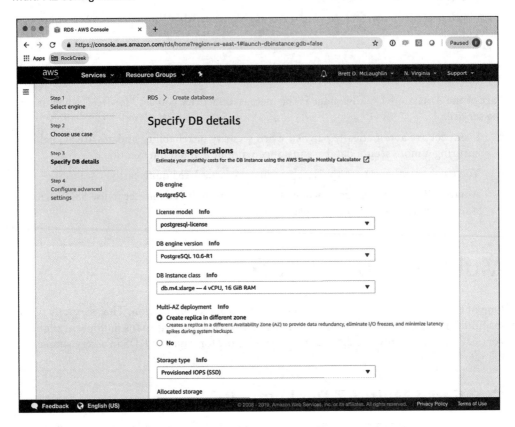

**WARNING**   You will almost certainly be asked questions about multi-AZ and read replicas on the exam. In general, AWS likes to ensure you understand that multi-AZ configurations are for disaster recovery and read replicas are for performance. They'll check this understanding by suggesting adding a multi-AZ setup to improve read capacity or adding read replicas to prevent data loss. You need to be comfortable recognizing the problems with these solutions in their wording.

## Failing Over to the Secondary Instance

Amazon RDS will initiate a failover to the secondary database instance when it considers the primary instance. A number of issues trigger this:

- Loss of network connectivity to the primary instance
- Disk failure of the storage volume on the primary instance

- Failure of the database instance itself
- Overall availability zone failure on the primary instance

In all of these cases, the secondary instance is brought online and made active. This failover takes less than a minute for Aurora and less than two minutes for other database engines.

 Amazon Aurora actually offers a number of advantages in the Amazon RDS realm. Those are discussed further in the later section on Amazon Aurora. In general, absent other factors like familiarity on your team or sunk license costs, Aurora is an excellent choice for a new Amazon RDS installation.

After failover is complete, the standby takes over all traffic. It should be up-to-date because of the synchronous replication already occurring since multi-AZ setup. To accommodate this change, AWS will update DNS entries pointing at your previous primary instance—which has now failed—to point at the secondary instance. At this point, the standby is considered to be the primary instance.

 In a failover situation, no IP addresses change. The IP address of the primary instance stays as it is, as does the IP address of the secondary instance. Only DNS changes to affect traffic redirection; in this case, the CNAME record is updated to use the IP address of the former standby instance. AWS will sometimes ask this on the exam, so be clear about exactly what changes in the event of a failover.

# Read Replicas

The complement to a multi-AZ setup for failover and disaster recovery is a read replica (or several of them) for performance gains. Just as a multi-AZ setup provides an additional database instance for failover, a read replica provides an additional instance for read performance. This is the preferred way to scale out your Amazon RDS instance when a significant portion of your database traffic is read-only.

## Replication to Read Replicas

Once you've set up a read replica, data is replicated to it asynchronously. When you write to your primary database instance, the updated data is eventually updated on all of your replicas as well. As the read replicas are (rather obviously) read-only, it's only the primary instance and this replication process that makes changes to them.

Most read replicas are set in the same region as the primary instance. In those cases, the replication is largely invisible to applications. However, you can also create read replicas in additional regions than that of the primary instance. In those cases, Amazon RDS sets up a secure channel and uses it for replication. The delay here can be slightly longer than that of a replica in the same region as the primary instance.

> The additional time it takes to replicate across regions is moot in most situations. An application in a region outside of the primary instance's region is going to have a similar lag in accessing the primary instance. In this case, though, the application sees less lag—accessing the read replica in the same region—and it's only on update that any lag occurs. That's invisible to the application consuming data, though, which is basically a net win for application users.

## Connecting to Read Replicas

You'll need to direct your applications to use these read replicas, though. A DNS endpoint will be created by Amazon RDS, and then you'll use that endpoint in your applications. This is an important point: if you don't tell your applications to use read replicas, they won't be used.

## Read Replicas' Requirements and Limitations

Because of the special nature of read replicas, you'll have to take a few things into account when using them:

- Read replicas work only with MySQL, PostgreSQL, MariaDB, and Aurora.
- You can't put a read replica behind an elastic load balancer.
- You can use up to 5 read replicas with MySQL and PostgreSQL, and up to 15 with Amazon Aurora.
- You can create a read replica of a read replica in certain cases (notably, MySQL).
- You cannot take a database snapshot of a read replica.

# Amazon Aurora

It's worth specifically mentioning Amazon Aurora. Although this book and the AWS certification exams are typically vendor-agnostic, Amazon Aurora tends to straddle the line between a vendor choice for a database and an AWS managed service. As such—and certainly because its tightly tied into the AWS development teams—it tends to match up with Amazon RDS very well.

Amazon Aurora essentially gives you a lot of redundancy and scalability "for free," notably:

- SSD-backed storage specifically targeted for database loads
- Automatic replication six ways across three availability zones
- Automatic fault tolerance; up to two copies of data can fail before data writing fails, and three can fail before data reading fails.
- Storage is "self-healing"; data blocks and disks are replaced automatically if they fail.

Aurora itself also provides specific compatibility with MySQL and PostgreSQL. So you'll find references in the AWS documentation to Aurora MySQL and Aurora PostgreSQL. These versions of Aurora are drop-in replacements for MySQL and PostgreSQL, respectively, encouraging users to take advantage of Aurora features without changing any MySQL- or PostgreSQL-specific code or table features.

Because Aurora always has replication occurring across availability zones, this effectively means that Amazon Aurora is *automatically* multi-AZ. This can cause some confusion. Just remember that by using Aurora, you're getting a number of failover and redundancy features that normally require multi-AZ configuration on a non-Aurora database instance.

## Aurora Volumes

Amazon Aurora handles storage slightly differently than normal Amazon RDS databases. Data for Aurora is stored in a cluster volume, a single virtual volume based on SSD (solid-state drive) technology. This cluster volume is virtual and spans multiple availability zones.

Each availability zone used by an Aurora instance then uses that data, or a replica of that data, ensuring high availability even if an AZ becomes unavailable. These clusters size up automatically as well, making them the only Amazon RDS instance type that currently does any sort of automatic scaling. These volumes can grow as large as 64 TB.

## Aurora Replicas

Aurora handles replicas in a slightly different way than normal as well. Like read replicas, Aurora replicas support only read operations. You can have up to 15 of them for a primary instance (making 16 database instances total). They can also be spread across availability zones.

Each replica inherits the same advantages in an RDS setup as the primary instance. The replicas are self-healing, they recover from crashes, and they can even be promoted to primary instances if needed.

# Summary

Amazon RDS is in many ways a middle ground in terms of exploiting the value proposition of AWS. It is easier to configure and manage than manually installing a database on an instance, and it is far easier to resize than a typical database instance. However, even when using Amazon Aurora, it is not a no-maintenance solution. Managed services in AWS require far less monitoring and intervention.

That said, unless you have custom plugins or very specialized needs, there is almost never a time when it's a good idea to install a relational database on AWS yourself. Amazon RDS reduces your overhead as a SysOps administrator, meaning you have time to worry about the many other concerns you'll have keeping applications and platforms running.

In terms of managing RDS—and answering questions about it—you'll need to understand that instance size and management is your job, not AWS'. You should be able to add read replicas and set up multi-AZ, and know when each option is appropriate. These two features are *not* identical or interchangeable, and your life (and exam) will be not go well if you can't easily distinguish between them.

# Resources to Review

Amazon RDS:

    https://aws.amazon.com/rds/

Amazon Aurora:

    https://aws.amazon.com/rds/aurora/

AWS Core Page for Databases:

    https://aws.amazon.com/products/databases/

AWS Documentation on Scaling RDS:

    https://aws.amazon.com/blogs/database/
    scaling-your-amazon-rds-instance-vertically-and-horizontally/

# Exam Essentials

**Explain the use of database instances by Amazon RDS.**   Amazon RDS provides database instances by setting up databases on instances. That seems obvious, but it is important to recognize that actual instances are used and that you have shared responsibility with AWS over those instances (compared to DynamoDB, where those instances are completely isolated from your control). AWS will patch your instances, but you will need to size them and handle security around and to them.

**Understand how Amazon RDS handles elasticity and scalability.**   Amazon RDS is not an elastic service. Database instances cannot be sized up or down quickly or on demand. Adding read replicas is the closest option to actual elasticity. Amazon RDS handles scalability by allowing you to size up an instance easily, without a lot of overhead.

**Know the database engines supported by Amazon RDS.**   Amazon RDS supports Amazon Aurora, MySQL, MariaDB, PostgreSQL, Oracle, and SQL Server. In general, Amazon Aurora has the most features, followed closely by PostgreSQL and MySQL.

**Explain the difference between read replicas and multi-AZ setups as it relates to high availability.**   Read replicas are replicas of the primary database instance and can be in the same or a different availability zone as well as the same or a different region. These replicas are read only and can improve read performance of applications that use them. Multi-AZ setups are for disaster recovery and involve adding a standby instance that replicates from the primary instance in a different availability zone, but the same region, as that instance. If the primary instance fails, the standby becomes the primary instance.

**Explain how read replicas can be used to improve performance.**   You can add up to 5 read replicas to a MySQL, MariaDB, or PostgreSQL Amazon RDS database, and up to 15 to an Aurora instance. These replicas are read-only and have a different connection string and DNS resolution than the primary instance. They can significantly improve performance by providing additional read capacity.

**Define the key features of Amazon Aurora as a database alternative to MySQL and PostgreSQL.**   Amazon Aurora is a particular flavor of a relational database. It provides up to 64 TB of storage per instance, up to 15 read replicas, and is fault-tolerant and self-healing. It also automatically handles backups (like all Amazon RDS instances if so configured) and replicates across a minimum of three availability zones. Further, it offers specific versions that are drop-in replacements for MySQL and PostgreSQL.

# Review Questions

You can find the answers in the Appendix.

1. Which of the following does Amazon RDS make most easy?
   A. Scalability of databases
   B. Elasticity of databases
   C. Automated scalability of data access
   D. Network access to databases

2. How is Amazon RDS similar to an Auto Scaling group?
   A. Both Amazon RDS and Auto Scaling policies will add instances in response to increased demand.
   B. Both Amazon RDS and Auto Scaling policies will fire off alerts when traffic thresholds are reached related to usage.
   C. Both Amazon RDS and Auto Scaling policies provide elasticity to your applications.
   D. None of these are true.

3. Which of the following statements is not accurate regarding databases created using Amazon RDS?
   A. Database utilization will never hit 100 percent due to Amazon RDS managing database instances.
   B. Database instances require sizing by the customer rather than being handled automatically by Amazon RDS.
   C. A portion of your Amazon RDS charges are related to the size of the database instance you have chosen.
   D. Amazon RDS makes database provisioning significantly simpler than manually installing a database on an instance.

4. When does Amazon RDS patch your managed database instances?
   A. Once a month
   B. Every time any new software patch is available
   C. Every time a patch related to security or instance reliability is available
   D. Never; you are responsible for instance patching.

5. How can you restrict access to an Amazon RDS instance? (Choose two.)
   A. By using IAM roles to limit resources' access to the database instance
   B. By using NACLs to limit access to the VPC in which the database resides
   C. By setting user permissions on the database running on the instance
   D. By using a bastion host to limit direct access to the database instance

6. Which of the following are backup methods supported by Amazon RDS? (Choose two.)

   **A.** Automated hourly snapshots

   **B.** Automated daily snapshots

   **C.** User-initiated snapshots at any time

   **D.** User-initiated snapshots in the set maintenance period for your database instance

7. What is the default Amazon RDS backup retention period?

   **A.** 3 days

   **B.** 7 days

   **C.** 10 days

   **D.** This value is set at instance creation.

8. Which of the following is not true about read replicas?

   **A.** Replication occurs asynchronously.

   **B.** Backups are configured on the replicas by default.

   **C.** A replica can be promoted to become a primary instance.

   **D.** A read replica can be created in the same availability zone as the primary instance.

9. Which of the following is not true about a multi-AZ configuration?

   **A.** Replication occurs synchronously.

   **B.** Backups are configured on the standby instance by default.

   **C.** A standby instance can be promoted to become a primary instance.

   **D.** A standby instance can be created in the same availability zone as the primary instance.

10. Which of the following is not true about a multi-AZ configuration?

    **A.** Replication occurs asynchronously.

    **B.** Backups are configured on the standby instance by default.

    **C.** A standby instance can be promoted to become a primary instance.

    **D.** Replication occurs synchronously.

11. When you're using a multi-AZ setup, if the primary database instance becomes unreachable, which of the following happens automatically? (Choose two.)

    **A.** The DNS CNAME is changed to point at the standby instance.

    **B.** Backups switch from the standby instance to the primary instance.

    **C.** The standby instance is promoted to become the primary instance.

    **D.** The primary instance is restarted.

12. Which of the following is the best solution for reducing the read workload on a database instance?

    A. Add read replicas to the database.

    B. Add a multi-AZ configuration to the database.

    C. Create a new database in a second region and set up replication between the original and the new database.

    D. Create a new database in a second availability zone and set up replication between the original and the new database.

13. Which of the following are allowed options for the deployment of a read replica?

    A. The same availability zone as the primary instance

    B. A different region than the primary instance

    C. The same region as the primary instance

    D. All of the above

14. Which of the following are allowed options for the deployment of a secondary instance of a multi-AZ setup?

    A. The same availability zone as the primary instance

    B. A different region than the primary instance

    C. The same region as the primary instance

    D. All of the above

15. Which of the following would be good uses for read replicas? (Choose two.)

    A. Database instances for a website with high volume displaying items for sale

    B. Database instances for a data warehouse focused on reporting

    C. Database instances for a website with high volume adding users to a mailing list

    D. Database instances to ensure that if network connectivity is lost, applications will continue to run

16. What is the largest sized table you can have on Amazon Aurora?

    A. 16 TB

    B. 32 TB

    C. 64 TB

    D. 128 TB

17. For which database engines can Amazon Aurora drop in as a direct replacement? (Choose two.)

    A. MariaDB

    B. SQL Server

    C. MySQL

    D. PostgreSQL

**18.** Which of the following will AWS automatically handle when you use RDS? (Choose two.)

    **A.** Patching the database server

    **B.** Optimizing queries received by the RDS instance

    **C.** Creating backups compliant with long-term retention requirements of your organization

    **D.** Taking point-in-time backups periodically

**19.** You are using Amazon RDS instances for your production and development environments. Both instances are running on db.t3.small instances. Lately, though development has been operating with no issues, the production environment is showing increased performance degradation, especially when writing new data to the production instance. What change would you consider to fix this issue?

    **A.** Set up ElastiCache in front of the production database to cache requests.

    **B.** Upgrade the production database to use a larger instance type.

    **C.** Set up read replicas on the production instance.

    **D.** Provision additional network bandwidth to the production database.

**20.** In a failover scenario from one RDS instance to another instance, using a multi-AZ setup, which of the following does *not* occur?

    **A.** All requests are re-routed to the new instance from the failed instance.

    **B.** DNS entries are pointed to the new instance.

    **C.** The IP address of the active instance can change.

    **D.** In-progress activity with the failing database completes before cutting over to the new instance.

# Auto Scaling

**THE AWS CERTIFIED SYSOPS ADMINISTRATOR – ASSOCIATE EXAM TOPICS COVERED IN THIS CHAPTER MAY INCLUDE, BUT ARE NOT LIMITED TO, THE FOLLOWING:**

**Domain 2.0: High Availability**

✓ **2.1** Implement scalability and elasticity based on use case

✓ **2.2** Recognize and differentiate highly available and resilient environments on AWS

**Domain 3.0: Deployment and Provisioning**

✓ **3.1** Identify and execute steps required to provision cloud resources

**Domain 7.0: Automation and Optimization**

✓ **7.1** Use AWS services and features to manage and assess resource utilization

✓ **7.2** Employ cost optimization strategies for efficient resource utilization

✓ **7.3** Automate manual or repeatable process to minimize management overhead

Amazon Web Services (AWS) has built most of its business on one basic principle: scalability. More core to their business than perhaps any other facet is the AWS ability to scale up to meet demand and then scale back down when demand increases to reduce costs. Easy to say but incredibly difficult to implement, Auto Scaling is the approach AWS takes to offering user control over this process.

While many AWS-managed services scale up and down automatically (think Lambda, DynamoDB, and the Simple Email Service, for example), many other services do not. Your fleet of EC2 instances, for example, will not magically grow to meet demand. And though you can launch 100 instances to handle a surge in traffic, AWS won't reduce this number when that surge ends.

It's in these instances that Auto Scaling is critical. Auto Scaling provides you with a mechanism to define policies to scale up and down your instances—primarily EC2 instances, but also many other things that AWS provides—to meet demand, decrease costs, and ultimately provide your application with the scalability for which AWS is so well known.

This chapter covers:

The basics of Auto Scaling, including key terminology and basic principles

The important difference between minimum capacity and desired capacity in an Auto Scaling policy

Launch configurations, Amazon Machine Images (AMIs), and the required components to start a new instance as part of Auto Scaling

The difference between launch templates and launch configurations and why you'd use one over the other

The various triggers that can cause a scaling event to occur

# Auto Scaling Terms and Concepts

*Auto Scaling* sounds almost deceptively simple. Turn it on and things automatically adjust to meet capacity needs. Seems reasonable, right? However, there's quite a bit more to the process, and you'll need to clearly understand the concepts involved before you can effectively set up Auto Scaling.

Auto Scaling is meant to handle scalability and, in the process, help manage your costs, but it can be a huge expense if not managed correctly. Scale up (or "scale out," as you'll soon learn) a large fleet of instances that aren't properly set to scale back down, and you could wake up at the end of the month with thousands of dollars in extra cost.

# Auto Scaling Groups

The most basic concept in Auto Scaling is that of the Auto Scaling group. An Auto Scaling group is, simply, a grouping of the things you're scaling automatically. So in a typical situation, an Auto Scaling group is a set of Amazon Elastic Compute Cloud (EC2) instances. That group could have zero instances, usually will have at least one, and can grow to the maximum you specify.

A group has a number of properties, which you'll learn about shortly: a minimum, a maximum, a desired capacity, and so forth. So Auto Scaling is the service or facility in AWS, and an Auto Scaling group is a specific case of that service in practice. You'll typically see Auto Scaling groups represented by a square for each instance, a long-dashed line around the members of the group, and a set of arrows, as shown in Figure 7.1.

**FIGURE 7.1**    A typical Auto Scaling group is shown using AWS notation.

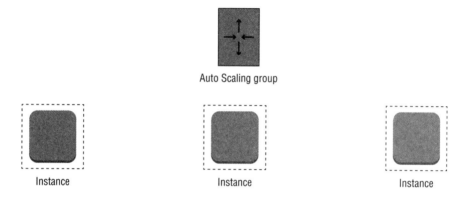

# Scaling In and Scaling Out

In Auto Scaling vocabulary, everything is built around scaling out and scaling in. Scaling out is typically thought of as "scaling up," and scaling in is thought of as "scaling back" or "scaling down." In other words, scaling out increases the bounds of your cluster, and scaling in shrinks those bounds. Figure 7.2 shows this in a simple form.

**FIGURE 7.2**    A set or cluster of instances in an Auto Scaling group can scale out and scale in, all based on triggers and the configuration you set up.

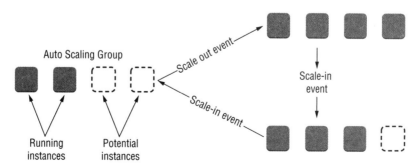

It's best to think of your cluster of instances as a horizontal line, rather than a grouping that isn't organized. That makes it easy to remember that scaling out means the width of the line of servers grows (outward) and scaling in means the width of the line of servers shrinks (inward).

It's also important to understand that when you scale out, you scale out with *more of the same thing*. In other words, if you have a cluster of EC2 instances that scale out, you're going to get more EC2 instances. When you scale in, you'll have fewer EC2 instances. A cluster is homogenous; they all are of the same type.

## Scaling More than EC2

It's almost always the case that when you hear or read "Auto Scaling"—whether in a meeting room or on a certification exam—that can be interpreted as "Auto Scaling EC2 instances." In fact, there's now a specific service, the *Amazon EC2 Auto Scaling service*, which handles EC2 instances. But it's almost entirely synonymous in public usage with Auto Scaling.

While that is true in practice, though, it's not true in reality. AWS provides a number of additional Auto Scaling options. Whenever you're not scaling EC2 instances, you can use the Application Auto Scaling API, which allows you to set up Auto Scaling for non-EC2 instances. You can scale:

- Amazon ECS services
- Amazon EC2 spot fleets
- Amazon EMR clusters
- Amazon AppStream 2.0 fleets
- Provisioned read/write capacity for Amazon DynamoDB tables and certain secondary indexes
- Amazon Aurora replicas
- Amazon SageMaker endpoints

These don't always behave in exactly the same way. This is especially true the more managed the service is. For example, scaling out an EC2 cluster provides a lot more control and options than scaling out Amazon Aurora replicas.

In general, the same concepts apply to both EC2 Auto Scaling and the Application Auto Scaling API. The parameters are likely to change, though.

It would be somewhat unusual for a certification exam to ask you which services were scalable via the application Auto Scaling API, although the exam is subject to change at any time. It's also likely that more services eventually get added to the Application Auto Scaling API, making the question even less likely; AWS tends to avoid questions that quickly grow stale.

It's better to understand that these services can scale in and out with Auto Scaling, and not get tripped up if you see a question that mentions (in a particular context) scaling out Aurora read instances or an ECS cluster.

# Minimums, Maximums, and Desired Capacity

When you're configuring an Auto Scaling group, arguably the most key concepts are the *minimum capacity*, *maximum capacity*, and *desired capacity* of your Auto Scaling group. The first two of these are incredibly straightforward: the minimum is the minimum number of instances you want your group to be capable of having, and the maximum is the highest number of instances you ever want to support.

Put another way, your Auto Scaling group always has a number of instances equal to or greater than the minimum and less than or equal to the maximum. So take a few example scenarios:

- With a minimum of 0 and a maximum of 5, your Auto Scaling group can have zero, one, two, three, four, or five instances.

- With a minimum of 1 and a maximum of 1, your Auto Scaling group will always have exactly one instance.

- With a minimum of 5 and a maximum of 10...well, you get the idea.

It's important to spend some time thinking through your minimum in particular. This will often be the "resting state" of your Auto Scaling group at its lowest usage (with a few exceptions discussed shortly), so you want to try to figure out the fewest number of instances you want to always have running. It's also correlated to the minimum cost of your group, which is nothing to take lightly.

If you set a minimum of 5, you will *always* be paying for at least five instances. As a rule, then, try to set your minimum low—ideally at 0. That would allow your costs to go to zero if there was no load at all.

Setting the maximum is a little less critical, because you can always increase that number as you see what the load looks like. In general, a higher maximum won't affect your costs negatively, because reaching that maximum indicates you needed extra capacity.

Desired capacity is a bit trickier, because unlike minimum or maximum, it is not a static value. The desired capacity of an Auto Scaling group is the target number of instances for that group; it is the number that the group is *currently* seeking to provide. If the desired capacity is greater than the number of instances in a group, the group will scale out. If the desired capacity is less, the group will scale in.

Desired capacity, then, is the key concept when you start to build a reactive Auto Scaling group. You will typically increase the desired capacity if load metrics get high and decrease the capacity if they reflect that not as many instances are needed. And, as you can surmise, desired capacity should always be at its lowest equal to the minimum for your group and its highest equal to the maximum.

# Auto Scaling Groups Auto Scale

Yes, saying that an Auto Scaling group automatically scales seems a bit silly, but it's a key point to understand. If at any point an Auto Scaling group has a different number of instances than its desired capacity, a scaling event occurs.

There are some slight exceptions to this statement. Auto Scaling and CloudWatch, the two main mechanisms for initiating a scaling event, perform checks periodically. These checks are frequent, but it is possible that desired capacity could be off for a minute or two before a check and then a scaling event occurs.

Auto Scaling performs health checks on your instances within groups frequently. If an instance is unhealthy, that instance is terminated and a new instance is launched—all in an attempt to keep the running instance count at desired capacity. If you manually stop an instance, or add another instance, Auto Scaling will also automatically adjust the group—by starting up a new instance or shutting down an instance.

Health checks occur only on instances in the InService state. They do not occur when an instance is starting up or shutting down to prevent false failures.

This means that manually adjusting the size of an Auto Scaling group cannot be effectively accomplished with manually adding or removing instances. Instead, you can manually update the desired capacity, and then let the Auto Scaling group add or remove instances to meet the new desired capacity.

Desired capacity is simple in its basic form; it's also essential and tied to almost every aspect of Auto Scaling. For now, focus on understanding its relationship to the minimum and maximum of an Auto Scaling group, and that it's the target number of instances for a group. You'll then layer on to that understanding of how it's used by various triggers and alarms to size a group dynamically.

## Auto Scaling Instances Must Be Maintained

An EC2 instance is not a managed service and must be maintained like any other instance. Auto Scaling provides a means of maintenance by allowing an instance to be moved from an InService state to the Standby state. When you move an instance to Standby, the following things occur:

1. The instance will remain in Standby until changed to a different state manually.

2. The Auto Scaling group will decrease its desired capacity by 1.

3. The instance is no longer sent traffic from load balancers associated with the Auto Scaling group.

When you move the instance back into InService, the following occurs:

1. The desired capacity is incremented by 1.

2. The instance is registered with the Auto Scaling group's load balancer.

# Launch Configurations

Fundamental to Auto Scaling is the idea that instances can easily be added or removed from the group. Removing an instance is trivial, but how can instances be added in a way that ensures they are more of the same kind as the existing instances? That's what a launch configuration provides: an instance configuration template (in AWS terminology). A *launch configuration* typically has:

- The ID of the AMI to use for instances
- The instance type
- A key pair for connecting to the instance
- One or more security groups
- A block device mapping

This should be information you have, as it's exactly what would have been required to launch the original instances in the group. In other words, a launch configuration is just capturing how you created the instances in the group initially, and it allows AWS Auto Scaling to launch more of those same instances.

 Although the exam won't always distinguish between EC2 Auto Scaling and the more generic term auto scaling, launch configurations only apply to EC2 Auto Scaling. Managed services, databases, and other non-instance-based Auto Scaling groups would not require this same information, although those various options each have some standard information required in a similar fashion.

## EC2 Instances Are Launch Configuration Templates

If you create a new Auto Scaling group by simply specifying an EC2 instance, AWS will create a launch configuration for you, based on that instance's properties. That's often the easiest way to create an Auto Scaling group: by creating a single instance and then letting AWS do the work.

There are a couple of key points when creating a launch configuration this way, though:

- The Auto Scaling group does not have tags applied to the original EC2 instance applied to the group. You would need to manually apply those tags to the group.
- Any EBS volumes or block mappings from the instance that were specified in the instance AMI are made a part of the launch configuration. However, if any devices were attached to the instance *after* the launch, they are *not* made a part of the launch configuration.

> This is a really big deal. It's incredibly easy to forget this detail and then pull your hair out trying to figure out why you can't get block mappings from a perfectly valid instance. Always go back to the AMI of the instance you're using as a template; the AMI is what is key, not the current running state of the instance. This is also a tricky but important exam question.

- No load balancer information about the instance is made a part of the launch configuration or Auto Scaling group. The group handles load balancing information in a separate process.

## One Auto Scaling Group Has One Launch Configuration

Each Auto Scaling group generally has one and only one launch configuration. (There is one possible exception to this, mentioned in the next section.) You will not find an Auto Scaling group with two launch configurations, because the whole point of Auto Scaling is to consistently create more of the same thing.

What isn't as obvious, though, is that once you've created and attached a launch configuration to an Auto Scaling group, you cannot modify that launch configuration. You have to create a new launch configuration—which you can base on your existing one—and then you can apply that to the Auto Scaling group.

But this actually creates an odd issue: new instances launched in the group will not match the old ones. They will instead be based on the newer launch configuration. This can be confusing. There are a few ways to reduce the chance of problems here:

- Simply create an entirely new Auto Scaling group with a new launch configuration and shut the old group down.
- Set the desired capacity for the group to 0, assign a new launch configuration, and then increase the desired capacity.
- Assign a new launch configuration, and then manually terminate the older instances.

None of these steps are required, but each of them tries to maintain consistency within the Auto Scaling group.

## Launch Templates: Versioned Launch Configurations

The one exception to an Auto Scaling group having a launch configuration is the case when it has a *launch template*. Launch templates are preferred by AWS to launch configurations, but they are nearly impossible to understand without first getting a grasp of launch configurations.

A launch template has all the information within it that a launch configuration does: an AMI ID, an instance type, key pair information, block mappings, and so on. However, launch templates are versioned, and they allow multiple versions to be created from a base template. You can use these versions within different groups, store older configurations and revert to them, and even set up variations in different versions for block mappings or network configuration while sharing common AMI IDs and key pairs.

Just as you can create a launch configuration from an instance, you can create a launch template from a launch configuration. Additionally, in recent years AWS is providing functionality via launch templates that is not available to launch configurations, such as use of unlimited instances (of the T2 class) and using spot instances alongside on-demand instances in an Auto Scaling group.

# Auto Scaling Strategies

As is the case with most things in AWS, you have more than one way to accomplish Auto Scaling within your group. Each variant of scaling is called an Auto Scaling strategy, and each behaves slightly differently.

## Manual Scaling

*Manual scaling* is somewhat of a contradiction in terms; if you use manual scaling, the only part of your Auto Scaling group that is truly auto(matic) is the creation of new instances. In this strategy, you can increase or decrease the desired capacity through the AWS Console or CLI, and the group will respond by creating or removing instances.

You can also attach or detach instances directly to the Auto Scaling group. In these cases, the desired capacity is changed to reflect your manual actions. If you add an instance, desired capacity increases by one, and if you remove an instance, it decreases by one. This is just a variation on manual scaling.

> To attach an instance to an existing Auto Scaling group, that instance must be running using an AMI that exists in your system. It cannot be a part of another Auto Scaling group, and it must be running in one of the availability zones allowed by the target Auto Scaling group.

## Scheduled Scaling

*Scheduled scaling* is only slightly more complex than manual scaling. In this strategy, you provide a certain time and a desired capacity to set on your Auto Scaling group at that time. Auto Scaling will adjust the desired capacity based on that schedule and then create or remove instances to match the updated desired capacity.

> You can also adjust the minimum or maximum of an Auto Scaling group on a schedule. This may not cause an actual change in the number of instances in your group.

There are some limitations associated with scheduling, but they are fairly extreme. For instance, you can have only 125 scheduled actions for an Auto Scaling group. Realistically, these are not commonly hit limitations, and they do not tend to appear on the exam either.

If you want to move beyond static schedules, other strategies are more appropriate. Scheduled scaling is a perfect fit for known workload spikes or batch processing, though.

## Dynamic Scaling

*Dynamic scaling* is by far the most common scaling strategy, and it has a number of sub-strategies supported. All are based on events within your AWS environment and reacting to those events.

*Target tracking scaling* allows you to set a particular metric—such as CPU utilization—and value—such as 80 percent. Your Auto Scaling group will then add or remove instances to attempt based on your policy. So you could set a policy to add instances if that utilization reaches 80 percent, until the target metric is no longer reached (say, utilization drops to 70 percent). You can also set lower bounds, perhaps removing instances when utilization drops below 50 percent.

You can also set *step scaling policies* to increase instances in degrees other than single instances. In addition to specifying that increases or decreases can be a particular value—like increasing by two instances—you can set up percentages, increasing the size of the group by 10 percent or 20 percent. This makes stepping incredibly valuable for groups that vary greatly in size.

There are a number of key parameters for step scaling:

- **ChangeInCapacity:** When scaling occurs, increase or decrease by the number of instances indicated in ChangeInCapacity.

- **ExactCapacity:** Scale to a specific number. You might indicate that if CPU utilization reaches 80 percent, scale to exactly 10 instances.

- **PercentChangeInCapacity:** Scale based on a percentage related to the current size of the group. A 25 percent change in capacity for a group of eight would be to add or remove two instances.

Percentage values greater than 1 are rounded down, so 8.7 would round down to eight instances. Values between 0 and 1 are rounded to 1, and values between 0 and -1 are rounded to -1. Values less than -1 are rounded up, so -8.2 is rounded to -8 (a decrease of eight instances).

## Cooldown Periods

One of the trickier aspects of Auto Scaling is the relationship between the triggering of a scaling event and the time it takes for that event to complete. Often, it takes time for an instance (or instances) to start up when scaling out, or to shut down when scaling in.

During this time, it's possible for an additional triggering to occur and more instances to be requested. You can quickly see that this can get out of hand. A need for a single instance to handle an uptick in requests could result in three or four instances starting, all in response to that single incident trigger.

To avoid this, AWS Auto Scaling uses a cooldown period. During this period, no additional events are triggered. The idea is that instances already triggered can complete startup or shutdown. Then, when the period ends, it is "safe" to see if more scaling events need to be triggered. This cooldown period is always on in a simple scaling policy and can be configured for all other policies.

The default cooldown period is 300 seconds (5 minutes) and is applied to all scaling events in simple scaling. You can use this same period for other scaling policies or configure your own.

A good cooldown period is tuned to the typical startup and shutdown time of the instances in your group. If your instances run a startup script and the time from request to running is 4 minutes, a good cooldown period would likely be 4.5 to 5 minutes. Much longer times will prevent your group from scaling as soon as it should, and shorter times will result in false triggering events.

## Instances Terminate in Order

When a scaling in event occurs, the Auto Scaling group does not pick an instance to terminate at random. Rather, it uses one of several ordering methods. By default, instances are terminated in order according to the following criteria:

1. An instance in the AZ with the most instances is terminated.

2. An instance that will bring the overall group in line with any stated allocation strategies related to on-demand versus spot instances is terminated.

3. An instance that has the oldest launch template is terminated.

4. An instance that has the oldest launch configuration is terminated.

5. The instance closest to the next billing hour is terminated.

6. Terminate an instance at random.

Each criterion follows from the previous one as well. In other words, if there are multiple "extra" instances in one AZ (criterion 1), then the next criterion (2) is applied to determine which instance to delete.

You can protect an instance from a scale-in event by setting its status in the console or CLI. That instance is not considered in the calculations listed.

You can also manually set your own termination policy from the following choices:

- `OldestInstance`: The oldest instance in the group is terminated first.
- `NewestInstance`: The newest instance in the group is terminated first.
- `OldestLaunchConfiguration`: The instance with the oldest launch configuration is terminated first.
- `OldestLaunchTemplate`: This is identical to `OldestLaunchConfiguration` but looks for a launch template instead.
- `ClosestToNextInstanceHour`: This terminates the instance in the group closest to the next billing hour.
- `AllocationStrategy`: This applies when you have spot and on-demand instances and will align the instances in the group as best as possible with the allocation strategy between spot and on-demand instances.
- `Default`: This simply uses the default criteria.

# When Auto Scaling Fails

As powerful and useful as Auto Scaling is, it's only as helpful as its configuration. And, unfortunately, there are a *lot* of ways to get Auto Scaling wrong. Here are just a few common mistakes:

- Your cooldown period is too short, and instances continue to spin up and spin down when that action is no longer needed.
- Your minimum is set too high, and costs are accrued when you don't need as many instances running as you have.
- You do not have enough variance between your minimum and maximum and are therefore not getting a lot of value out of scaling in and out.
- You are using a scaling policy that doesn't correlate to the size of your Auto Scaling group. The larger the group, the more you should favor changing capacity by larger amounts or using percentage-based scaling.

There are certainly many more ways that you can make mistakes when setting up an Auto Scaling group. Most importantly, though, you should constantly be examining your Auto Scaling group and tuning it. If you set your group up and then forget about it, it will happily run—but it may not run optimally.

Many of the exam questions on Auto Scaling focus on poor setups—desired capacity is confused with minimum, a cooldown period is too short, or the change in capacity doesn't reflect the needs of the system. The more you get comfortable tuning your Auto Scaling group, the more likely you'll be able to quickly and clearly answer questions about Auto Scaling on the exam.

# Summary

Auto scaling is arguably one of the most important things you can understand about AWS—and that goes for actual practice as well as when taking an AWS certification exam. Although there is an increasing move to serverless technologies—API gateways, Lambda, DyanmoDB, GraphQL, and so on—you'll likely never find yourself in a situation where virtual servers have no effect on your daily life as a SysOps administrator. If you can scale your resources well, you'll save costs and extend the value and life of the applications for which you're responsible.

Further, Auto Scaling is easy to foul up. An Auto Scaling group is only as useful as its launch configuration or template and capacity settings, and those are things you're going to have to set. Get these right, and your applications will be boring and predictable; get them wrong, and you're likely to get a call in the middle of the night from an executive who wants to know why the company front end is slow—or worse, not responding at all.

A good Auto Scaling policy is a living thing. Monitor it and tweak it frequently to ensure its good health. Reduce instance sizes when it makes sense, and use multiple Auto Scaling groups. Your applications—and your management chain—will thank you for it.

# Resources to Review

Amazon Auto Scaling:

    https://aws.amazon.com/autoscaling/

AWS management tools blog (lots on scaling and related topics here):

    https://aws.amazon.com/blogs/mt/

AWS documentation specifically on scaling EC2 instances:

    https://aws.amazon.com/ec2/autoscaling/

Getting started with AWS Auto Scaling:

    https://docs.aws.amazon.com/autoscaling/plans/userguide/auto-scaling-
    getting-started.html

# Exam Essentials

**Understand how Auto Scaling groups scale in and out.**   Fundamentally, an Auto Scaling group grows (scales out) and shrinks (scales in) based on demand. The most useful groups have tuned policies for the scaling process and have carefully set parameters controlling the size and elasticity of the group.

**Know that Auto Scaling groups have a minimum, maximum, and desired capacity.**   A group cannot scale in beyond its minimum or scale out beyond its maximum. The desired capacity is the number of instances intended to be running at any given time. Instances are added when desired capacity increases and removed when it decreases.

**Understand how Auto Scaling groups react to outside triggers.** While you can manually change your Auto Scaling group parameters, the most common use case for modifying the desired capacity of an Auto Scaling group is through outside triggers, such as when a CloudWatch alarm goes off. That alarm might be monitoring the CPU utilization of instances, and when a threshold is overshot, it tells the Auto Scaling group to scale out.

**Explain how instances in an Auto Scaling group can still be manually controlled.** You can still stop, start, and change the status of instances. Most commonly, instances are put into a Standby state for maintenance. The Auto Scaling group will react to these changes. If an instance is removed, a new one is started; if one is added, an instance is removed. If an instance is put into a Standby state, the group will (by default, which can be overridden) reduce the group's desired capacity by 1.

**Know how launch configurations and launch templates provide repeatable setups for launching new instances.** Both launch configurations and launch templates can be used to indicate key parameters for starting up new instances—key pairs, security groups, network setup, and block storage mappings can all be captured in a launch configuration or a launch template. Launch templates also offer versioning and are now the preferred means of storing launch information for instances.

**Explain how to terminate and scale instances through default and custom policies.** Both scaling policies and termination policies are configurable for each Auto Scaling group. Defaults for both exist and are predictable and typically tuned to maintain a group's provided configuration and then to save money when possible.

# Exercises

These exercises are based on the assumption that you have a basic network set up and that you have at least at least two subnets, each assigned to a different availability zone. For this example, I will use Private 1 (10.0.10.0/24) and Private 2 (10.0.11.0/24).

**EXERCISE 7.1**

### Create a Launch Configuration

The first step to creating Auto Scaling groups is to create the launch configuration. The launch configuration is where you configure the AMI you want to use, networking, roles, and any bootstrap data you want to add.

1. Log into the AWS Management Console.

2. Under Compute, choose EC2.

3. From the EC2 Dashboard menu, scroll down to Auto Scaling, and choose Launch Configurations.

4.   Click the blue Create Launch Configuration button.

5.   You are asked to select an AMI; choose whatever you'd like. For this exercise, I will choose the Amazon Linux 2 image. Click Select next to the image that you want.

6.   Choose the instance type you want, I will choose t2.micro. Click Next: Configure Details.

7.   For the name, type **StudyGuideLC**. Click Next: Add Storage.

8.   Click Next: Configure Security Group.

9.   Click Review, and then click Create Launch Configuration.

10.  Acknowledge that you have access to the key pair by selecting the check box and click Create Launch Configuration.

11.  On the Creation Status screen where you see "Successfully created launch configuration: StudyGuideLC," click Close.

Once you have completed these steps, you have a launch configuration. Now let's create an Auto Scaling group.

---

**EXERCISE 7.2**

## Create an Auto Scaling Group

For this exercise, you will create an Auto Scaling group that will scale up.

1.   From the EC2 Dashboard menu, under Auto Scaling, choose Auto Scaling Groups.

2.   Click Create Auto Scaling Group.

3.   On the Create Auto Scaling Group screen, keep the default Launch Configuration checked, and select the check box next to the launch configuration you created in the previous exercise, shown in Figure 7.3.

4.   Click Next Step.

5.   Give your group a name. I called mine **StudyGuideASG**.

6.   For group size, set two instances.

7.   Under Network, select your VPC.

8.   Click Subnet, and choose the subnets that are available for multiple availability zones, Private 1 and Private 2 in my case.

9.   Click Next: Configure Scaling Policies.

10.  Choose "Use scaling policies to adjust the capacity of this group." Choose to scale between one and four instances.

**FIGURE 7.3**   You will need to select the launch configuration that you chose previously to use the Launch Configuration option.

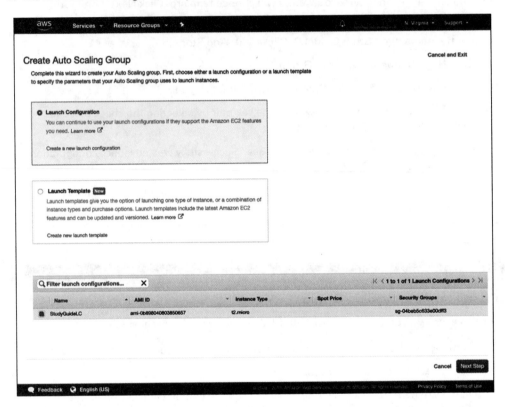

11. Click the blue hyperlink that says "Scale the Auto Scaling group using step or simple scaling policies."

12. Under Increase Group Size, click Add New Alarm. (Shown in Figure 7.4)

   a.   Uncheck the Send A Notification To check box.

   b.   Set Whenever to Average Of CPU Utilization.

   c.   Set Is to **>= 75%**.

   d.   Set For At Least to 2 Consecutive Period(s) Of 5 Minutes.

   e.   Assign the name of the alarm: **High-CPU-Utilization**.

   f.   Click Create Alarm.

**FIGURE 7.4**    Creating the alarm for the step policy is pretty simple—you just need to decide what to measure to auto scale.

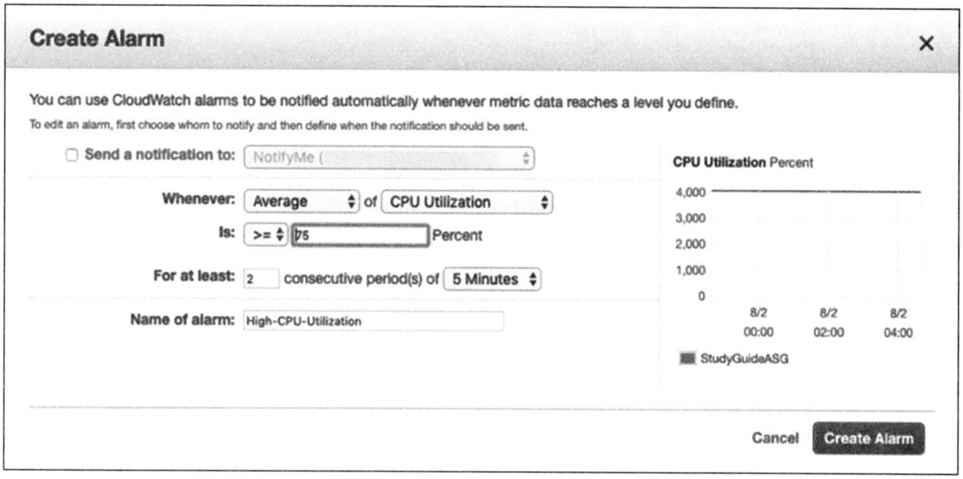

13. For Instances Need, type **300**.

14. Under Decrease Group Size, click Add New Alarm.

   a.    Uncheck the Send A Notification To check box.

   b.    Set Whenever to Average Of CPU Utilization.

   c.    Set Is to **<= 40%**.

   d.    Set For At Least to 2 Consecutive Period(s) of 5 Minutes.

   e.    Assign the name of the alarm: **Low-CPU-Utilization**.

   f.    Click Create Alarm.

15. For Take The Action, select Remove One Instance When 40 >= CPUUtilization > -Infinity.

16. Click Next: Configure Notifications.

17. Click Next: Configure Tags.

18. Click Review.

19. Click Create Auto Scaling Group.

20. Click Close once the wizard completes.

If you had no Amazon EC2 instances created before these exercises, you will find that you now have one instance that is being spun up. This is due to the fact that the minimum capacity was set to 1.

When you clean up after this exercise, remember to delete the Auto Scaling group first, and then terminate the instance. If you terminate the instance first, the Auto Scaling group will kick off another instance because it no longer has the minimum capacity met.

# Review Questions

You can find the answers in the Appendix.

1. Which of the following can an EC2 Auto Scaling group contain?

    **A.** On-demand instances

    **B.** Spot instances

    **C.** Containers

    **D.** A and B but not C

2. Which of the following are part of a launch configuration? (Choose two.)

    **A.** AMI ID

    **B.** EBS volume mapping

    **C.** NFS mount points

    **D.** IAM group for connectivity

3. An Auto Scaling group has a minimum of 2, a maximum of 5, and a desired capacity of 3. How many instances are running in the group if the network has reached peak capacity in the VPC in which the group is running?

    **A.** 2

    **B.** 5

    **C.** 3

    **D.** There is not enough information to answer this question.

4. Why might you choose a launch template over a launch configuration? (Choose two.)

    **A.** You want to create the template directly from an existing EC2 instance.

    **B.** You want to create copies of the template that share key information but differ in slight ways.

    **C.** You want to use both on-demand and spot instances in your Auto Scaling group.

    **D.** You want to have a group with multiple launch templates.

5. You have an Auto Scaling group serving EC2 instances running web servers. You have set CloudWatch to monitor network traffic and, at a threshold of 80 percent, to scale the group up. Which of the parameters of the Auto Scaling group will change when your CloudWatch trigger executes?

    **A.** Minimum

    **B.** Maximum

    **C.** Desired Capacity

    **D.** ScaleBy

6. Which of the following is not possible to specify as part of a launch template?

   A. Security group

   B. Key pair

   C. AMI ID

   D. Target availability zone

7. Which of the following is not a required parameter for a launch template?

   A. Security group

   B. Key pair

   C. AMI ID

   D. None of these are required.

8. You are responsible for a high-value web application that should be "always available." It is currently supported by an Auto Scaling group running with a desired capacity of 50 instances. Based just on this information, and the need to ensure responsiveness of the application, what Auto Scaling policy would you likely implement?

   A. Simple scaling

   B. Dynamic scaling using `ExactCapacity`

   C. Dynamic scaling using `ChangeInCapacity`

   D. Dynamic scaling using `PercentChangeInCapacity`

9. You have an Auto Scaling group of EC2 instances set up and serving web content. Web traffic increases and additional instances are created through Auto Scaling, but no traffic is going to those instances. Which of the following could result in this behavior?

   A. The new instances have been launched with a different key pair than the existing instances.

   B. The next instances have been launched in a different availability zone than the existing instances.

   C. The new instances have been launched with a different security group than the existing instances.

   D. The new instances have not yet had time to completely start; just wait a little longer.

10. You have an Auto Scaling group that has been functioning quite well until recently. You learn that thousands of new customers have been introduced to the hosted application lately, and they typically access the application between 4 and 8 p.m. During these hours, the application's performance suffers for all users. What changes could you make to your Auto Scaling policy to restore performance? (Choose two.)

   A. Set up a scheduled scaling policy to increase the desired capacity significantly at 4 p.m. and reduce the desired capacity back down at 8 p.m.

   B. Set up a dynamic scaling policy with a large value for the capacity percentage to increase by.

   C. Investigate using CloudFront to provide caching to the data used in the application.

   D. Increase the maximum value for the Auto Scaling group.

**11.** What is the default cooldown period for an EC2 Auto Scaling group?

    **A.** 2 minutes

    **B.** 5 minutes

    **C.** 8 minutes

    **D.** There is no default cooldown period.

**12.** Which of the following does a launch template offer but a launch configuration does not?

    **A.** The ability to specify a key pair for new instances

    **B.** The ability to version a specific launch setup

    **C.** The ability to specify a security group for new instances

    **D.** The ability to back up a specific launch setup

**13.** Which of the following is a common reason for an Auto Scaling group not scaling out fast enough to handle a large increase in demand? (Choose two.)

    **A.** The cooldown period is too long.

    **B.** The cooldown period is too short.

    **C.** The step size for scaling out is too small.

    **D.** The step size for scaling in is too small.

**14.** Which of the following is a good reason to use a launch template instead of a launch configuration? (Choose two.)

    **A.** You want to use on-demand instances in your Auto Scaling group.

    **B.** You want to use spot instances in your Auto Scaling group.

    **C.** You want to use T2 instances in your Auto Scaling group.

    **D.** You want to use reserved instances in your Auto Scaling group.

**15.** Which of the following is not a default in an EC2 Auto Scaling group?

    **A.** A cooldown period of 300 seconds

    **B.** Health checks on running instances

    **C.** Automatic startup of a new instance when a running instance fails

    **D.** Automatic restarting of instances that fail health checks

**16.** When does the first health check on a new instance within an Auto Scaling group take place?

    **A.** As soon as the instance starts

    **B.** As soon as the cooldown period ends

    **C.** As soon as the instance enters the `InService` state

    **D.** An indeterminate time after the instance starts but before the cooldown period ends

**17.** You are running an Auto Scaling group with both on demand and spot instances. You are seeing what appear to be random shutdowns of instances in the group. You cannot find any failed health checks or triggered scaling events, and instances are started to replace the shutdown instances. What might be causing these shutdowns?

   **A.** The health check is configured incorrectly.

   **B.** You have a process on the shutting down instance that is locking up the processor on the instance.

   **C.** The instances are spot instances and the spot price has changed beyond tolerance.

   **D.** The instances are spot instances and Auto Scaling groups often recycle spot instances to keep costs low.

**18.** When you put an `InService` instance into `Standby`, which of the following would happen? (Choose two.)

   **A.** Health checks of the instance stop.

   **B.** The desired capacity of the Auto Scaling group is decreased by 1.

   **C.** Another instance is launched to replace the `Standby` instance.

   **D.** The minimum of the Auto Scaling group is decreased by 1.

**19.** You have 3 instances in availability zone 1, 2 in availability zone 2, and 4 in availability zone 3. There are no spot instances being used, and no instances are protected. An instance in availability zone 1 is closest to the next billing hour, and an instance in availability zone 2 is using the oldest launch configuration. On a scale-in event, which instance would be terminated first?

   **A.** The instance in availability zone 1 closest to the next billing hour

   **B.** The instance in availability zone 2 using the oldest launch configuration

   **C.** The instance in availability zone 3 that has the oldest launch template, launch configuration, or is closest to the next billing hour (in that order of precedent)

   **D.** There is not enough information to know.

**20.** Which of the following termination policies might not always be applicable to an Auto Scaling group? (Choose two.)

   **A.** `OldestInstance`

   **B.** `OldestLaunchTemplate`

   **C.** `ClosestToNextInstanceHour`

   **D.** `AllocationStrategy`

# Deployment and Provisioning

# Chapter

# 8

# Hubs, Spokes, and Bastion Hosts

---

**THE AWS CERTIFIED SYSOPS ADMINISTRATOR – ASSOCIATE EXAM TOPICS COVERED IN THIS CHAPTER MAY INCLUDE, BUT ARE NOT LIMITED TO, THE FOLLOWING:**

**Domain 3.0: Deployment and Provisioning**

✓ 3.1 Identify and execute steps required to provision cloud resources

**Domain 7.0: Automation and Optimization**

✓ 7.1 Use AWS services and features to manage and assess resource utilization

✓ 7.3 Automate manual or repeatable process to minimize management overhead

As a SysOps administrator, you know that connectivity is one of the most important things to have once your basic infrastructure is in place.

Connectivity between virtual private clouds (VPCs), for example, can be very important, and although multiple methods allow you to let traffic traverse VPCs, for instance, VPC peering keeps your traffic internal to AWS rather than traversing the Internet to access your other AWS resources.

VPCs get a lot of visibility, but remote access to your instances is also critical. One option that allows you to remotely access your AWS resources without having to open multiple IP addresses is a bastion host.

This chapter includes:

Introducing VPC peering

Choosing VPC peering

Using VPC peering across regions

Introducing the concept of bastion hosts

Architecting your AWS environment to use a bastion host

Understanding the options you have for bastion hosts

# VPC Peering

A virtual private cloud (VPC) is a logical network that you create within AWS. Your many AWS components reside within the VPC, typically within their own subnets.

---

VPCs aren't going to be covered in depth in this chapter. If VPCs are a new concept to you, I suggest checking out Chapter 16: Virtual Private Cloud (VPC) which focuses on VPCs.

---

It would be unusual for a large organization to have a single VPC only. There may be VPCs for environments like production, development, and research and development (R&D), or VPCs may be split based on zones in order to create network segmentation, such as a zone for management services, a zone for systems containing sensitive information, and a zone for web services. It is considered desirable—especially with management services and systems that contain sensitive data—to reduce the amount of data that is traveling via the Internet. By peering a VPC, the systems in one VPC can talk to systems in another VPC directly through AWS' low-latency backbone rather than over the Internet.

VPC peering allows bidirectional communication between VPCs. The peering connection must be added to the routing tables so that the traffic bound for the peered VPC will be directed to the correct destination. The entry in the routing tables for VPC peers is prefixed with *pcx* and is followed by a dash and a randomly generated string of numbers. Security groups or network access control lists (NACLs) may also need to be updated to allow the traffic through. It is important to remember that VPC peering is nontransitive. This means that if VPC A is peered to VPC B, and VPC B is peered to VPC C, that VPC A can't talk to VPC C. Instead, VPC A would also need to be peered to VPC C to allow communication.

Before you can peer a VPC, you must ensure that the IP space of the VPCs that you want to peer do not have any overlap. If they do overlap, then they can't be peered. Assuming there is no overlap, you can request the VPC peering connection from one VPC, and then accept the request in the other VPC.

Once you have accepted the peering request, you need to update the route table with the information for the peered network. One of the great things about this is that you can specify whole ranges or individual IP addresses. You can see an example of this in Figure 8.1, where I have allowed the IP addresses for one of the subnets in VPC1 to communicate with VPC2.

**FIGURE 8.1**    Setting up the routing for traffic to traverse over the VPC peering connection

# Understanding the Use Case for Hub-and-Spoke Architecture

The hub-and-spoke architecture seeks to remedy an issue that organizations face when they need all systems to be able to share a central VPC. This is common when there are shared services or management services that need to reach into the other VPCs. This model is referred to as *hub and spoke*—the central VPC is the hub where the shared services reside, and the other VPCs that are set up as VPC peers are the spokes. Each of the "spokes" can speak to the hub, but not to the other spokes.

By using hub-and-spoke architecture, you can make things like file servers, Active Directory, and orchestration tools available to the spoke VPCs that are connected to the hub VPC. You can achieve a high degree of granularity and allow full access between the VPCs, or if desired, you can be more specific as to what types of traffic are allowed across the peered connection. You can get an idea of what this looks like in Figure 8.2.

**FIGURE 8.2** Hub-and-spoke architecture is very useful in supporting shared services scenarios.

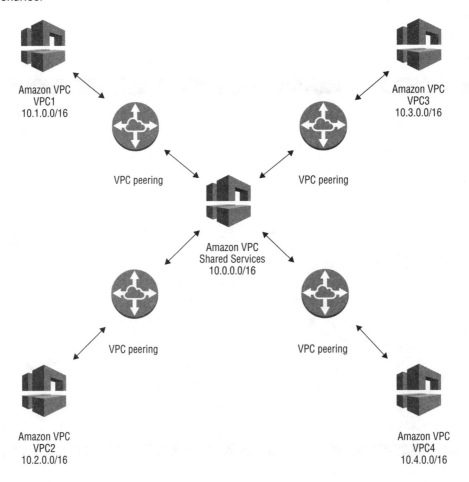

## Using a VPC Peering Connection Across Multiple Regions (Interregion Peering)

It's easy to see why VPC peering is a win for organizations that have moved their resources to the cloud. The ability to peer VPCs used to be limited to VPCs within the same region; however, AWS removed that requirement and you can now use interregion peering to peer VPCs across separate regions.

The same rules that apply to traditional VPC peering connections still apply with interregion VPC peering. For instance, the network ranges defined in the VPC can't overlap. The great thing about interregion VPC peering over traditional methods of connectivity like VPNs is that they leverage AWS' low-latency network and don't require the additional purchase of hardware or software VPN appliances. Using an interregion VPC peering connection is also more secure as traffic does not traverse the public Internet.

Interregion VPC peering does have some limitations above and beyond the limitations of a traditional VPC peering connection. Let's look a few of those:

- You can't reference a security group that is available in a peered VPC.
- You can't route IPv6 traffic across an interregion peered VPC connection.
- There is no support for *jumbo frames*.
- You have to ensure that DNS resolution will work properly for systems in both VPCs—that is, private hostnames must resolve to private IP addresses.

It is important to note that VPC peering is not available in all regions, so you will want to check to see if it is available in your regions.

# Bastion Hosts

For SysOps administrators, one of the most important aspects of working with their systems is the ability to access them remotely. Although many methods are available, the one that will be discussed here is the Linux bastion host. A *bastion host* is a system that is used to remotely access other systems. It resides in a public subnet, and the systems it provides access to reside in other public and/or private subnets. By using the bastion host, you can limit the amount of connections that you need to allow into your network.

As you might imagine, the bastion host must be a secure system since it is exposed to the Internet. You can build your own system from scratch and secure it, but other options are available in the AWS Marketplace. Some options, like the Bastion Host SSH Amazon Machine Image (AMI), are free-tier eligible, whereas others are pay as you go or bring your own license. The great thing about these AMIs is that they are purpose-built to be bastion hosts and, as such, are security-hardened images. As of this writing, 10 options were available in the AWS Marketplace when I searched for the word "bastion."

## Architecting for Bastion Host Use

The most obvious architectural need when looking at a bastion host is the need for a public IP address. I recommend that you use an elastic IP address. If you ever need to upgrade or replace your instance, you can attach the elastic IP address to the new instance.

If a bastion host is your main method to remotely administer your Linux systems, you will want to ensure that it is highly available. To ensure high availability, you should have more than one bastion host placed in an Auto Scaling group. If an instance becomes unhealthy and has to be replaced, the elastic IP address can be moved to the new instance that the Auto Scaling group creates.

Having a publicly accessible system can be challenging from a security perspective. Creating security groups for the bastion hosts that allow only connections from your organizational IP range on specific ports is a great way to lock down access. Configuring *Multi-Factor Authentication* (MFA) to access the host adds a layer of protection and can be accomplished with software tokens or certificate-based authentication.

## Options for Bastion Hosts

You may be wondering how to get started with bastion hosts, and what your options are for installation and configuration. Let's look at some of the options.

The simplest method to deploy a bastion host is to use the AWS Quick Start for Linux Bastion Hosts. The Quick Start allows you to build out the bastion hosts either into a new VPC or into an existing VPC and follows AWS best practices for high availability and security. You can also view the CloudFormation template so that you can see what the Quick Start is doing and make any modifications that you want before deploying it. The Quick Start when deployed to a new VPC will install and configure the following:

- An architecture that will utilize two availability zones with an Auto Scaling group
- A VPC with both public and private subnets in each availability zone
- An Internet gateway that will allow traffic to and from the Internet for systems in the public subnets
- Network address translation (NAT) gateways that reside in the public subnets to allow your instances out to the Internet through the Internet gateway
- A Linux bastion host in each public subnet with an elastic IP address and a security group already configured to allow Secure Shell (SSH)
- A log group in Amazon CloudWatch Logs that will hold all the shell history logs from your Linux bastion hosts

If you choose to build your own bastion host, I recommend that you use one of the purpose-built bastion host images (shown in Figure 8.3), though doing so is not a requirement. Either way, you will want to choose a Linux-based image and ensure that only the necessary services are running on the system. Don't forget to restrict access to the bastion host by IP address ranges and port numbers and ensure that you have made your bastion host highly available with the use of Auto Scaling groups and elastic IP addresses. Ensure that shell history is being logged so that you can see who did what and when if there is ever an issue. Amazon CloudWatch Logs is a great solution for that. You can create a log group for the shell history logs and configure the bastion host to send its logs to Amazon CloudWatch Logs.

**FIGURE 8.3**    Options for purpose-built bastion host appliances are available from the AWS Marketplace.

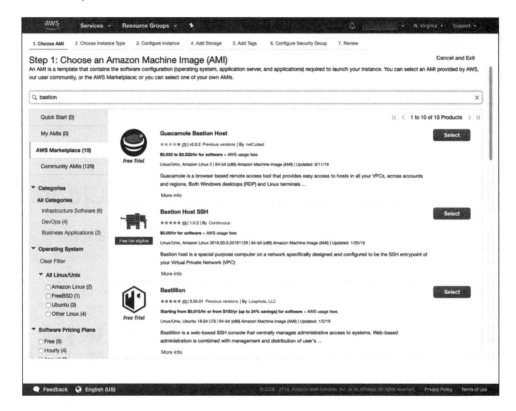

# Summary

VPC peering allows you to connect two VPCs together so that traffic can pass between them on AWS' low-latency internal links. For a VPC to be able to be peered, the IP address space in the VPCs can't overlap. VPC peering is nontransitive, meaning that a VPC can communicate only with another VPC that is directly peered to it. You can peer VPCs in separate regions; this is called interregion VPC peering, and it does have a few restrictions that regular VPC peering does not.

A bastion host, often referred to as a "jump host," is used to gain remote access to systems and resources in other networks. There are purpose-built network appliances for this task that are already security hardened, or you can create your own bastion host. Security groups should be used to restrict access to the bastion host, and Auto Scaling groups should be used to make bastion hosts highly available.

# Resources to Review

VPC Peering Basics:

   https://docs.aws.amazon.com/vpc/latest/peering/vpc-peering-basics.html

VPC Peering Scenarios:

   https://docs.aws.amazon.com/vpc/latest/peering/peering-scenarios.html

# Linux Bastion Hosts on the AWS Cloud:

https://docs.aws.amazon.com/quickstart/latest/linux-bastion/welcome.html

# Exam Essentials

**Know the use cases for VPC peering.**   Since traffic is not leaving the VPC, VPC peering can be used to save money (egress costs) and increase security. It may also improve performance since traffic is traversing AWS' low-latency network.

**Understand what a nontransitive peering connection is.**   VPC peering in AWS is nontransitive, meaning that a peering connection must be established directly between VPCs in order to facilitate communication. Communication can't pass through one VPC to get to another VPC.

**Know why you would use a bastion host and how to secure it.**   A bastion host provides the ability to remotely access other systems in the network and is publicly available. To protect the bastion host, I recommend that the image be hardened (unnecessary services are stopped, operating system is kept up to date, etc.), security groups are used to restrict access, and logs are maintained with a history of what has occurred in the shell.

# Exercises

### Create a VPC Peering Connection

In this exercise, you will create two VPCs named VPC1 and VPC2. You will then peer these VPCs to allow systems and resources in one VPC to talk to the other VPC.

First, let's create the VPCs. You will be using the VPC Wizard in this example as it makes setup simpler for the exercise.

1.  Sign in to the AWS Management Console.

2.  Click Services, then click VPC under Networking & Content Delivery.

3.  Click Elastic IPs.

4.  Click Allocate New Address.

5.  Leave IPv4 Address Pool set to Amazon Pool and click Allocate.

6.  Click Close.

7.  Repeat steps 4–6 so that you have two elastic IP addresses.

8.  Click VPC Dashboard.

9.  Click Launch VPC Wizard.

10. Click VPC With Public And Private Subnets; then click the Select button.

11. In the IPv4 CIDR Block box, type **10.1.0.0/16**.

12. In the VPC Name box, type **VPC1**.

13. In the Public Subnet's IPv4 CIDR box, type **10.1.0.0/24**.

14. In the Private Subnet's IPv4 CIDR box, type **10.1.1.0/24**.

15. Click in the Elastic IP Allocation ID box and select one of the elastic IP addresses you created earlier. Your settings should look similar to Figure 8.4.

16. Click Create VPC. The creation process will take a few minutes to complete.

17. Click VPC Dashboard.

18. Click Launch VPC Wizard.

19. Click VPC With Public And Private Subnets; then click the Select button.

**FIGURE 8.4** VPC1 settings should look like this once you have followed the instructions.

20. In the IPv4 CIDR block box, type **192.168.0.0/16**.

21. In the VPC Name box, type **VPC2**.

22. In the Public Subnet's IPv4 CIDR box, type **192.168.1.0/24**.

23. In the Private Subnet's IPv4 CIDR box, type **192.168.2.0/24**.

24. Click in the Elastic IP Allocation ID box, and select one of the elastic IP addresses you created earlier, shown below in Figure 8.5.

25. Click Create VPC. The creation process will take a few minutes to complete.

**FIGURE 8.5**    VPC2 settings should look like this once you have followed the instructions.

Now that the VPCs are created, it's time to set up the peering agreement from VPC1 to VPC2.

1. From within the VPC Dashboard, choose Peering Connections.

2. Click Create Peering Connection.

3. In the Peering Connection Name Tag box, enter **My-VPC-Peer**.

4. Click the arrow in the VPC (Requester) drop-down box and select VPC1 by it's VPC ID.

5. Under Select Another VPC To Peer With, select My Account and This Region.

6. Click the arrow in the VPC (Accepter) drop-down box and select VPC2 by it's VPC ID.

7.  When your screen looks similar to Figure 8.6, click Create Peering Connection.

**FIGURE 8.6**    At this point the Create Peering Connection screen should look like mine in this figure.

8.  Click OK.

9.  Select My-VPC-Peer, then click Actions.

10. Select Accept Request, then click Yes, Accept.

11. Click Close and notice that Status is now Active.

Now we need to add the peering connection to the route tables being used by both VPCs.

1.  Click Route Tables in the VPC Dashboard menu.

2.  Select the route table for the private subnet of VPC1. This will be marked as Main: Yes.

3.  Click the Routes tab and then click Edit Routes.

4.  Click the Add Route button.

5.  In the Destination box, type **192.168.2.0/24**.

6. Click the arrow in the Target drop-down box and choose Peering Connection. Choose the peering connection created earlier in the suggestion box that will appear. Your route table should look similar to mine in Figure 8.7.

**FIGURE 8.7**   Adding the peering connection in your route table enables communication between networks.

7. Click Save Routes.

8. Select the route table for the private subnet of VPC2. This will be marked as Main: Yes.

9. Click the Routes tab and then click Edit Routes.

10. Click the Add Route button.

11. In the Destination box, type **10.1.1.0/24**.

12. Click the arrow in the Target drop-down box and choose Peering Connection. Choose the peering connection created earlier in the suggestion box that will appear.

13. Click Save Routes.

You now have a peering connection set up between VPC1 and VPC2. Remember that you may need to update security groups and/or NACLs to enable instances and other resources to talk to the IP address space in the other VPC.

**EXERCISE 8.2**

## Create a Bastion Host and Configure for Use

In this exercise, you will create a bastion host using an image from the AWS Marketplace. It is assumed that you have a VPC configured with a public and private subnet for this exercise.

1. Log into the AWS Management Console.

2. Click Services; then click EC2 under Compute.

3. Click Launch Instance.

4. Select AWS Marketplace, and type **bastion** in the search field.

5. Click the Select button for the Bastion Host SSH AMI.

6. Click Continue on the information screen that appeared.

7. Select the check box next to t2.micro and click Next: Configure Instance Details.

8. Choose the VPC you want to deploy the bastion host into from the Network drop-down list.

9. Choose a public subnet from the Subnet drop-down list.

10. Click Next: Add Storage.

11. Click Next: Add Tags.

12. Click Next: Configure Security Group.

13. In the SSH rule in the security group shown, add your organization's IP address or CIDR range in the Source box. The Source box should be set to Custom.

14. Click Review And Launch.

15. Click Launch.

16. Select the applicable key pair and select the check box to acknowledge that you have access to the key pair.

17. Click Launch Instances.

18. On the EC2 Dashboard, click Elastic IPs under Network & Security.

19. Click Allocate New Address.

20. Leave Amazon Pool selected, and click Allocate.

21. Select the new elastic IP address and click Actions, then Associate Address.

22. Click the Private IP Label drop-down box and select the private IP address of the bastion host.

23. Click Associate, and then click Close.

**24.** On the EC2 Dashboard, select Instances. Note the public IP address that is assigned (this is the elastic IP you just associated to the instance).

**25.** Connect to the bastion host using your key pair.

To connect using Windows, download PuTTY from here: www.chiark.greenend.org .uk/~sgtatham/putty/latest.html; then follow these steps:

**1.** Open PuTTYgen.

**2.** Click Load.

**3.** Select your key pair file, and click OK. (You may have to change the drop-down from the PuTTY format to All Files.)

**4.** Click OK in the dialog that appears.

**5.** Click Save Private Key, give the private key a name, ensure the file type is the PuTTY PPK format, and click OK.

**6.** Open PuTTY.

**7.** Under Category, click SSH, then Auth, and under Authentication Parameters, browse to your PPK key file. This is shown in Figure 8.8.

**FIGURE 8.8**    You need to configure PuTTY to use the private key of your key pair to connect.

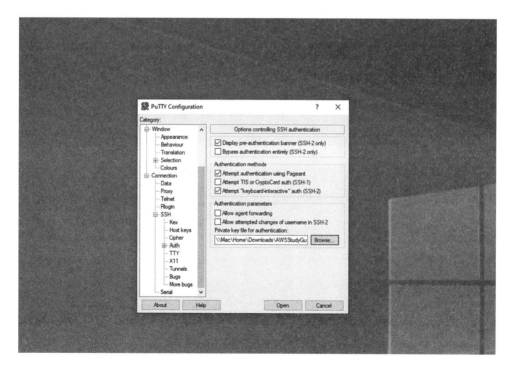

8.  Click Session in the Category pane, and enter the public IP address in the Host Name (Or IP Address) field, shown in Figure 8.9. Ensure that SSH is configured; then click Open.

**FIGURE 8.9**    Enter the hostname or IP address that you want to connect to and click Open.

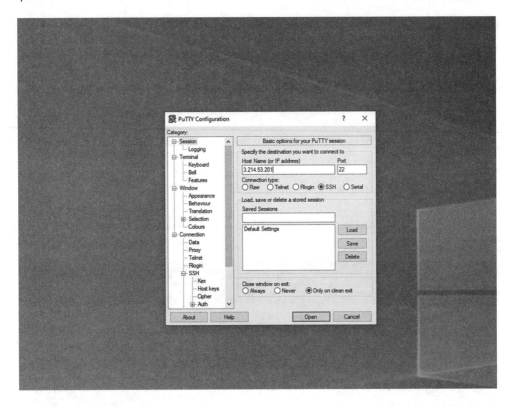

9.  If you get the PuTTy security alert, click Yes.

10. In the Username field, type **ec2-user** and press Enter, as shown in Figure 8.10.

**FIGURE 8.10** Once you are successfully authenticated on your Windows system, you will see the EC2 splash screen.

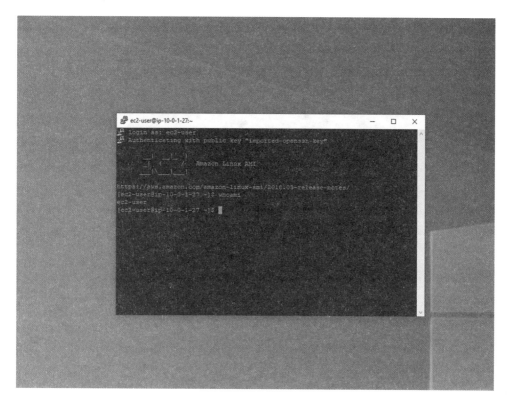

To connect using Linux/macOS:

1. Open Terminal.

2. Type the following command, as shown in Figure 8.11:

   **ssh <public_ip_address> -i <keypair_file>**

**EXERCISE 8.2** *(continued)*

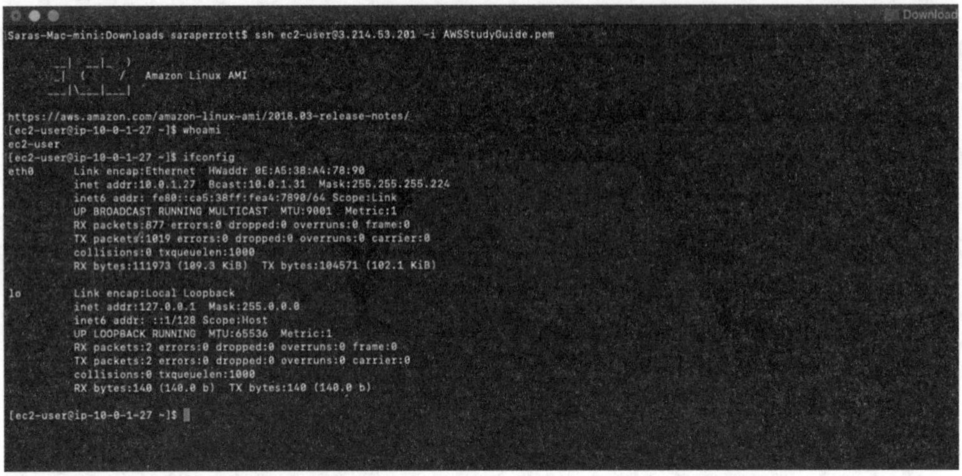

**FIGURE 8.11**    Once you are successfully authenticated on your Linux/MacOS system, you will see the EC2 splash screen.

# Review Questions

You can find the answers in the Appendix.

1. VPCs that are peered have connection names that look like which of the following?

    **A.**  vpc-11112222

    **B.**  pcx-11112222

    **C.**  11112222-pcx

    **D.**  pcx-vpc1vpc2

2. Which of the following does a bastion host provide to a private VPC?

    **A.**  Access to the resources in the VPC through a host outside the VPC

    **B.**  Access to the resources in the VPC through a host inside the VPC

    **C.**  Access to the public resources in the VPC through assigning each an elastic IP address

    **D.**  Access to the private resources in the VPC through assigning each an elastic IP address

3. Which of the following are good security practices for a bastion host? (Choose two.)

    **A.**  Set up Multi-Factor Authentication on the bastion host.

    **B.**  Use a security group that limits traffic on port 80 to the bastion host.

    **C.**  Use an administrative key pair for access to the bastion host.

    **D.**  Whitelist a known set of addresses for access to the bastion host.

4. Does VPC peering have any effect on cost in your environments?

    **A.**  Yes, if you have traffic flowing from one VPC to another, that traffic will not leave the AWS network and use your peering connection.

    **B.**  Yes, if your users are downloading from a peered VPC, no egress costs will be incurred.

    **C.**  Yes, if your users are accessing hosts in two VPCs that are peered, those two hosts will not incur CPU usage costs.

    **D.**  No, VPC peering has no effect on cost.

5. Can two VPCs in different regions be peered?

    **A.**  Yes, if the two VPCs are in the same AWS account.

    **B.**  Yes, regardless of what accounts the VPCs are in.

    **C.**  Yes, if the two VPCs are not peered to any other VPCs.

    **D.**  No, VPCs cannot be peered across regions.

6. Which of the following is a limitation of interregion VPC peering? (Choose two.)

    **A.**  IPv6 traffic cannot flow across the connection.

    **B.**  IPv4 traffic cannot flow across the connection.

    **C.**  There is no support for jumbo frames.

    **D.**  Spot instances cannot be in the peered VPCs.

**7.** Which of the following are true of bastion hosts? (Choose two.)

    **A.** They must reside in a private subnet.

    **B.** They must reside in a public subnet.

    **C.** They must have an elastic IP address.

    **D.** They must have a public IP address.

**8.** Which of the following is not allowed in two peered VPCs?

    **A.** The two VPCs cannot have multiple public IP addresses.

    **B.** The two VPCs cannot have multiple elastic IP addresses.

    **C.** The two VPCs cannot have overlapping CIDR blocks.

    **D.** The two VPCs cannot have IPv6 addresses.

**9.** Which of the following are best practices for bastion hosts? (Choose two.)

    **A.** Security groups should be used to restrict access to the hosts.

    **B.** The host should have a non-elastic IP address.

    **C.** The host should be in a VPC that is peered to at least one other VPC.

    **D.** The host should be in an Auto Scaling group for high availability.

**10.** VPC A is peered with VPC B and VPC C. Can traffic flow across these peered connections from VPC B to VPC C?

    **A.** No. This is not allowed.

    **B.** Yes, as long as the traffic is IPv4 and not IPv6.

    **C.** Yes, as long as the traffic is IPv6 and not IPv4.

    **D.** No, unless the traffic is smaller than 64KB.

**11.** VPC A is peered with VPC B and VPC C. Can traffic flow across these peered connections from VPC B to a host in VPC A, and then in a second transmission from that host in VPC A to VPC C?

    **A.** No. This is not allowed.

    **B.** Yes, as long as the traffic is IPv4 and not IPv6.

    **C.** Yes, as long as the traffic is IPv6 and not IPv4.

    **D.** Yes, this is allowed.

**12.** How many VPCs can connect to a shared services VPC?

    **A.** There is no set limit.

    **B.** 25

    **C.** 5

    **D.** There is a default limit of 125, but this limit can be raised on request.

**13.** What hardware is required to set up a VPC peering connection between two VPCs in the same AWS account?

   **A.** A customer gateway

   **B.** An Internet gateway

   **C.** A virtual private gateway

   **D.** No hardware is required.

**14.** What is the main difference between a bastion host and a NAT device?

   **A.** A bastion host allows traffic into a private VPC whereas a NAT device allows traffic out to the Internet.

   **B.** A bastion host relies on NACLs for security whereas a NAT device relies on security groups.

   **C.** A bastion host should be in a public VPC whereas a NAT device should be in a private VPC.

   **D.** A bastion host should be in a private VPC whereas a NAT device should be in a public VPC.

**15.** You have just inherited a new network architecture that has a private VPC with numerous resources within it and a bastion host for administrative access. Which of the following would you do first?

   **A.** Set up MFA on the hosts in the private VPC.

   **B.** Remove any Internet gateways on the private VPC.

   **C.** Whitelist any IPs that need to access the bastion host.

   **D.** Set up logging on all shell activity on the bastion host.

**16.** Which of the following protocols would typically be allowed to access your bastion host? (Choose two.)

   **A.** SSH

   **B.** HTTP

   **C.** HTTPS

   **D.** RDP

**17.** You have a peering connection between VPC A and VPC B. Additionally, VPC B has a hardware VPN connection with your internal corporate network. You are trying to communicate from VPC A to the internal network but connections are being refused. What is the most likely issue?

   **A.** You need to set up a peering connection between VPC B and your internal network using the VPN connection.

   **B.** You need to ensure that route propagation is turned on in VPC B.

   **C.** You need to ensure that route propagation is turned on in VPC A.

   **D.** This is an example of edge-to-edge routing and is disallowed by AWS.

**18.** You have just been put in charge of a network configuration described as using the hub-and-spoke model. There are five total VPCs. How many peering connections would you expect to find?

    **A.** 3

    **B.** 4

    **C.** 5

    **D.** It is impossible to answer this question without more information.

**19.** VPC A has a logging aggregator within it. VPC B has a web server and VPC C has an application server, both of which log events. VPC D has software that can visualize log data. How would you connect these VPCs?

    **A.** Peer VPC A to VPC D, and peer both VPC B and C to D. Log data within each VPC and visualize it using the software in VPC D.

    **B.** Peer VPCs B, C, and D to VPC A. Have VPCs B and C send log data to VPC A, and VPC D connect to VPC A to load and visualize data.

    **C.** Peer VPC D to both VPC B and C, and then pair VPC B and C to VPC as well. Log data to VPC A, and use the existing peering connections to deliver that data to VPC D for visualization.

    **D.** Peer VPC B to VPC C, and VPC C to VPC A. Route all logs from both B and C into A. Then peer VPC D to VPC A to visualize the log data.

**20.** What additions to your route table would you expect to need to add in a situation where you have two VPCs peered?

    **A.** Destination IPs for IPs within the peered VPC would have a target of the VPC peering connection (pcx-11112222, for example).

    **B.** Destination IPs for IPs within the source VPC would have a target of the VPC peering connection (pcx-11112222, for example).

    **C.** Destination IPs for IPs within the peered VPC would have a target of the CIDR block within the peered VPC (10.0.0.0/28, for example).

    **D.** Destination IPs for IPs within the source VPC would have a target of the CIDR block within the peered VPC (10.0.0.0/28, for example).

# Chapter 9

# AWS Systems Manager

---

**THE AWS CERTIFIED SYSOPS ADMINISTRATOR – ASSOCIATE EXAM TOPICS COVERED IN THIS CHAPTER MAY INCLUDE, BUT ARE NOT LIMITED TO, THE FOLLOWING:**

**Domain 3.0: Deployment and Provisioning**

✓ 3.1 Identify and execute steps required to provision cloud resources

✓ 3.2 Identify and remediate deployment issues

**Domain 5.0: Security and Compliance**

✓ 5.1 Implement and manage security policies on AWS

✓ 5.2 Implement access controls when using AWS

**Domain 7.0: Automation and Optimization**

✓ 7.3 Automate manual or repeatable process to minimize management overhead

For most SysOps administrators, the challenge in their day-to-day work is not in building servers but in maintaining them. As organizations put more emphasis on keeping their systems secure, it is that much more crucial to keep systems up-to-date on patches and to keep an eye on the overall state of your infrastructure.

AWS Systems Manager gives you the ability to centrally manage, install, update, and configure software for your AWS systems and on-premises systems in addition to some other useful administrative features that will be covered in this chapter.

This chapter includes:

How AWS Systems Manager works

Managing EC2 instances with AWS Systems Manager

Creating documents in AWS Systems Manager

Using the Insights Dashboard

Patching your systems with AWS Systems Manager

Storing secrets and configurations with AWS Systems Manager

Connecting to your EC2 instances...no SSH or RDP required

# AWS Systems Manager

*AWS Systems Manager* (SSM) is a free service offered by AWS that provides patching automation, software inventory, and software installation and configuration. It allows you to group systems logically, and it integrates with both AWS Config and Amazon CloudWatch. It can monitor both Windows and Linux operating systems by utilizing the *SSM agent*. You can see the AWS Systems Manager console in Figure 9.1.

The SSM agent must be installed on the systems that you want AWS Systems Manager to monitor, install, configure, and update software on. If you choose one of the Windows or Amazon Linux Amazon Machine Images (AMIs) in the Amazon Marketplace, the SSM agent is already installed. Other operating systems in AWS and on-premises will need to have the agent installed before you can use AWS Systems Manager to administer them.

**FIGURE 9.1**   The AWS Systems Manager Console is where you will configure the Systems Manager services.

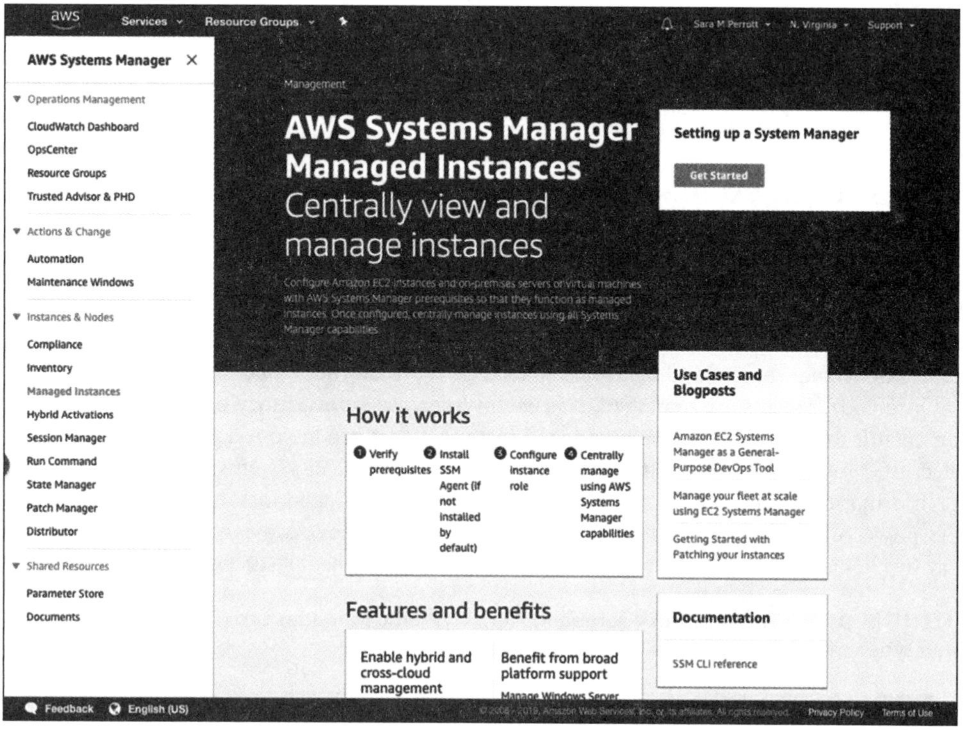

## Communication with AWS Systems Manager

To communicate with AWS Systems Manager, you must install the SSM agent. As just mentioned, for the Windows and Amazon Linux AMIs (2017.09 and later) in the Amazon Marketplace, the SSM agent is already installed. If you want to use another distribution of Linux, however, or if you want to use a non-AMI image, you will have to install the agent first. You can download the SSM agent from the aws/amazon-ssm-agent GitHub repository here: https://github.com/aws/amazon-ssm-agent.

Once the agent is installed on the system, create an Identity and Access Management (IAM) role that will allow the Amazon EC2 instance to communicate with SSM. When you create the role, you need only attach one policy to the role, the AmazonEC2RoleforSSM policy. Once the role has been created with this policy, and the role has been attached to an EC2 instance, you will be able to manage it with AWS Systems Manager.

Remember that you can use AWS Systems Manager for your AWS resources and on-premises systems. The examples in this chapter will focus on using it to manage Amazon EC2 instances. If you would like to know more about how to use it to manage your on-premises systems as well, please check out the "Setting Up AWS Systems Manager for Hybrid Environments" page listed in the "Resources to Review" section.

## AWS Managed Instances

When looking at AWS Systems Manager, a *managed instance* is an Amazon EC2 instance or an on-premises server that is being managed by AWS Systems Manager. This means that it has the SSM agent installed, the role that grants needed access is attached, and it will be visible within the AWS Systems Manager console. Managed instances can be both physical servers or virtual servers and can even be located with another cloud provider.

Once your systems are managed, it is useful to create an inventory of the systems. You can default to selecting all of the managed instances that are in your account, you can select EC2 instances based on tags, or you can manually select systems. The inventory gathers information about current software versions on the managed instances and is a first and very powerful step toward centrally managing your instances. You can configure the inventory by clicking Inventory in the AWS Systems Manager console (see Figure 9.2).

**FIGURE 9.2**    The Inventory screen in AWS Systems Manager provides insights into what types of components are being monitored.

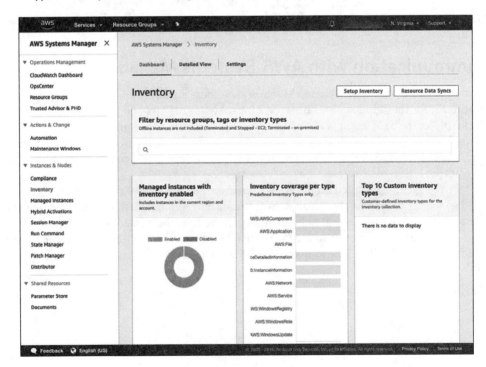

When you set up an inventory, you will notice that some of the options are specific to Windows. If you only have Linux servers that are being scanned by the inventory feature, then it is best to disable the Windows-specific functionality.

# AWS Resource Groups

One of the stellar integrations with AWS Systems Manager is AWS resource groups. By using AWS resource groups, you can logically group your systems, which can simplify management. Systems can be in more than one group, and they can be used for everything from software installation and patching to better monitoring and reporting. For instance, you might create a resource group based on whether a system is Production or Development, or by application, or maybe even by department if you are using tags.

You can execute documents, discussed in the next section, against specific resource groups. Think of a situation where you had to ensure that you patched only the Development systems in your environment, and not the Production. You could use an AWS resource group to query for all systems with a tag of Environment:Dev and then execute a document that installs patches against that resource group.

AWS resource groups are created on a per-region basis, so if you have resources in more than one region, you will need to create the AWS resource groups in each region.

# Taking Action with AWS Systems Manager

AWS Systems Manager uses *documents* to allow you to use configuration as code. Quite a few documents are available from Amazon, and you can also create your own using either JavaScript Object Notation (JSON) or YAML Ain't Markup Language (YAML). Documents can do everything from running commands like installing software from a repository on a Linux box to ensuring a desired configuration state. Documents can be used on both Windows and Linux, though compatibility may depend on what you are asking the document to do. For instance, a script that is being used to install Apache (httpd) with apt on Linux would not work on a Windows system.

There are three types of documents that you can use within AWS. Each type has a specific purpose in mind:

**Command Document**   A document that is meant to be used with the Run command or State Manager (which is part of AWS Systems Manager). Maintenance windows can also take advantage of command documents to apply desired configurations on a schedule that you set.

**Policy Document**    A document that is meant to be used with State Manager and is used to enforce your policies on the systems that you are targeting within AWS Systems Manager

**Automation Document**    A document that is meant to be used for automation and that can also be utilized by State Manager, as well as by maintenance tasks during scheduled maintenance windows

## *Run* Command

The *Run command* uses command documents to execute actions against one or more managed EC2 instances. You can use it to run commands like ls to gather information on a Linux system or dir on a Windows system, or to install software. For instance, I can use a command document to install the Apache web server on my Linux web servers with the Run command.

## Patch Manager

The *Patch Manager* is the component of AWS Systems Manager that allows you to patch whole fleets of EC2 instances and on-premises systems automatically. You can patch operating systems as well as the applications that are installed on those systems.

 On Windows Server, it is important to note that you can patch only Microsoft applications. This limitation does not exist with Linux-based systems.

Using maintenance tasks, you can schedule the installation of patches to install only approved patches during a maintenance window. AWS Systems Manager uses *patch baselines*, which list all approved and rejected patches and can contain rules that can automatically approve patches after they have been out for a certain number of days. Why would you want to automatically approve patches? This automates your patching process so that you need to intervene only if there is a patch that is known to cause issues. Think of how much time you could save using SSM Patch Manager to automate patches to be approved and then installed with your AWS and on-premises systems. For some systems, of course, automatic patching may not be appropriate. For instance, applications that rely on a very specific version of .NET Framework could break if you update the .NET Framework on them, so this is a type of patch that you would not want to automatically approve. Regarding Patch Manager, use your best judgment and your knowledge of the application to determine whether automatic patching is the best option.

## Parameter Store

For many organizations, one of the challenges in implementing automation is how to safely store the secrets used for authentication purposes. The *Parameter Store* provides the ability to not only securely store or call secrets (think passwords and certificates), but also store items like database strings and license codes. Did a change occur and now the new secret doesn't work properly? The Parameter Store also includes the ability to use versioning, which allows you to retrieve the old password. All of this can be called by tasks running within AWS Systems Manager. It should be noted that the use of the Parameter Store is free.

Many of the services you will use in AWS already support the use of the Parameter Store, including Amazon EC2, Amazon ECS, AWS Lambda, and Amazon CloudFormation. If you support developers, they will be very happy to find that both *AWS CodeBuild* and *AWS CodeDeploy* also include support for the Parameter Store. Additionally, if you want to be able to call certificates the Parameter Store seamlessly integrates with the AWS Key Management Service (KMS).

For your administrators and developers to be able to leverage the Parameter Store, you will need to grant them the appropriate permissions within IAM. The policy that is written in JSON should look something like the following code for a trusted administrator. In this example, you would replace the region, account ID, and prefix with whatever you wanted to use. The region is where you want the account to be able to create, modify, and delete policies; the account ID is the ID of the AWS account, and the prefix is what you want your parameters to start with. For the prefix, you might use labels like Prod and Dev, or you might use an organizational identifier of some kind if you want them to be able to work with custom-built policies. Alternatively, you could simply use a wildcard to allow them to work with all parameters in the Parameter Store.

```
{
    "Version": "2012-10-17",
    "Statement": [
        {
            "Sid": "VisualEditor0",
            "Effect": "Allow",
            "Action": [
                "ssm:PutParameter",
                "ssm:DeleteParameter",
                "ssm:GetParameterHistory",
                "ssm:GetParametersByPath",
                "ssm:GetParameters",
                "ssm:GetParameter",
                "ssm:DeleteParameters"
            ],
            "Resource": "arn:aws:ssm:<region:account-id>:parameter/<prefix>-*"
        },
        {
            "Sid": "VisualEditor1",
            "Effect": "Allow",
            "Action": "ssm:DescribeParameters",
```

```
        "Resource": "*"
      }
  ]
}
```

## Session Manager

Remote access to your Amazon EC2 instances can be a security hole if not implemented properly. Windows servers, for instance, need Remote Desktop Protocol (RDP) open if you want to connect to their consoles, and Linux servers need Secure Shell (SSH). One small misconfiguration could open your systems up to the world. This is where Session Manager comes in.

*Session Manager* allows you to connect remotely to your Amazon EC2 managed instances with no exceptions needed in the security group for that remote access. This feature is currently available for all Amazon EC2 managed instances, but you can use Session Manager only for on-premises servers that are in the advanced-instances tier. The Session Manager Console lists all of your managed instances, similar to what is shown in Figure 9.3.

**FIGURE 9.3** You can remotely administer your EC2 instances from AWS Session Manager.

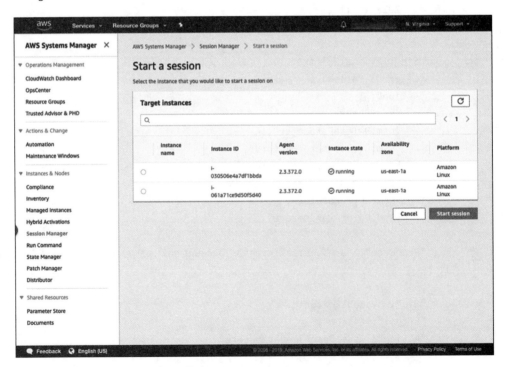

Actions performed with Session Manager can optionally be logged to Amazon S3 and/ or Amazon CloudWatch, and you can also choose to leverage AWS KMS to encrypt session data.

## State Manager

*State Manager* is a compliance tool that allows you to ensure that your instances are running the appropriate versions of software, to define security groups settings that are permissible, and to join systems to Windows domains or run scripts against Windows and Linux systems.

You create an association that allows State Manager to use documents that define what you want to have happen, set the targets for the documents, and schedule how often you want State Manager to run. If you run the initial inventory job, you will see an association already created in State Manager that uses the AWS-GatherSoftwareInventory document, as shown in Figure 9.4.

**FIGURE 9.4**   Associations allow State Manager to run actions against your AWS resources.

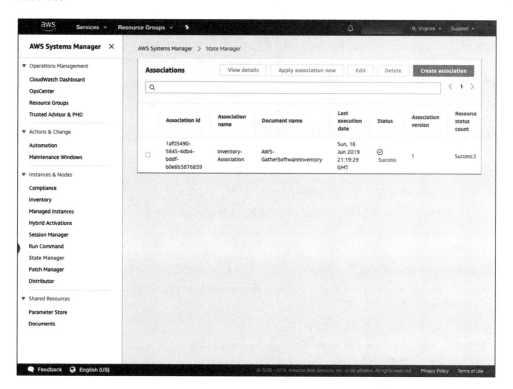

State Manager will make your security admins very happy, as you can confirm that security applications like antivirus are installed and running the latest versions. It can ensure that systems are joined to a Windows domain and, by extension, receive settings through Group Policy. You can even use State Manager to bootstrap all new instances so that they must download and install all the new security updates right after the OS is installed.

# Summary

AWS Systems Manager allows you to perform maintenance tasks such as patching, application updates, and policy enforcements on your AWS and on-premises systems. With the Run command, you can run commands against one or more AWS resources, making configuration a breeze. Using Patch Manager, you can ensure that your systems are patched automatically according to schedules that you define. The Parameter Store makes storing secrets, license keys, and so forth secure and simple, and it integrates seamlessly with a large number of AWS services. Session Manager allows you to remotely administer your systems from their consoles without having to open any ports to the outside world. Finally, State Manager provides a simple method for SysOps administrators to ensure that their systems are compliant with organizational standards related to configuration and software installation.

# Resources to Review

AWS Systems Manager FAQs:

> https://aws.amazon.com/systems-manager/faq/

Setting Up AWS Systems Manager for Hybrid Environments:

> https://docs.aws.amazon.com/systems-manager/latest/userguide/
> systems-manager-managedinstances.html

Running Commands Using Systems Manager Run Command:

> https://docs.aws.amazon.com/systems-manager/latest/userguide/
> run-command.html

Working with Patch Manager (Console):

> https://docs.aws.amazon.com/systems-manager/latest/userguide/
> sysman-patch-working.html

AWS Systems Manager Parameter Store:

> https://docs.aws.amazon.com/systems-manager/latest/userguide/
> systems-manager-parameter-store.html

AWS Systems Manager Session Manager:

> https://docs.aws.amazon.com/systems-manager/latest/userguide/
> what-is-session-manager.html

AWS Systems Manager State Manager:

```
https://docs.aws.amazon.com/systems-manager/latest/userguide/
systems-manager-state.html
```

# Exam Essentials

**Explain how AWS Systems Manager is able to help with operational tasks.** AWS Systems Manager provides tools that allow you to monitor and maintain your instances, while allowing for the creation of patch baselines and compliance monitoring.

**Explain the use of the various components of AWS Systems Manager.** Know what the various components of AWS Systems Manager do. The Run command allows you to execute command documents against AWS resources. Patch Manager allows you to automate the installation of security patches and application updates. The Parameter Store creates a central location to store secrets and other parameters like license keys. Session Manager allows you to remotely administer your systems without opening up ports in your security groups. State Manager helps you monitor the compliance of your systems in regard to versioning and proving that baseline software is installed.

# Exercises

These exercises make the assumption that you have the basic networking components set up that will allow systems to communicate with one another. I will also assume that you have set up two EC2 instances. For my examples, I am using the Amazon Linux image since it has the SSM agent already installed.

---

**EXERCISE 9.1**

### Create a Role for SSM and Attach It to Your EC2 Instances

Before you can manage your EC2 instances, you need to give them permissions to talk to AWS Systems Manager. First, you will need to create a role that the EC2 instance can use.

1. In the AWS Management Console, click Services and then click IAM.

2. Click Roles, then Create Role.

3. Under Select Type Of Trusted Entity, choose AWS Service.

4. Under Choose The Service That Will Use This Role, choose EC2.

5. Click Next: Permissions.

6. In the Filter Policies box, search for **AmazonEC2RoleforSSM**. Click the check box next to it, and then click Next:Tags.

7. Click Next:Review.

8. On the Review screen, name your role **EC2toSSM** and then click Create Role.

**EXERCISE 9.1** *(continued)*

Now that the role is created, you will need to attach the role to your EC2 instances:

1. In the AWS Management Console, click Services and then click EC2.

2. Choose Instances from the Navigation menu to view your EC2 instances.

3. Click the check box next to one of your EC2 instances, click the Actions button, choose Instance Settings, and then click Attach/Replace IAM Role.

4. Click the IAM Role drop-down box and select the EC2toSSM role that you created earlier, shown in Figure 9.5.

**FIGURE 9.5** Attaching the EC2toSSM role allows the EC2 instance to communicate with AWS Systems Manager.

5. Click Apply.

Repeat steps 3–5 for any other EC2 instances you have that you want to manage with AWS Systems Manager.

**EXERCISE 9.2**

## Tag Your EC2 Instances

Tagging your EC2 instances allows you to target them together for use with resource groups, the Run command, the Inventory screen, and so forth. Tags should be used to group like systems.

1.   On the EC2 Dashboard, select Instances.

2.   Click the check box next to your EC2 instance, click Actions, choose Instance Settings, and then click Add/Edit Tags.

3.   Click Create Tag. For Key, type **Env** and for Value, type **Prod**.

4.   Click Save.

Repeat steps 2–4 for all of your EC2 instances that you want to manage with AWS Systems Manager.

---

**EXERCISE 9.3**

## Set Up Your Resource Groups Based on Tags

The resource group can be used for patching, among other things. Separating out Prod from Dev systems, for instance, is an excellent use of a resource group.

1.   On the AWS Management Console, select Services, then Systems Manager.

2.   Click Resource Groups.

3.   Click Create A Resource Group.

4.   For Group Type, select Tag Based.

5.   For Grouping Criteria, click the Resource Types drop-down box and select AWS::EC2::Instance.

6.   Type **Env** in the Tags field, and type **Prod** in the Optional Tag Value field. Click Add.

7.   In the Group Details field, enter a name for the resource group. I will use **Prod-EC2-Instances**.

8.   Click Create Group.

Once the resource group has been created, your screen should look similar to Figure 9.6 below.

**EXERCISE 9.3** *(continued)*

**FIGURE 9.6**   Resource groups allow you to organize like systems in AWS Systems Manager.

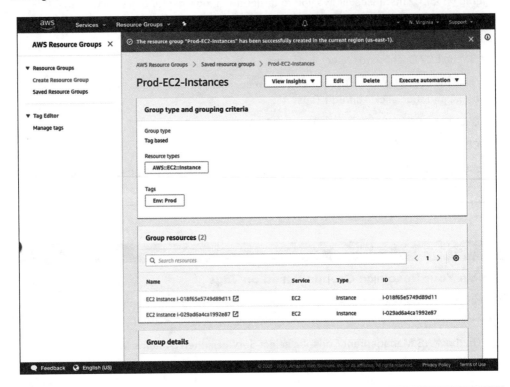

**EXERCISE 9.4**

### Use the *Run* Command to Install Apache on Web Servers

Being able to install software without having to log into individual systems is a huge timesaver for most SysOps admins. In this exercise, you'll install Apache on an Amazon Linux EC2 instance.

1. On the AWS Systems Manager Console, select Run Command.

2. Click Run Command.

3. Select the radio button next to AWS-RunShellScript.

4. Scroll down to Command Parameters, and type the following commands:

   ```
   sudo yum update -y
   sudo yum install -y httpd
   sudo service httpd start
   ```

5. Scroll down to Targets, and choose Manually Selecting Instances. Click the check box next to the system you want to do the installation on.

6. Under Output Options, deselect Enable Writing To An S3 Bucket.

7. Click Run.

When installation is successful, the instances you selected will say Success under Overall Status, as in Figure 9.7.

**FIGURE 9.7** A successful install of Apache using the Run command in AWS Systems Manager

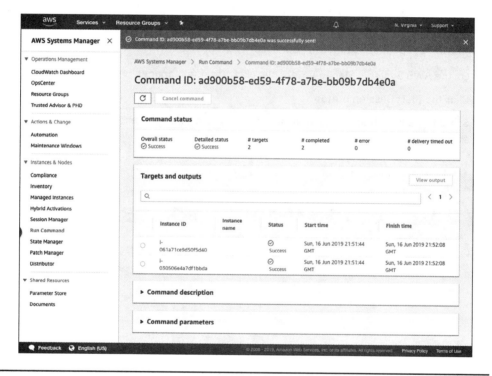

---

**EXERCISE 9.5**

## Create a Parameter for a License Key

Creating a parameter for a license key allows you to call the parameter when installing software so that the license key can be applied automatically.

1. On the AWS Systems Manager Console, select Parameter Store.

2. Click Create Parameter.

3. For Name, enter **LicenseKey_MyApp**.

4. For Tier, select Standard.

**EXERCISE 9.5** *(continued)*

5. Under Type, select String.

6. Enter a string of characters in the Value box; it doesn't matter for this exercise what it is. In a production environment, this would be your actual license key.

7. Click Create Parameter.

**EXERCISE 9.6**

## Connect to Your EC2 Instance with Session Manager

Connecting to your systems via Session Manager is an excellent way to enable administration without opening up holes in your security groups.

1. On the AWS Systems Manager Console, click Session Manager.

2. Click the Start Session button.

3. Select the radio button next to the instance you want to connect to and click Start Session, shown in Figure 9.8.

**FIGURE 9.8** You can select the EC2 instance you want to manage from AWS Systems Manager.

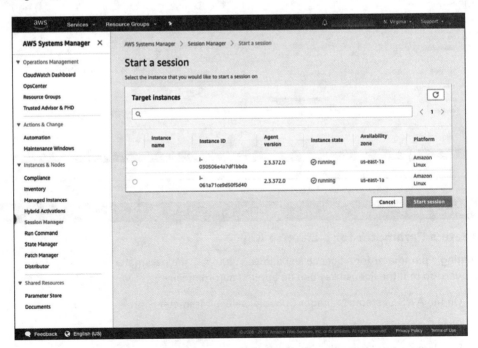

4. Your remote session through AWS Session Manager will open to the Linux or Windows console.

**EXERCISE 9.7**

## Configure Patch Manager for Your EC2 Instances

Setting your systems up for patching ensures that patching is done automatically and on a schedule that you define.

1. On the AWS Systems Manager Console, choose Patch Manager.

2. Click Configure Patching. You will see a screen similar to Figure 9.9.

3. Under Instances To Patch, choose Enter Instance Tags. Type **Env** in the Tag field and **Prod** in the Tag Value field. Click Add.

4. Under Patching Schedule, choose Schedule In A New Maintenance Window.

5. Choose Use A CRON Schedule Builder, and set the window to run every Saturday at 11:00 p.m.

**FIGURE 9.9**   Setting a patching schedule for your production server allows patching to be separate from development servers.

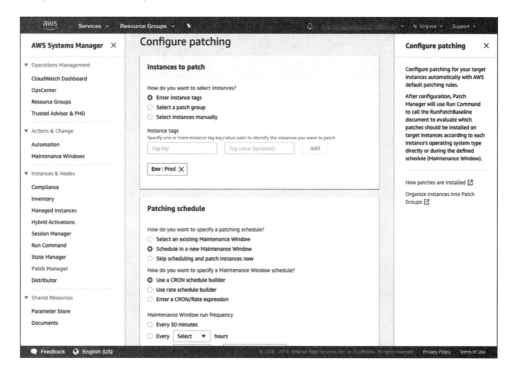

6. Set the maintenance window duration to 4 hours.

7. Give the maintenance window a name. In my example, I used **Prod-EC2-Instances**.

**EXERCISE 9.7** *(continued)*

8. For Patching Operation, choose Scan And Install.

9. Click Configure Patching.

You will be dropped into the Patch Baselines area. From here, you can configure baselines and approve patches. The patches that you approve will be installed during the maintenance window that you have specified.

1. Click the patch baseline that corresponds to your instance types. For this example, I chose AWS-AmazonLinuxDefaultPatchBaseline.

2. Click Actions and then click Modify Patch Groups.

3. In the Patch Groups box, enter the name of the patching configuration that you created earlier. Then click Add.

4. Click Close.

# Review Questions

You can find the answers in the Appendix.

1. Which of the following does AWS Systems Manager *not* provide?

   **A.** Patching automation

   **B.** Software installation

   **C.** Software configuration

   **D.** Critical vulnerability notification

2. Which of the following AMIs will not automatically have AWS Systems Manager installed?

   **A.** A Windows 7 AMI from the Amazon Marketplace

   **B.** A Windows 2000 AMI from the Amazon Marketplace

   **C.** A Linux AMI from the Amazon Marketplace

   **D.** A macOS AMI from the Amazon Marketplace

3. You have a number of instances based on AMIs with AWS Systems Manager agent installed, but none are able to communicate to the SSM service. What is likely the source of this issue?

   **A.** You need to create an IAM group and assign that group to each instance you want communicating with AWS Systems Manager.

   **B.** You need to create an IAM role and have each instance assume that role to communicate with the AWS Systems Manager service.

   **C.** You need to add the AWSSystemsManager policy to each instance running an SSM agent.

   **D.** You need to use a Linux-based AMI on each instance to ensure it can communicate with the SSM service.

4. Which of the following policies is required for an SSM agent on an instance to communicate with the AWS Systems Manager service?

   **A.** AmazonEC2RoleforSSM

   **B.** AmazonEC2RoleforASM

   **C.** AWSEC2RoleforAWSSM

   **D.** AWSEC2RoleforSSM

5. Which of the following has the capability to be a managed instance? (Choose two.)

   **A.** An on-premises server

   **B.** An EC2 instance running in AWS

   **C.** A container running in AWS via ECS

   **D.** A Lambda triggered by an API; gateway running in an AWS VPC

6. Which of the following are valid ways to filter or organize a resource group? (Choose two.)

   **A.** By resource tag

   **B.** By AWS account number

   **C.** By IAM role

   **D.** By environment

7. Which of the following is a limitation of a resource group?

   **A.** They cannot contain resources based on resource tag.

   **B.** They cannot contain resources based on environment.

   **C.** They cannot contain resources in different regions.

   **D.** They cannot query resources based on a specific tag.

8. Which of the following are supported document types within AWS Systems Manager? (Choose two.)

   **A.** Command document

   **B.** Role document

   **C.** Policy document

   **D.** Resource document

9. Which of the following are supported notation formats for documents in AWS Systems Manager? (Choose two.)

   **A.** YAML

   **B.** JSON

   **C.** CSV

   **D.** Text

10. Which of the following document types can be used by State Manager?

    **A.** Policy documents

    **B.** Automation documents

    **C.** Command documents

    **D.** All of the above

11. With which command does a command document typically deal?

    **A.** The Run command

    **B.** The Patch command

    **C.** The Halt command

    **D.** The Update command

**12.** Which of the following encryption options is supported by session manager?

   **A.** CMKs

   **B.** KMS

   **C.** Customer-provided keys

   **D.** CMS

**13.** Which of the following can State Manager help to enforce? (Choose two.)

   **A.** Messaging

   **B.** Inventory

   **C.** Security

   **D.** Compliance

**14.** Which of the following are designed to work with the Parameter Store? (Choose two.)

   **A.** GitHub

   **B.** AWS CodeBuild

   **C.** AWS CodePipeline

   **D.** AWS CodeDeploy

**15.** You are responsible for a fleet of EC2 instances and have heard that a recently released patch has known issues with Rails, which your instances are all running. How would you prevent the patch from being deployed to the instances, given that they are all running the SSM agent?

   **A.** Remove the patch from the automation pipeline.

   **B.** Remove the patch from the patch baseline.

   **C.** Add the patch as an exclusion to the patch baseline.

   **D.** Add the path as an exclusion to the automation pipeline.

**16.** Which of the following is possible to do in an AWS Systems Manager maintenance window? (Choose two.)

   **A.** Execute AWS Lambda functions

   **B.** Update patches

   **C.** Remove a bad patch

   **D.** Restart an instance

**17.** You have a command document written in JSON for your instances running a Windows AMI and communicating with the AWS Systems Manager Service. You now have inherited several Linux-based instances and want to use the same command document. What do you need to do to use this document with the Linux instances?

   **A.** Convert the document from JSON to YAML and reload it.

   **B.** Copy the document and assign the copy to the Linux-based instances.

   **C.** You cannot use a document written for Windows-based instances with Linux-based instances.

   **D.** Nothing; documents will work across platform operating systems.

**18.** Your organization has mandated that all code running on your macOS EC2 instances must either be part of an approved AMI or open source. You have been using the AWS Systems Manager agent on your instances. What will you need to do to ensure compliance with this new policy?

    **A.** You will need to remove the agent and reinstall it using the Open Source option within the agent's installation script.

    **B.** You will need to remove the Systems Manager agent and find another option.

    **C.** Nothing; the Systems Manager agent is part of the default macOS AMI in AWS.

    **D.** Nothing; the Systems Manager agent is open source and available on GitHub.

**19.** You need to ensure that a compliance script is executed on all of your managed instances every morning at 1 a.m. How would you accomplish this task?

    **A.** Create a new Execute command and use Systems Manager to set it up on your instances.

    **B.** Create a new Run command and use Systems Manager to set it up on your instances.

    **C.** Create a new compliance policy document and ensure that all instances' agents reference the document.

    **D.** Create a new action document and ensure that all instances' agents reference the document.

**20.** Which of the following are ways to customize the default patching procedures used by AWS Systems Manager Patch Manager? (Choose two.)

    **A.** Write a custom Run command to install patches on your own schedule.

    **B.** Write an automation document describing your preferred patching levels and schedule.

    **C.** Write your own AWS Systems Manager command to refine the default automation.

    **D.** Write a policy document for each instance you want customized.

# Storage and Data Management

# Chapter

# 10

# Amazon Simple Storage Service (S3)

**THE AWS CERTIFIED SYSOPS ADMINISTRATOR – ASSOCIATE EXAM TOPICS COVERED IN THIS CHAPTER MAY INCLUDE, BUT ARE NOT LIMITED TO, THE FOLLOWING:**

**Domain 2.0: High Availability**

✓ 2.2  Recognize and differentiate highly available and resilient environments on AWS

**Domain 3.0: Deployment and Provisioning**

✓ 3.1  Identify and execute steps required to provision cloud resources

**Domain 4.0: Deployment and Provisioning**

✓ 4.1  Create and manage data retention

✓ 4.2  Identify and implement data protection, encryption, and capacity planning needs

**Domain 5.0: Security and Compliance**

✓ 5.2  Implement access controls when using AWS

One of the components that SysOps administrators generally have to work with as part of their daily jobs is storage. In a traditional on-premises environment, that may be locally attached storage, network-attached storage (NAS), or even storage area network (SAN) storage.

These traditional modes of storage have their counterparts in AWS, and this chapter is going to discuss object storage solutions like Amazon Simple Storage Service (S3) and Glacier.

This chapter includes:

An introduction to object storage basics

What is S3 and how to use it

Naming conventions used in S3

Choosing the right level of availability

How to secure access to S3

Encrypting your data in S3

Archiving your data with Amazon Glacier

Managing the life cycle of your data

Using hybrid cloud storage with storage gateways

# Object Storage and Amazon S3

Before we begin any conversation regarding *Amazon Simple Storage Service* (S3), I would like to make sure that you understand what object storage is. The differentiator with object storage from other forms of storage is that services within AWS interact with object storage via APIs. AWS has full visibility into your object storage and you can interact with objects that reside within your object storage via API.

*Object storage* in AWS is offered by services like S3 and Glacier. Amazon S3 is a service that offers high durability and varying levels of availability, depending on which class of S3 you choose. Amazon Glacier is a low-cost solution for archiving data. It is especially helpful for those organizations that need to keep data for compliance reasons but that don't expect to have to access the data.

So why access data via an API? Simply put, it enables greater flexibility and automation down the road. Data put into S3 can be used as the data set for queries using Amazon

Athena; it can also be used to trigger other events or workflows. For instance, a common use case is where you upload an image into S3, and a process is kicked off that takes that image and resizes it so that it will work with a variety of mobile devices. This is all made possible because object storage is accessible via APIs to other AWS services or applications you build to interact with it. Some other use cases for Amazon S3 in particular might be for backups, hybrid storage with storage gateways, and disaster recovery capabilities due to the high durability of Amazon S3.

Amazon S3 (see Figure 10.1) stores objects in containers that are referred to as *buckets*. You can set access controls specific to an individual bucket, and/or you can use buckets to organize the types of objects that are being uploaded into Amazon S3.

**FIGURE 10.1**    The Amazon S3 Console is where you create and configure buckets.

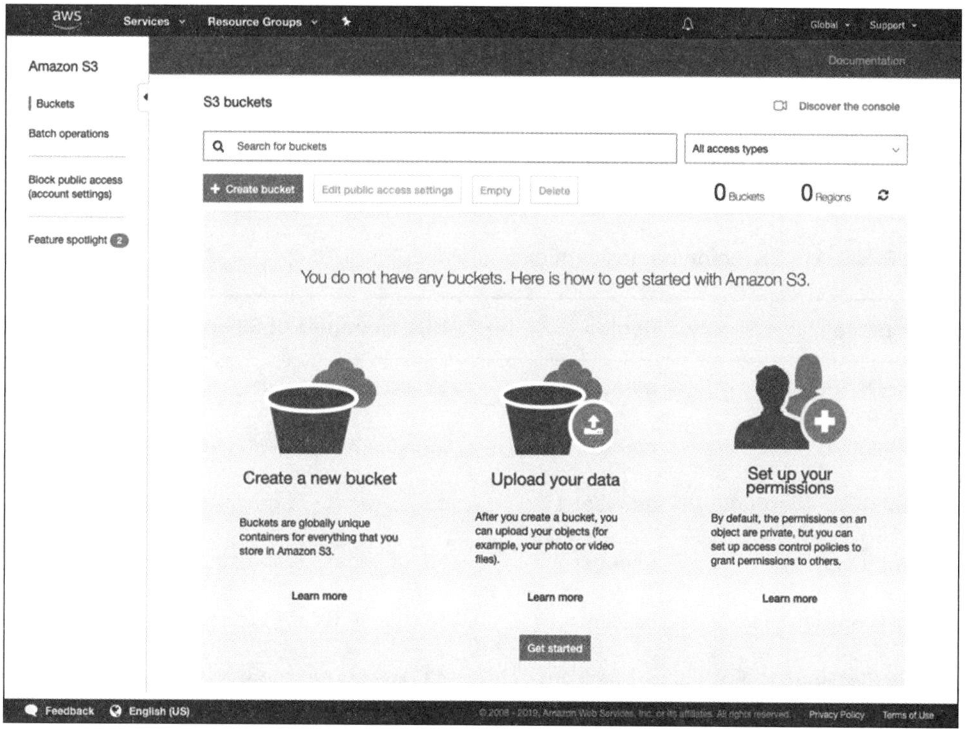

Objects stored in S3 can be up to 5 TB in size individually, and there is no limit on how much you can upload to an S3 bucket. Keep in mind that you are charged for what you use, and that charge will vary depending on which S3 storage class you are using. Individual objects are identified by an *object key*, which is made up of the bucket name, a key, and a version. For instance, say that you have uploaded an image by the name of mypicture .jpg to a bucket named example. The full URL would look something like this: http:// example.s3.amazonaws.com/2019-07-07/mypicture.jpg. As you can see the bucket's name (example) is in the URL, and the key in this case would be 2019-07-07/mypicture.jpg.

# What's in a URL?

You can access your S3 bucket through the AWS Management Console, of course. However, you can also access your S3 bucket directly with a URL. There are two methods to access your S3 buckets: virtual-hosted URLs and path-style URLs.

With the virtual-hosted URL, the bucket's name is included as part of the domain name in the URL. An example of this would be: `http://<bucketname>.s3.amazonaws.com` or `http://<bucketname>.s3.<regionname>.amazonaws.com`.

With the path-style URL, the bucket's name is not part of the domain name, and the addresses look like this: `http://s3.amazonaws.com/<bucketname>` or `http://s3.<regionname>.amazonaws.com/<bucketname>`.

Looking at these examples, you might be wondering why one URL has no region specified and the other URL does have a region specified. When no region is specified in an S3 URL, it is because the S3 bucket resides in the US East (N. Virginia) region. Any other region will have a region name specified. Table 10.1 lists the region names that are available as of this writing, with examples of what the S3 URL would look like as well. If you want to use virtual-hosted URLs, add the name of the bucket before the domain name and separate the bucket name and the domain name with a period. If you want to use path-style URLs, add the bucket name at the end after a forward slash.

**TABLE 10.1**   S3 region names with example endpoint URLs

| Region name | Region | URL examples of S3 endpoints |
| --- | --- | --- |
| US East (N. Virginia) | us-east-1 | s3.amazonaws.com |
| US East (Ohio) | us-east-2 | s3.us-east-2.amazonaws.com |
| US West (N. California) | us-west-1 | s3.us-west-1.amazonaws.com |
| US West (Oregon) | us-west-2 | s3.us-west-2.amazonaws.com |
| Canada (Central) | ca-central-1 | s3.ca-central-1.amazonaws.com |
| Asia Pacific (Hong Kong) | ap-east-1 | s3.ap-east-1.amazonaws.com |
| Asia Pacific (Mumbai) | ap-south-1 | s3.ap-south-1.amazonaws.com |
| Asia Pacific (Osaka) | ap-northeast-3 | s3.ap-northeast-3.amazonaws.com |
| Asia Pacific (Seoul) | ap-northeast-2 | s3.ap-northeast-2.amazonaws.com |
| Asia Pacific (Singapore) | ap-southeast-1 | s3.ap-southeast-1.amazonaws.com |

| Region name | Region | URL examples of S3 endpoints |
| --- | --- | --- |
| Asia Pacific (Sydney) | ap-southeast-2 | `s3.ap-southeast-2.amazonaws.com` |
| Asia Pacific (Tokyo) | ap-northeast-1 | `s3.ap-northeast-1.amazonaws.com` |
| China (Beijing) | cn-north-1 | `s3.cn-north-1.amazonaws.com.cn` |
| China (Ningxia) | cn-northwest-1 | `s3.cn-northwest-1.amazonaws.com.cn` |
| EU (Frankfurt) | eu-central-1 | `s3.eu-central-1.amazonaws.com` |
| EU (Ireland) | eu-west-1 | `s3.eu-west-1.amazonaws.com` |
| EU (London) | eu-west-2 | `s3.eu-west-2.amazonaws.com` |
| EU (Paris) | eu-west-3 | `s3.eu-west-3.amazonaws.com` |
| EU (Stockholm) | eu-north-1 | `s3.eu-north-1.amazonaws.com` |
| South America (Sao Paulo) | sa-east-1 | `s3.sa-east-1.amazonaws.com` |

For the most current version, go to `https://docs.aws.amazon.com/general/latest/gr/rande.html`.

You may have noticed that the Chinese S3 addresses end with the country code "cn," but that the other countries conform to the standard "amazonaws.com." Remember that these differences do exist and that they are valid S3 addresses.

# Availability and Durability

Most organizations have two major concerns when it comes to storing their data. The first concern, durability, has to do with ensuring that their data exists and is resilient to outages. In fact, S3 will not report back a successful write operation until the data that was written has been copied to multiple facilities (usually three). The second, availability, focuses on the ability to access their data even in the event of an outage at one of the AWS datacenters.

The durability of S3 is the same across all of the S3 storage classes. Amazon guarantees eleven 9s of durability (99.999999999 percent). Essentially if you were to store 10,000 objects within Amazon S3, you might lose one object every 10 million years or so. That's pretty durable! This is a popular question that you may run into on the exam…and also the easiest. Just remember that all storage classes in S3 provide eleven 9s of durability.

Availability in S3 is where you run into some fluctuation. The availability is determined by which storage class you are using in Amazon S3. The availability promised is also defined in a *service level agreement* (SLA). If at any point in time, the promised availability is not met, and it is the fault of Amazon, you receive service credits in return. In the next section, we will examine each of the storage classes and what to expect from each.

# S3 Storage Classes

No chapter in Amazon S3 would be complete without a conversation regarding storage classes; why you would want one storage class over another, what the pros and cons are of each, and so forth.

There are four storage classes in total that we will discuss. They are S3 Standard, S3 Intelligent-Tiering, S3 Standard-Infrequent Access (IA), and S3 One Zone-Infrequent Access (IA).

## S3 Standard

S3 Standard is that Swiss Army knife of S3 storage classes. It's a great fit for any data that might be frequently accessed such as websites, applications, analytics, and even content distribution. It has the highest availability of all the S3 storage classes at 99.99 percent, and multiple copies of your data are stored across numerous availability zones, providing a high degree of durability.

## S3 Intelligent-Tiering

If your organization is concerned about cost and their focus is on cost optimization, S3 Intelligent-Tiering is a good option. You load your data to S3 Standard, and if it is not accessed for 30 days, it is moved to S3 Standard-IA. When it is accessed, it is moved back to S3 Standard. There are no tiering fees for moving data between the tiers; you pay only a small monitoring and auto-tiering fee for the service. S3 Intelligent-Tiering offers 99.9 percent availability and offers the same capabilities that S3 Standard does.

This S3 storage class is perfect for organizations that need to retain data for a very long time but want to optimize costs in doing so. With this tier you can still use lifecycle policies (covered later in this chapter) to archive data to Amazon Glacier for even more cost savings. It is also good if you are unsure of how often data will be accessed because it will automatically move less frequently accessed data into a less expensive tier.

## S3 Standard-IA

S3 Standard-Infrequent Access (IA) offers 99.9 percent availability and in many respects is similar to S3 Standard. The biggest difference is that data put into S3 Standard-IA is data that you are not going to access often but need to be able to access immediately if the need should arise. It is less expensive to store data in S3 Standard-IA than S3 Standard, but there is a per-GB retrieval fee if you need to recover your data from S3 Standard-IA.

This storage class is perfect for saving things like backup files and disaster recovery files...things that you shouldn't need to access often. You can also use lifecycle policies to move data to Amazon Glacier for long-term archiving from this tier, just as you can with S3 Standard.

### S3 One Zone-IA

In many ways, S3 One Zone-IA is similar to S3 Standard-IA. The biggest and most important difference is that this tier will store your data in only *one* availability zone as opposed to a minimum of three with the other storage classes. This does make it less expensive than S3 Standard-IA, but it does reduce the availability guaranteed by Amazon to 99.5 percent.

### Choosing a Storage Class

There is no easy way to remember these other than to memorize them. For the exam, you should know what the promised availability is for the various tiers of S3 storage.

**TABLE 10.2** Availability of S3 Storage Classes

| Class | Availability |
|---|---|
| S3 Standard | 99.99 percent |
| S3 Intelligent-Tiering | 99.9 percent |
| S3 Standard-IA | 99.9 percent |
| S3 One Zone-IA | 99.5 percent |

# Securing and Protecting Data in S3

As with any storage solution, security is important. You must be able to control access to your data and ensure that it is protected from unauthorized access. Amazon gives you a number of options to secure the data in your S3 buckets, including robust access controls, versioning, and data encryption.

## Access Control

When an S3 bucket is first created, it is private, meaning that only the owner of the bucket can access it. To allow others to use the S3 bucket, you need to allow the access to happen. You can do that through a multitude of ways, including user policies, bucket policies and ACLs.

## User Policies

*User policies* are written in JSON and, as you might imagine from the name, affect users interacting with your S3 buckets. You can use them to allow specific IAM users access to a bucket or to a specific folder in your bucket. In this example, I am allowing an IAM user access to a folder named FudgeRecipes in my mytopsecretstuff S3 bucket.

```json
{
    "Version":"2012-10-17",
    "Statement":[
        {
            "Effect":"Allow",
            "Action":[
                "s3:PutObject",
                "s3:GetObject",
                "s3:GetObjectVersion",
                "s3:DeleteObject",
                "s3:DeleteObjectVersion"
            ],
            "Resource":"arn:aws:s3:::mytopsecretstuff/FudgeRecipes/*"
        }
    ]
}
```

## Bucket Policies

*Bucket policies* are written in JSON, but you can also leverage the *AWS Policy Generator* to create your bucket policy if you are not familiar with JSON. As you might imagine, bucket policies affect the entire bucket, and you can do quite a few things with them. In the following example, I am using a bucket policy for my S3 bucket called mytopsecretstuff to enforce multifactor authentication (MFA) on the FudgeRecipes folder so that someone must enter a one-time PIN (OTP) to access the objects in that particular folder in that bucket.

```json
{
    "Id": "<unique_string>",
    "Version": "2012-10-17",
    "Statement": [
        {
            "Sid": "<unique_sid>",
            "Action": "s3:*",
```

```
        "Effect": "Deny",
        "Resource": "arn:aws:s3:::mytopsecretstuff/FudgeRecipes/*",
        "Condition": {
          "Null": {
            "aws:MultiFactorAuthAge": "true"
          }
        },
        "Principal": "*"
    }
  ]
}
```

## Access Control Lists (ACLs)

At the beginning of this section, I mentioned that by default only the owner of the S3 bucket has access to it. This is accomplished by the default ACL that is created when a new bucket is created.

In an ACL, you can grant read, write, read_acp, write_acp, and full control. Read allows you to list the contents of a bucket or read the contents of an object. Write allows you to create, modify, or delete an object in the bucket. Read_acp and write_acp allow you to work with the ACLs themselves; read allows a person to read an ACL and write allows you to modify the ACL for a bucket or object. Full control gives you all of the permissions that we just discussed.

You can grant multiple permissions inside of an ACL, within the body of a grant. Each person or AWS group given access within the grant is referred to as a grantee, and a single ACL can have up to a maximum of 100 grants.

## Public Access Settings

It was mentioned earlier that public access is restricted by default and that only the owner of the S3 bucket has access initially. This can be overridden by bucket policies and permissions that are set on the buckets or folders within the buckets to allow access to other users.

As a SysOps administrator, you probably want to ensure that public access is restricted for an entire bucket and that your users can't accidentally open up your S3 buckets to the Internet. S3 provides the ability to restrict this with the Permissions tab. Only account administrators or bucket owners can change the Public Access settings.

To access the public access settings, all you need to do is click on your S3 bucket, and then choose the Permissions tab. Block public access is the first option in the list after that, as shown in Figure 10.2.

**FIGURE 10.2**   Public Access settings can be made by account administrators and bucket owners.

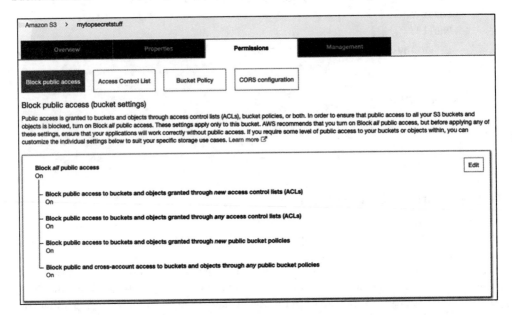

You can adjust four settings here:

- **Block Public Access To Buckets And Objects Granted Through *New* Access Control Lists (ACLs):** This setting will prevent public access from being granted by a new ACL by blocking the creation of an ACL that allows public access, but it will not impact existing ACLs.

- **Block Public Access To Buckets And Objects Granted Through *Any* Access Control Lists (ACLs):** This setting will cause S3 to ignore any ACL that is granting public access, new or existing.

- **Block Public Access To Buckets And Objects Granted Through *New* Public Bucket Policies:** This setting will prevent public access from being granted by new bucket policies by blocking the creation of a bucket policy that allows public access, but it will not impact existing bucket policies.

- **Block Public And Cross-Account Access To Buckets And Objects Through *Any* Public Bucket Policies:** This setting will cause S3 to ignore any bucket policy that is granting public or cross-account access to S3 buckets.

## Versioning

If you are concerned about data getting corrupted or deleted, one of the simplest controls you have at your disposal with Amazon S3 is *versioning*. Any time an object is uploaded, a new version is created. If an object is deleted, you can still retrieve the old version of that object. You can't disable versioning once it has been enabled—you can only suspend it—so be sure that you want to use versioning before you turn it on. Versioning can be in three states at any given time:

**Versioning Disabled (Default)**    Uploading an object with the same key will overwrite the existing object. Deleting an object will permanently delete it.

**Versioning Enabled**    When you upload an object that has the same key as an existing object, S3 creates a new object with a brand-new version ID. When you delete an object, it will show that it was deleted, but the old versions of the object are still available. You can reference old versions of the object by their version ID.

**Versioning Suspended**    Any previous versions that were created while versioning was enabled will be kept, but further versions will not be created as objects are uploaded or deleted.

Keep in mind that with Amazon S3, you pay for the storage you use. If you enable versioning, you will be paying for the space the versioned documents take up as well as the space needed by the current version.

# Encryption

Amazon has tried to make encrypting your S3 buckets simpler with Amazon S3 default encryption. You can enable *default encryption* on new or existing buckets, and you can choose to use either Amazon S3–managed keys (SSE-S3) or, if you need an audit trail for who is accessing your keys, you can use AWS-KMS-managed keys (SSE-KMS). You can also choose to use your own keys with Customer-Provided Keys (SSE-C), though this is not included in the default encryption categories.

The SSE in SSE-S3 and SSE-KMS stands for server-side encryption, meaning that the encryption is handled by the server rather than the client. KMS stands for Key Management Service, which refers to the AWS managed service for issuing and managing keys.

## Amazon S3–Managed Keys (SSE-S3)

With SSE-S3, Amazon manages key rotation and key usage. Every single object loaded into Amazon S3 has its own key used to encrypt it, and that key is encrypted by a master key, which is regularly rotated behind the scenes. SSE-S3 uses the industry standard AES-256 encryption algorithm to encrypt all of your data.

## AWS KMS-Managed Keys (SSE-KMS)

While SSE-KMS behaves similarly to SSE-S3, there are some important differences. The master key which is used to encrypt the keys has separate permissions from the keys used to encrypt your objects, and when using SSE-KMS you get an audit trail that established not only when your master key was used but also who used it. For organizations with strict compliance requirements, SSE-KMS may be the best choice.

An easy way on the exam to distinguish encryption types is if the question specifies that auditing is required. If the question mentions auditing, SSE-KMS is most likely your answer.

## Customer-Provided Keys (SSE-C)

Customer-Provided Keys is not one of the default encryption methods available in Amazon S3, but it is an option that you should be aware of. For organizations that need to maintain control over their private key at all times, SSE-C is a good solution. You manage your encryption keys, and Amazon S3 will manage the encryption of the objects within the S3 bucket that you have enabled SSE-C on.

# Amazon Glacier

Amazon S3 is a great solution for data that must be retrieved quickly when needed. As we discussed already, tiers allow you to optimize the cost of storage but still maintain the ability to retrieve data at a moment's notice. Some organizations, however, are required to maintain data for years (medical records are a great example of this) but won't likely need to access that data. If a request comes in for the older data, it is generally not required to retrieve it quickly. For use cases like this, where data needs to be saved at the lowest cost possible and does not need to be retrieved immediately, Amazon Glacier is a great fit.

Amazon Glacier is an archiving solution within AWS. Unlike many of the services, you can't interact with Amazon Glacier through the AWS Management Console. You can move objects between S3 and Glacier with lifecycle policies, or you can interact with Glacier with the Glacier API.

Retrieving objects can be done in a few different ways, depending on how the data got into Amazon Glacier. If the data was moved to Glacier through lifecycle policies in S3, then you can restore the archived files within the Amazon S3 Management Console or through the Amazon S3 API. If you saved the data to Amazon Glacier using the API, then the only way to retrieve it is with the API—you can't retrieve it through the S3 Management Console because S3 won't have visibility into it.

You have three different options for retrieving data from Amazon Glacier, and they all have to do with how quickly you need the data back. Standard is the default retrieval option and is used if no other option is specified when you retrieve your data. The retrieval options are:

- **Expedited:** Most expensive option, usually available within 1–5 minutes
- **Standard (default):** Usually available in 3–5 hours
- **Bulk:** Lowest-cost option, usually available within 5–12 hours

## Amazon Glacier Deep Archive

Amazon Glacier has been the archiving solution of choice for AWS environments for quite a while; however, Amazon released a similar solution created specifically for long-term retention of data (think 7–10+ years). That solution is referred to as Amazon Glacier Deep Archive.

Amazon Glacier Deep Archive is very similar to Amazon Glacier, though it is less expensive and has fewer retrieval options. The retrieval time promised is 12 hours, and it is assumed that customers who use Amazon Glacier Deep Archive will most likely need to access their data only one to two times a year.

# S3 Lifecycle Management

If you have worked with traditional storage, you know that you can more effectively use it when you use tiered storage. Things that are accessed often are kept on the faster, more expensive storage, whereas things that aren't accessed as often can be saved onto the slower spinning disks.

S3 Lifecycle Management lets you follow a similar process in AWS. However, it is greatly simplified, and you have lots of options as far as which tiers you want data moved to and when. You can specify when you want your objects to be moved to lower-cost tiers and when you want your data to be marked expired. When an object is marked as expired, it is deleted by Amazon. In the example in Figure 10.3, I have set up a lifecycle policy that will transfer objects to S3 Standard-IA after 90 days, and then to Amazon Glacier after 180 days. These are completely customizable as far as which tier you want to transfer to and when you want to transfer.

**FIGURE 10.3**    A lifecycle rule allows you to define when and where you want objects to transition to.

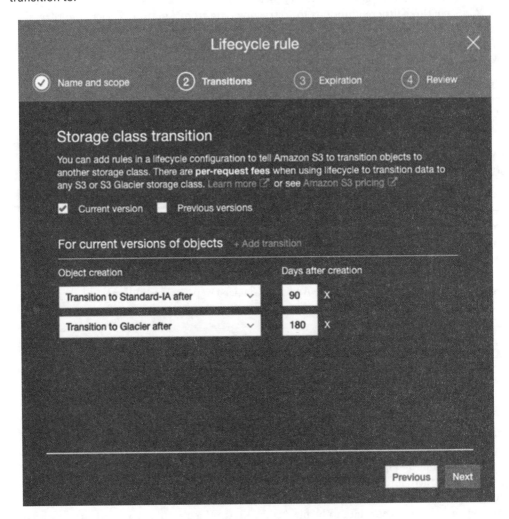

# Storage Gateways

For some organizations, cutting over to purely cloud storage may not be an acceptable solution. They may have concerns about cloud storage in general, or they may have concerns about performance issues. The storage gateway solutions offer a great way to begin using cloud-based storage in AWS with your on-premises resources.

Storage gateways are software appliances that you install in your on-premises datacenter. These appliances securely transfer your data to Amazon S3, Amazon Glacier, and Amazon EBS. You can connect using an array of protocols, including Network File System (NFS), Internet Small Computer Systems Interface (iSCSI), and Server Message Block (SMB). There are three types of storage gateways, each with its own use case:

**File Gateway**   Your files are stored in Amazon S3 as objects and are accessible via either NFS or SMB. You can take advantage of the features we have discussed within Amazon S3.

**Volume Gateway**   The volume gateway appears to your applications like normal block-level storage. Storage on a volume gateway is accessed via the iSCSI protocol. These volumes are backed up in the form of Amazon EBS snapshots. The volume gateway can be run in two different ways:

**Cached Mode**   Data is stored in S3, but frequently used data is cached locally on the appliance to improve performance.

**Stored Mode**   All data is stored locally, then replicated to Amazon S3.

**Tape Gateway**   Backup applications that require a tape backup device are presented with a virtual tape library when you use the tape gateway. Virtual tapes are stored in Amazon S3 and can be archived into Amazon Glacier.

# Summary

Amazon S3 is a regional service that provides high availability and durability for your data. It has robust security features, including access controls, versioning, and encryption. With Amazon S3, organizations can choose the tier that is the most cost effective for them. Amazon Glacier provides an affordable means to archive important data and can be used in conjunction with S3 lifecycle policies to automatically move older data into the archive. Storage gateways allow you to embrace a hybrid cloud storage model in which you have on-premises storage and cloud-based storage as well. The three types of storage gateways are file gateways, volume gateways, and tape gateways.

# Resources to Review

Getting Started with Amazon Simple Storage Service:

```
https://docs.aws.amazon.com/AmazonS3/latest/gsg/GetStartedWithS3.html
```

Amazon S3 Storage Classes:

    https://aws.amazon.com/s3/storage-classes/

Protecting Data Using Server-Side Encryption:

    https://docs.aws.amazon.com/AmazonS3/latest/dev/serv-side-encryption.html

Object Lifecycle Management:

    https://docs.aws.amazon.com/AmazonS3/latest/dev/object-lifecycle-mgmt.html

What Is AWS Storage Gateway?:

    https://docs.aws.amazon.com/storagegateway/latest/userguide/
    WhatIsStorageGateway.html

# Exam Essentials

**Know what a valid S3 endpoint address looks like.**   Valid S3 endpoint addresses look like this: `s3.<region_name>.amazonaws.com`, with the exception of the S3 endpoint in us-east-1, which is simply `s3.amazonaws.com`, and the two endpoints in China that end with the Chinese country code.

**Understand the different storage classes in S3.**   S3 Standard is great for frequently accessed data. Less frequently accessed data can be moved to another class such as S3 Standard-IA, S3 One Zone-IA, or Amazon Glacier, depending on availability and retrieval time requirements.

**Understand the use cases for Amazon Glacier.**   Amazon Glacier is for data archiving. It has three retrieval options offering faster, more expensive retrieval or slower, less expensive retrieval. Amazon Glacier Deep Archive is intended for long-term retention and has only one retrieval option.

**Know what a lifecycle policy is and how to use it.**   Lifecycle policies can be used to move objects between classes of storage based on age or can expire documents after a certain amount of time.

# Exercises

These exercises don't assume that anything exists outside of S3 for you to complete them. The entirety of these exercises occurs inside of Amazon S3.

**EXERCISE 10.1**

## Create an S3 Bucket

Creating an S3 bucket is one of the first things that you will most likely do in S3. In this exercise, you will create your first S3 bucket. This bucket will be used in the rest of the exercises.

1. On the AWS Management Console, select Services, then S3 under Storage.

2. Click the Create Bucket button.

3. Enter a name for your bucket; it has to be unique across all of S3. Click Next.

4. Leave the options blank for now and click Next.

5. Leave Block All Public Access checked and click Next.

6. Click Create Bucket.

When your bucket is created, your screen will look similar to Figure 10.4.

**FIGURE 10.4**   Buckets are displayed on the S3 dashboard once created.

**EXERCISE 10.2**

## Enable Default Encryption

In this exercise, you will enable S3-managed keys encryption on the bucket that you created earlier.

1. On the S3 Dashboard, click the bucket you created in Exercise 10.1.

2. Click the Properties tab, and then click the Default Encryption box.

3. Choose AES-256, and then click Save.

**EXERCISE 10.2** *(continued)*

Default encryption is now enabled with S3-managed keys (SSE-S3). The default encryption box should look like the image in Figure 10.5.

**FIGURE 10.5** Default encryption has been enabled with S3-managed keys.

# Default encryption

**Automatically encrypt objects when stored in Amazon S3**

Learn more

 **AES-256**

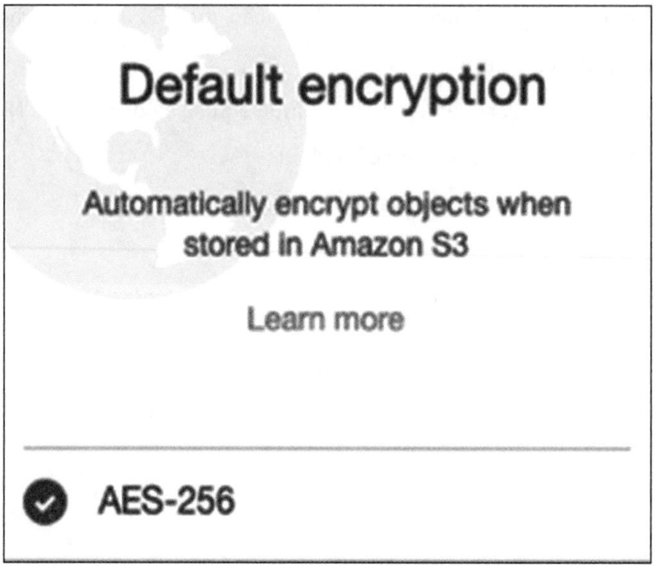

**EXERCISE 10.3**

## Enable Versioning

In this exercise, you will enable versioning on your S3 bucket.

1. On the S3 Dashboard, click the bucket you created in Exercise 10.1.

2. Click the Properties tab, and then click the Versioning box.

3. Choose Enable Versioning, and then click Save.

Versioning is now enabled for this S3 bucket. The Versioning box should look like the image in Figure 10.6.

**FIGURE 10.6**    Versioning has been enabled for our S3 bucket.

# Versioning

### Keep multiple versions of an object in the same bucket.

Learn more

 **Enabled**

---

**EXERCISE 10.4**

## Create and Apply a Bucket Policy

In this exercise, you will create a bucket policy that will require MFA when someone tries to access a folder in your S3 bucket.

1.  On the S3 Dashboard, click he bucket you created in Exercise 10.1.

2.  Click the Permissions tab, and then click the Bucket Policy box.

3.  Make note of the full ARN next to where it says Bucket Policy Editor. You may want to copy it to your clipboard by pressing Ctrl+C or, if you are on a Mac, Cmd+C.

4.  Scroll down to the bottom of the screen and click Policy Generator.

5.  From the Select Policy Type drop-down, select S3 Bucket Policy.

6.  In Add Statements, set the following:

    **Effect**: Deny

    **Principal**: *

**AWS Service:** Amazon S3

**Actions:** All Actions ('*')

**Amazon Resource Name (ARN):** <ARN value from step 3>

7. Click Add Conditions (Optional) and set the following:

   **Condition:** Null

   **Key:** AWS:MultiFactorAuthAge

   **Value:** true

8. Click Add Condition, then click Add Statement.

9. Click Generate Policy.

10. Copy the generated policy and click Close.

11. Go back to the Bucket Policy Editor screen and paste the generated policy.

12. Click Save.

You may not require the Policy Generator, but it is a very useful tool for those SysOps administrators who are just being introduced to policies, or those who are not familiar with JSON.

---

**EXERCISE 10.5**

## Create a Lifecycle Policy

In this exercise, you will create a lifecycle policy that will transition objects at 90 days to S3 Standard-IA, then to Glacier at 180 days, and finally expire them at 720 days.

1. On the S3 Dashboard, click the bucket you created in Exercise 10.1.

2. Click the Management tab; the Lifecycle tab will already be selected.

3. Click Add Lifecycle Rule.

4. Name the lifecycle rule **Age out old documents**, and click Next.

5. In the Storage class transition window, select the Current Version check box.

6. Click Add Transition.

7. In the Object Creation drop-down, select Transition To Standard-IA After.

8. Change Days After Creation to **90**.

9. Click Add Transition again.

10. From the drop-down box, select Transition To Glacier After.

11. Change Days After Creation to **180**, as shown in Figure 10.7.

**FIGURE 10.7** Creating the transition rules in the lifecycle rule allows S3 to move objects between S3 classes.

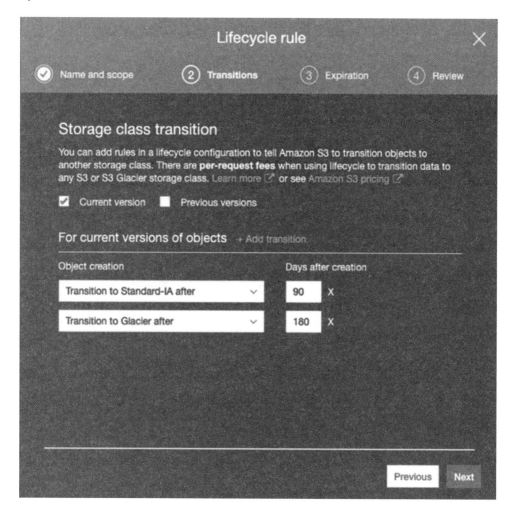

12. Click Next.

13. On the Configure Expiration screen, select the Current Version check box.

14. Expire Current Version Of Object will be checked; change the text field to **720** so that it reads After 720 Days From Object Creation.

15. Click Next.

16. Click Save.

# Review Questions

You can find the answers in the Appendix.

1. You are responsible for a team of engineers storing large documents in S3, often 10 GB or larger. The team has begun to receive the following error: "Your proposed upload exceeds the maximum allowed object size." What change should you make to resolve this issue?

   A. Use a different S3 bucket for additional uploads.

   B. Request a change to the maximum upload size by contacting AWS support.

   C. Switch to using S3-IA, which supports larger file uploads.

   D. Select the Multipart Upload option for all of the uploaded documents and ensure their code uses this API.

2. You have an S3 bucket named `compliance_docs` in the US East 2 region and created a folder at the root level of the bucket called `nist/`. You've turned on website hosting and asked your content team to upload documents to the `nist/` folder. At what URL will these documents be available through a web browser?

   A. `https://compliance_docs.s3-website-us-east-2.amazonaws.com/nist`

   B. `https://s3-website-us-east-2.amazonaws.com/compliance_docs/nist`

   C. `https://s3-us-east-2.amazonaws.com/compliance_docs/nist`

   D. `https://compliance_docs.s3-website.us-east-2.amazonaws.com/nist`

3. For which of the following HTTP methods does S3 have eventual consistency? (Choose two.)

   A. PUTs of new objects

   B. UPDATEs

   C. DELETEs

   D. PUTs that overwrite existing objects

4. What is the smallest file size that can be stored on standard class S3?

   A. 1 byte

   B. 1 MB

   C. 0 bytes

   D. 1 KB

5. You've just created a new S3 bucket named `rasterImages` in the US East 2 region. You need the URL of the bucket for some programmatic access. What is the correct bucket URL?

   A. `https://s3-us-east-2-rasterImages.amazonaws.com/`

   B. `https://s3-east-2.amazonaws.com/rasterImages`

   C. `https://s3-us-east-2.amazonaws.com/rasterImages`

   D. `https://amazonaws.s3-us-east-2.com/rasterImages`

6. You want to store your documentation in S3 and have it easily and quickly available. However, you also are concerned that some documents are not accessed except in bursts. When a document is accessed, it is usually accessed multiple times by the same team. Which S3 storage class would be a good option here?

   **A.** S3 Standard

   **B.** S3 Intelligent-Tiering

   **C.** S3 One Zone-IA

   **D.** Glacier

7. What availability does S3 Standard storage provide?

   **A.** 99.99 percent

   **B.** 99.9 percent

   **C.** 99.5 percent

   **D.** 99.999999999 percent

8. What durability does S3 Standard-IA storage provide?

   **A.** 99.99 percent

   **B.** 99.9 percent

   **C.** 99.5 percent

   **D.** 99.999999999 percent

9. What availability does S3 One Zone-IA storage provide?

   **A.** 99.99 percent

   **B.** 99.9 percent

   **C.** 99.5 percent

   **D.** 99.999999999 percent

10. If a document is stored in S3 Standard-IA, how many availability zones is that document replicated across?

    **A.** 1

    **B.** 2

    **C.** 3

    **D.** At least 3, but may be more

11. When a new S3 bucket is created, who can access that bucket without any additional permission changes?

    **A.** Only the bucket creator

    **B.** Any users with the S3AllBucket policy

    **C.** The bucket creator and all administrative users

    **D.** The bucket creator and anyone in the same IAM groups or roles as the bucket creator

12. Which of the following are valid ways to limit and control access to S3 resources? (Choose two.)

    A. IAM policies

    B. KMS

    C. Access keys

    D. Access control lists

13. Which of the following are valid ways to encrypt data on S3? (Choose two.)

    A. SSE-IAM

    B. SSE-S3

    C. SSE-KMS

    D. Amazon Client Encryption Toolkit

14. If you need to encrypt resources in S3 but require complete control of your keys, which option for encryption would you use?

    A. SSE-KMS

    B. Amazon S3 Encryption Client

    C. SSE-S3

    D. SSE-C

15. Which of the following are actual differences between Amazon Glacier and Amazon Glacier Deep Archive? (Choose two.)

    A. Amazon Glacier Deep Archive is less expensive than Amazon Glacier.

    B. Amazon Glacier Deep Archive is faster to retrieve files from than Amazon Glacier.

    C. Amazon Glacier Deep Archive has fewer access options than Amazon Glacier.

    D. Amazon Glacier Deep Archive is more expensive than Amazon Glacier.

16. Which of the following is a good reason to use S3 Intelligent-Tiering for an S3 bucket? (Choose two.)

    A. The bucket has data that is accessed only once a month.

    B. The bucket has unknown access patterns.

    C. The bucket has changing access patterns that are difficult to learn.

    D. The bucket has access patterns that change once each month.

17. Which of the following statements is true? (Choose two.)

    A. S3 Standard and S3 One Zone-IA have the same durability.

    B. S3 Standard-IA and S3 One Zone-IA have the same availability.

    C. S3 Standard and S3 One Zone-IA have the same availability.

    D. S3 Standard-IA has greater availability than S3 One Zone-IA.

**18.** In terms of performance, what does S3 Intelligent-Tiering most resemble?

   **A.** S3 Standard

   **B.** S3 Standard-IA

   **C.** S3 One Zone-IA

   **D.** Amazon Glacier

**19.** What is the availability of S3 Intelligent-Tiering?

   **A.** 99.99 percent

   **B.** 99.9 percent

   **C.** 99.5 percent

   **D.** 99 percent

**20.** Your organization has a large amount of compliance data stored in Amazon Glacier. For the next few weeks, your team needs to access this data frequently, but you do not want to move the data out of Glacier and then back in a month later. What should you do to speed up access to this data temporarily?

   **A.** Turn on S3 Lifecycle Management and set up a policy to move the data into S3 Standard and then back out again in a month.

   **B.** Select the Expedited option for data retrieval on Amazon Glacier.

   **C.** Select the Bulk option for data retrieval on Amazon Glacier.

   **D.** Set up a Lambda to pull all the data from Glacier and stage it on an EBS volume for the month.

# Chapter

# 11

# Elastic Block Store (EBS)

---

**THE AWS CERTIFIED SYSOPS ADMINISTRATOR – ASSOCIATE EXAM TOPICS COVERED IN THIS CHAPTER MAY INCLUDE, BUT ARE NOT LIMITED TO, THE FOLLOWING:**

**Domain 2.0: High Availability**

✓ 2.2   Recognize and differentiate highly available and resilient environments on AWS

**Domain 3.0: Deployment and Provisioning**

✓ 3.1   Identify and execute steps required to provision cloud resources

✓ 3.2   Identify and remediate deployment issues

**Domain 4.0: Storage and Data Management**

✓ 4.1   Create and manage data retention

✓ 4.2   Identify and implement data protection, encryption, and capacity planning needs

**Domain 7.0: Automation and Optimization**

✓ 7.2   Employ cost-optimization strategies for efficient resource utilization

Most SysOps administrators are familiar with working with the storage on their servers. Some have even worked with the traditional storage backends like network-attached storage and storage area networks and are well versed in administering block storage systems. If you have worked with block storage in the past, or if you haven't touched block storage at all, this chapter will serve as an introduction to block storage and will then dive into Amazon Elastic Block Storage (EBS).

This chapter includes:

Understanding what block storage is

Introducing Elastic Block Store (EBS)

Exploring the types of EBS storage

Understanding the differences between EBS and instance stores

Understanding how to secure your EBS volumes

Backing up your EBS volumes

# Understanding Block Storage and EBS

In Chapter 10: Simple Storage Service (S3) we discussed object storage and how it is an API-based storage solution. Block-based storage is not API driven, and unlike object storage, Amazon has no visibility into block storage volumes. Block storage is designed to be attached to a computer and gets its name from the fact that data is stored in blocks. Multiple blocks may be needed to store a file, and block storage systems are able to intelligently combine the blocks when a file is requested.

*Amazon Elastic Block Store (EBS)* is the AWS product offered for block storage. You can choose multiple types of volumes depending on the speed that you need and the cost that you want to maintain. Faster storage like the solid-state drive (SSD) storage is going to be more expensive than the spinning disk storage (hard disk drive [HDD]) in most cases, but that's what you will want for applications that need high-performance drives that support a large number of *input/output operations per second (IOPS)*. For applications that are not dependent on high IOPS but that do require a large amount of throughput, the HDD offerings are what you would want.

When you provision an EBS volume, you choose which volume type you want and what size you want to provision. You pay for the size of the drive that you provision. You can create EBS volumes independently of an Amazon EC2 instance and then attach the volume at a later time, or you can create EBS volumes when you create your Amazon EC2 instance. You can also detach a drive and attach it to a different Amazon EC2 instance. It's important to remember that an Amazon EBS volume can be attached to only one Amazon EC2 instance at a time.

> Amazon EBS volumes are used in many different AWS services. For the sake of clarity, the coverage in this chapter will focus on the use of EBS with EC2 instances. Remember that it can be used with other services.

Amazon EBS is considered persistent storage. Persistent storage is storage that can survive the termination of the Amazon EC2 instance that it is attached to. If the EBS volume is serving as the root partition on an EC2 instance, you need only ensure that the DeleteOnTermination flag is set to false. This setting can be modified using the AWS CLI. On a Linux system with an SSD identified as sda, you can set the flag to false by running the following command:

```
aws ec2 modify-instance-attribute --instance-id <instance_id_number>
--block-device-mappings "[{\"DeviceName\": \"/dev/sda\",
\"Ebs\":{\"DeleteOnTermination\":false}}]"
```

Interestingly, DeleteOnTermination is set to true by default on the root volume but to false on the other volumes. You will need to remember that when working with Amazon EBS.

## Types of EBS Storage

There are four volume types available for Amazon EBS as of this writing. Two of the volume types are SSD storage, and two are HDD storage. The SSD volume types can be used as boot volumes or data volumes. The HDD volume types can't be used as boot volumes; they can be used only as data volumes. The different types of EBS storage are detailed below in Table 11.1

**TABLE 11.1**  Amazon EBS volume types

| Name | Description | Use cases |
| --- | --- | --- |
| General-purpose SSD (gp2) | Good balance for performance and cost; supports up to 16,000 IOPS | Boot volumes<br>Most applications and systems will perform well with this type of volume. |
| Provisioned IOPS SSD (io1) | Best-performing SSD; supports up to 32,000 IOPS; 64,000 is possible on Nitro-based instances. | Any application that needs consistent IOPS above 16,000<br>Database workloads |

**TABLE 11.1**    Amazon EBS volume types *(continued)*

| Name | Description | Use cases |
| --- | --- | --- |
| Throughput-optimized HDD (st1) | Low-cost solution designed for applications that are throughput intensive; supports IOPS up to 500 | Data warehousing<br>Video/data streaming |
| Cold HDD (sc1) | Low-cost storage for infrequently accessed data; supports IOPS up to 250 | Lowest-cost storage is desirable |

The most recent version of this information can be found at https://docs.aws.amazon.com/AWSEC2/latest/UserGuide/EBSVolumeTypes.html.

## General-Purpose SSD (gp2)

A *general-purpose SSD* volume offers good performance and is cost effective for most applications. You can size general-purpose volumes to be anywhere between 1 GB to 16 TB, and these volumes can offer up to 16,000 IOPS (assuming they are at least 5.3 GB in size).

## Provisioned IOPS SSD (io1)

A *provisioned IOPS SSD* volume offers higher performance and is perfect for I/O-intensive applications and databases. Provisioned IOPS volumes can range in size from 4 GB to 16 TB, and they can support up to 32,000 IOPS in most cases. For Nitro-based instances, provisioned IOPS SSD volumes can reach 64,000 IOPS. There are specific Amazon EC2 instance types that are Nitro-based. For a full listing, check out this page: https://docs.aws.amazon.com/AWSEC2/latest/UserGuide/instance-types.html#ec2-nitro-instances.

> Nitro instances are built by AWS and are used to enable very high performance, availability and security.

## Throughput-Optimized HDD (st1)

While the focus of the SSD drives is on IOPS, the focus of the HDD drives is on throughput. *Throughput-optimized HDD* volumes are a low-cost form of magnetic storage that is great for workloads that are sequential in nature, like transactional jobs, log processing, and data warehousing. These drives are meant to be used for data that is accessed often. You can't use throughput-optimized HDD volumes as the boot volume for an Amazon EC2 instance.

## Cold HDD (sc1)

The *cold HDD* volume type is similar to the throughput-optimized HDD, but it is designed to store data that is not accessed very often. You can't use cold HDD volumes as the boot volume for an Amazon EC2 instance.

When you create your EBS volume, you will select which type of volume you want it to be as well as other important attributes like size, location, snapshot ID (if you're restoring from a snapshot), and whether or not you want to encrypt the volume. The options are shown in Figure 11.1.

**FIGURE 11.1**   You can choose the volume type when you create an EBS volume. The older magnetic type has been deprecated but is still visible as a choice.

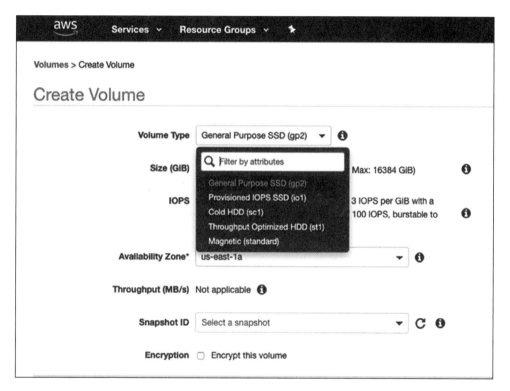

## EBS vs. Instance Stores

Amazon EBS isn't the only type of block storage that your instances can use. The *Amazon EC2 instance store* is also a form of block-level storage that is available to you. Instance stores do not persist when an instance has been stopped or terminated, and they can't be detached from one instance and then attached to a new instance. This is in contrast to Amazon EBS, which is persistent storage that can survive an instance being stopped or terminated; also, the storage can be detached from an instance and then reattached to another instance.

You might be wondering why you should use an Amazon EC2 instance store if it isn't a persistent means of storage. These types of drives are great for storing data that changes often. That might be a temporary drive or even a place for an application to cache data that it is using while the application is operational.

An Amazon Machine Image (AMI) created from an Amazon EC2 instance with an instance store will not contain any data on its instance store volume, even if there was data in the source Amazon EC2 instance.

# Encrypting Your EBS Volumes

Securing data at rest and in transit is important in today's environments. By choosing to *encrypt* your EBS volume, you are encrypting all of the data stored on the volume, the data moving between the instance and the volume (even if the source instance is not encrypted), any snapshots you might create to back up the volume, and of course any volumes you create from the encrypted snapshots.

If you want to ensure that all of your EBS volumes are encrypted, you can change the setting on your account. Doing so will ensure that all volumes are encrypted going forward. The setting does not encrypt existing EBS volumes, however. Also, it is a per-region setting, so if you have EBS volumes in more than one region, you need to update the setting for each region. Once this setting is updated, new EBS volumes will automatically be encrypted, and new snapshots will also be encrypted, even if the volume they are from is not encrypted.

There is no direct mechanism at this time to encrypt an existing EBS volume that is not encrypted, or to decrypt an EBS volume that is encrypted. You can use snapshots to encrypt a snapshot of an unencrypted volume as the snapshot is created. Using the encrypted snapshot, you can restore the EBS volume from the encrypted snapshot, which will ensure that the EBS volume is then encrypted as well.

To move data from an unencrypted volume to an encrypted volume, you can copy the data from the unencrypted volume to the encrypted volume. As an example, let's say you want to copy data from an unencrypted volume to an encrypted volume on an Amazon Linux instance. Using the AWS CLI, you can issue the rsync command to copy the information; here's an example:

```
sudo rsync -avh --progress /mnt/src /mnt/dst
```

If you want to move your data from an unencrypted volume to an encrypted volume, you can also use EBS snapshots to back up and restore the data. This topic is covered in more detail in the "EBS Snapshots" section a bit later in this chapter.

Amazon EBS uses a customer-managed key (CMK) for each EBS volume. It is created by AWS Key Management Service (KMS) automatically, or you can create it manually. Select Encrypt This Volume when creating an EBS volume, and you are given the option to choose the encryption key that you want to use, as shown in Figure 11.2.

**FIGURE 11.2**   When you choose to encrypt your EBS volume, you need to select the key you want it to encrypt the volume with.

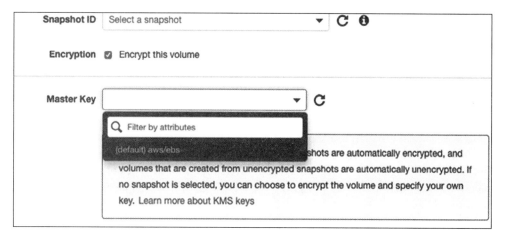

Once the EBS volume has been created, you can validate that it is encrypted by selecting the volume and checking the information pane. (Encrypted) will appear by the volume name, and if you look at the attributes, you will see that Encrypted appears next to Encryption and that the information for the KMS key you are using is populated, as shown in Figure 11.3.

**FIGURE 11.3**   You can validate that your volume is encrypted by selecting the volume and looking at the information pane.

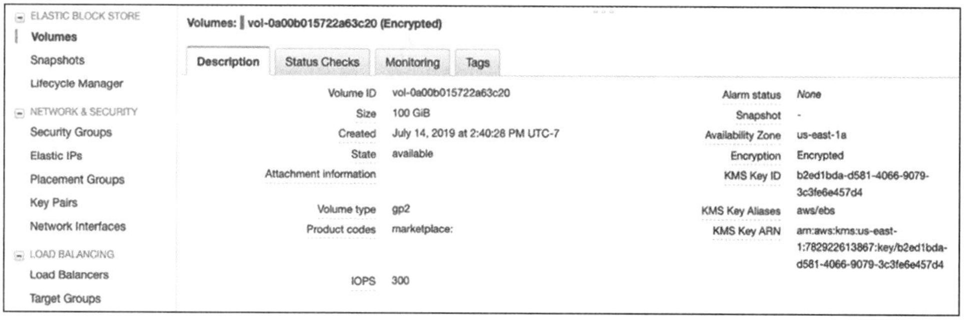

# EBS Snapshots

EBS snapshots are incremental point-in-time backups for an EBS volume. You can share snapshots across other AWS accounts, as long as they are within the same region.

The first snapshot done on an EBS volume is similar to a traditional full backup, and subsequent snapshots are incremental backups. If you are creating a snapshot from an encrypted volume, that snapshot will also be encrypted. If you create a snapshot from an unencrypted volume, the snapshot will also be unencrypted.

To convert an unencrypted snapshot to an encrypted snapshot, you can select Snapshots within the Elastic Block Store section of the EC2 Dashboard and select Actions ➢ Copy. A dialog box opens that offers you the option to encrypt the copy. Once the copy is encrypted, any volume restored from that encrypted copy will also be encrypted.

# Summary

Block storage stores data in blocks. Files may take up several blocks, and a block storage system knows how to reassemble the blocks properly to retrieve the file. Amazon EBS is the AWS solution for persistent block storage and offers four volume types to meet the needs of its customers: general-purpose SSD, provisioned IOPS SSD, throughput-optimized HDD, and cold HDD.

An instance store is also block storage, but it's designed to be nonpersistent. It is good for quickly changing or temporary data. Data on an instance store does not survive the stopping or termination of the Amazon EC2 instance to which it is attached.

Amazon EBS offers default encryption, which allows you to automatically encrypt EBS volumes when they are created. Unencrypted volumes can't be encrypted directly; you can copy a snapshot to encrypt it, and then use the encrypted snapshot to restore if you need the data to be secured.

# Resources to Review

Amazon EBS Volume Types:

    `https://docs.aws.amazon.com/AWSEC2/latest/UserGuide/EBSVolumeTypes.html`

Amazon EC2 Instance Store:

    `https://docs.aws.amazon.com/AWSEC2/latest/UserGuide/InstanceStorage.html`

Amazon EBS Encryption:

    `https://docs.aws.amazon.com/AWSEC2/latest/UserGuide/EBSEncryption.html`

Amazon EBS Snapshots:

    `https://docs.aws.amazon.com/AWSEC2/latest/UserGuide/EBSSnapshots.html`

# Exam Essentials

**Know the various EBS volume types and when to use them.** There are four types of EBS volume types you should know for the exam: general-purpose SSD, provisioned IOPS SSD, throughput-optimized HDD, and cold HDD. The general-purpose SSD is the most commonly recommended drive for the majority of applications, but the provisioned IOPS SSD drive is best for I/O-intensive applications. Throughput-optimized HDD is perfect for real-time data when throughput is more important than I/O, and cold HDD is similar to throughput-optimized HDD but is designed for less frequently accessed data.

**Know the difference in IOPS between the SSD EBS volumes.** General-purpose SSD can go up to 16,000 IOPS and provisioned IOPS SSD can go up to 32,000 (64,000 on Nitro-based instances) IOPS.

**Understand how to encrypt unencrypted EBS volumes.** Remember that you can't directly encrypt an EBS volume. You can copy a snapshot and encrypt it during the copy process. That encrypted snapshot can be used to restore to an unencrypted volume, which will encrypt the volume once the snapshot is complete.

# Exercises

It is assumed for these exercises that you have an Amazon EC2 instance available to attach the EBS volume to once it has been created. The instructions will walk you through how to attach the EBS volume but not how to create an Amazon EC2 instance.

### EXERCISE 11.1

### Create an Unencrypted EBS Volume

This exercise walks you through creating an unencrypted volume. Although it would be desirable to create only encrypted volumes, chances are that you will run into unencrypted volumes and will be asked to encrypt them.

1. Log into the AWS Management Console.

2. Click Services, and then select EC2 under Compute.

3. In the EC2 Dashboard, select Volumes under Elastic Block Store.

4. Click Create Volume.

5. Accept the defaults and click Create Volume.

6. Click Close.

You may need to click the refresh icon to get your EBS volume to show up. Once your EBS volume has been created and is available under State, proceed to Exercise 11.2.

**EXERCISE 11.2**

## Use a Snapshot to Encrypt EBS Volumes

This exercise walks you through creating a snapshot on the unencrypted volume. You will then copy that snapshot to an encrypted snapshot. From there you will create a new encrypted volume. In a production environment, it is likely that the EBS volume would be attached to an EC2 instance. You would want to power down the instance and detach the EBS volume before following these steps.

1.  In the area where you created the volume in Exercise 11.1, select the volume.

2.  Click Actions ➢ Create A Snapshot.

3.  For Description, enter **unencrypted snapshot**.

4.  Click the Create Snapshot button.

5.  Click Close once the snapshot is created.

6.  In the EC2 Dashboard, click Snapshots under Elastic Block Store.

7.  Select the snapshot that is now listed with the description Unencrypted Snapshot.

8.  Click Actions ➢ Copy.

9.  For Description, enter **encrypted snapshot**, and then select the Encryption check box, as shown in Figure 11.4.

**FIGURE 11.4**    Encrypting a snapshot enables you to create an encrypted EBS volume.

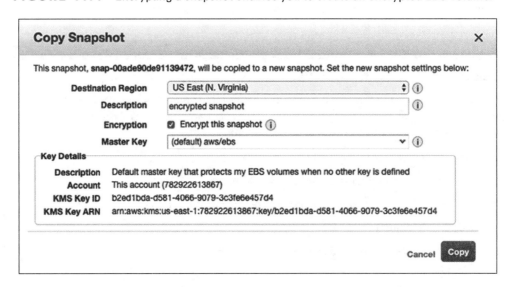

10. Click Copy, and then click Close.

11. Select the snapshot that has Encrypted Snapshot in its description.

**12.** Click Actions ➢ Create Volume.

**13.** Accept the defaults and click Create Volume.

**14.** Click Close.

It is worth noting that you can in fact create an encrypted volume using the unencrypted snapshot. If you select the unencrypted snapshot and choose Create Volume from the Actions menu, you will have the option to encrypt the volume at that time. I prefer the method in the procedure as it ensures that the source snapshot is encrypted. I can delete the unencrypted one once I confirm that the encrypted snapshot is good.

---

### EXERCISE 11.3

### Attach the Encrypted EBS Volume to an Amazon EC2 Instance

Now that we have an encrypted EBS volume, we will attach it to an existing EC2 instance.

**1.** Select Volumes from the EC2 Dashboard.

**2.** Select the newly encrypted volume

**3.** Click Actions ➢ Attach Volume.

**4.** Click in the Instance field and select your EC2 instance from the drop-down list.

**5.** Click Attach.

The instance ID and the drive mapping will now show up in the volume attributes under Attachment Information, and the drive will be available for use with your instance.

---

### EXERCISE 11.4

### Turn On Default EBS Encryption for Your Account

For the last exercise of this chapter, let's look at how to turn on default encryption for all EBS volumes.

**1.** Click where it says EC2 Dashboard.

**2.** Under the Account Attributes section to the right, click Settings.

**3.** Select the Always Encrypt New EBS Volumes check box, and then click Save Settings.

**4.** Click Close.

Remember this only makes this change for the region that you are in, you will need to change this setting for each region that you have EBS storage in.

# Review Questions

You can find the answers in the Appendix.

1.  What does IOPS stand for?
    A.  Input operations per second
    B.  Input/output operations per second
    C.  Input and output per second
    D.  Input/output overhead per second

2.  Which EBS volume type has the highest maximum IOPS?
    A.  General-purpose SSD
    B.  Provisioned IOPS SSD
    C.  Throughput-optimized HDD
    D.  Cold HDD

3.  Which EBS volume type supports the largest volume size?
    A.  General-purpose SSD
    B.  Provisioned IOPS SSD
    C.  Throughput-optimized HDD
    D.  All volume types support the same maximum volume size.

4.  Which EBS volume type is best suited for a system boot volume?
    A.  General-purpose SSD
    B.  Provisioned IOPS SSD
    C.  Throughput-optimized HDD
    D.  Cold HDD

5.  Which EBS volume type is well suited for data warehousing?
    A.  General-purpose SSD
    B.  Provisioned IOPS SSD
    C.  Throughput-optimized HDD
    D.  Cold HDD

6.  Which EBS volume type is well suited for large database workloads?
    A.  General-purpose SSD
    B.  Provisioned IOPS SSD
    C.  Throughput-optimized HDD
    D.  Cold HDD

**7.** Which of the following EBS volume types cannot be boot volumes? (Choose two.)

   **A.** General-purpose SSD

   **B.** Provisioned IOPS SSD

   **C.** Throughput-optimized HDD

   **D.** Cold HDD

**8.** If you create an EBS volume type using the console, what type will that volume be by default?

   **A.** General-purpose SSD

   **B.** Provisioned IOPS SSD

   **C.** Throughput-optimized HDD

   **D.** Cold HDD

**9.** You want to create a lot of EBS volumes and are not concerned about performance, but you're very concerned about cost. These volumes will need to be bootable. What is your best option?

   **A.** General-purpose SSD

   **B.** Provisioned IOPS SSD

   **C.** Throughput-optimized HDD

   **D.** Cold HDD

**10.** If you create an EBS volume type using the console, what type will that volume be by default?

   **A.** General-purpose SSD

   **B.** Provisioned IOPS SSD

   **C.** Throughput-optimized HDD

   **D.** Cold HDD

**11.** Which of the following are true about EBS snapshots? (Choose two.)

   **A.** They are incremental.

   **B.** They are stored on S3.

   **C.** They are available through the S3 API.

   **D.** EBS volumes are unmounted before snapshots are taken.

**12.** You create a new snapshot from an encrypted EBS volume. What will the result be?

   **A.** An unencrypted snapshot of the encrypted volume

   **B.** An encrypted snapshot of the encrypted volume

   **C.** You will be able to create the snapshot only if you have the encryption keys to the original volume.

   **D.** You cannot create a snapshot from an encrypted volume.

**13.** How do you create an encrypted snapshot from an unencrypted snapshot?

  **A.** Encrypt the unencrypted snapshot using the AWS Client Encryption tool.

  **B.** Create a snapshot of the original volume and encrypt that snapshot after it completes.

  **C.** Make a copy of the unencrypted snapshot and select the option to encrypt the copy.

  **D.** You cannot encrypt an unencrypted snapshot once it has been taken.

**14.** You are consistently finding that EBS snapshots of your volumes do not contain all of the data that you are seeing reflected in applications that connect to those volumes. What could be the issue?

  **A.** You should make sure your EBS volumes are unmounted before taking snapshots.

  **B.** You should make sure that you stop any EC2 instances connected to your EBS volumes before taking snapshots.

  **C.** Your application may be caching content and not writing it to the EBS volume at the time of the snapshot.

  **D.** Your application may have written the data to the volume but the snapshot captures only data that has been on the volume for 60 seconds prior to snapshot.

**15.** What type of encryption key is applied to encrypted EBS snapshots?

  **A.** A unique 128-bit AES key

  **B.** A unique 256-bit AES key

  **C.** A unique 512-bit AES key

  **D.** A shared key is used for encryption, but that key is 256-bit AES.

**16.** You want to launch a new instance from an unencrypted snapshot, but you want the launched instance to be encrypted. How do you accomplish this? (Choose two.)

  **A.** You can select encryption of the instance during creation, regardless of the encryption status of the snapshot.

  **B.** You need to create the instance unencrypted and then encrypt it using the AWS Instance Encryption tool.

  **C.** You need to encrypt the snapshot and then launch the instance from the encrypted snapshot.

  **D.** You can't. You need to launch an encrypted instance from an encrypted snapshot.

**17.** What happens to the data on an EBS volume when the instance it is mounted to terminates?

  **A.** If the EBS volume persists, the data on it will also persist.

  **B.** All data on the EBS volume is deleted when the instance is terminated.

  **C.** If the EBS volume is a boot drive, all data on it is deleted when the instance is terminated.

  **D.** Data is persisted on the EBS volume if Persist Data is checked when the volume is attached to the instance.

**18.** What do you need to do to a root EBS volume if you want it to persist beyond the life of the EC2 instance booting from it?

   **A.** Set the Persist Data flag on the volume to Yes.

   **B.** Set the Live Past Instance flag on the volume to Yes.

   **C.** Set the Delete Data flag on the volume to No.

   **D.** Set the Delete on Termination flag on the volume to No.

**19.** Which of the following allows you to change the capacity and performance of an in-use EBS volume?

   **A.** Change the volume type using the AWS Console.

   **B.** Change the volume type using the AWS CLI.

   **C.** Change the volume type using the AWS API.

   **D.** All of these

**20.** It takes AWS about 3 minutes to snapshot your EBS volumes with approximately 2 TB of data on them. How long would you expect it to take to snapshot of 16 TB of data, given that the data is of the same type, on average?

   **A.** 24 minutes

   **B.** 5 minutes

   **C.** 3 minutes

   **D.** It is impossible to know given the information in the question.

# Chapter

# 12

# Amazon Machine Image (AMI)

---

**THE AWS CERTIFIED SYSOPS ADMINISTRATOR – ASSOCIATE EXAM TOPICS COVERED IN THIS CHAPTER MAY INCLUDE, BUT ARE NOT LIMITED TO, THE FOLLOWING:**

Domain 2.0: High Availability

✓ 2.1 Implement scalability and elasticity based on use case

✓ 2.2 Recognize and differentiate highly available and resilient environments on AWS

Domain 3.0: Deployment and Provisioning

✓ 3.1 Identify and execute steps required to provision cloud resources

✓ 3.2 Identify and remediate deployment issues

Domain 4.0: Storage and Data Management

✓ 4.2 Identify and implement data protection, encryption, and capacity planning needs

Domain 5.0: Security and Compliance

✓ 5.2 Implement access controls when using AWS

Domain 7.0: Automation and Optimization

✓ 7.3 Automate manual or repeatable process to minimize management overhead

It's been a standard practice in many organizations to define a gold image. This gold image is used to create servers and workstations and to ensure that they are built to an organization's requirements.

Images will typically include a patched operating system and the basic applications that are defined by the organization as standard applications. This may include things like monitoring agents and antivirus software.

In this chapter, we will discuss AWS images, referred to as Amazon Machine Images (AMIs). You will learn what they are and how to use them.

This chapter includes:

An introduction to AMIs

Differences between public and private AMIs

What you can find on the AWS Marketplace

Configuring storage types for AMIs

Defining launch permissions for AMIs

Configuring encryption on your AMIs

Moving AMIs between regions

Troubleshooting issues with AMIs

# Amazon Machine Images (AMIs)

As I mentioned in the introduction, AWS uses *Amazon Machine Images (AMIs)* as an image to build an instance from. The AMI, unlike a traditional image, is more of a template for what to build than simply a copy of something already built. It contains a template (if instance stores are used) or an EBS snapshot (if EBS volumes are used) for the root volume. The template typically contains the operating system and possibly applications, as well as the volumes that need to be attached to the instance and the launch permissions that define who can use the AMI. Launch permissions are explained later in this chapter.

AMIs are created and made available to you in one of four ways. They are created by AWS or by a third party, and then placed on the AWS Marketplace; created by another user and then made available in the AWS Community; or they are made by you from an existing Amazon EC2 instance. When you use an AMI, you specify the instance type and size, network settings, storage, and the key pair to use to gain access to the instance. The AMI already contains the other necessary information, including the template for how to build the instance, such as the launch permissions that need to be set and the block device mappings for any additional storage that the instance will need.

## Accessibility of AMIs

Being able to access AMIs is the starting point for any SysOps administrator building systems in AWS. After all, to build an Amazon EC2 instance you will most likely use one of the AMIs provided to you by AWS to get started.

### Public

A *public AMI* is one that is available to all AWS accounts. You should keep a few caveats in mind. AMIs are specific to the region that they are in. The AMI ID will change between regions, even though it is the same AMI. So if you have a CloudFormation template that is using an AMI ID in US-East-1, for instance, and you want the template to also be usable in US-West-1, you will need to ensure that the template has AMI IDs for that AMI from each region. Additionally, if an AMI contains an encrypted volume, it can't be made public. After all, the other companies or individuals using the AMI won't have access to your encryption keys.

### Shared

A *shared AMI* is one that has been made available to you and your organization by someone else. This is different from a public AMI in that you must be granted permissions to launch the AMI by its owner—it is not open to all AWS accounts. It has the same limitation when it comes to sharing across regions. The AMI ID will vary depending on the region in which you are building your systems.

### Private

AMIs that you generate are considered private. They are available only within your account unless you change the launch permissions on the AMI. *Private AMIs* are great for when you want to create a base image for your company's systems that includes all of the patches and third-party applications that the various teams within your company require.

### AWS Marketplace

The AWS Marketplace opens up a whole world of AMIs—everything from purpose-built servers to network appliances built by some of the biggest names out there. You can see a selection of the AMIs available in the AWS Marketplace in Figure 12.1.

**FIGURE 12.1**  There is a wide selection of AMIs on the AWS Marketplace.

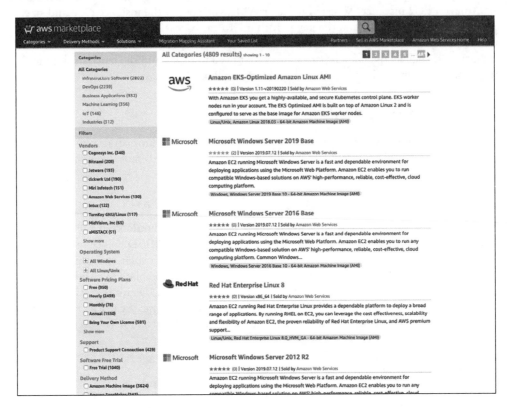

One of the things that I love about the AWS Marketplace is that it allows you to find what you are looking for quickly with a robust set of premade filters and a search box in case you either know exactly what you want or are having difficulty finding it. For instance, if you need an AMI that is free (meaning in this case that there are no additional charges above what the instance will cost) and is running CentOS 7, you can select free under Software Pricing Plans and then CentOS under Operation System ➢ All Linux/Unix.

Some of the items in the AWS Marketplace have a subscription fee that you will need to account for. This is common with the AMIs that are providing a service with frequent security updates. If you click an AMI, you can get more information regarding that AMI, including cost. For instance, Figure 12.2 shows an AWS Marketplace offering for an F5 BIG-IP appliance. It tells you which bundle comes with which features and offers insights into pricing so that you can have an idea how much you will need to pay to use the service.

**FIGURE 12.2**    When you click the name of an AMI in the AWS Marketplace, you can get more information about the AMI.

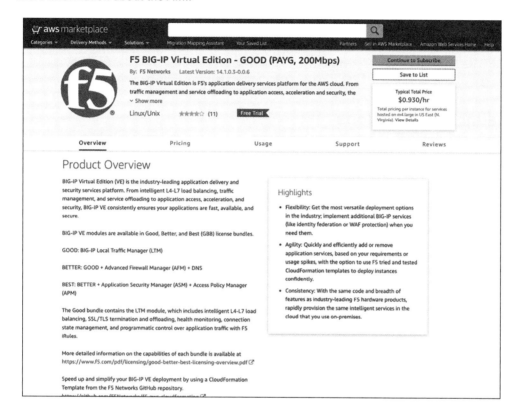

# AMI Storage

AMIs on AWS are said to be either instance-backed or EBS-backed. The option you choose will depend on your use case and may differ from AMI to AMI.

*Instance-backed AMIs* are perfect for short-lived workloads because the storage is destroyed when the instance is terminated. So for applications that are taking advantage of containers, short-lived instances like auto-scaled instances or spot instances, instance-backed storage may be a perfect fit.

*EBS-backed AMIs* are a great solution for when you need to ensure that data can persist even once an Amazon EC2 instance is terminated. While the root volume by default will be deleted when an instance is terminated, this behavior can be avoided by setting the DeleteOnTermination flag to false.

# AMI Security

Ensuring that your AMI is secure means that you need to understand how a few things work. Launch permissions allow you to define who can use your AMI. AMIs that are EBS-backed can have encryption applied, which ensures that systems deployed from the AMI always have encrypted volumes as well. Let's explore each of these topics a little more in depth.

## Launch Permissions

AWS provides three types of *launch permissions* that you can use for your AMIs: public, explicit, and implicit.

Public is the most permissive as it allows any AWS account to use the AMI. The public launch permission is typically used by AMIs that are in the AWS Marketplace or that are shared by the AWS Community.

Explicit allows you to identify a few AWS accounts that can have access to the AMI. This is useful for organizations that have different accounts for different departments or environments (Development, Test, Production) as it allows for the use of the same approved AMI across all the organization's AWS accounts. This type of launch permission is used for shared AMIs.

The implicit launch permission grants the owner of the AMI permissions to use the AMI. This means that if you create an AMI, you have permissions to it since you created it.

## Encryption

If you are using an EBS-backed AMI, you can also ensure that encryption is set using the AMI. Remember that you can't set an AMI's launch permissions to public if you have enabled encryption for the EBS volumes. You might be wondering why you would want to set encryption on an EBS volume through an AMI. The simple answer is that you can't directly encrypt an EBS volume after it has been created. So if you create encrypted EBS volumes and attach them to an Amazon EC2 instance, and then create an AMI from that instance, your custom AMI will use encrypted EBS snapshots to accommodate the encrypted EBS volumes, and they will use whichever key you specified at the time that you created the custom AMI.

If you are using an EBS-backed AMI that is not encrypted, all is not lost! You can specify encryption of the EBS volumes when you launch an Amazon EC2 instance from the AMI.

# Moving AMIs Between Regions

So you've created an awesome AMI in US-East-1, but you need to use it in US-West-1 as well. You could build another AMI from scratch; however, the simplest solution is to copy your AMI to another region.

## AWS Management Console

Copying an AMI from the AWS Management Console is the simplest method for most SysOps administrators who are learning AWS. You can access the list of AMIs by entering the EC2 Dashboard and then choosing AMIs under Images.

From the AMI screen, you can perform the majority of AMI management tasks, including copying an AMI to another region. The default setting is Owned By Me, but you can switch that to Public Images if you want to launch directly from the AMI, as shown in Figure 12.3.

**FIGURE 12.3** You can browse the available Public AMIs from within the Amazon EC2 Dashboard.

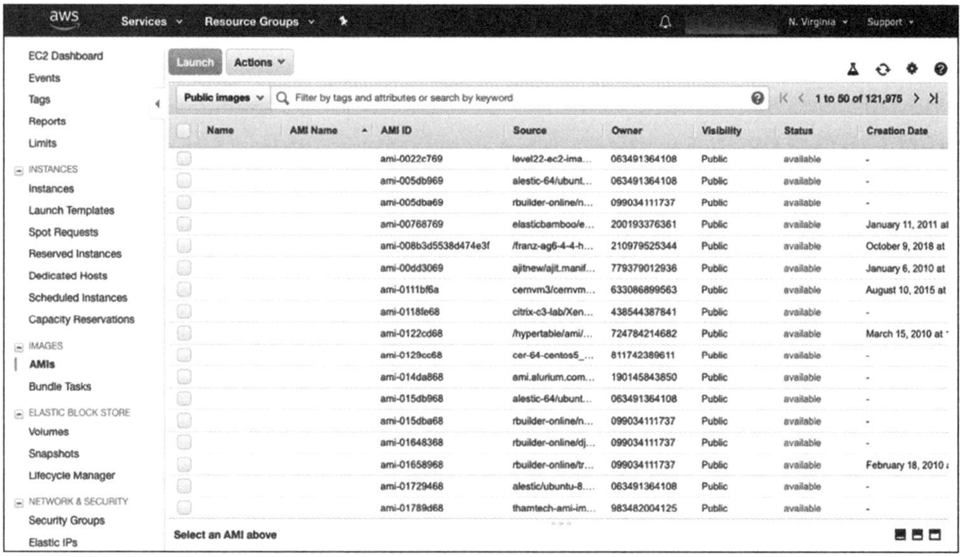

## AWS CLI

If you prefer to use the AWS CLI to perform your administrative tasks, you can use it to copy an AMI to another region with the copy-image command.

For instance, if you want to copy an AMI from US-East-1 to US-West-1, you would use a command similar to the following:

```
aws ec2 copy-image --source-image-id ami-1234567a --source-region us-east-1
--region us-west-1 --name "MyAwesomeAMI"
```

After you run the command, you will get the new AMI ID for the AMI that has been copied to US-West-1. You can then add this AMI ID to any CloudFormation templates or scripts that you might be using.

# Common AMI Issues

When you use Amazon CloudFront, you can set the AMI ID as a resource that can be used within the template. One of the most common issues is when a template is referencing the wrong AMI ID for a region. Remember that AMIs are region specific, so you will need to copy or re-create the AMI in all regions where you want to use it. You can specify within the Amazon CloudFront template to use a particular AMI ID based on the region that you have selected.

The other common issue is when an AMI has been deleted but you have scripts, templates, or Auto Scaling groups that depend on that AMI. With Auto Scaling, for example, you will receive an error similar to "The AMI ID *actual AMI ID* does not exist. Launch EC2 instance failed." It's important to ensure that any automation processes that exist have been updated to a new version of the AMI before the old version is deleted.

# Summary

An Amazon Machine Image (AMI) is a template that contains instructions on how to build the root volume of an Amazon EC2 instance, including the launch permissions and the block device mappings. AMIs are specific to the region in which they are created. They can be copied to another region and will be assigned a new ID in the destination region once copied.

AMIs can be instance-backed or EBS-backed, and the EBS-backed AMIs offer support for encryption. AMIs with encrypted volumes may not be copied to other regions.

You can use either the AWS Management Console or the AWS CLI to copy an AMI from one region to another. Copying can be done in the AMI section of the EC2 Dashboard if using the AWS Management Console or with the copy-image command within the AWS CLI.

# Resources to Review

Amazon Machine Images:

https://docs.aws.amazon.com/AWSEC2/latest/UserGuide/AMIs.html

Creating an Instance Store-Backed Linux AMI:

https://docs.aws.amazon.com/AWSEC2/latest/UserGuide/
creating-an-ami-instance-store.html

Creating an Amazon EBS-Backed Linux AMI:

https://docs.aws.amazon.com/AWSEC2/latest/UserGuide/creating-an-ami-ebs.html

Using Encryption with EBS-Backed AMIs:

https://docs.aws.amazon.com/AWSEC2/latest/UserGuide/AMIEncryption.html

Copying an AMI:

https://docs.aws.amazon.com/AWSEC2/latest/UserGuide/CopyingAMIs.html

Creating a Custom Windows AMI:

https://docs.aws.amazon.com/AWSEC2/latest/WindowsGuide/
Creating_EBSbacked_WinAMI.html

# Exam Essentials

**Understand what an AMI is and what it is not.**   An AMI is a template used to build a system; it is not an image in the traditional sense. The template may contain a snapshot to build the root volume, launch permissions for the AMI, and block device mappings.

**Be familiar with the types of AMIs.**   Remember that an AMI can be public, shared, or private. Public AMIs are available to all AWS accounts, shared AMIs are available to some AWS accounts, and private AMIs are available to the owner of the AMI, in the owner's AWS account.

**Know how to secure AMIs.**   Understand the different launch permissions: public, explicit, and implicit. Public allows the AMI to be accessed by any AWS account; this is typical of AWS Marketplace AMIs and AWS Community AMIs. Explicit launch permissions allow AWS accounts that have specifically been granted permissions to use the AMI. Implicit launch permissions allow AMI owners to use their AMI.

# Exercises

These exercises assume that you have basic networking functionality set up in your AWS environment.

### EXERCISE 12.1

### Create an EC2 Instance from an AMI

We will start these exercises by creating an EC2 instance from one of the Community AMIs.

1. Log on to the AWS Management Console.

2. Under Compute, choose EC2.

3. On the EC2 Dashboard, choose Instances under Instances.

4. Click the blue Launch Instance button.

5. In Step 1: Choose An Amazon Machine Image (AMI), select Community AMIs.

6. Click the Select button next to the Amazon Linux 2 AMI that is toward the top of the list.

**EXERCISE 12.1 *(continued)***

7.  For Instance Type, choose t2.micro and click Next: Configure Instance Details.

8.  In Step 3, accept the defaults and choose Next: Add Storage.

9.  In Step 4, accept the default and select Review And Launch.

10. Click the blue Launch button.

11. In the dialog box for choosing your key pair, select the appropriate key pair, select the check box to acknowledge that you have access to the private key file, and then click Launch Instances.

12. Click View Instances.

As you can see, creating an EC2 instance from an AMI can be simple. There are multiple ways to customize the EC2 instance that we did not touch in this exercise as that topic is out of scope for the purposes of these exercises.

**EXERCISE 12.2**

### Create a Custom AMI

In this exercise, let's assume that you have logged into this EC2 instance and have installed some software and made configuration changes. Now you want to create a custom AMI.

1.  In the EC2 Dashboard, select Instances.

2.  Select the check box next to the instance that you created in Exercise 12.1.

3.  Click Actions ➢ Image ➢ Create Image, as shown in Figure 12.4.

**FIGURE 12.4**   Creating an AMI from an existing EC2 instance is a common practice for an AWS system administrator.

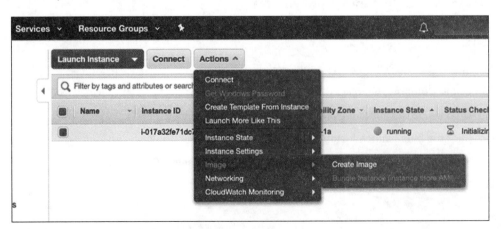

4.  In the Create Image dialog box, fill in the image name. I will call mine **MyAwesomeAMI**.

5.  Click Create Image.

6.  Click Close.

7.  From the EC2 Dashboard menu, choose AMIs under Images. Once the AMI has a status of Available, move on to Exercise 12.3.

---

**EXERCISE 12.3**

### Change the Launch Permissions of the AMI

Now we will change the launch permissions of the AMI to Public. You will notice when you first open the Modify Image Permissions dialog that it is set to Private. If you wanted to make it Shared, you would add an AWS account number in the field.

1.  From the EC2 Dashboard, select AMIs under Images.

2.  Select the check box next to the AMI you created in Exercise 12.2.

3.  Click Actions ➤ Modify Image Permissions.

4.  Click Public, and then click Save.

5.  Click the refresh icon, and notice that Visibility is now set to Public, as shown in Figure 12.5.

**FIGURE 12.5**    A publicly available AMI will show Public under Visibility.

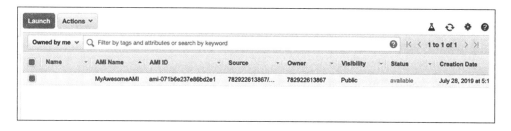

# Review Questions

You can find the answers in the Appendix.

1. Which of the following is not an AMI accessibility level?
   A. Public
   B. Private
   C. Protected
   D. Shared

2. You have created a custom AMI and launched a number of instances into the US-West-1 region. Recently, you've been instructed to re-create the entire environment in US-East-2 for redundancy. What steps are required to use this AMI in US-East-2?
   A. None; AMIs are available to all regions as long as the same account is used.
   B. Ensure that the AMI is set to the Shared accessibility and it will be usable in US-East-2.
   C. Copy the AMI to US-East-2 and then it will be available in that region.
   D. AMIs cannot be used in multiple regions. You will need to create a new AMI in US-East-2.

3. Which of the following are valid ways to obtain an AMI? (Choose two.)
   A. Create one yourself from an existing EC2 instance.
   B. Obtain one from the Global AMI Marketplace.
   C. Obtain one from the AWS Marketplace.
   D. Obtain one from a third-party vendor's GitHub repository.

4. Which of the following are storage options to back an AMI? (Choose two.)
   A. Instance-backed AMI
   B. Volume-backed AMI
   C. EMS-backed AMI
   D. EBS-backed AMI

5. Who can grant permissions for the use of a shared AMI?
   A. The AMI owner
   B. Anyone who already has permissions to use the AMI
   C. Anyone with the `AmiAdmin` policy attached to an IAM user, group, or role
   D. Anyone within an IAM group who has the `AmiDistributor` permission

**6.** You have created a private AMI in your own AWS account. You have a coworker who wants to use the same AMI in their own development account. How can you allow this? (Choose two.)

   **A.** Grant permissions to the coworker to use the AMI.

   **B.** Convert the AMI to a shared AMI.

   **C.** Add the coworker to a group with the `AmiDistributor` permission.

   **D.** Set the permissions on the AMI to include the account that the coworker is using.

**7.** You are responsible for setting up a new Auto Scaling group with a number of instances and want to choose the correct type of AMI storage. Which AMI storage is most appropriate for an Auto Scaling group, given that you expect the group to be quite volatile in terms of scaling in and scaling out?

   **A.** Instance-backed AMIs

   **B.** EBS-backed AMIs

   **C.** Transient-backed AMIs

   **D.** The storage used by an AMI is unrelated to the use of Auto Scaling groups, so any storage would be fine.

**8.** Which of the following use cases would not be a good fit for an EBS-backed AMI instance?

   **A.** A database server running SQL Server

   **B.** Container-based applications

   **C.** An application that typically runs 24/7 for weeks at a time

   **D.** An instance dedicated to long-term data storage

**9.** Who is billed when an AMI you create and share is launched within another user's account?

   **A.** You are billed, as well as the owner of the account in which the AMI is launched.

   **B.** Only you are billed, as you are the AMI owner.

   **C.** Only the owner of the account in which the AMI is launched is billed.

   **D.** Anyone who is using the AMI is billed.

**10.** What happens when you copy an AMI to a new region? (Choose two.)

   **A.** The source API is available for immediate usage as is in the new region.

   **B.** An identical but distinct AMI is created in the new region.

   **C.** A new AMI is created with the same identifier as the source AMI.

   **D.** A new unique identifier is assigned to the new AMI.

**11.** How can a deregistered AMI be used to start a new instance?

    **A.** You can start an instance from a deregistered AMI just as you would from a registered AMI.

    **B.** You have to re-register the AMI and then start the instance.

    **C.** You have to choose the Available For Launch option from the AWS Console on the deregistered AMI.

    **D.** It cannot.

**12.** What options do you have for encrypting an EBS-backed AMI? (Choose two.)

    **A.** By using a KMS customer master key

    **B.** By using an SSE customer-provided master key

    **C.** By using a customer managed key

    **D.** You cannot encrypt an EBS-backed AMI.

**13.** What action would you use to launch an EC2 instance from an AMI?

    **A.** The LaunchInstances action

    **B.** The RunInstances action

    **C.** The RunAMI action

    **D.** The LaunchAMI action

**14.** By default, what encryption state is used when the RunInstances action is executed?

    **A.** The resulting instance is encrypted.

    **B.** The resulting instance is unencrypted.

    **C.** The resulting instance maintains the encryption state of the AMI's source snapshot.

    **D.** The resulting instance uses the encryption set as default in the AWS console.

**15.** How can you ensure that an instance launched from an AMI based on an unencrypted snapshot is encrypted at all times? (Choose two.)

    **A.** Set the Encryption By Default setting to True.

    **B.** Supply an encryption parameter to encrypt when using the RunInstances action.

    **C.** Encrypt the instance after creation.

    **D.** Use a different AMI.

**16.** How can you recognize an Amazon public image, as compared to non-Amazon images?

    **A.** Amazon images have a header of amazon-.

    **B.** Amazon images have an aliased owner, which will appear as amazon in the account field.

    **C.** Amazon images have names beginning with amazon-.

    **D.** You cannot reliably determine if an image is from Amazon.

**17.** What do you need to do to share an AMI with specific AWS accounts?

    **A.** Make the AMI public.

    **B.** Add the AWS account IDs to the AMI's permissions.

    **C.** Add the AWS account owner IAM usernames to the AMI's permissions.

    **D.** Add the AWS IAM permission `shared` to the AMI's permissions.

**18.** Within how many accounts can an AMI be used?

    **A.** 5

    **B.** 25

    **C.** 100 by default, but this limit can be raised upon request.

    **D.** Unlimited

**19.** Which of the following are included when you copy a source AMI to a new region?

    **A.** Launch permissions

    **B.** User-defined tags

    **C.** Amazon S3 bucket permissions

    **D.** None of these

**20.** You create a new AMI, and then copy it into a new account owned by your coworker. Who is the owner of the copied AMI?

    **A.** You are.

    **B.** Your coworker is.

    **C.** You and your coworker have joint ownership of the AMI.

    **D.** There is not enough information to answer.

# Security and Compliance

# Chapter

# 13

# IAM

**THE AWS CERTIFIED SYSOPS ADMINISTRATOR – ASSOCIATE EXAM TOPICS COVERED IN THIS CHAPTER MAY INCLUDE, BUT ARE NOT LIMITED TO, THE FOLLOWING:**

**Domain 2.0: High Availability**

✓ **2.2** Recognize and differentiate highly available and resilient environments on AWS

**Domain 3.0: Deployment and Provisioning**

✓ **3.1** Identify and execute steps required to provision cloud resources

**Domain 5.0: Security and Compliance**

✓ **5.1** Implement and manage security policies on AWS

✓ **5.2** Implement access controls when using AWS

✓ **5.3** Differentiate between the roles and responsibility within the shared responsibility model

It's no secret that in today's organizations, security is a critical component of protecting your infrastructure. Within the traditional datacenter model, responsibilities were clear. With the transition to a cloud service provider (CSP) like AWS, the lines aren't so clear. This is where the Shared Responsibility Model comes in.

We'll begin this chapter by digging into what the Shared Responsibility Model is and how it can help you secure your infrastructure. Then, we'll discuss identities. An *identity* can be a user, a system, or a service. Managing identities falls under the purview of Identity and Access Management (IAM).

In this chapter you will learn about IAM, as well as the services that can be used to manage identities across your AWS ecosystem.

This chapter includes:

An introduction to the Shared Responsibility Model

Components of Identity and Access Management on AWS

Management of passwords and access keys

Best practices recommended to secure AWS accounts

Introduction to other identity services

# Shared Responsibility Model: A Cloud Security Primer

Many organizations make the transition to the cloud in part due to the perception that by moving to the cloud their systems will be more secure. Though that is certainly possible, many of the systems or services are not 100 percent secure out of the box. The services that are secure can easily be made insecure with a simple misconfiguration. So how do you know which components of the cloud services are the responsibility of the cloud provider and which services are your responsibility?

To answer this important question, AWS uses their Shared Responsibility Model to illustrate the concept. Simply put, AWS is responsible for the security of the cloud, whereas you are responsible for security in the cloud. You can get an idea of what the Shared Responsibility Model looks like with Figure 13.1.

**FIGURE 13.1** The Shared Responsibility Model defines where responsibilities lie in cloud security.

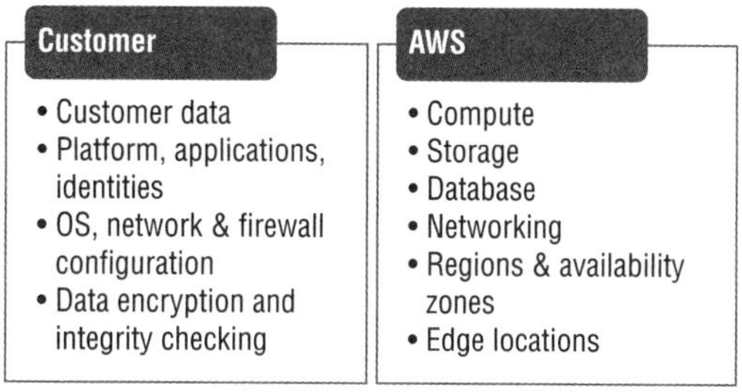

Let's expand these concepts. The Shared Responsibility Model states that AWS is responsible for the security of the cloud. That includes the datacenters that they own, the physical servers, networking equipment and racks within the datacenters, as well as the security of some of their managed services. When we talk about the customer responsibility—security *in* the cloud—we are looking at things like securing data, using encryption, using secure configurations, keeping operating systems and applications up-to-date, Identity and Access Management (IAM), and finally the network configuration.

There is also the concept of shared controls within the Shared Responsibility Model. For instance, AWS is responsible for patching the host servers that Amazon EC2 instances are launched on, but the patching of the Amazon EC2 instances themselves (the operating system and applications) is the customer's responsibility.

# Building Blocks of IAM

You may have noticed that one of the customer responsibilities is IAM. It's all about controlling access to your AWS account and its resources. Whenever you think of IAM, you should think of "least privilege," meaning that a user, group, or role should have only the permissions to do what they need to perform their function–and nothing more than that. AWS IAM makes practicing the concept of least privilege simple by allowing for very granular access control policies.

## Users

Within AWS, there are two types of users that you need to be aware of. The root user account is the first account that exists in an AWS account. It can't be removed or disabled, and you can't remove permissions from it. It is the most privileged account type in AWS and, as such, needs to be properly protected. Protection recommendations are covered later in this chapter in the section called "Securing Your AWS Accounts."

The other type of user account is the IAM user account. This is an account that is created within IAM in your AWS account. IAM users can be assigned to roles or groups that grant them the necessary permissions to do what they need to do. These are the users with whom you want to ensure you follow the concept of *"least privilege."* As mentioned previously, least privilege means that they have the permissions needed to perform their duties but nothing in addition to what they actually need to have.

Users in AWS have several types of credentials that they can use to access their account. Let's examine each type of credential and what they are used for:

**Email Address**   You can use an email address rather than a username. You should make the choice early on as to whether you want your user identities to be based on email or username.

**Username and Password**   The username and password are used by IAM users. Normally, IAM users will have their own link that they will use to access AWS rather than going straight to the AWS portal.

**Access Keys**   Access keys can be used to authenticate via the APIs or when working with the SDK. The root account has access keys, which should be removed. IAM users can have an access key created for them when they are provisioned. Access keys can be created after a user has been provisioned as well.

**Key Pairs**   Key pairs are used to access various services. One of the most common services is when you are remotely accessing a system via Remote Desktop Protocol (RDP) or Secure Shell (SSH). You use a key pair to authenticate to the server.

**Multifactor Authentication (MFA)**   It's been known for some time that username and password is a weak credential by itself. Best practice is to add some form of MFA. MFA can consist of something you know, like a password; something you are, like biometrics; and something you have (like a token). AWS supports both hardware tokens and software (virtual) tokens. These tokens generate a one-time PIN (OTP) that you use in addition to your username and password. Hardware tokens include the Gemalto SafeNet token, YubiKeys, and Gemalto SafeNet Display Cards. Google Authenticator and Authy are supported software token programs available on both Android and iOS.

## Groups

Although you can grant permissions to individual users, that method of permissions management doesn't scale well in an enterprise. Groups provide a simple way to uniformly apply permissions to users with similar functions or jobs across the enterprise. It is worth noting that users can be members of multiple groups but groups can't be members of other groups.

## Roles

Roles are different from users and groups. A role is used to define the permissions that AWS services can use when they assume the role. They can in many cases take the place of service accounts used in traditional datacenters. For instance, a role can be used to grant access for an EC2 instance to communicate with S3. No usernames or passwords are required. Instead, the EC2 instance assumes the role and is able to communicate to all of S3 or to a specific bucket, depending on what the role is granting. Roles work their magic by taking advantage of policies, which we explore in the next section.

 You are limited to 1,000 roles for each AWS account you own. You can request to have that limit raised.

# Policies

The power of roles ultimately comes from the policies that define the permissions that entities consuming the role will be able to use. Of course, policies are not limited to roles. You can also apply them to users and groups. The policies in IAM allow you to get specific about what you want to access and how you want to access it.

There are two types of policies within AWS IAM: *managed policies* and *inline policies*.

- Managed policies can be attached to multiple users, groups, and/or roles. Managed is the preferred type of policy in AWS as it is reusable, rather than being a one-off, like an inline policy.

- Inline policies are generally not recommended. They are attached directly to single user, group, or role. As this creates a special case, it can make managing permissions more difficult.

Policies have multiple elements, and for the exam you should know what they do and what they look like. Those elements are as follows:

**Version**   If you think this is the date that the policy is created, you'd be mistaken (however, it's a common mistake with beginners). In fact, you'll get errors when you try to use it. Version in an IAM policy refers to the version of the policy language that you want to use. The most current and recommended version as of this writing is 2012-10-17.

**Statement**   The Statement element is essentially a container for all the elements below. As policies become more complex, they can contain multiple statements.

**Sid**   This field is optional; however, it is very useful if you have multiple statements inside of your policy. Sid refers to "statement identifier," and it is a unique number that helps you tell the difference between the individual statements in a policy.

**Effect**   This is one of the most basic elements of an IAM policy. Effect is used to specify that you are either allowing or denying access.

**Principal**   This element lets you specify what identity you are allowing or denying access to. This may be an IAM user, a role, or even a federated user.

**Action**   This element is where you specify precisely what you are allowing or denying. For instance, if you want to allow List permission on an S3 bucket, Action would be s3:List.

**Resource**   The Resource element allows you to specify what the action will be allowed on. In the instance of an S3 bucket, for example, you can choose S3 as a whole or you can specify a specific S3 bucket.

**Condition** The Condition element is optional and allows you to choose when the policy should grant permission. For instance, you can use condition to enforce a password reset when an IAM user first logs in.

Now let's take a look at an actual IAM policy. Remember for the exam, that you need to understand what the various elements do so that you can interpret what the policy is doing. I can almost guarantee that you will get at least one or two questions on policies. The following example shows a policy—using all of the elements that we just discussed—that allows users to list and get S3 buckets but requires MFA if you access an S3 bucket named confidential-data. This fantastic sample is provided by AWS at https://docs.aws.amazon.com/IAM/latest/UserGuide/access_policies.html.

```
{
  "Version": "2012-10-17",
  "Statement": [
    {
      "Sid": "FirstStatement",
      "Effect": "Allow",
      "Action": ["iam:ChangePassword"],
      "Resource": "*"
    },
    {
      "Sid": "SecondStatement",
      "Effect": "Allow",
      "Action": "s3:ListAllMyBuckets",
      "Resource": "*"
    },
    {
      "Sid": "ThirdStatement",
      "Effect": "Allow",
      "Action": [
        "s3:List*",
        "s3:Get*"
      ],
      "Resource": [
        "arn:aws:s3:::confidential-data",
        "arn:aws:s3:::confidential-data/*"
      ],
      "Condition": {"Bool": {"aws:MultiFactorAuthPresent": "true"}}
    }
  ]
}
```

Reading a policy is one thing; for SysOps administrators new to AWS, it can be intimidating to write one. Here comes the AWS Policy Generator to the rescue! The AWS Policy Generator (see Figure 13.2) gives you a simple graphical interface where you can choose your options from drop-down boxes and radio buttons, and enter account-specific items into text fields. This tool can be used to create policies for multiple AWS services, and the type of policy you choose is ultimately what will determine the options that you have to work with in crafting your policy. The AWS Policy Generator can be found at `https://awspolicygen.s3.amazonaws.com/policygen.html`.

**FIGURE 13.2**   The AWS Policy Generator makes building custom JSON policies for AWS services less intimidating for newer SysOps administrators and is also convenient for experienced administrators.

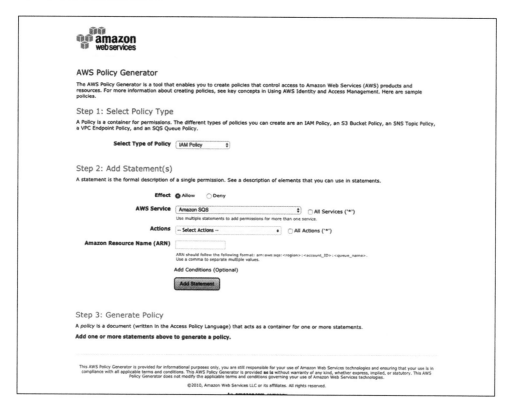

Once you have built your policy, you may want to test it to see if it has the desired effect. For that use case, you have the AWS Policy Simulator. The AWS Policy Simulator is great for testing new policies and is also very handy if you find yourself troubleshooting an access issue that you believe a policy may be causing. You can access the AWS Policy Simulator Console at `https://policysim.aws.amazon.com/`.

# Managing IAM

Now that you understand the foundational concepts needed to work with and understand how IAM works, let's see how to manage password policies and access keys within AWS.

## Managing Passwords

Most organizations have a password policy set in their Active Directory environment. If the choice has been made to use IAM users rather than connecting to your Active Directory, you can set a password policy within the IAM Console. You can define several different items, including password length, complexity, expiration, and reuse shown in Figure 13.3.

**FIGURE 13.3**    The password policy allows you to set up the password requirements for your organization's IAM users.

Let's examine each of the settings in greater detail and why you might want to set them:

**Minimum Password Length**   This specifies the minimum length your IAM users must set their passwords to.

**Require At Least One Uppercase Letter**   This setting deals with password complexity. It ensures that users must have at least one uppercase letter in their password.

**Require At Least One Lowercase Letter**   This setting deals with password complexity. It ensures that users must have at least one lowercase letter in their password.

**Require At Least One Number**   This setting deals with password complexity. It ensures that users must have at least one number in their password.

**Require At Least One Non-Alphanumeric Character**   This setting deals with password complexity. It ensures that users must have at least one special character in their password.

**Allow Users To Change Their Own Password**   Allows IAM users to change their passwords as they can in most traditional on-premises environments.

**Enable Password Expiration**   This setting allows you to set how long a user can use the same password before it will expire and they will be forced to change it.

**Prevent Password Reuse**   It is important to set the reuse high enough that it keeps your users from simply cycling through their passwords until they are able to reuse the old password they know and love. This helps ensure that expired passwords are expired properly and not reused.

**Password Expiration Requires Administrator Reset**   When an IAM user's password expires, the administrator must reset the password.

Remember to make your password policy robust and ensure that you are enforcing your organization's requirements. Additionally, always use MFA with your IAM users. Best practice is to always require it with administrative users, but I would go a step further and encourage that you require it for all users.

## Managing Access Keys

While the passwords attached to IAM users are governed by the password policy, some users may also have a set of long-term credentials that they can use to work with AWS services programmatically. These credentials are referred to as *access keys*. Since these keys are long-lived, you need to ensure that they are kept secure.

An access key consists of both an access key ID and a secret access key. These are analogous to a username and password in the sense that they are both used together to authenticate your API or AWS command-line interface/software development kit (CLI/SDK) requests.

You should use roles rather than access keys whenever possible.

WARNING

Remove the access keys from the root AWS account as soon as possible. You should not use access keys to authenticate to the root account—if someone were to get your root account access keys, they could gain permanent privileged access to your account.

You can manage access keys via the AWS Management Console or via the AWS CLI. For instance, when creating an access key for a specific user, you can go to the Security Credentials tab in their IAM account and click Create Access Key. This is shown in Figure 13.4. You can inactivate an access key by clicking Make Inactive, or you can delete an access key by clicking the X on the Access Keys row.

**FIGURE 13.4** You can generate access keys for single users within their account on their Security Credentials tab.

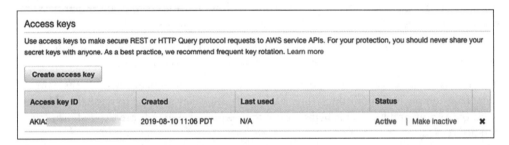

To create an access key through the AWS CLI, you use the command `aws iam create-access-key`. You can also remove an access key through the CLI by issuing the `aws iam delete-access-key` command.

## Safeguarding Access Keys

Since access keys are long-lived credentials, you want to ensure that they are changed regularly. The recommendation from AWS is to practice *key rotation*, which means that you periodically change out the access key. The process is similar between the AWS Management Console and the AWS CLI, but let's explore how to perform key rotation in the AWS Management Console. By practicing key rotation, you can change out this long-lived credential without causing any outages.

### Key Rotation Process

The process to rotate keys is the same regardless of whether you use the AWS Management Console or the AWS CLI.

1. Create a new access key.

2. Update applications to use the new key.

3. Look at the Last Used column in the console to see if the old access key is still in use.

4. Inactivate the old access key.

5. Delete the old access key once you have confirmed it is no longer in use.

By following this process, you can safely rotate keys with less risk of taking things offline.

# Securing Your AWS Accounts

Since your users have access to your resources, one of the most important things you can do as a SysOps administrator is provide the best protections possible for their accounts and safeguard the root account as much as possible.

## Protecting the Root Account

The root account is the most privileged account in your AWS account, and its permissions can't be removed. The first step in protecting your overall AWS account and resources is to protect the root account. Here are some best practices for protecting the root account:

- Remove the access key from the root account. If you can't remove it, rotate it regularly.

- Set a very long and complex password.

- Set up MFA on the root account.

- Do not use the root account for daily administrative work.

- Never, ever, ever share your root account credentials with anyone.

- Change the password on the root account whenever an admin with access to the credentials has left the organization.

## IAM Best Practices

You've secured the root account; now what? Here are some of the recommendations that you should keep in mind when looking at AWS IAM:

- Create individual named IAM users rather than shared user accounts.

- Use groups to manage permissions, rather than granting permissions directly to users.

- Use roles when possible instead of users or access keys.

- Grant only the permissions necessary for the user, group, or role to accomplish their task.

- Enable MFA whenever possible.

- Do not share credentials for access keys.

- Change passwords and access keys often.
- Remove accounts that are not needed.
- Monitor the activities of your IAM users with tools like AWS CloudTrail, Amazon CloudWatch, and AWS Config.

## Trusted Advisor

Trusted Advisor is an excellent resource to help you secure your AWS resources properly, including IAM. The free version will check for your IAM usage and for whether or not you are using MFA on your root account. The free version checks are shown in Figure 13.5. The paid version offers checks against your IAM password policy, SSL certificates, access key rotation, and exposed access keys. What I like most is that it makes it very simple for you to see if you have done all of the things that you needed to do.

**FIGURE 13.5**   Trusted Advisor security checks include multiple checks for IAM-related settings.

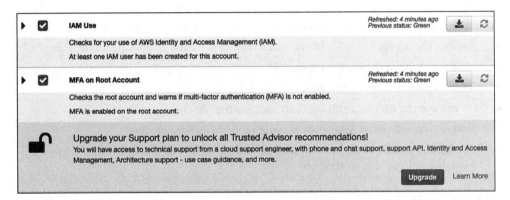

# Other Identity Services

Of course, IAM isn't the only game in town when we talk about managing identities in AWS, so I would like to use this section to ensure that you understand the other services related to identities.

## Cognito

Amazon Cognito offers a way for you to add the ability to manage identities for your mobile or web applications. It allows users to log in with their accounts from Facebook, Google, and Amazon, and to take advantage of identity providers that utilize Security Assertion Markup Language (SAML) 2.0.

With Cognito, you have a user directory service that can be different from your internal directory service. It also provides MFA to the users of your web and mobile applications, which helps to protect the users' data.

## Federation

With Federation, you can offer your internal users a seamless single sign-on (SSO) experience when logging into AWS. By taking advantage of standards like SAML 2.0, you can authenticate your users against your internal directory service like Active Directory, rather than have separate credentials to manage within AWS IAM.

To support multiple AWS accounts, you can use AWS Single Sign-On, which allows you to centrally manage your SSO options. It can become an identity provider for other applications as well, like Salesforce and Office365.

## AWS KMS

The AWS Key Management Service (KMS) simplifies the administration and storage of encryption keys. When you use AWS KMS, you can easily audit anyone who has used your keys and where the keys were used.

With AWS KMS, you can grant access to certain IAM users for certain keys within KMS. You can also import your own keys or allow KMS to create the keys for you. AWS KMS can even be set up to rotate your keys automatically.

The great thing about AWS KMS is that it is integrated into just about every AWS service. This makes encryption at scale easy to implement for every organization, regardless of the size.

# Summary

The Shared Responsibility Model defines where responsibilities lie. AWS is responsible for security of the cloud, and you are responsible for security in the cloud.

AWS IAM allows you to secure your AWS resource using users, groups, roles, and policies. Users are individual identities; groups can be used to manage permissions for users with similar needs; roles can be used in place of credentials; and policies are used to grant permissions. The concept of least privilege should be followed when creating policies.

You can use a password policy to help safeguard your user accounts in AWS IAM. The policy can enforce minimum length, complexity, and how many passwords have to be used before a user can reuse a password.

Access keys are long-term credentials that are used for doing things that require programmatic access, such as working with APIs or the AWS CLI and SDK. They consist of two parts: the access key ID and the secret access key. These should never be shared. It is a best practice to rotate access keys often.

There are several ways to secure AWS accounts. These include using password policies, using the concept of least privilege, and enforcing MFA.

Other identity services exist that are available depending on the use case. Cognito allows you to manage identities for your web and mobile applications, Federation allows you to offer SSO for your internal users and the directory service of your choice, and AWS KMS manages and stores encryption keys.

# Resources to Review

Shared Responsibility Model:

https://aws.amazon.com/compliance/shared-responsibility-model/

Multifactor Authentication:

https://aws.amazon.com/iam/details/mfa/

Policies and Permissions:

https://docs.aws.amazon.com/IAM/latest/UserGuide/access_policies.html

Testing IAM Policies with the IAM Policy Simulator:

https://docs.aws.amazon.com/IAM/latest/UserGuide/
access_policies_testing-policies.html

Amazon Cognito:

https://aws.amazon.com/cognito/

AWS Single Sign-On:

https://aws.amazon.com/single-sign-on/

AWS Key Management Service (KMS):

https://aws.amazon.com/kms/

# Exam Essentials

**Understand the Shared Responsibility Model.** You need to remember that AWS is responsible for the security of the cloud, whereas you are responsible for security in the cloud. A misconfigured S3 bucket, for instance, would be your responsibility, not AWS'.

**Know the difference between users, groups, roles, and policies.** Remember that users are individual IAM accounts. They can be part of multiple groups. Groups are used to grant permissions and reduce management overhead. Roles can be used in place of IAM users to grant access to AWS services. Policies are used to define the permissions that should be given to whichever service assumes the role.

**Understand MFA.** Multifactor authentication uses multiple methods of authentication to identify an authorized user from an unauthorized user. MFA can take advantage of something you know (passwords), something you are (biometrics), or something you have (tokens). AWS supports Gemalto and Yubico hardware as well as virtual MFA apps like Google Authenticator and Authy for iOS and Android.

**Understand access keys and key rotation.**   Access keys are long-term credentials that are used to complete programmatic tasks through APIs, the AWS CLI, or the AWS SDKs. Keys should be rotated regularly; AWS will allow two keys to be active at the same time to allow for rotation. To rotate keys, you create the new key, update the applications to use the new key, deactivate the old key, and then delete the old key once you are sure it's no longer in use.

# Exercises

To complete these exercises, you should download and install Authy on to your mobile device for the MFA exercise.

**EXERCISE 13.1**

### Create an IAM User

The first step in this IAM journey is to create a user in IAM. Let's get started!

1.   Log into the AWS Management Console.

2.   Click Services; then choose IAM under Security, Identity And Compliance.

3.   On the IAM Dashboard, choose Users.

4.   Click Add User.

5.   For Username, type **jsmith**.

6.   Select the AWS Management Console Access check box. Accept the default to let AWS set a password for the user.

7.   Click Next: Permissions.

8.   Click Create Group.

9.   Name the group **System_Admin**.

10.   In the search box, type **administrator**.

11.   Select the AdministratorAccess check box, and then click Create Group.

12.   Click Next: Tags.

13.   Click Next: Review.

14.   Click Create User.

15.   Click Close.

Just like that, you have your first user. Note that you could have selected an existing group at step 8 if one existed in your environment and then followed steps 12–14 to create your user and add them to an existing group.

**EXERCISE 13.2**

### Generate an Access Key

Our user jsmith from Exercise 13.1 now needs programmatic access so that he can take advantage of the AWS CLI. Let's give him his access key.

1. On the IAM Dashboard, click Users.

2. Click the jsmith link.

3. Select the Security Credentials tab and scroll down to the Access Keys section.

4. Click Create Access Key.

5. Download the comma-separated values (CSV) file, and then click Close.

The CSV file contains both the access key ID and the secret access key. Creation is the only time you can get the secret access key. If it is ever lost, you will need to create a new access key.

**EXERCISE 13.3**

### Enable MFA

Our user jsmith has logged into the console and now wants to set up MFA on his account.

1. On the IAM Dashboard, click Users.

2. Click the jsmith link.

3. Select the Security Credentials tab and go to Assigned MFA Service.

4. Click Manage.

5. Select Virtual MFA Device and click Continue.

6. Click Show QR Code in the box on your screen.

7. Open the Authy app on your mobile device.

8. Click the + symbol and select Scan QR Code. You may need to grant Authy access to your camera.

9. Hold your mobile device up so that it can capture the QR code.

10. The account name should be displayed; click Done.

11. On the AWS screen, enter the six-digit code displayed on your phone in the MFA Code 1 box.

**12.** Once the code refreshes, add the second six-digit code displayed on your phone in the MFA Code 2 box, shown in Figure 13.6.

**13.** Click Assign MFA.

**FIGURE 13.6**    Enter the two consecutive codes from the virtual software token to enroll your device in MFA for the AWS account (the QR code is blanked out for security reasons).

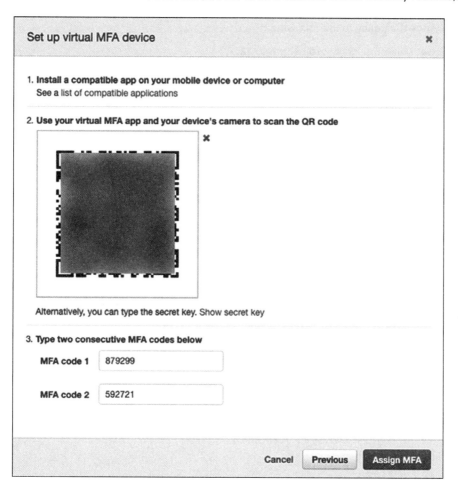

**14.** Click Close.

Just like that, we've now added MFA to jsmith's administrator account.

**EXERCISE 13.4**

## Create a Password Policy

Now we need to create a password policy to ensure that IAM users are meeting our organizational password requirements.

1. On the IAM Dashboard, select Account Settings.

2. Change the policy to the following:

   ▪ Set Minimum Password Length to **12**.

   ▪ Select the following options:

   Require At Least One Uppercase Letter

   Require At Least One Lowercase Letter

   Require At Least One Number

   Require At Least One Non-Alphanumeric Character

   Allow Users To Change Their Own Password

   ▪ Select Password Expiration, and set it to **90** days.

   ▪ Select Prevent Password Reuse, and set it to **10**.

3. Click Apply Password Policy.

**EXERCISE 13.5**

## Create a Role

Roles can be used to allow services the permissions that they need to do specific tasks. In this case, we will create a role that will allow an EC2 instance to reach into an S3 bucket. To do that, we will create the policy that defines the permissions, then create the role and assign that policy to it.

1. On the IAM Dashboard, select Policies.

2. Click Create Policy.

3. For Service, choose S3.

4. For Actions, choose List ≻ Read And Write.

5. Expand Resources and choose All Resources.

6. Click Review Policy.

7. Name the policy **EC2toS3All**, and click Create Policy.

**8.** Return to the IAM Dashboard and select Roles from the menu.

**9.** Click Create Role.

**10.** For Select Type Of Trusted Entity, select AWS Service.

**11.** For Choose The Service That Will Use This Role, click EC2.

**12.** Click Next: Permissions.

**13.** Type the name of the policy that you created into the search box. Select the check box next to EC2toS3All.

**14.** Click Next: Tags.

**15.** Click Next: Review.

**16.** Name the role **EC2toS3All**, and click Create Role.

In a production environment, you would choose a specific S3 bucket rather than choosing All Resources as you did in step 5. Once the role is created, you simply add it to the IAM Role drop-down menu available when you create an EC2 instance or when you choose to modify the instance.

# Review Questions

You can find the answers in the Appendix.

1.  Which of the following are you responsible for?
    A.  Security on the cloud
    B.  Security of the cloud
    C.  Security in the cloud
    D.  Security beyond the cloud

    Users of AWS are responsible for security *in* the cloud, whereas AWS is responsible for security *of* the cloud.

2.  Which of the following is AWS responsible for? (Choose two.)
    A.  Networking equipment
    B.  Application authentication
    C.  Networking port security
    D.  Physical servers

3.  Which of the following are you responsible for? (Choose two.)
    A.  Encrypting data
    B.  Keeping operating systems on EC2 instances up-to-date
    C.  Keeping operating systems on RDS instances up-to-date
    D.  AWS datacenters

4.  Which of the following is an example of shared responsibility between AWS and a user?
    A.  Keeping RDS instances up-to-date
    B.  Securing access to resources below the hypervisor
    C.  Maintain EC2 instances at a host and a server level
    D.  Application authorization

5.  How might encryption of data be considered an example of the Shared Responsibility Model?
    A.  AWS maintains S3, whereas the user encrypts data that is stored on S3.
    B.  AWS handles the actual mechanism of encrypting data, whereas the user chooses what data that encryption should apply to.
    C.  AWS provides encryption requirements and the user implements those requirements.
    D.  None of these are examples of shared responsibility.

6. Which of the following are user types when considering an AWS account? (Choose two.)

   **A.** Account owner

   **B.** Root user

   **C.** IAM user

   **D.** IAM role

7. What does the principle of least privilege mean?

   **A.** Users should have minimal privileges and only be granted additional privileges through IAM roles.

   **B.** Users should only gain privileges through group membership.

   **C.** Users should have the permissions they need to perform their duties, but nothing more than that.

   **D.** Users should have permissions to perform their duties and possible future duties, but nothing more than that.

8. Which of the following are valid types of identifiers for IAM users? (Choose two.)

   **A.** Username

   **B.** Access key

   **C.** Secret key

   **D.** MFA

9. For what purpose would an IAM user need to use a key pair?

   **A.** Accessing the AWS web console

   **B.** Accessing the AWS SDK

   **C.** Accessing the AWS CLI

   **D.** Accessing a running EC2 instance

10. You have come on as an AWS consultant and need to audit software running on EC2 instances. There is no CloudFormation, so you need to examine each instance individually. What credential should you ask of your AWS administrator?

    **A.** An access key

    **B.** A username and password

    **C.** A key pair

    **D.** A secret key

11. Which of the following is true of an IAM role but not an IAM group?

    **A.** Permissions can be granted through this mechanism.

    **B.** Users can be assigned multiples of each mechanism.

    **C.** Permissions assumed through this mechanism are temporary.

    **D.** All of these are true of both roles and groups.

12. Which of the following would you apply to an EC2 instance that needs to communicate with a standard S3 bucket in the same region?

    **A.** An IAM group

    **B.** An IAM role

    **C.** An IAM policy

    **D.** All of these can provide an instance access to S3.

13. To which of the following can you assign IAM policies?

    **A.** An IAM role

    **B.** An IAM user

    **C.** An IAM group

    **D.** All of these

14. Which of the following is a difference between a managed and inline policy? (Choose two.)

    **A.** A managed policy can be attached to multiple users whereas an inline policy cannot.

    **B.** An inline policy can be attached to multiple users whereas a managed policy cannot.

    **C.** AWS recommends using inline policies rather than managed policies.

    **D.** AWS recommends using managed policies rather than inline policies.

15. To what does the version of a policy refer?

    **A.** The date and time the policy was created

    **B.** The date and time the policy was updated

    **C.** An arbitrary identifier assigned by the policy author

    **D.** The version of the policy language used in the policy

16. Which of the following are parts of a valid IAM policy? (Choose two.)

    **A.** Effect

    **B.** Sid

    **C.** Id

    **D.** Affect

17. Which of the following is an acceptable entry for an IAM policy's principal? (Choose two.)

    **A.** Another policy's sid

    **B.** An IAM user

    **C.** An AWS account ID

    **D.** A federated user

18. Why are access keys a potentially greater security risk than passwords? (Choose two.)

    **A.** They are long-lived compared to user passwords.

    **B.** They are not governed by password policies.

    **C.** They provide programmatic access to the AWS SDK or CLI.

    **D.** They expire every 90 days.

**19.** When AWS uses the term *access key*, to which of the following are they referring? (Choose two.)

  **A.** A username

  **B.** A key pair

  **C.** An access key ID

  **D.** A secret access key

**20.** What options does AWS KMS provide for key creation? (Choose two.)

  **A.** AWS KMS can generate keys.

  **B.** AWS KMS can read keys from another AWS account.

  **C.** AWS KMS allows you to import your own keys.

  **D.** AWS KMS can import keys from an existing AWS user.

# Chapter 14

# Reporting and Logging

---

**THE AWS CERTIFIED SYSOPS ADMINISTRATOR – ASSOCIATE EXAM TOPICS COVERED IN THIS CHAPTER MAY INCLUDE, BUT ARE NOT LIMITED TO, THE FOLLOWING:**

**Domain 1.0: Monitoring and Reporting**

✓ 1.1 Create and maintain metrics and alarms utilizing AWS monitoring services

✓ 1.2 Recognize and differentiate performance and availability metrics

✓ 1.3 Perform the steps necessary to remediate based on performance and availability metrics

**Domain 3.0: Deployment and Provisioning**

✓ 3.2 Identify and remediate deployment issues

**Domain 6.0: Networking**

✓ 6.3 Gather and interpret relevant information for network troubleshooting

**Domain 7.0: Automation and Optimization**

✓ 7.1 Use AWS services and features to manage and assess resource utilization

Getting visibility into what is going on in your environment is an essential part of securing and troubleshooting your network. After all, as a system administrator you need to be able to tell when your systems are having performance issues as they may impact uptime. As a security administrator, you need to be able to tell who logged in, at what time, and what they did when they were logged in. AWS provides several monitoring and reporting tools to meet the needs of system admins and security admins in today's cloud and hybrid environments.

This chapter includes:

An introduction to reporting and monitoring in AWS

Monitoring API calls with AWS CloudTrail

Log monitoring with Amazon CloudWatch

Reporting on baselines with AWS Config

# Reporting and Monitoring in AWS

In the traditional on-premises datacenters, you had products that could monitor and alert on performance metrics, and if you enabled auditing to include successful/failed logins, you could track login activity. Organizations that must meet compliance requirements must be able to extend capabilities such as these to the cloud, and even organizations that don't need to meet strict compliance or regulatory requirements can benefit from enabling reporting and monitoring features in the cloud.

When we talk about monitoring in AWS, we are really looking at real-time and historical data: performance metrics over time, user activity over time, and so forth. You can choose to get even more detail about EC2 instances and the applications installed on them with Amazon CloudWatch Logs Agent. You can get a record of every API call made by a user with AWS CloudTrail, which can be helpful when you're investigating whether something was changed when you're troubleshooting an active incident.

We'll look at each of these topics in more detail in the following sections. We'll start with AWS CloudTrail, and then discuss Amazon CloudWatch and AWS Config.

# AWS CloudTrail

Have you ever wondered what your users were doing? It's common to monitor for failed logins and, in some cases, successful logins. In a traditional on-premises environment, however, the majority of organizations don't get much more insight than that. Tools are available that can correlate user activity data, but they can be expensive to purchase and difficult to maintain. That's where *AWS CloudTrail* comes in (see Figure 14.1). Not only is it simple to use, but if you use the defaults you are able to view 90 days' worth of account activity free of charge as long as the event is a management event and is a create, modify, or delete operation.

**FIGURE 14.1**    The free AWS CloudTrail monitoring captures create, modify, and delete operations and retains the information for 90 days.

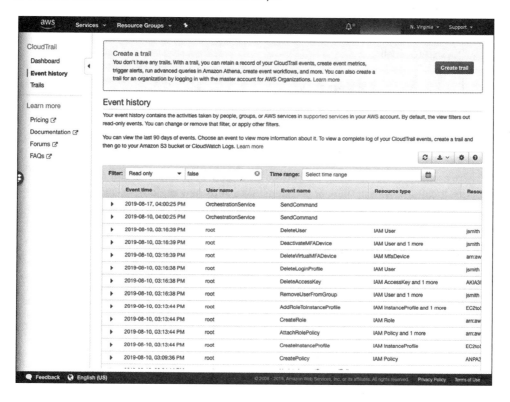

Do you want to collect more data? You can do so easily by creating a trail. You can create a *trail* that will allow you to gather management and data events from all regions and put that information into an S3 bucket of your choosing. Additionally, if you create a trail you can create custom event metrics and trigger alerts with the integration into Amazon CloudWatch. The trail is able to deliver events to both Amazon CloudWatch Logs and Amazon CloudWatch Events.

Management and data events are collected every time there is an API call. One of the most important things to remember is that everything that is done within AWS generates an API call. This includes activity within the AWS Management Console, the AWS CLI, and AWS SDKs, including other AWS services. In fact, you may notice in Figure 14.1 that there are two entries where the username is OrchestrationService. This is an example of an AWS service initiating an API call.

## Applying a Trail to All Regions

Having an active trail in AWS CloudTrail is the best way to get a full picture of the activity happening in your account. What's even better is that you can manage that one trail and have it apply to all regions where there is activity within your AWS account. You can do that by clicking the Yes radio button for Apply Trail To All Regions, as shown in Figure 14.2, or by setting IsMultiRegionTrail to true if you're using the AWS CLI.

**FIGURE 14.2**    You can apply a trail to all regions.

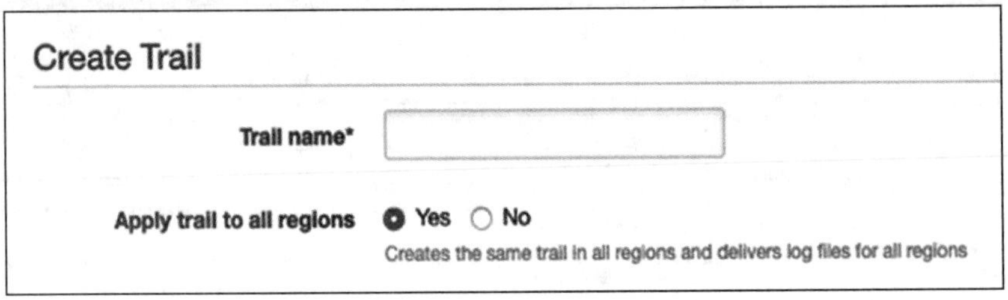

### Create Trail

Trail name*    [                    ]

Apply trail to all regions    ● Yes    ○ No

Creates the same trail in all regions and delivers log files for all regions

There are benefits to applying the trail to all regions. For one, you can manage the trail from one location. Another benefit is that as AWS adds new regions, your trail will automatically apply to the new regions—no intervention required.

## Management Events

By default, AWS CloudTrail records management events as long as the operation is create, modify, or delete, for a period of 90 days. *Management events* relate to things that are done to the resources in your AWS account.

When you create a trail, you are given the option to select All, Read-Only, Write-Only or None. Let's look at each of these in more detail.

- **All:** This setting configures AWS CloudTrail to collect all management events.
- **Read-Only:** This setting configures AWS CloudTrail to collect management events related to read actions like Describe* (for example, DescribeSecurityGroups).
- **Write-Only:** This setting configures AWS CloudTrail to collect management events related to actions that can cause changes to your resources such as Create* (for example, createTags), RunInstances, and TerminateInstances.
- **None:** This setting ensures that AWS CloudTrail does not collect any management events.

## Data Events

By default, data events are not recorded. *Data events* are related to events that might change data objects in your account. These might include Get* and Put* in S3, or the invocation of an AWS Lambda function. You can choose to monitor all the S3 buckets in your account or just specific buckets. For instance, you may choose to monitor specific buckets that contain sensitive information like personally identifiable information (PII) or personal healthcare information (PHI). Typical API activity for S3 buckets might include GetObject, PutObject, and DeleteObject. As shown below in Figure 14.3, you can choose to record read activities, write activities, or both.

**FIGURE 14.3**    You can choose to log read activities, write activities, or both for S3 bucket data events.

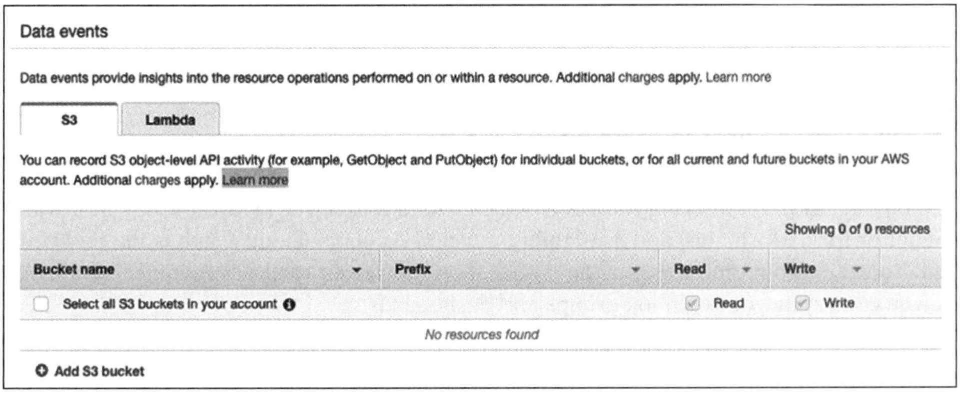

You can also log events from AWS Lambda. You can select specific functions to monitor, or you can choose to monitor all functions. Typical activity for AWS Lambda might include the use of Invoke to kick off a Lambda function. You have the option to monitor your current region or all regions for Lambda events, shown below in Figure 14.4.

**FIGURE 14.4**    You can choose to log activity for all regions or specific regions for AWS Lambda data events.

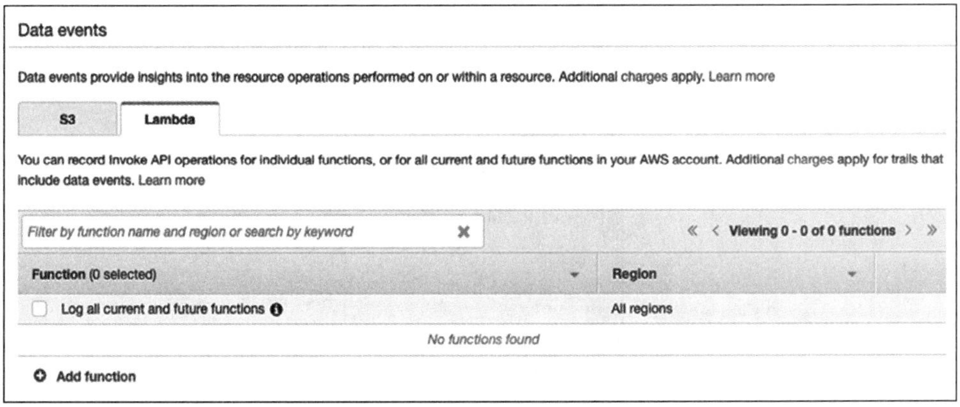

## But You Said CloudTrail Was Free...

If you are using the default setup for AWS CloudTrail, you will get a 90-day history of management events as long as they are related to create, modify, or delete operations. This is completely free.

If you create your own trail, the first copy of any management events in each region is free. However, you must pay for the usage of the S3 bucket that they are stored in. You are also charged for:

- Additional copies of management events
- Data events

# Amazon CloudWatch

Next on our list of monitoring tools is Amazon CloudWatch (see Figure 14.5). If you want to monitor for performance and availability metrics, Amazon CloudWatch is the tool you need. You can also monitor for custom application metrics (if the Logs Agent is installed), and you can create your own log groups and dashboards.

**FIGURE 14.5** The Amazon CloudWatch console gives you easy access to alarms, events, and logs within your environment.

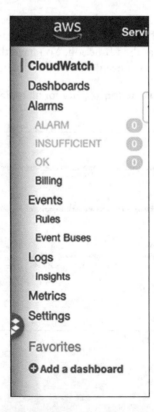

Amazon CloudWatch has a lot of different components, all managed from within the same console. We will talk about each of these in more detail in this section, starting with Amazon CloudWatch Alarms, then moving into Amazon CloudWatch Logs, Amazon CloudWatch Events, and finally the Amazon CloudWatch Dashboard.

# Amazon CloudWatch Alarms

An Amazon CloudWatch alarm is responsible for monitoring a single metric. That may be as simple as an alarm that monitors for a CPU to reach 95 percent or an alarm that takes an average of a 5-minute period to see if the CPU stays at 95 percent and, if so, goes into an alarm state. Amazon CloudWatch alarms are a powerful tool in your AWS arsenal; they can be used to drive actions like telling an Auto Scaling group to scale based on that CPU metric I mentioned.

Alarms have three possible states that they can be in at any given point in time:

- OK: If your Amazon CloudWatch alarm says it is OK, that means that the metric or the mathematical expression behind the metric is within the defined threshold.

- ALARM: If your Amazon CloudWatch alarm says it is in an ALARM state, that means that the metric or the mathematical expression behind the metric is below or above the defined threshold.

- INSUFFICIENT_DATA: There are a couple of reasons that your CloudWatch alarm might have INSUFFICIENT_DATA as its state. The most common reasons are that the alarm has only just started/been created, the metric it is monitoring is not available, or there is simply not enough data at this time to determine whether the alarm should be in an OK or an ALARM state.

When you create an alarm, you will have to decide what you want to set for the period, evaluation period, and the Datapoints To Alarm. The *period* is the amount of time that CloudWatch will assess a metric. For instance, if you set your period to 60 seconds, then you will have a new data point every 60 seconds. The *evaluation period* is the number of data points the alarm should consider before determining which state it should be in. For instance, if the period is set to 60 seconds (1 minute) and your evaluation period is set to 5 minutes, then you could potentially get a different alarm state every 5 minutes. The *Datapoints To Alarm* specifies the number of data points that would need to be outside of the threshold, referred to as "breaching," for the alarm to go into an ALARM state. In the case where the period is 60 seconds and the evaluation period is 5 minutes, there are two ways Datapoints To Alarm could go:

- **Datapoints To Alarm is equal to the evaluation period:** The CloudWatch alarm will go into an ALARM state when the number of Datapoints To Alarm has been reached. For example, with the period set to 1 minute, the evaluation period set to 5 minutes, and Datapoints To Alarm set to 5, you will get an ALARM state if the metric is outside of the defined threshold for 5 data points.

- **Datapoints To Alarm is less than the evaluation period:** The CloudWatch alarm will go into an ALARM state when the number of Datapoints To Alarm has been reached. For example, with the period set to 1 minute, the evaluation period set to 5 minutes, and Datapoints To Alarm set to 3, you will get an ALARM state if the metric is outside of the defined threshold for three of the five data points within the evaluation period.

What happens if you are missing data points? For each alarm, you can set how you want Amazon CloudWatch to treat missing data points. This allows you to customize your alarms to meet your expectations as far as how missing data points are handled. There are four possible settings:

- notBreaching: If you set the alarm to treat missing data points as notBreaching, it will consider missing data points to be good.

- breaching: If you set the alarm to treat missing data points as breaching, it will consider missing data points to be bad.

- ignore: If you set the alarm to ignore, it will ignore the missing data points and maintain the current alarm state.

- missing: If you set the alarm to missing, it will simply not consider the missing data points when it decides whether or not to change alarm states.

You will get to see these settings when we set up a CloudWatch alarm in Exercise 14.2 at the end of the chapter.

## Amazon CloudWatch Logs

Amazon CloudWatch Logs is a one-stop shop for all things having to do with logging. Not only does it store logs from AWS systems and resources, it can also handle the logs for on-premises systems as long as they have the Amazon Unified CloudWatch Agent installed. If you have chosen to monitor AWS CloudTrail activity through Amazon CloudWatch, the activity that is monitored is sent to Amazon CloudWatch Logs.

If you need to have a long retention period for your logs, then Amazon CloudWatch Logs is also a good fit. By default, logs are kept forever and will never be expired. You should adjust this based on your organization's retention policies. You can choose to keep logs for only a single day or go up to 10 years.

### Log Groups and Log Streams

Getting logs in a single destination is a great start; however, to make it more useful, one of the first things most system admins want to do is to put like data with like data. For example, say you have some EC2 instances that handle web traffic. You want the logs to be grouped together since they are serving a similar purpose. This is where a log group comes into play.

Each web server that sends logs into Amazon CloudWatch Logs is using a log stream. A *log stream* is a collection of the events that have happened on a single source, like an EC2 instance or an AWS service. A *log group* in Amazon CloudWatch is a collection of log streams that will share the same settings in regard to retention and monitoring, as well as

IAM settings. In our example, the EC2 instances handling the web traffic would each have a log stream in Amazon CloudWatch, and those log streams would be grouped together into a log group.

### Unified CloudWatch Agent

While you can get basic information regarding availability and performance for your Amazon EC2 instances, you can get far more detailed information if you have installed the unified *CloudWatch agent.* You can also gather logs from your on-premises servers in the case of a hybrid environment with the CloudWatch agent, and centrally manage and store them from within the Amazon CloudWatch console. The agent is supported for multiple Windows and Linux operating systems, including the 64-bit versions of Windows Server 2008, 2012, and 2016 and multiple versions of Amazon Linux, Amazon Linux 2, Ubuntu Server, CentOS, RHEL, Debian, and SLES.

By installing the CloudWatch agent on a Windows machine, you can gather in-depth information from the Performance Monitor, which is built into the operating system. When CloudWatch is installed on a Linux system, you can get more in-depth metrics related to CPU, memory, network, processes, and swap memory usage. You can also gather custom logs from applications installed on servers.

To install the CloudWatch agent, you need to set up the configuration file. Amazon provides a wizard to make the creation of the configuration file simple. For more information on how to set up the agent, refer to this document: `https://docs.aws.amazon.com/ AmazonCloudWatch/latest/monitoring/ create-cloudwatch-agent-configuration-file-wizard.html`.

## Amazon CloudWatch Events

At the beginning of the chapter, I mentioned real-time monitoring. This function is provided by Amazon CloudWatch Events. One of the big wins with CloudWatch Events is the ability to use an event as a trigger to kick off something else. For instance, an event related to an HTTP 500 error from a web server might kick off notifications to the administrator or could be used to reboot a backend application server that is having problems. There are quite a few services that can be targeted by CloudWatch Events.

## Amazon CloudWatch Dashboard

The Amazon CloudWatch Dashboard is a fully customizable method to view the data that is most meaningful to you. You can create dashboards with your own custom metrics so that you are presented with the data you need to call attention to. If you create a dashboard and name it CloudWatch-Default, it is displayed in the Overview dashboard, shown in Figure 14.6.

**FIGURE 14.6**   The overview page houses default metrics as well as a CloudWatch-Default dashboard if you choose to make one.

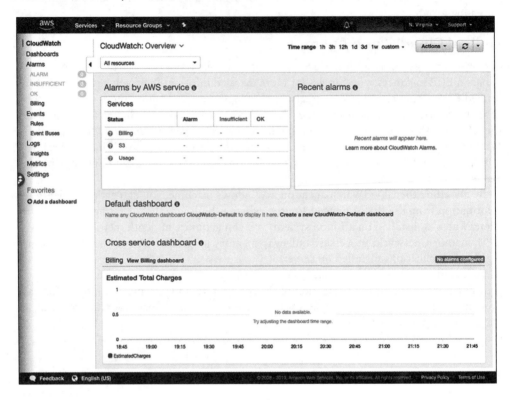

You will create your own dashboard in Exercise 14.3.

# AWS Config

So far in this chapter, we have discussed monitoring account activity and performance and availability metrics. Now it's time to look at monitoring for and alerting on changes to configuration.

*AWS Config* provides a solid change management solution within AWS. It allows you to track the change history on individual resources and configure notifications when a resource has been changed. It does this by using config rules. A *config rule* is essentially the desired state that the resource should be in. By using config rules, you can monitor for systems that fall outside of organization baselines and even see which changes caused the system to fall out of compliance with the baseline, assuming that it was within the baseline at a certain point in time. AWS Config is enabled per-region, so you will need to enable it for every region that you want to use it in.

It is important to note the AWS Config is a monitoring tool. It will not enforce baselines, nor will it prevent a user from making changes that take a system out of compliance.

# Summary

There are several products within AWS that allow you to monitor your AWS environment and report the things that you find. Central to monitoring and reporting in AWS are AWS CloudTrail, Amazon CloudWatch, and AWS Config.

AWS CloudTrail is used for monitoring API activity within your account. Every action taken generates an API call regardless of whether the action occurred in the AWS Management Console, in the AWS CLI, or through the AWS SDKs. By default, 90 days of management events are kept for free, but you can set up custom trails that allow you to capture data events. Data events are not free, and custom trails also incur cost from the S3 buckets where they are stored.

Amazon CloudWatch is a monitoring solution that you can use within AWS to track various metrics related to performance and availability. Certain events that occur can trigger actions such as getting an Auto Scaling group to scale up when CPU usage is too high. You can create a custom dashboard within Amazon CloudWatch that allows you to make the events you care about front and center.

AWS Config is a tool that enables you to monitor for compliance with organizational baselines. You can be alerted when a system has fallen out of compliance, and you can view the change history of the resource.

# Resources to Review

What Is AWS CloudTrail?

https://docs.aws.amazon.com/awscloudtrail/latest/userguide/
cloudtrail-user-guide.html

Using Amazon CloudWatch Alarms:

https://docs.aws.amazon.com/AmazonCloudWatch/latest/monitoring/
AlarmThatSendsEmail.html

What Is Amazon CloudWatch Logs?

https://docs.aws.amazon.com/AmazonCloudWatch/latest/logs/
WhatIsCloudWatchLogs.html

Working with Log Groups and Log Streams:

https://docs.aws.amazon.com/AmazonCloudWatch/latest/logs/
Working-with-log-groups-and-streams.html

Collecting Metrics and Logs from Amazon EC2 Instances and On-Premises Servers with the CloudWatch Agent:

https://docs.aws.amazon.com/AmazonCloudWatch/latest/monitoring/
Install-CloudWatch-Agent.html

Using Amazon CloudWatch Dashboards:

https://docs.aws.amazon.com/AmazonCloudWatch/latest/monitoring/CloudWatch_
Dashboards.html

What Is AWS Config?

https://docs.aws.amazon.com/config/latest/developerguide/WhatIsConfig.html

# Exam Essentials

**Understand what AWS CloudTrail is monitoring.**   Everything that happens in AWS is an API call and AWS CloudTrail monitors API calls. For the exam, remember that AWS CloudTrail can give you the who behind events that happened in your AWS account.

**Understand what Amazon CloudWatch does.**   Amazon CloudWatch provides a central area to monitor logs for both AWS systems and on-premises systems (assuming the unified CloudWatch agent is installed). It gives you the ability to set up actions that can be triggered off certain events and allows you to create custom dashboards based on logs or events of interest.

**Understand the role of log groups and log streams.**   Remember that data from a single source is referred to as a log stream and that a log group is a logical collection of similar log streams.

**Understand how AWS Config can help baseline monitoring.**   AWS Config uses config rules to define the expected baseline for a system and will then monitor for compliance with that baseline. It tracks configuration history, which is great for troubleshooting issues or trying to determine why a system went out of compliance with a baseline. AWS Config can also send a notification if a system goes out of compliance with the baseline.

# Exercises

**EXERCISE 14.1**

### Set Up a Trail in AWS CloudTrail

In this exercise, we will configure a trail in AWS CloudTrail to monitor for both management and data events.

1. Log into the AWS Management Console.

2. Click Services; then select CloudTrail under Management & Governance.

3. Click Create Trail.

4. For the name, type **MyCTTrail**.

5. For Apply To All Regions, select Yes.

6. Under Management Events, select All.

7. Under Data Events on the S3 tab, select the option Select All S3 Buckets In Your Account. Ensure that Read and Write are both selected.

8. Click the Lambda tab and select the Log All Current And Future Functions option.

9. Under Storage Location, select Yes to create a new S3 bucket, and then give the bucket a unique name.

10. Click Create.

Now you will see your trail in the console.

---

**EXERCISE 14.2**

## Set Up an Amazon CloudWatch Alarm

Now we will set up a CloudWatch alarm. This exercise assumes that you have an S3 bucket that can be used. If you do not have an S3 bucket created in your environment, you can easily create one so that you can follow along.

1. From the AWS Management Console, click Services and then choose CloudWatch under Management & Governance.

2. Click Alarms, and then select Create Alarm.

3. Click Select Metric, select S3, and then click Storage Metrics.

4. You will have two metrics to choose from. Select the NumberOfObjects option and then click Select Metric.

5. Change Statistic to Sum and set Period to 1 Day.

6. Under Conditions, set the threshold type to Static.

7. Under Whenever NumberofObjects Is, choose Greater/Equal and set Than to 2.

8. Click Next.

9. Under Configure Actions, click Notification and choose In Alarm.

10. Under Select An SNS Topic, choose Create New Topic.

11. Add the email address where you want to receive the notification.

12. Click Create Topic.

13. Click Next.

**EXERCISE 14.2** *(continued)*

**14.** Name the alarm something that makes sense to you. I called mine S3 Objects Greater Than Or Equal To 2. Click Next.

**15.** On the next screen, if everything looks correct click Create Alarm.

Your new alarm should now display INSUFFICIENT_DATA for the state. Assuming you have fewer than two objects in your S3 bucket, it will transition to OK during the next evaluation period. In Figure 14.7, you can see what it will look like when your alarm is in an OK state. If you have two or more objects, it will send an email.

**FIGURE 14.7**   My S3 bucket currently has one item in it, so the alarm is in an OK state.

If I add another object, the alarm threshold will have been reached since I will have two objects and it will go into an alarm state.

**EXERCISE 14.3**

### Set Up an Amazon CloudWatch Dashboard

Now that we have our S3 object alarm, let's create a new dashboard and add the alarm to the dashboard.

**1.** In the CloudWatch console, click Dashboards.

**2.** Click Create Dashboard.

**3.** Name the dashboard **My-Awesome-Dashboard**.

**4.** In the Add To This Dashboard box, select Text, and then click Configure.

**5.** Add the following to the box and then click Create Widget.

```
# My Awesome Dashboard

This dashboard is home to my S3 alarm I made in Exercise 14.2.
```

Now let's add the alarm that we created in Exercise 14.2.

**6.** Click Alarms, and then select the check box next to the alarm you created earlier.

**7.** Click Add To Dashboard.

**8.** Ensure that the dashboard you created is listed under Select A Dashboard, and click Add To Dashboard.

**9.** Click Save Dashboard.

Now if you go back to your dashboard, you'll see your text widget and your alarm. This is a simple example, of course, but it gives you a general idea of how to create dashboards and customize their content. You can see an example of the dashboard in Figure 14.8.

**FIGURE 14.8**    A custom dashboard can hold different widgets and alarms, limited only by the metrics available within Amazon CloudWatch.

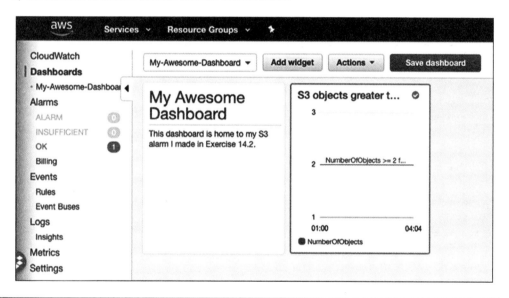

---

**EXERCISE 14.4**

### Configure a Rule in AWS Config

To close this chapter, we will set up AWS Config.

**1.** In the AWS Management Console, click Services and then choose Config under Management & Governance.

**2.** Under Settings, ensure that both check boxes are selected next to All Resources under Resource Types To Record.

3. Scroll down to Amazon S3 bucket and choose Create A Bucket.

4. Scroll down to the bottom of the page and click Next.

5. Under AWS Config rules, type **cloudtrail** in the search box and click Cloudtrail-Enabled.

6. Click Next and then click Confirm.

As simple as that, you've created your first rule, and you can evaluate your AWS environment against it. Hundreds of rules are available to you within AWS Config, and I recommend looking through them to find the ones you are most interested in. Figure 14.9 shows you what a noncompliant resource will look like. In this case, I went back to AWS CloudTrail and disabled the trail we created earlier.

**FIGURE 14.9**   When a resource is noncompliant, it shows up on the AWS Config dashboard.

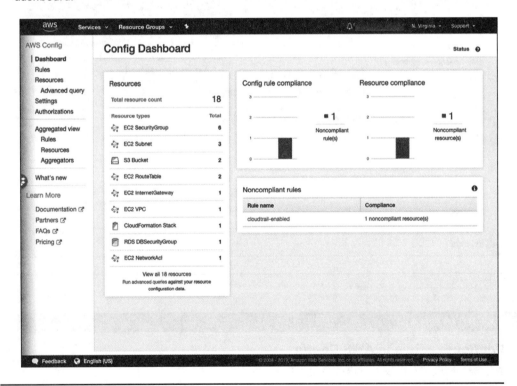

# Review Questions

You can find the answers in the Appendix.

1. Which of the following is the most important usage of reporting and monitoring?

   **A.** Security

   **B.** Compliance

   **C.** Performance of applications

   **D.** All of the above

2. Which AWS tool would you use to collect metrics from a running EC2 instance that has multiple EBS volumes attached?

   **A.** AWS Config

   **B.** Amazon CloudWatch

   **C.** AWS CloudTrail

   **D.** All of the above

3. You suspect that an application client is nonperformant because it is making more calls than normal to a REST-based API on your application estate. What AWS tool would you use to verify this information and validate any changes you make to correct this issue?

   **A.** AWS Config

   **B.** Amazon CloudWatch

   **C.** AWS CloudTrail

   **D.** AWS NetReporter

4. You have a number of metrics collecting via Amazon CloudWatch on your fleet of EC2 instances. However, you want to gather additional metrics on a number of instances that do not seem to be performing as well as the majority of running instances. How can you gather additional metrics not available through Amazon CloudWatch's stock configuration?

   **A.** Turn on detailed monitoring.

   **B.** Install the Amazon CloudWatch Logs Agent.

   **C.** Create a new VPC flow log.

   **D.** Turn on detailed statistics in Amazon CloudWatch.

5. How long does AWS CloudTrail retain information on API calls?

   **A.** 60 days

   **B.** 90 days

   **C.** 6 months

   **D.** 1 year

6. Which of the following activities will not generate a management and/or data event in AWS CloudTrail?

   **A.**  An AWS CLI call initiated by a developer

   **B.**  A AWS SDK call initiated by Java code running in another cloud provider

   **C.**  An interaction between an EC2 instance and RDS

   **D.**  A login to the AWS web console

7. Which of the following statements about an AWS CloudTrail trail with regard to regions is true? (Choose two.)

   **A.**  A trail applies to all your AWS regions by default.

   **B.**  A trail collects both management and data events.

   **C.**  A trail can apply only to a single region.

   **D.**  A trail applies to a single region by default.

8. Which of the following is not an example of a management event?

   **A.**  An AttachRolePolicy IAM operation

   **B.**  An AWS CloudTrail CreateTrail API operation

   **C.**  Activity on an S3 bucket via a PutObject event

   **D.**  A CreateSubnet API operation for an EC2 instance

9. How are management events different from data events? (Choose two.)

   **A.**  Data events are typically much higher volume than management events.

   **B.**  Data events are typically lower volume than management events.

   **C.**  Data events are disabled by default when creating a trail, whereas management events are enabled by default.

   **D.**  Management events include Lambda execution activity whereas data events do not.

10. Which of the following options for a trail would capture events related to actions such as RunInstances or TerminateInstances? (Choose two.)

    **A.**  All

    **B.**  Read-Only

    **C.**  Write-Only

    **D.**  None

11. Which of the following will not incur a charge for usage?

    **A.**  The first copy of a management event

    **B.**  The first copy of a data event

    **C.**  The second copy of a data event

    **D.**  The second copy of a management event

**12.** How many different performance metrics can an Amazon CloudWatch alarm monitor?

   **A.** One

   **B.** Two

   **C.** One or more

   **D.** Amazon CloudWatch alarms do not monitor performance metrics.

**13.** Which of the following is not a valid Amazon CloudWatch alarm state?

   **A.** OK

   **B.** INSUFFICIENT_DATA

   **C.** ALARM

   **D.** INVALID_DATA

**14.** You have a CloudWatch alarm with a period of 2 minutes. The evaluation period is set to 10 minutes, and Datapoints To Alarm is set to 3. How many metrics would need to be outside the defined threshold for the alarm to move into an ALARM state? (Choose two.)

   **A.** Three out-of-threshold metrics out of five within 10 minutes

   **B.** Three out-of-threshold metrics out of five within 2 minutes

   **C.** Two out-of-threshold metrics out of five within 5 minutes

   **D.** Three out-of-threshold metrics out of eight within 16 minutes

**15.** Which of the following settings are allowed for dealing with missing data points within Amazon CloudWatch? (Choose two.)

   **A.** notBreaching

   **B.** invalid

   **C.** missing

   **D.** notValid

**16.** Which of the following statements accurately describes a CloudWatch log stream?

   **A.** A collection of logs that share the same retention and monitoring settings

   **B.** A collection of logs that share the same IAM settings

   **C.** A collection of events from a single source

   **D.** A collection of events from a single VPC

**17.** Which of the following does AWS Config not provide?

   **A.** Remediation for out-of-compliance events

   **B.** Definition of states that resources should be in

   **C.** Notifications when a resource changes its state

   **D.** Definition of compliance baselines for your system

**18.** Which of the following would you use to ensure that your S3 buckets never allow public access? (Choose two.)

    **A.** AWS Config

    **B.** Amazon CloudWatch

    **C.** AWS Lambda

    **D.** AWS CloudTrail

**19.** Which of the following is not part of an AWS Config configuration item (CI)?

    **A.** An AWS CloudTrail event ID

    **B.** A mapping of relationships between the resource and other AWS resources

    **C.** The set of IAM policies related to the resource

    **D.** The version of the configuration item

**20.** You want to ensure the minimum amount of time for any resource that moves out of compliance. You do not care about costs associated with configuration monitoring. What evaluation approach should you use for your config rules?

    **A.** Immediate

    **B.** Periodic

    **C.** Tagged

    **D.** Change-triggered

# Chapter

# 15

# Additional Security Tools

THE AWS CERTIFIED SYSOPS
ADMINISTRATOR – ASSOCIATE EXAM
TOPICS COVERED IN THIS CHAPTER MAY
INCLUDE, BUT ARE NOT LIMITED TO, THE
FOLLOWING:

Domain 2.0: High Availability

✓ 2.2 Recognize and differentiate highly available and
resilient environments on AWS

Domain 5.0: Security and Compliance

✓ 5.1 Implement and manage security policies on AWS

✓ 5.2 Implement access controls when using AWS

✓ 5.3 Differentiate between the roles and responsibility
within the shared responsibility model

There are some additional security tools that you'll most likely see on the SysOps Administrator – Associate exam. These tools help to round out your security tool arsenal to provide better visibility and better protection against threats. Seeing vulnerabilities in your environment, for instance, allows you to patch or reconfigure before someone is able to exploit those vulnerabilities. In this chapter, we'll discuss two types of tools available for you in AWS that are likely to show up on the exam. They are similar to services you most likely have running on-premises right now, like vulnerability scanners and network intrusion detection systems (NIDSs)/network intrusion prevention systems (NIPSs).

This chapter includes:

Monitoring for vulnerabilities

Checking your systems and configurations against baselines

Gaining visibility on your network

Defending your network against common threats

# Amazon Inspector

An important part of security at any organization is making sure that you have visibility into your systems. You need to know about open ports and out-of-date software. As organizations get larger, you also need a way to automate security assessments, rather than relying on manual scanning and other processes. With AWS, you have the ability to create automated security assessments with a product called Amazon Inspector.

*Amazon Inspector* is an AWS offering that allows the automation of security assessments. You can have assessments run on a schedule or when an event occurs that is monitored by Amazon CloudWatch, or you can even kick off the assessment with an application programming interface (API) call. The dashboard gives you a simple view for assessments that have run, as well as findings from various scans. It also gives you a quick method to view the last scan.

Amazon Inspector makes use of *assessment templates* that define which sets of rules you want to run against your environment. Two types of assessments are offered by Amazon Inspector: *network assessments* and *host assessments*. Network assessments don't require an agent to be installed on your systems, though if you want to find out about processes running on a specific port you'll need the Inspector Agent for that. Host assessments require the Inspector Agent to be installed. These assessments are much more detailed and can look for things like vulnerable versions of software, security best practices, and industry-standard host-hardening practices. You can choose one or both of these when you set up Amazon Inspector. The template shown in Figure 15.1 includes both the network and host assessments.

**FIGURE 15.1**   The default assessment template created by Amazon Inspector includes CVEs and CIS benchmarks.

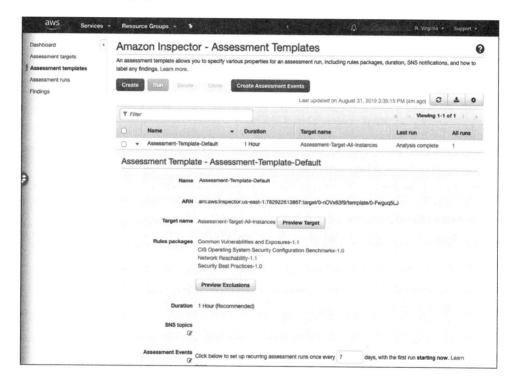

CVE stands for Common Vulnerabilities and Exposures. It is a listing of known vulnerabilities, each identified with a unique number.

The Center for Internet Security (CIS) publishes benchmarks for operating system and application hardening.

Once you have set up your assessment template, you can use it to assess your environment. An *assessment run* is when you scan your environment using the assessment template that you set up previously. Once the assessment run has completed, you'll be able to view any of the findings that were discovered.

You may be wondering what makes up a template. Templates contain one or more rules packages. A *rules package* defines specifically what you are checking for in your environment. It is worth noting that you can't create custom rules packages; you can use only the rules packages provided by AWS. As of this writing, these are the rules packages available, listed by assessment type:

- Network assessments

  - **Network Reachability:** This rules package can examine your environment's network configurations. Specifically, it is able to review the configurations for security groups, network access control lists (NACLs), route tables, subnets, virtual private cloud (VPC), VPC peering, AWS Direct Connect and virtual private gateways (VPGs), Internet gateways (IGW), EC2 instances, elastic load balancers (ELBs), and elastic network interfaces (ENIs).

- Host assessments

  - **Common Vulnerabilities and Exposures (CVE):** This rules package will check your systems to see if they are vulnerable to any of the CVEs reported.

  - **Center for Internet Security (CIS) Benchmarks:** This rules package will assess your systems against CIS benchmarks specific to your operating system. There are Level 1 and Level 2 checks. Level 1 is typically safe to implement; Level 2 tends to be more risky as the settings in Level 2 may "break" things. Level 2 is usually used in environments where the security of the system is paramount.

  - **Security Best Practices:** This rules package is looking at security best practices in general. For instance, if you have a Linux instance it will verify that you can't log in with root over SSH. This particular rules package does not apply to EC2 instances running Windows at this time.

  - **Runtime Behavior Analysis:** This rules package identifies risky behaviors on your systems, such as using protocols that are insecure to connect or open ports that aren't being used.

I'm sure you can see how Amazon Inspector is a powerful tool in your AWS arsenal that will give you better insight into how well your environment as a whole is configured against security best practices.

# Amazon GuardDuty

In an AWS ecosystem, *Amazon GuardDuty* is analogous to your traditional intrusion detection system (IDS) or intrusion prevention system (IPS) that you may have on-site. It uses various threat intelligence feeds and analyzes logs from several sources, including VPC flow logs, AWS CloudTrail event logs, and DNS logs. It can alert you to different kinds of malicious activity that could indicate issues with leaked user account credentials, privilege escalation attacks, and command-and-control type behavior. There are three types of activity that Amazon GuardDuty looks for specifically:

- Reconnaissance
- Instance compromise
- Account compromise

*Reconnaissance* is often a first step toward an attack. In fact, it is the first step defined in the Cyber Kill Chain, which was developed by Lockheed Martin. During the reconnaissance phase, an attacker is trying to learn about your environment. This is typically when you'll see vulnerability scans being conducted against your environment. The attacker is looking for IP addresses, hostnames, open ports, and/or misconfigured protocols. If they have a list of usernames and passwords, you may also have a larger than normal number of failed logins from a single source. Amazon GuardDuty is able to detect all these behaviors and is able to use the threat intelligence feeds to detect IP addresses that are known to be malicious. Even better, you can use findings that are detected by Amazon GuardDuty to automatically remediate the issue before it becomes an incident. The event in Amazon CloudWatch that generated the finding can trigger a function in AWS Lambda that can be used to resolve the issue.

The next type of activity is instance compromise. *Instance compromise* has several indicators that may be present. Some of them are similar to what you would expect to see on-site if a system was compromised, such as malware command and control, crypto miners, unusual amounts of traffic or unusual network protocols, or even communication with a known bad IP. Amazon GuardDuty is able to spot this activity and will report it as a finding. As you can see in the Cyber Kill Chain shown in Figure 15.2, this type of activity will typically fall under weaponization, delivery, exploitation, installation, and command and control. It may also include the last step, Actions on Objective, if Amazon GuardDuty alerts to data exfiltration.

**FIGURE 15.2**    The Cyber Kill Chain outlines the various stages of attack.

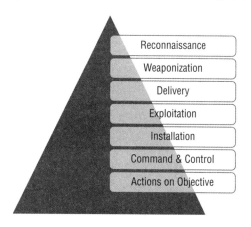

The last type of activity we'll examine is account compromise. *Account compromise* is usually going to be identified by events like logins from strange places, especially IP addresses known to belong to anonymizing services and attempts to disable the monitoring services that you may be using within AWS. The phases of the Cyber Kill Chain involved with this activity type would be delivery and actions on objective. This activity is most commonly seen when administrative accounts are not protected by multifactor authentication.

# Summary

Amazon Inspector uses assessment templates to define which sets of rules will be used to assess your AWS environment. The assessment templates can include both network assessments and host assessments. For the network assessments, you can choose to run it with or without the Inspector Agent; however, you must install the Inspector Agent for the host assessments. An assessment run refers to when you are using your assessment template to assess your AWS environment against the rulesets that you configured.

Amazon GuardDuty can be used to monitor instances and your network for potentially malicious activity. It is able to detect typical reconnaissance behavior, instance compromise, and account compromise. When it detects these events, it generates a finding. You can automatically remediate the events that created the findings by using Amazon CloudWatch to trigger an AWS Lambda function.

# Resources to Review

Amazon Inspector FAQs:

> https://aws.amazon.com/inspector/faqs/

Amazon Inspector Rules Packages and Rules:

> https://docs.aws.amazon.com/inspector/latest/userguide/
> inspector_rule-packages.html

What Is Amazon GuardDuty?:

> https://docs.aws.amazon.com/guardduty/latest/ug/what-is-guardduty.html

Amazon GuardDuty FAQs:

> https://aws.amazon.com/guardduty/faqs/

# Exam Essentials

**Know what Amazon Inspector is used for.**   Amazon Inspector is used to run automated security assessments against your AWS environment. It works similarly to a vulnerability scanner and on the exam may be referred to in a similar fashion.

**Understand Amazon Inspector terminology.**   Amazon Inspector uses assessment templates, which contain predefined rules packages. The rules packages define what baselines your systems will be tested against, such as CIS benchmarks or specific CVEs. An assessment run is when Amazon Inspector uses an assessment template to analyze whether a system is compliant with the rules packages in the assessment template.

**Know what Amazon GuardDuty does.**    You'll most likely not have any in-depth questions on the exam about Amazon GuardDuty. Just remember that it is used to monitor your AWS infrastructure for known bad activities and that you can use AWS Lambda to automate remediation.

# Exercises

To follow along with these exercises, you'll need to have a network properly configured in AWS, as well as an EC2 instance. The default VPC will work well for this, or you can use a VPC of your own design if you prefer. I highly recommend using the Amazon Linux AMI with Amazon Inspector Agent for your instance, as it comes with Inspector Agent already installed. If you choose to install it on a different system, you'll find these instructions helpful:

```
https://docs.aws.amazon.com/inspector/latest/userguide/
inspector_installing-uninstalling-agents.html
```

Given the large number of systems and installation methods, I will not cover the installation of the Inspector Agent in these exercises.

### EXERCISE 15.1

**Set Up and Configure Amazon Inspector**

For these steps to work properly, you must have the Amazon Inspector Agent installed on the Amazon EC2 instance that you'll assess.

1. Log into the AWS Management Console.

2. Click Services; then under Security, Identity And Compliance, click Inspector.

3. On the Amazon Inspector screen, click Get Started.

4. Leave both check boxes for network assessments and host assessments selected and click Advanced Setup.

5. On the Define An Assessment Target screen, click Next.

6. On the Define An Assessment Template screen, open the Duration drop-down menu and change the entry from 1 hour to 15 minutes.

   This will make the scan complete in 15 minutes—which is great for the exercise. However, in a production environment you'd want it to run long enough to complete. A safe bet would be to start with the default hour and extend the time if needed.

7. Deselect the Assessment Schedule option at the bottom. Click Next.

8. Scroll down and click Create.

9. On the Amazon Inspector - Assessment Runs screen, click the arrow just to the left and below Start Time to expand the settings for this assessment run.

10. Click the Refresh button after 15 minutes to verify the scan is complete. Once complete, it will look like Figure 15.3.

**FIGURE 15.3** The assessment run compares your network configurations and your EC2 host against the recommendations made by the rules packages in the assessment template you created.

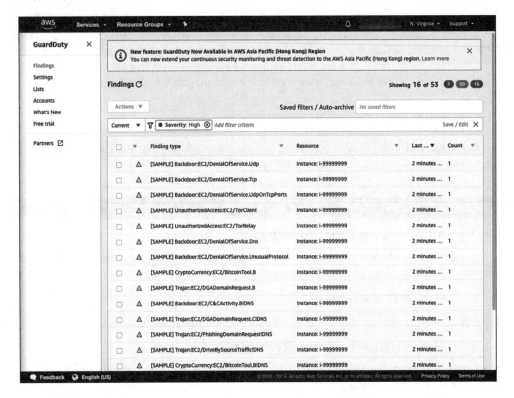

11. Now that the assessment run has finished, click Findings in the Inspector Console navigation menu.

12. Click the arrow next to one of the findings to expand it. In my case, one of the High Severity findings is that core dumps aren't restricted. You can see the description and the recommendation to resolve the issue in Figure 15.4.

**FIGURE 15.4**    A High Severity finding from Amazon Inspector gives me information on why it is an issue and how to resolve it.

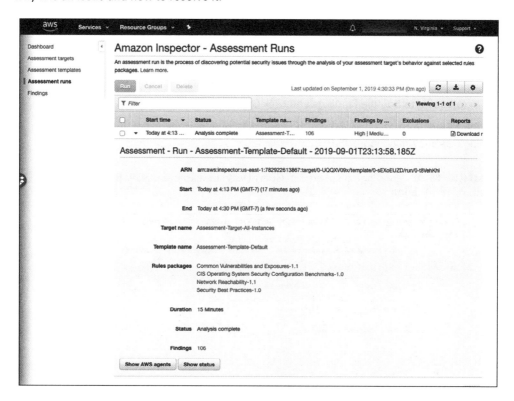

Experiment with this view to become familiar with some of the findings you might see. You are charged per run, so be careful not to run it too often. Many organizations do monthly scans, which should be sufficient. You should check the guidelines of your organization to determine whether you must meet scanning requirements.

If you would like to reset Amazon Inspector to where it was before, delete the assessment run, the assessment template, and the assessment targets by clicking the corresponding menu item, selecting the check box next to the item you want to delete, and then clicking Delete.

---

**EXERCISE 15.2**

## Set Up and Configure Amazon GuardDuty

1.  Log into the AWS Management Console.

2.  Click Services then under Security, Identity And Compliance, click GuardDuty.

3.  Click the Get Started button.

4.  Click Enable GuardDuty.

5.  Let's generate some test findings so that you can see what they would look like. From the GuardDuty Console navigation menu, click Settings.

6.  Scroll down to Sample Findings and click Generate Sample Findings.

7.  Click Findings in the GuardDuty Console navigation menu and you'll see some findings, as shown in Figure 15.5.

**FIGURE 15.5**   Findings displayed in GuardDuty are expandable, which allows you to get more information.

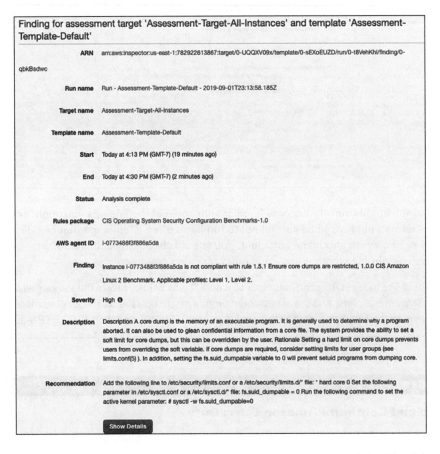

Finding for assessment target 'Assessment-Target-All-Instances' and template 'Assessment-Template-Default'

| | |
|---|---|
| **ARN** | arn:aws:inspector:us-east-1:782922613867:target/0-UQQXV09x/template/0-sEXoEUZD/run/0-t8VehKhi/finding/0-qbkBsdwc |
| **Run name** | Run - Assessment-Template-Default - 2019-09-01T23:13:58.185Z |
| **Target name** | Assessment-Target-All-Instances |
| **Template name** | Assessment-Template-Default |
| **Start** | Today at 4:13 PM (GMT-7) (19 minutes ago) |
| **End** | Today at 4:30 PM (GMT-7) (2 minutes ago) |
| **Status** | Analysis complete |
| **Rules package** | CIS Operating System Security Configuration Benchmarks-1.0 |
| **AWS agent ID** | i-0773488f3f886a5da |
| **Finding** | Instance i-0773488f3f886a5da is not compliant with rule 1.5.1 Ensure core dumps are restricted, 1.0.0 CIS Amazon Linux 2 Benchmark. Applicable profiles: Level 1, Level 2. |
| **Severity** | High ❶ |
| **Description** | Description A core dump is the memory of an executable program. It is generally used to determine why a program aborted. It can also be used to glean confidential information from a core file. The system provides the ability to set a soft limit for core dumps, but this can be overridden by the user. Rationale Setting a hard limit on core dumps prevents users from overriding the soft variable. If core dumps are required, consider setting limits for user groups (see limits.conf(5) ). In addition, setting the fs.suid_dumpable variable to 0 will prevent setuid programs from dumping core. |
| **Recommendation** | Add the following line to /etc/security/limits.conf or a /etc/security/limits.d/* file: * hard core 0 Set the following parameter in /etc/sysctl.conf or a /etc/sysctl.d/* file: fs.suid_dumpable = 0 Run the following command to set the active kernel parameter: # sysctl -w fs.suid_dumpable=0 |

Show Details

8.  Click any of the findings to open an informational screen up on the right side of the screen. This is shown in Figure 15.6.

**FIGURE 15.6**  Additional details on specific findings are available in the console by clicking on an individual finding.

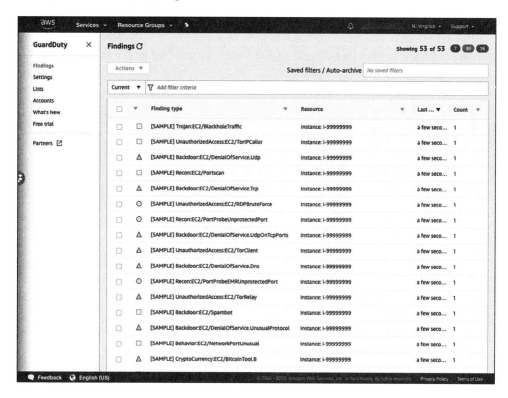

That's all there is to setting up GuardDuty. To avoid being charged for this service in your lab environment, make sure you disable it after this exercise. Here's how:

1.  Choose Settings from the GuardDuty Console menu.

2.  Scroll all the way down to Suspend GuardDuty. Select the Disable GuardDuty option and click the Save Settings button.

3.  Click the Disable button to confirm.

# Review Questions

You can find the answers in the Appendix.

1. Which of the following are not types of assessments offered by Amazon Inspector? (Choose two.)

   A. Port assessments

   B. Network assessments

   C. VPC assessments

   D. Host assessments

2. How does Amazon Inspector determine the rules to use in assessing your environment?

   A. Through AWS Config configuration items

   B. Through Trusted Advisor template settings

   C. Through Amazon Inspector assessment templates

   D. All of the above

3. Which of the following require agents to be installed on your systems?

   A. Network assessments

   B. Host assessments

   C. Both network and host assessments

   D. Neither network nor host assessments

4. You are concerned about open ports on your system. A previous administrator was known to neglect shutting off unused ports. Which AWS rules package might you use to determine if unused ports are still open?

   A. The CVE rules package

   B. The CIS Benchmarks package

   C. The Security Best Practices package

   D. The Runtime Behavior Analysis package

5. Which of the following is not assessed by the Network Reachability rules package?

   A. VPC peering

   B. Route tables

   C. Virtual private gateways

   D. All of these are assessed by the Network Reachability rules package.

6. Which of the following are types of activity that Amazon GuardDuty looks for? (Choose two.)

    **A.** Host compromise

    **B.** Instance compromise

    **C.** Account compromise

    **D.** Service compromise

7. You have been tasked with securing your system against attacks. Specifically, your environments have been vulnerable in the past to vulnerability scans. Which of the following are areas into which you should look to protect from malicious vulnerability scans? (Choose two.)

    **A.** Open ports

    **B.** Dated operating systems

    **C.** Passwords that don't meet current password policies

    **D.** Misconfigured protocols

8. You have instances running in three different AWS regions. You are running Amazon GuardDuty in each region. How many collections of security findings will you have?

    **A.** One; security findings are aggregated into the first region in which you set up Amazon GuardDuty.

    **B.** One; security findings are aggregated into a region of your choosing.

    **C.** Three; security findings are kept in the region to which they apply.

    **D.** Two; security findings are aggregated but kept in two regions for redundancy.

9. You have responsibility for eight different AWS accounts. Each account has Amazon GuardDuty enabled. How many accounts will have security findings within them?

    **A.** Only the master account will have findings.

    **B.** Each account will have its own findings but the findings will be aggregated into the master account.

    **C.** Findings will remain in the account to which they apply.

    **D.** None of these

10. Which of the following are analyzed by the Amazon GuardDuty service? (Choose two.)

    **A.** AWS CloudTrail

    **B.** AWS DNS logs

    **C.** Amazon CloudWatch

    **D.** Amazon Inspector

11. You are responsible for setting up Amazon GuardDuty at a global firm with applications and instances running in every available AWS region. How can you set up GuardDuty so that all your security findings are aggregated into a single account? Which of the following tools would you need to use? (Choose two.)

    **A.** Amazon S3

    **B.** Amazon RDS

    **C.** Amazon CloudWatch

    **D.** Amazon Inspector

12. Which of the following services is not available to be consumed and analyzed by Amazon GuardDuty?

    **A.** AWS CloudTrail

    **B.** AWS DNS logs

    **C.** VPC flow logs

    **D.** AWS EC2 instance logs

13. You have set up an extensive network within AWS and are using Amazon GuardDuty to analyze VPC flow logs and DNS logs. You also have a requirement to maintain your VPC flow logs for at least 12 months. What do you need to meet this requirement?

    **A.** Nothing; Amazon GuardDuty will maintain those logs for two years automatically.

    **B.** Configure Amazon GuardDuty to maintain the VPC flow logs for 12 months rather than the default of 90 days.

    **C.** Amazon GuardDuty does not maintain logs; you'll need to use another AWS logging and monitoring service such as CloudWatch.

    **D.** Turn on log retention in Amazon GuardDuty and set the Keep value to 12 months.

14. You need to delete all previous findings from Amazon GuardDuty and ensure the service is no longer running on your system. How can you stop GuardDuty and make sure findings are deleted?

    **A.** You cannot delete GuardDuty findings manually.

    **B.** Suspend the GuardDuty service, which will also delete all findings and configurations.

    **C.** Disable the GuardDuty service, which will also delete all findings and configurations.

    **D.** Tear down all instances and devices in the target region, turn off GuardDuty, and rebuild your environment.

15. Which of the following is a means of viewing findings from Amazon GuardDuty? (Choose two.)

    **A.** AWS CloudWatch events

    **B.** Amazon Inspector

    **C.** The Amazon GuardDuty console

    **D.** The Amazon GuardDuty CLI

**16.** Which of the following does Amazon GuardDuty threat intelligence store?

   **A.** IP addresses

   **B.** Subnets

   **C.** CIDR blocks

   **D.** None of these

**17.** You are a consultant asked to assess a client's AWS network. However, you have no access to individual hosts. Which of the following can you perform using Amazon Inspector?

   **A.** Only host assessments

   **B.** Only network assessments

   **C.** Both host and network assessments

   **D.** Nothing; you need access to hosts for running any Amazon Inspector assessments.

**18.** You want to set up Amazon Inspector to automatically assess new instances launched through an Auto Scaling scale-out event. Which of the following services would you use to set a security assessment to run when that happens?

   **A.** Amazon CloudWatch Events

   **B.** Amazon CloudWatch

   **C.** Amazon Inspector, which provides native access to Auto Scaling events

   **D.** You cannot monitor events using Amazon Inspector.

**19.** Which of the following is not a valid security finding level for an Amazon Inspector rule?

   **A.** High

   **B.** Low

   **C.** Informational

   **D.** Notification

**20.** Which of the following services gives you access to Amazon Inspector assessment metrics?

   **A.** Amazon CloudWatch

   **B.** Amazon CloudWatch Events

   **C.** Amazon CloudTrail

   **D.** None of these

# Networking

# Chapter

# 16

# Virtual Private Cloud

**THE AWS CERTIFIED SYSOPS ADMINISTRATOR – ASSOCIATE EXAM TOPICS COVERED IN THIS CHAPTER MAY INCLUDE, BUT ARE NOT LIMITED TO, THE FOLLOWING:**

**Domain 1.0: Monitoring and Reporting**

✓ 1.2   Recognize and differentiate performance and availability metrics

**Domain 2.0: High Availability**

✓ 2.1   Implement scalability and elasticity based on use case

✓ 2.2   Recognize and differentiate highly available and resilient environments on AWS

**Domain 3.0: Deployment and Provisioning**

✓ 3.1   Identify and execute steps required to provision cloud resources

✓ 3.2   Identify and remediate deployment issues

**Domain 6.0: Networking**

✓ 6.1   Apply AWS networking features

✓ 6.2   Implement connectivity services of AWS

✓ 6.3   Gather and interpret relevant information for network troubleshooting

There is nothing more fundamental to a datacenter environment than its network. Migrating to the cloud does require some changes in how things function, but networking is still a core component that, when done properly, can contribute to a successful cloud deployment. Although AWS manages the underlying network hardware, it is your responsibility as a system administrator to ensure that your networking is configured properly and securely. To do that, you need to understand the basic components of AWS networking, how they all tie together, and of course, how to troubleshoot when things aren't going according to plan.

This chapter includes:

A refresher on CIDR notation

Fundamentals of VPCs and their components

Connecting outside of your VPC

Using security groups to protect your instances

Using network access control lists (NACLs) to defend your networks

Troubleshooting AWS networking issues

# Understanding AWS Networking

When you think about networking in a traditional datacenter, you probably think about the physical infrastructure that is used. Devices like firewalls, routers, and switches make up the core backbone of your datacenter. When you move to the AWS cloud, you are separated from the hardware layer completely. AWS manages the underlying hardware, and you are responsible for configuring the networking components that are exposed to you. For example, you can configure your logical network, referred to as a virtual private cloud (VPC), with subnets to allow for more efficient use of your available IP space. You can configure routing and pathways to the Internet or other VPCs.

AWS networking supports both IPv4 and IPv6. Certain features, such as NAT devices, are not available if you wish to use IPv6. You can get functionality similar to NAT devices with an egress-only Internet gateway, which we will discuss later in this chapter.

IP stands for Internet Protocol. This is how we identify devices on a network. An IPv4 address consists of 32 bits, whereas an IPv6 address consists of 128 bits.

Network address translation (NAT) is a technology that was invented to help with the shortage of IPv4 addresses in the public address space. It allows you to map nonroutable internal IP addresses to a single or a pool of external public IP addresses.

They say you have to walk before you can run, so let's review an important networking concept and then dive into the AWS components.

## Classless Inter-Domain Routing Refresher

*Classless Inter-Domain Routing* (CIDR) is a form of notation used to tell you how many bits in an IP address are being used for the network as opposed to being used for the host part of the address. It is appended to the end of an IP address in the form of /*XX*, where *XX* is the number of network bits, and it can help you easily determine what the subnet mask is. A *subnet mask* is used to divide an IP address into network bits and host bits. A simpler way to think of it is that CIDR notation is shorthand for subnet masks—/24, for instance, is much simpler to write repeatedly than 255.255.255.0.

As the number used for the CIDR notation grows larger, the number of host bits gets smaller, which in turn reduces the number of IP addresses available. For instance, in Figure 16.1 you'll notice that the /16 CIDR notation uses 16 bits for the network address, which leaves 16 bits for the host part of the address. This equates to 65,536 IP addresses total, of which 65,534 are usable. The /24 notation, on the other hand, uses 24 bits for the network, leaving only 8 bits for the host part of the address. This equates to 256 IP addresses total, of which 254 are usable.

The first address and last address of every network range is reserved. The first address is a network identification address and the last address is the network's broadcast address.

**FIGURE 16.1** Using CIDR notation to identify network bits versus host bits is a common practice.

**IP Address with CIDR notation: 192.168.0.0/16**

- Subnet Mask in Decimal: 255.255.0.0
- Subnet Mask in Binary: <u>11111111 11111111</u> 00000000 00000000

**IP Address with CIDR notation: 192.168.10.0/24**

- Subnet Mask in Decimal: 255.255.255.0
- Subnet Mask in Binary: <u>11111111 11111111 11111111</u> 00000000

**Underlined bits are the network part of the address. Each grouping consists of 8 bits.**

# Virtual Private Cloud

The *virtual private cloud* (VPC) is the most basic networking component in AWS. It defines the address space of a logical network and can be set to allow IPv4 and IPv6 addresses. Within the VPC, you can create subnets, route tables, Internet gateways, NAT gateways, and NAT instances. You can customize your network to a great degree.

Don't worry if you don't understand these topics yet—by the end of the chapter, you'll understand them well enough to configure your network in AWS!

Once your VPC is ready to go, you can connect to your on-premises datacenter through virtual private network (VPN) connections or AWS Direct Connect. Your VPC in AWS can act as an extension of your on-premises datacenter if you want to use a hybrid model, or you can use it to enable more secure and potentially better-performing connections to all your workloads in the cloud.

When you first create an AWS account, you are given a default network. That default network has most of the basic components available for you to hit the ground running, though you may wish to provision your own, especially if you want to keep to a particular IP address range. When building a VPC, you can certainly do it from scratch, but it is much simpler to use the VPC Wizard provided by Amazon to put the basic building blocks into place and then customize them to meet your needs. There are four options when using the VPC Wizard:

**Amazon VPC With A Single Public Subnet Only**    This option is great for hosting systems that are meant to be publicly accessible, such as web servers that have no need to connect to a backend system in a private subnet.

**Amazon VPC With Public And Private Subnets**    Use this option to build your lab environment. It provisions a public and a private subnet, with all the basic routing set up automatically.

**Amazon VPC With Public And Private Subnets And AWS Site-To-Site VPN Access**    This option is the same as the second one except that it is already configured to allow you to set up your VPN connection.

**Amazon VPC With Private Subnet Only And AWS Site-to-Site VPN Access**    This option is great for hosting internally accessible systems, and is already configured to allow you to set up your VPN connection.

VPCs are free to create, but keep in mind that the resources within them may not be. Amazon EC2 instances incur costs, as does data transfer through a VPN connection.

When you create your VPC, you can choose how large the IP address space will be. With IPv4 addressing, you can use anything from /16 to /28. If you are using IPv6, then by default you'll use /56. Make certain that you have sized your VPC appropriately for the current state, and be sure to factor in growth. Although you can add secondary IPv4 CIDR ranges to a VPC to grow it, you can't do that with an IPv6 address range.

# Subnets

Once your VPC is created, the next step is to carve out the large IP space within the VPC into smaller chunks of address spaces. These smaller chunks are referred to as *subnets*. Although the VPC spans all availability zones, subnets are assigned to specific availability zones. If you are trying to achieve a highly available infrastructure, you'll want to create at least two subnets, each in its own availability zone. For instance, say you want to create highly available web servers. Create two subnets, each in its own availability zone; call them **Subnet1A** and **Subnet1B**. Then, when you set up load balancing and/or Auto Scaling, you ensure that you include both subnets. This will route traffic to either availability zone in the case of a load balancer or will automatically scale capacity depending on demand across both availability zones. If one availability zone goes down, these mechanisms will either route traffic to the active availability zone or add more instances to the active availability zone.

Subnets in AWS are referred to as private or public. A private subnet is typically used for resources within the VPC that have no Internet connection and do not contain Internet gateways.

A public subnet has an Internet gateway and allows for Internet traffic. As a best practice, the public subnet should not contain instances, with the exception of bastion hosts, discussed in a moment. It will instead contain things like NAT gateways and instances, which are discussed later in this chapter. In Figure 16.2 below, you can see six subnets that have been defined in a single VPC. Each of those subnets has its own IP range assigned to it.

**FIGURE 16.2** Subnets created in a VPC spanning six different availability zones are all listed with their IPv4 ranges and CIDR notation.

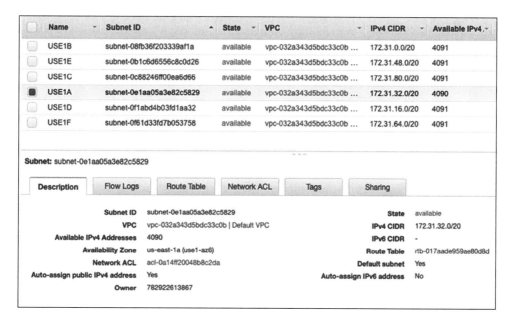

Bastion hosts are publicly accessible hosts that allow you to access your other resources within AWS. Private subnets with hosts that need to download patches and/or software updates from the Internet but that don't require inbound access can add a NAT gateway or NATinstance ID to their route table (the NAT gateway or instance resides in a public subnet). Doing so allows their outbound traffic to be routed through the NAT device but will not allow any inbound traffic from the Internet (other than returning traffic, of course).

## Route Tables

In an on-premises network, you use *route tables* to define the next destination (hop) for traffic going outside a local network. In AWS, it works similarly, though there are a few differences.

In an AWS network, the next "hop" is usually going to be a device ID of some sort rather than a network address. You start by defining the target destination, and then you choose the actual target. For instance, Internet gateways can be target devices and are prefixed with *igw*. Local traffic may be set up with the VPC CIDR as the destination address, and the target will be set to local. This allows any subnets associated with this route table to talk to one another. In Figure 16.3, you can see a typical routing table setup for a default VPC. The destination is anything bound for 172.31.0.0/16 and the target is local. So any subnets associated with this routing table that are sending traffic to this network will be allowed to do so. Notice the 0.0.0.0/0—that's essentially a catch-all. Anything that doesn't match the routes specified will match on this rule and, in this case, will be forwarded to an Internet gateway.

**FIGURE 16.3** This is a typical routing table in AWS with a simple entry for the VPC's address space and an entry to route traffic not destined for that address space out to the Internet.

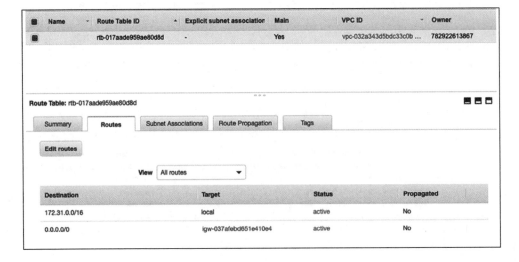

| | Name | Route Table ID | Explicit subnet association | Main | VPC ID | Owner |
|---|------|----------------|----------------------------|------|--------|-------|
| ■ | | rtb-017aade959ae80d8d | - | Yes | vpc-032a343d5bdc33c0b ... | 782922613867 |

Route Table: rtb-017aade959ae80d8d

| Summary | **Routes** | Subnet Associations | Route Propagation | Tags |

Edit routes

View | All routes ▼

| Destination | Target | Status | Propagated |
|-------------|--------|--------|------------|
| 172.31.0.0/16 | local | active | No |
| 0.0.0.0/0 | igw-037afebd651e410e4 | active | No |

I've mentioned a few times that the routes in the route table only apply to subnets that are associated with them. You may be wondering what I mean by that. When a subnet is associated with a route table, it is able to use the routes that are defined within that route table. By default, new subnets end up in the main route table. You can explicitly assign them to that route table or to a different route table. A route can be associated with many subnets, but a subnet can be associated with only one route table. In Figure 16.4, you can see the subnets associated with the chosen routing table. This is the main routing table, so they are associated with it by default. If they were explicitly associated with this routing table, they would show up in the top section, right under the Edit Subnet Associations button.

**FIGURE 16.4**    You can view associated subnets for a routing table on the Subnet Associations tab.

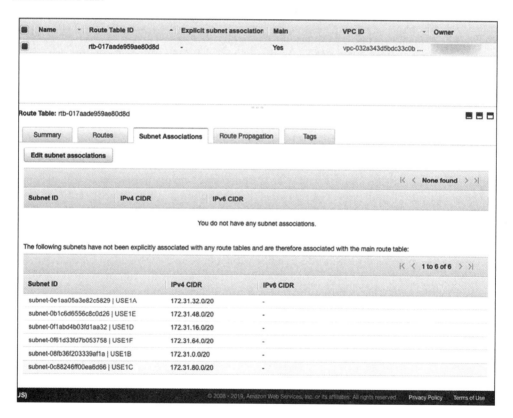

## Internet Gateways

An *Internet gateway*, when added to a subnet, makes it possible for systems and/or services in that subnet to access the Internet or be accessed from the Internet. When a subnet has an

Internet gateway in it, it is referred to as a public subnet. Without firewalls, security groups, or NACLs, systems in a public subnet are accessible from the Internet. Public subnets are typically used for systems and/or services that need to be publicly exposed. This includes things like NAT gateways, NAT instances, and bastion hosts.

An *egress-only Internet gateway* is a special use case. If you are using IPv4, then you don't need an egress-only Internet gateway. With IPv4 addressing, if you want to ensure that systems can reach out to the Internet for patches, for example, you can use a NAT gateway or instance to ensure that the system can reach outbound traffic but that it is not accessible from the Internet. With IPv6 addresses, however, you can't use NAT gateways or NAT instances. The egress-only Internet gateway takes care of that need, allowing systems with IPv6 addresses to reach out for updates and so forth without allowing inbound traffic to those systems.

## NAT Gateways and Instances

NAT has been mentioned several times in this chapter. Before we dive into NAT gateways and instances, let's review what NAT is and how it works. NAT stands for *network address translation*. Simply put, NAT translates one or more internal addresses to an external address and back. It has several uses:

- Allows multiple internal systems to use one IP address outbound
- Protects internal IP address space from reconnaissance activities

One of the main reasons that NAT was invented was because we were running low on IPv4 addresses. The IPv4 address pool has, in fact, been exhausted for several years now. With NAT, organizations can use whatever IP addressing scheme they want to use, as long as they are private IP addresses. NAT ensures that outbound traffic uses a single IP, or a small pool of IP addresses, and is also stateful in that it will ensure that traffic will get back to the appropriate system.

In AWS, you have two options in relation to setting up NAT for use. In either case, the NAT device needs to be deployed into a public subnet (a subnet with an Internet gateway). The NAT device will use the Internet gateway to actually access the Internet; think of it like a translation device sitting between the traffic from the private subnets and the Internet. Private subnets will be directed via the route tables to send any unmatched traffic to the NAT gateway or NAT instance. The entry in the route table for a NAT device has a prefix of *nat*. Now let's look at the two options we have for NAT and why you may want to use one over the other.

NAT is supported on IPv4 networks only. If you need NAT functionality but you have an IPv6 network, an egress-only Internet gateway is your best option. This was discussed earlier in the "Internet Gateways" section.

### NAT Gateways

The NAT gateway is a managed service provided by AWS (Figure 16.5). When you create it, you specify which public subnet it will live in, and you assign an elastic IP address to it as well. Once created, the private subnets that need to route to the NAT gateway will need an entry added to the route table that they are associated with pointing them at the NAT gateway for egress out to the Internet.

**FIGURE 16.5**   The NAT Gateway can be managed in the AWS Console. It is created with a private IP address and the elastic IP address it was assigned at creation time.

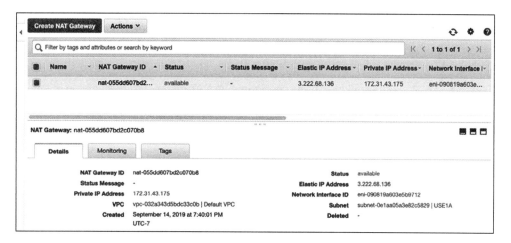

NAT gateways exist only in the availability zone in which they were created. If you are supporting a highly available architecture, you'll need to create a NAT gateway in each availability zone; otherwise, if the availability zone that hosts the NAT gateway goes down, your systems will lose outbound Internet connectivity.

A NAT gateway is a good fit for you if:

- You want a managed service to reduce administrative overhead.
- You do not need to support anything greater than 45 Gbps bandwidth.

Once you have created your NAT gateway and updated your route tables, you can use a simple ping test to ensure that outbound traffic is being allowed from your private subnet. If everything is configured correctly, your ping will be allowed to traverse your network to the Internet site and return a reply.

 The ping test involves logging on to a system in the private subnet that has been routed to through the NAT device and pinging a publicly accessible resource to ensure that traffic is allowed out and return traffic is allowed back in. For instance, from the command line on a Windows or Linux host, type **ping www.wiley.com**. If you get a response, you have configured your NAT device properly.

## NAT Instances

If you want to have fine-grained control over your NAT capabilities or you want to be able to scale it up to handle even higher bandwidth demands, then a NAT instance may be a better choice for you.

A NAT instance is a special-purpose EC2 instance that provides NAT capabilities just as the NAT gateway does. In this case, you have access to the operating system and can change configurations just as you would with a traditional server.

Getting a NAT instance set up on a regular Linux server can be challenging, so AWS simplifies the process by providing readymade Amazon Linux Amazon Machine Images (AMIs) that are configured and ready to be used as NAT instances. Simply search for the AMI name **amzn-ami-vpc-nat** in Community AMIs (Figure 16.6) and you'll find them; then choose the instance type and size as you would with a normal EC2 instance. Amazon recommends choosing the latest version that is available.

**FIGURE 16.6**   Amazon Linux AMIs configured as NAT instances are available in the Community AMIs section.

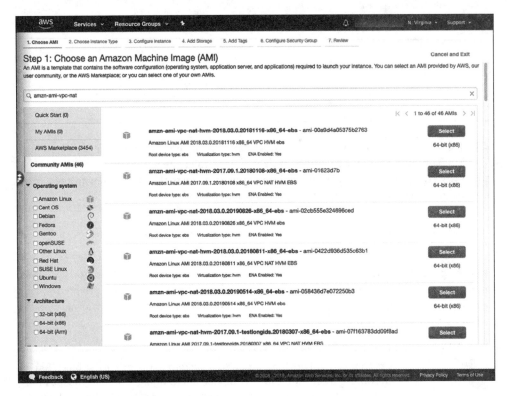

## VPC Endpoints

Once your basic network connectivity is working, there are things you can do to optimize and scale your networks. For instance, keeping traffic internal to your network can result in cost savings and improve security since your traffic is not traversing the Internet.

Several AWS services are available that allow you to keep traffic internal, and that is accomplished using VPC endpoints. *VPC endpoints* allow you to connect to AWS services within your network over the high-speed AWS backbone, rather than routing your traffic to the Internet and back in. Since your systems don't have to traverse the Internet to reach necessary services, you don't need to give them public IPs or worry about Internet gateways or NAT—they can simply connect to the VPC endpoint.

There are two types of VPC endpoints: interface endpoints and gateway endpoints. You create the type of VPC endpoint that you need to support the service that you want to consume. Once you create your VPC endpoint, you create and attach an endpoint policy that determines how much of the service is accessible to your systems.

Each type of VPC endpoint has a different use case. which we will examine next.

## Interface Endpoints

An *interface endpoint* serves as a method to access various AWS services. When you create an interface endpoint, you are creating an *elastic network interface* (ENI) that has a private IP address within the IP address range of your subnets. This private IP address is what is used to connect to the service. As of this writing, you can use an interface endpoint to access these key services and several more:

- Amazon API Gateway
- Amazon Athena
- Amazon CloudFormation
- AWS CloudTrail
- Amazon CloudWatch, CloudWatch Logs, and CloudWatch Events
- AWS CodeBuild, CodeCommit, and CodePipeline
- AWS Config
- Amazon Elastic Container Service (ECS) and Elastic Container Registry (ECR)
- AWS Key Management Service (KMS)
- Amazon Kinesis Data Firehouse and Kinesis Data Streams
- AWS Security Token Service (STS)
- Amazon Simple Notification Service (SNS)
- Amazon Simple Queue Service (SQS)

For a full, current listing of available services using interface endpoints, check out the VPC Endpoints documentation here:

https://docs.aws.amazon.com/vpc/latest/userguide/vpc-endpoints.html.

## Gateway Endpoints

A gateway endpoint differs from an interface endpoint. Rather than creating an elastic network interface, you are creating a gateway that you can reference in your route tables as a target for traffic. When you create a gateway endpoint, it is automatically added to the route table that you select. The following services are supported for use with a gateway endpoint:

- Amazon S3
- Amazon DynamoDB

## Connecting to the Outside

For many organizations, the move to the cloud is a gradual migration. The end goal may be to have all systems in the cloud, or a hybrid datacenter may be the desired outcome. Whatever the case, to support the move to the cloud you need to be able to establish a connection from your datacenter on-premises to your datacenter in AWS. There are a few options to do that; we'll explore using a virtual private network (VPN) and AWS Direct Connect.

### Virtual Private Network (VPN)

AWS supports site-to-site virtual private network (VPN) connections. A VPN is a method that allows you to create a protected "tunnel" for your data to traverse the Internet to its end destination. It offers both authentication and encryption for your data. Typically a VPN is established between two edge devices, most commonly firewalls. The AWS implementation is a little different.

To create a VPN on AWS, you need a virtual private gateway on the AWS side and a customer gateway on the other end of the connection.

A *virtual private gateway* is the terminating end of the VPN tunnel on the AWS side of the network. It allows a connection to one VPC on your AWS network. You can have up to five virtual private gateways per AWS account, per region. This makes sense when you take into account that you can have only five VPCs per region by default.

 Five VPCs per region is a soft limit, which you can raise by filling out an Amazon VPC limits form.

A *customer gateway* is the terminating end of the VPN tunnel on the customer side. This can be a hardware or software appliance, and it will quite commonly be a firewall that you have on-premises. There are some fantastic example scenarios with various types of firewalls being used as customer gateways in the AWS Network Administrator Guide. The section on customer gateways can be found here:

https://docs.aws.amazon.com/vpc/latest/adminguide/Introduction.html.

### AWS Direct Connect

Although site-to-site VPNs have been standard for years, newer technology has given you a method to connect directly to the AWS network rather than relying on an Internet connection to gain access to your resources. That method is called AWS Direct Connect. *AWS*

*Direct Connect* allows you to connect directly from your datacenter to AWS. This can result in a less expensive connection, while also providing a steadier and more reliable connection to your infrastructure on AWS.

If you need your connection to be highly available, then you'll need to provision at least two routers to talk to the AWS datacenter routers. The routers when provisioned in AWS are already redundant, so no further action is required on the AWS side. You may also use a site-to-site VPN as a backup solution to AWS Direct Connect in the event of a failure.

# Securing Your Network

On the forefront of most people's minds is the security of their network and its assets. Security professionals like to take the approach of "defense-in-depth," meaning that they have layers of security. No one tool is the silver bullet when it comes to protecting their datacenter.

Although we've discussed the various security tools in other chapters, we'll cover the network-specific features here that help you secure your infrastructure.

## Security Groups

A *security group* acts like a software firewall and is attached at the instance level. When you create your instances, you are prompted to either attach a security group or create a security group. If you opt to create a security group, it will by default have a rule that will allow remote access—Remote Desktop (RDP) for Windows, Secure Shell (SSH) for Linux, or from any source, 0.0.0.0/0. If you leave the security group with the wide-open source, you'll be warned that it is a security risk to do so. You can attach up to five security groups to any one instance.

Keep in mind that security groups are stateful, meaning that if traffic is allowed outbound, return traffic will be allowed in automatically as it is part of the same session. You don't need to specify individual rules for inbound and outbound traffic to facilitate communication. Additionally, all rules are evaluated that are in the security group before the decision is made whether or not to allow traffic to pass.

To increase security in tiered infrastructures—think web, application, and database—you can chain security groups. This approach allows you to define a security group that allows only traffic from instances assigned in another security group. This is common with elastic load balancers. For instance, you may have a security group called sg_webelb that is used for the elastic load balancer in front of your web servers and another security group called sg_web that gets assigned to your web servers. If you set the inbound rule of sg_web to allow only traffic from sg_webelb, you ensure that it will accept only traffic from the elastic load balancer in the sg_webelb security group. This strategy provides a great deal of protection against malicious traffic.

The default security group (shown below in Figure 16.7) created for the default VPC has basic rules. Essentially, inbound traffic will be allowed from instances that are in the same security group, and outbound traffic is allowed to go anywhere, on any port. You can, of course, alter the rules in the default security group, though I recommend creating your own and giving them descriptive names for their purpose.

**FIGURE 16.7** The default security groups allow traffic between instances attached to the same security group inbound.

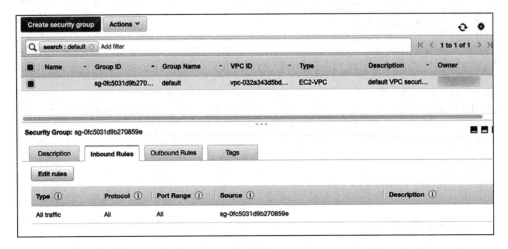

When you create a security group, you define not only the source of the traffic, but also the application and port or port range of the traffic. Well-known applications like HTTPS, MS SQL, and MySQL are already defined and, when selected, will fill in the appropriate port numbers. From there, for source you can select one of three options:

- **Custom:** This allows you to specify a specific IP address or IP address range that you expect to receive traffic from.

- **Anywhere:** This is essentially 0.0.0.0/0. It is not safe to use this, so be very careful if you leave it open.

- **My IP:** This captures the public IP address that is assigned to you at the moment (this is my favorite for my home lab).

Outbound rules similarly allow you to choose a well-known application or specify a port or port range. The biggest difference is that you specify a destination IP address or IP address range rather than a source.

## Network Access Control Lists

Whereas security groups are applied to individual instances, a *network access control list* (NACL) is applied at the subnet level. NACLs allow you to secure your individual subnets down to specific ports. They are stateless, meaning that they are not aware of sessions and must have rules defined for inbound and outbound traffic. Return traffic is not automatically allowed. This is a common issue and a favorite topic on AWS exams.

The default NACL allows all inbound traffic into the subnet and all outbound traffic out of the subnet. You can edit the default NACL if you choose to do so; just remember that the default NACL is automatically applied to any subnet that does not have an association specific to another NACL. This factor may result in denied traffic if it is not taken into account.

NACLs evaluate traffic in order from top to bottom. The default ACL has the Allow All rule set as Rule 100, shown below in Figure 16.8. If you wanted a rule to get evaluated before that rule, you would need to set the rule number to before 100. If you wanted it to be evaluated afterward, you would need a rule number higher than 100. In the case of the Allow All rule in the default NACL, if you put a rule after that it would never be matched as the Allow All rule would match everything.

**FIGURE 16.8** The default NACL allows all traffic from any source inbound to pass through it into the subnet.

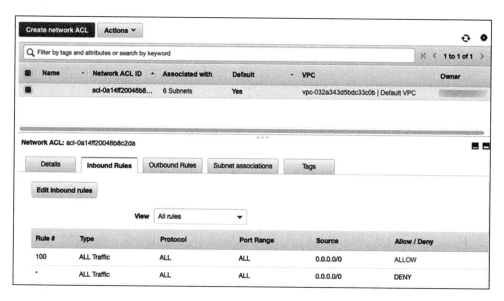

# Troubleshooting Network Issues

In this last section of our chapter on VPC, I felt it important to discuss how to troubleshoot the inevitable issue one day where your network traffic is not behaving in the way that you are expecting it to. Part of being a good system administrator, after all, is being able to resolve issues when they arise. One of the tools I'll highlight is the VPC flow log.

## VPC Flow Logs

*VPC flow logs* allow you troubleshoot traffic at several different levels, which can be handy if you're trying to figure out why traffic isn't reaching a specific end destination. They can help you recognize if you have security groups that are so restrictive they are blocking traffic, they can let you know what traffic is getting to your instances, and they can help you determine directionality of traffic if that is a concern. The great thing about VPC flow logs is that they can be applied at the VPC level (as the name implies) and can also be applied to a subnet or specific network interface on a system, which allows for more targeted troubleshooting.

You can save your flow logs to either Amazon CloudWatch Logs or Amazon S3. Flow logs can be captured for EC2 instances and other AWS services and will continue to be collected until the flow is deleted. It is important to remember that flow logs are not real time, and when you create one it may be several minutes before you have any data to review.

## Other Resources

Although VPC flow logs are your best friend when it comes to troubleshooting your AWS networks, there are a few other places you can look as well. If you suspect issues are related to DNS, you can check the Route 53 logs in Amazon CloudWatch. You may also be able to narrow down issues with web servers with Amazon CloudWatch where the issue may be related to the application rather than the network. Last but not least, if your network was working but is suddenly having issues, AWS CloudTrail will allow you to see if anything was changed recently, as well as who made the change.

# Summary

CIDR notation is used as shorthand to identify the network portion of an IP address versus the host portion of an IP address.

A virtual private cloud (VPC) is the logical network that you create within AWS. VPCs are free and consist of many resources, some of which are free like subnets and NACLs, and some that are not free like Amazon EC2 instances and Amazon RDS. Egress out of the VPC will typically incur costs as well. VPCs support both IPv4 (/16 to /28) and IPv6 (/56) addresses. Subnets are used to break up VPCs into smaller, more manageable chunks and to aid in setting up high availability. Route tables allow subnets to communicate with other subnets and other networks via devices like Internet gateways, NAT devices, and peering connections.

Internet gateways allow for systems in a public subnet to access the Internet. You can tell that a subnet is public as the route table it is attached to will have a route directing all unmatched traffic to an Internet gateway that is prefixed with *igw*. Egress-only Internet gateways give NAT-like capability to IPv6 networks.

NAT gateways and NAT instances are only used for IPv4 traffic—they do not support IPv6 traffic. NAT gateways are a managed service provided by AWS to simplify the administration of NAT technology on your network. NAT instances provide more granular control over configurations than a NAT gateway does and run as Amazon EC2 instances.

VPC endpoints allow you to connect to various Amazon services without having to go through the Internet. There are two types of VPC endpoints: interface endpoints and gateway endpoints. Interface endpoints use an ENI and a private IP to interface with your systems and support a wide range of services. Gateway endpoints are used by S3 and DynamoDB, and they create a gateway that can be targeted in your routing tables.

VPNs allow for external access to your AWS infrastructure. Site-to-site VPNs can be creating using virtual private gateways and customer gateways. You are limited to five virtual private gateways, which can each connect to one VPC. AWS Direct Connect is another connectivity option that can be used. It consists of a private link directly to the AWS datacenter, which provides a cost-effective and stable link between your on-premises systems and the AWS datacenter.

Security groups are similar to software firewalls, and they are applied at the instance level. They are stateful, meaning that the traffic needs to be allowed only one way and return traffic will be allowed automatically. All rules are evaluated before traffic is allowed or denied. NACLs are applied at the subnet level. Rules must be created for both directions to allow traffic flow, and they are evaluated in order, top to bottom.

VPC flow logs can be applied to a VPC, subnet, or network interface and can be stored and reviewed from either Amazon CloudWatch Logs or Amazon S3. They are perfect for troubleshooting network issues regarding traffic flow.

# Resources to Review

What Is Amazon VPC?

https://docs.aws.amazon.com/vpc/latest/userguide/what-is-amazon-vpc.html

VPCs and Subnets:

https://docs.aws.amazon.com/vpc/latest/userguide/VPC_Subnets.html

Internet Gateways:

https://docs.aws.amazon.com/vpc/latest/userguide/VPC_Internet_Gateway.html

Egress-Only Internet Gateway:

https://docs.aws.amazon.com/vpc/latest/userguide/
egress-only-internet-gateway.html

NAT Gateways:

https://docs.aws.amazon.com/vpc/latest/userguide/vpc-nat-gateway.html

NAT Instances:

https://docs.aws.amazon.com/vpc/latest/userguide/VPC_NAT_Instance.html

VPC Endpoints:

https://docs.aws.amazon.com/vpc/latest/userguide/vpc-endpoints.html

AWS VPN FAQs:

https://aws.amazon.com/vpn/faqs/

Your Customer Gateway:

   https://docs.aws.amazon.com/vpc/latest/adminguide/Introduction.html

AWS Direct Connect FAQs:

   https://aws.amazon.com/directconnect/faqs/?nc=sn&loc=6

Security Groups for Your VPC:

   https://docs.aws.amazon.com/vpc/latest/userguide/VPC_SecurityGroups.html

Network ACLs:

   https://docs.aws.amazon.com/vpc/latest/userguide/vpc-network-acls.html

VPC Flow Logs:

   https://docs.aws.amazon.com/vpc/latest/userguide/flow-logs.html

# Exam Essentials

**Understand what a VPC is and what its components do.**   The VPC is a logical network that contains your AWS infrastructure. It is broken down into smaller, more manageable chunks called subnets. Route tables define how traffic moves through a VPC.

**Remember the role of the Internet gateway, NAT gateway, and NAT instance.**   The Internet gateway sits inside a public subnet. This allows systems in the public subnet to reach out to the Internet and to be accessible from the Internet. NAT gateways and NAT instances both reside in a public subnet, but they are used to allow outbound connections from systems in a private subnet while restricting inbound connections.

**Understand the importance of VPC endpoints and why you would use them.**   With VPC endpoints, you can set up your systems to access services without having to traverse the Internet. VPC endpoints use AWS' backbone to provide low-latency links that can be more stable and more cost-effective.

**Understand connection options like VPN and Direct Connect.**   VPNs use virtual private gateways and customer gateways to establish connections between AWS and on-premises. Direct Connect is a direct connection between your router and AWS. It provides a cost-effective, and often more stable, connection to AWS than going over the Internet can.

**Remember the differences between security groups and NACLs.**   This is a favorite topic on AWS exams. Remember that security groups are stateful, so you don't need explicit rules on both inbound and outbound to allow traffic. NACLs are stateless and do require both inbound and outbound rules to allow traffic to pass.

**Know what VPC flow logs offers for troubleshooting.** VPC flow logs aid in troubleshooting efforts and can be applied at the VPC, subnet, or interface level. This can help you determine directionality of traffic and identify security groups that are too strict.

# Exercises

To do the exercises in this chapter, you need a login to the AWS Management Console that has permissions to complete the tasks.

**EXERCISE 16.1**

### Create a VPC

In this first exercise, I will walk you through creating a VPC called "MyLab." The VPC, which will use the VPC Wizard, will create a NAT gateway and two subnets (one public and one private).

1. Log into the AWS Management Console.

2. Click Services and then choose VPC under Networking & Content Delivery.

3. Click Elastic IPs in the VPC Dashboard menu.

4. Click Allocate New Address, accept the default settings, and click Allocate.

5. Click Close.

6. Click VPC Dashboard at the top of the navigation menu, and then click Launch VPC Wizard.

7. Select the second tab, VPC With Public And Private Subnets, and click Select.

8. To configure the VPC:

   a. VPC name: **MyLab**

   b. Public subnet's IPv4 CIDR: **10.0.1.0/27**

   c. Public subnet name: **Public1**

   d. Private subnet's IPv4 CIDR: **10.0.10.0/24**

   e. Private subnet name: **Private1**

   f. Elastic IP Allocation ID: Click the field and select the elastic IP you created in step 4.

   Your settings should appear similar to Figure 16.9.

**EXERCISE 16.1** *(continued)*

**FIGURE 16.9** Configure your VPC with the VPC Wizard to have a public and a private subnet provisioned automatically.

9. Click Create VPC.

10. Click OK once you see the VPC Successfully Created screen.

Now that your VPC is set up, you have your basic AWS network in place. Let's refine it a little more and make a subnet!

**EXERCISE 16.2**

### Create a Subnet and Add It to a Route Table

In the previous exercise, you created a VPC with a single public and private subnet. In this exercise, you'll create another private subnet and add it to the route table with the other private subnet.

1. In the VPC Dashboard, click Subnets.

2. Click Create Subnet.

3. For Name Tag, type **Private2**.

4. Click the VPC field and select the VPC you created in the previous exercise.

5. In the IPv4 CIDR Block, type **10.0.11.0/24**, and then click Create.

6. Click Close.

Now that the subnet is created, let's get it added to the route table.

1. Click Route Tables in the VPC Dashboard menu.

2. You'll see two route tables listed. Select the one associated with the VPC you created in the previous exercise that contains Yes in the Main column.

3. Select the Subnet Associations tab and click Edit Subnet Associations.

4. Select both of the private subnets on the next screen by clicking their check boxes, and click Save.

You may be wondering why we associated the subnets to the routing table when they were already associated with it. The main routing table is where subnets will show up by default; they are implicitly associated with it. If you wanted to associate a subnet with a routing table that was not Main, you would need to manually associate it as we just did.

---

**EXERCISE 16.3**

## Create a VPC Endpoint for S3

In this exercise, we will create a VPC endpoint for S3. Remember that S3 VPC endpoints are referred to as gateway endpoints.

1. On the VPC Dashboard, click Endpoints.

2. Click Create Endpoint.

3. In the Service Name list, search for **com.amazonaws.<*regionname*>.s3**, where **<*regionname*>** is the name of the region you are in currently.

4. Under VPC, select the VPC that you created in our first exercise.

5. Select the route table that contains our two private subnets. It will have Yes in the Main column and will say that it is associated with two subnets.

6. Click Create Endpoint.

7. Click Close.

Just like that, you have created your first VPC endpoint for S3.

**EXERCISE 16.4**

### Create a Security Group

In this exercise, you'll create a security group that will be used for your web servers to communicate over HTTP and HTTPS.

1. On the VPC Dashboard, click Security Groups.

2. Click Create Security Group.

3. For Security Group name, type **Web Servers**.

4. For Description, type **Allow HTTP/HTTPS**.

5. Click VPC, and select the VPC you created in the first exercise.

6. Click Create.

7. Click Close.

Now that the security group is created, you can apply it when you create an EC2 instance. You can, of course, also create security groups during EC2 creation time if you forget to do it ahead of time.

---

**EXERCISE 16.5**

### Create a NACL

Last but not least, let's look at NACLs. Remember that NACLs are stateless, so you have to define inbound and outbound rules. Let's create a NACL that could be associated with the subnets the web servers are in that we currently have a security group protecting.

1. On the VPC Dashboard, click Network ACLs.

2. Click Create Network ACL.

3. For Name, type **WebSubnet**.

4. Click the VPC field and select the VPC you created in the first exercise.

5. Click Create.

Let's edit the inbound rules:

1. On the Inbound Rules tab, click Edit Inbound Rules.

2. Click Add Rule.

3. For Rule Number, type **100**.

4. For Type, choose HTTP.

**5.**   Click Add Rule.

**6.**   For Rule Number, type **101**.

**7.**   For Type, choose HTTPS.

**8.**   Click Save.

Now we'll edit the outbound rules:

**1.**   On the Outbound Rules tab, click Edit Outbound Rules.

**2.**   Click Add Rule.

**3.**   For Rule Number, type **100**.

**4.**   For Type, select All Traffic.

**5.**   Click Save.

You've created your first NACL. Remember that NACLs are applied at the subnet layer, so they are ideal as a first level of defense, with security groups providing the next layer of defense at the host level.

# Review Questions

You can find the answers in the Appendix.

1. Which of the following are not available to IPv6 networks? (Choose two.)

   A. NAT instances

   B. VPCs

   C. VPC endpoints

   D. NAT gateways

2. How many IP addresses are available in a CIDR block with a /16 mask?

   A. 256

   B. 4,096

   C. 65,536

   D. 1,048,576

3. You need to support 16 hosts in a new subnet and want to assign the very smallest possible CIDR block in which these hosts will all reside. What is the size of the CIDR block you'd choose?

   A. /30

   B. /29

   C. /28

   D. /27

4. You have a CIDR block that has a /20 sized pool of IP addresses. How many bits are available for the host part of an address in this scenario?

   A. 20

   B. 10

   C. 12

   D. 22

5. You have a new VPC and are launching an EC2 instance into the VPC with the intent of serving IPv6 requests. However, incoming IPv6 requests are not being handled by the new instance. What could be the problem? (Choose two.)

   A. There is no IPv6 CIDR block associated with the VPC.

   B. There is no IPv6 CIDR block associated with the target EC2 instance.

   C. There is no IPv6 IP address assigned to the VPC.

   D. There is no IPv6 IP address assigned to the target EC2 instance.

**6.** What is the default size of an IPv6 CIDR block?

   **A.** /32

   **B.** /48

   **C.** /56

   **D.** IPv6 does not use CIDR blocks.

**7.** You are responsible for converting an IPv4 subnet with multiple instances to use IPv6 addresses. You have a specific set of IPv6 addresses you want to use. How do you set up a VPC to use these specific IPv6 addresses?

   **A.** You configure the IPs you want to use during VPC creation.

   **B.** You can only configure IPv6 addresses using the AWS CLI.

   **C.** You can't; IPv6 addresses are supplied by the Internet registrar at random.

   **D.** You can't; IPv6 addresses are supplied by AWS from the pool of IPv6 addresses owned by Amazon.

**8.** You are responsible for converting an IPv4 subnet with multiple instances to use IPv6 addresses. You have a specific set of IPv6 addresses you want to use. How do you set up a VPC to use these specific IPv6 addresses?

   **A.** You configure the IPs you want to use during VPC creation.

   **B.** You can only configure IPv6 addresses using the AWS CLI.

   **C.** You can't; IPv6 addresses are supplied by the Internet registrar at random.

   **D.** You can't; IPv6 addresses are supplied by AWS from the pool of IPv6 addresses owned by Amazon.

**9.** You have inherited over 22 VPCs from a previous SysOps administrator, many of which are very small—ranging in size from /26 to /28. You want to consolidate the VPCs into a single, large new VPC and then use multiple subnets. What is the largest allowable VPC you can create?

   **A.** /24

   **B.** /16

   **C.** /8

   **D.** There is no limit to the size of the netmask allowed for custom VPCs.

**10.** You are newly responsible for a number of operational applications. Each application should have a development, testing, and production environment, with both public and private components such as web servers (public) and database servers (private). There are nine applications and you want to limit a VPC to having no more than three applications hosted. You also don't want to have different environments within the same VPC. You want redundancy for every resource, so what is the minimum number of subnets you'd need?

   **A.** 9

   **B.** 18

   **C.** 36

   **D.** 54

**11.** Which of these must be present for a subnet to be considered public? (Choose two.)

    **A.** It exists within a VPC that has an Internet gateway attached.

    **B.** It has a CIDR block with public IP addresses.

    **C.** It has a route to a public subnet.

    **D.** It has a route to an Internet gateway.

**12.** You are administrating a well-configured AWS network that has a VPC that uses an egress-only Internet gateway. Why would this type of Internet gateway be necessary? (Choose two.)

    **A.** A public subnet within the VPC must communicate outward to the Internet.

    **B.** A private subnet within the VPC must communicate outward to the Internet.

    **C.** A subnet within the VPC uses only IPv4 addresses.

    **D.** A subnet within the VPC uses only IPv6 addresses.

**13.** Traffic is set up to flow from an instance within a private subnet out to the public Internet. Which of the following is a possible path that traffic could take?

    **A.** Instance ➤ Internet

    **B.** Instance ➤ NAT device ➤ Internet gateway ➤ Internet

    **C.** Instance ➤ NAT device ➤ virtual private gateway ➤ Internet

    **D.** Instance ➤ Internet gateway ➤ Internet

**14.** You have a private subnet with multiple instances within it, and you want several of these instances to be able to access the Internet. You also want to schedule all outbound access within a brief 10-minute window at 2:00 a.m. When that access occurs, the instances will download hundreds of gigabytes of patch definitions. What device is most appropriate for this scenario?

    **A.** NAT instance

    **B.** Internet gateway

    **C.** Virtual private gateway

    **D.** NAT gateway

**15.** You have an S3 bucket that stores documents and records that are required by one of your high-volume applications. You want to maximize performance and minimize network latency. What might you use to speed access from the applications to the S3 bucket?

    **A.** Multipart transfer

    **B.** Interface endpoint

    **C.** Gateway endpoint

    **D.** S3 transfer acceleration

**16.** For which of the following services could you not use an interface endpoint to access?

   **A.** Amazon CloudFormation

   **B.** Amazon DynamoDB

   **C.** Amazon Kinesis

   **D.** AWS CloudTrail

**17.** Which of the following are required components of an AWS VPN connection? (Choose two.)

   **A.** Internet gateway

   **B.** Direct Connect gateway

   **C.** Customer gateway

   **D.** Virtual private gateway

**18.** You are securing a subnet that contains a number of private instances. You want to ensure that databases are reachable by web servers in AWS. However, these web servers also have security groups that you want to respect and that have been set up by another AWS SysOps administrator. What is the best approach to use for securing the database-containing subnet?

   **A.** Use elastic IPs for the database servers and use those IPs in the subnet's NACLs.

   **B.** Do not provide a default route in the database instances' security groups.

   **C.** Use the security group of the instances containing the web servers as the incoming source for allowing traffic to the databases.

   **D.** Ensure port 3306 is open but all other ports are closed for AWS traffic.

**19.** In what order are rules in a NACL evaluated?

   **A.** Top to bottom

   **B.** Bottom to top

   **C.** From the lowest-numbered rule to the highest-numbered rule

   **D.** From the highest-numbered rule to the lowest-numbered rule

**20.** You have created a new subnet within the default VPC. You then added a new rule, numbered 150, to reject all incoming traffic. You are still seeing traffic allowed into the subnet. What is the problem with your configuration?

   **A.** You also need to reject traffic at the security group level.

   **B.** The default VPC always allows in all traffic and this cannot be changed.

   **C.** You need to remove the Internet gateway on the default VPC.

   **D.** Your NACL rule is higher than rule 100, which by default allows in all traffic. You need to move your deny rule to a number lower than 100 to take effect before rule 100.

# Chapter

# 17

# Route 53

THE AWS CERTIFIED SYSOPS
ADMINISTRATOR – ASSOCIATE EXAM
TOPICS COVERED IN THIS CHAPTER MAY
INCLUDE, BUT ARE NOT LIMITED TO, THE
FOLLOWING:

Domain 2.0: High Availability

- ✓ 2.1 Implement scalability and elasticity based on use case

- ✓ 2.2 Recognize and differentiate highly available and resilient environments on AWS

Domain 3.0: Deployment and Provisioning

- ✓ 3.1 Identify and execute steps required to provision cloud resources

- ✓ 3.2 Identify and remediate deployment issues

Domain 6.0: Networking

- ✓ 6.1 Apply AWS networking features

- ✓ 6.2 Implement connectivity services of AWS

As you work more and more with networks, and the IP addresses that systems use to communicate with one another, it is easy to see that tracking IP addresses and the systems they map to can quickly become a nightmare. IP addresses aren't easily memorable for most people, and even a small organization can quickly outgrow static IP addresses and Excel spreadsheets tracking their names, as well as custom host files.

Domain Name System (DNS) is a service that has been around for many years at this point, and the simplest way to think of it is like our Contacts list on our mobile devices. We remember the names of our friends and family, but we may not remember their phone numbers. When we want to call someone, we click their name, and the phone knows based on the name we selected which phone number needs to be called. DNS does something very similar in that it allows us to use easy-to-remember names like `www.wiley.com` rather than having to find out or remember the IP address for the site that we want to reach.

This chapter is focused on the AWS implementation of DNS, which is referred to as Route 53, and what you will need to know about Route 53 to pass the exam.

This chapter includes:

Understand what domain name system (DNS) does

The difference between private and public DNS

How AWS uses routing policies in Amazon Route 53

Using health checks in Amazon Route 53

# Domain Name System

The *Domain Name System* (DNS) provides a method to translate between human-readable (and easily remembered) addresses with the IP addresses that systems use to communicate over an IP-based network. You might be wondering how DNS is able to convert between friendly names and IP addresses. If you are, then read on for a little DNS 101.

When you look up a site, say like `www.wiley.com`, your system will reach out to its local DNS server with a DNS query to see if the local DNS server knows what the IP address is for this site. If your local DNS server knows the answer, then it will respond with the IP address. If it doesn't know the answer, it sends a query to the *top-level domain* (TLD) DNS server for `.com`. The TLD DNS server will respond with the address of the authoritative

DNS server for `wiley.com`. Your DNS server then sends the query to the DNS server for `wiley.com`, which responds with the IP address for `www.wiley.com`.

DNS operates over the network using both Transmission Control Protocol (TCP) and User Datagram Protocol (UDP) over port 53. UDP has historically been used for DNS queries, but large packets like what you get with IPv6 and/or DNS Security (DNSSEC) signed records have to go over TCP. TCP is also used for zone transfers. Knowing this, now you can understand the humor in the name Route 53, which is Amazon's DNS service. It also makes it easier to remember. If you can remember that DNS operates over port 53, then it is simpler to remember that Route 53 is the DNS service in AWS.

# DNS Records

Amazon Route 53 supports many of the DNS record types that you might expect, and perhaps a few more. In case you aren't familiar with what each of these types of records is used for, let's examine each as there are usually a few DNS-related questions on the exam.

- **A/AAAA:** The A record is used to map a hostname to an IP address. An A record is an IPv4 address whereas an AAAA record is used for IPv6 addresses.

- **CAA:** A CAA record is used to identify valid certificate authorities for your domain. This can prevent unauthorized certificate authorities from being used to issue certificates for your domain.

- **CNAME:** A canonical name (CNAME) is used to create an alias name to a true (canonical) name. This is commonly used in web hosting to map an alias like `www.stuff.com` to the actual server that hosts the website. When people type **`www.stuff.com`**, DNS is able to resolve the address to the web hosting server due to the CNAME record.

- **MX:** Mail exchange (MX) records are used to identify email servers for a given domain. They can also be used to set the priority of the email servers. For instance, you may have a primary email server with a priority of 10 and a secondary with a priority of 20.

- **NAPTR:** You will typically find Name Authority Pointer (NAPTR) records linked with service records (SRV). They are used to in effect "chain" multiple records together to create rewrite rules which can create things like uniform resource identifiers (URIs) or domain labels. This is most commonly used to support the Session Initiation Protocol (SIP) with Internet telephony.

- **NS:** Name Server (NS) records are used to identify the DNS servers for a given hosted zone. This will typically be expressed as the fully qualified domain name (FQDN) of the server.

- **PTR:** A pointer (PTR) record is used to do reverse DNS lookups. The traditional lookup gives you an IP address from a hostname; the PTR does the opposite and gives you the hostname from the IP address.

- **SOA:** The Start of Authority (SOA) record is used to define the authoritative DNS servers for an individual DNS zone.

- **SPF:** The Sender Policy Framework (SPF) is used to identify the sender of email messages and validate that the identity presented is the true identity. Due to interoperability issues with SPF v1, AWS recommends that you use TXT records to present the necessary information rather than SPF records.

- **SRV:** The Service Record (SRV) is used to identify hostnames and port numbers for servers that provide services with a DNS zone.

- **TXT:** The text (TXT) record is used to provide information in a text format to systems outside of your domain. It has many purposes, one of which is to present the information for identity validation for SPF, rather than using SPF records.

This is not an exhaustive list of every single type of DNS record that exists, but it is (as of this writing) a list of the record types that are supported by Amazon Route 53. This list will no doubt grow over time.

 AWS also supports alias records, not to be confused with CNAME records. An alias record in AWS is used to route traffic to AWS resources such as Amazon S3 buckets, VPC interface endpoints, elastic load balancers, Amazon CloudFront distributions, and more. This is a popular topic on the AWS exams, so keep in mind that alias records are used for routing to AWS services, not CNAMES.

# Amazon Route 53

Route 53's DNS acts in the way you would expect it to if you have worked with DNS in the past. You can create the record types that we discussed previously for both IPv4 and IPv6 addresses. When a query is made, as long as Route 53 is authoritative for the DNS record it can return the appropriate response. Additionally, you can choose to block certain IP addresses through Route 53 if you know that they resolve to malicious domains. Route 53 can do much more than just simple DNS, however. It can manage traffic, which is covered in the "Amazon Traffic Flow" section; domain registration; and availability monitoring, which are covered later in this chapter. As you can see in Figure 17.1, Amazon Route 53 offers four distinct services that allow you to more effectively manage your DNS and routing capabilities.

**FIGURE 17.1** The main console for Amazon Route 53 makes it simple to choose a service to manage.

Route 53 is able to function as a registrar for domain names in addition to the DNS capabilities already discussed. You can register new domain names or transfer existing domain names. AWS gives you the ability to add privacy protection for free, unlike other registrars who typically charge you for this service. Your registration is good for a year and is set to automatically renew at the end of the one-year cycle. You can manage a grand total of 50 domains by default using Route 53, though you can request a higher limit if needed.

You may be wondering how your services within AWS are able to use the DNS services provided by Route 53 and how they can resolve addresses outside of AWS. Route 53 Resolver is the key. *Amazon Route 53 Resolver* provides recursive lookups for both systems hosted on AWS as well as systems on the Internet. It also supports conditional forwarding rules, which can help provide support for multiple domain names and situations where you are running a hybrid datacenter with systems on-premises and in the cloud.

## Amazon Traffic Flow

Wouldn't it be great if there was a way to manage your traffic on a global scale and be able to reduce latency so that your users or customers have a positive experience? With Amazon Traffic Flow, you can do exactly that.

Amazon Traffic Flow allows you to create traffic policies that can route requests to your application's endpoints. You then use a policy record to assign the traffic policy to a specific domain name. In this way, you can potentially associate a policy with multiple endpoints and use Amazon Traffic Flow to route your customers or users to the best endpoint for them based on best latency, closest geographical endpoint, or even endpoint health (that is, if the closest endpoint is in a degraded state, they are routed to the next closest endpoint).

## AWS Private DNS

You may be wondering what the best way would be to host your internal DNS when your infrastructure resides in AWS. Although you may be more comfortable with installing DNS on a server, it is not necessary if all the systems that are using DNS are within a VPC. Instead, you can use what AWS refers to as Private DNS. *Private DNS* is a feature that allows you to create a special hosted "private" zone in Route 53. Once the hosted zone is created, it can even be shared with other VPCs. The best part about using Private DNS is that your records are not exposed to the Internet, much as you would have with traditional internal DNS, but they are still managed by the same highly available and manageable service in AWS that manages public DNS. Additionally, you can use the same Private DNS zone across multiple accounts and multiple regions, and you can configure DNS failover just as you can for public DNS.

# Routing Policies

For each record you create in Amazon Route 53, you choose a routing policy. The routing policy is what determines how to return the results of a DNS query, and each type of policy has a different use case. These routing policies can do some very interesting things, including performance and availability improvements. Let's examine each of the types of routing policies and what they are used for.

## Simple Routing Policy

If you just want Amazon Route 53 to route traffic without any special considerations like priorities or geolocation, then a *simple routing policy* is the best fit. Simple routing policies do allow you to apply more than one IP address to a record, but the results are returned in a random order. When you create a record using a simple routing policy, configure it as follows:

- **Name:** This field holds the name of the record plus the name of the hosted zone that the record resides in. The hosted zone will be the default value, so you don't need to specify it if you want the record in the hosted zone. An example for a value would be www for the name, and wiley.com would be the hosted zone.

- **Type:** Select the type of DNS record that you want to create. These were covered earlier in this chapter.

- **Alias:** No

- **TTL (Time to Live):** AWS recommends starting with a lower value like 300 seconds (5 minutes) until you are sure that everything is working properly. DNS won't be queried again until the TTL has expired.

- **Value:** This should hold the value that you want the record to hold. For example, if you are creating an A record, you would enter an IPv4 address.

- **Routing Policy:** Simple

## Failover Routing Policy

You can use a failover routing policy to direct traffic to a primary instance while it's healthy but divert traffic to a secondary instance if the primary becomes unhealthy. When you create a record for a failover routing policy, configure it as follows:

- **Name:** This field holds the name of the record plus the name of the hosted zone that the record resides in. The hosted zone will be the default value, so you don't need to specify it if you want the record in the hosted zone. An example for a value would be www for the name, and wiley.com would be the hosted zone.

- **Type:** Select the type of DNS record that you want to create. These were covered earlier in this chapter.

- **Alias:** No

- **TTL (Time to Live):** AWS recommends starting with a lower value like 300 seconds (5 minutes) until you are sure that everything is working properly. DNS won't be queried again until the TTL has expired. If you are using health checks, you should drop this down to 60 seconds or less. This reduces downtime if a host becomes unhealthy.

- **Value:** This should hold the value that you want the record to hold. For example, if you are creating an A record, you would enter an IPv4 address.

- **Routing Policy:** Failover

- **Failover Record Type:** You will need to create at least two records, one for primary and one for secondary.

- **Set ID:** This is a value that identifies the individual records that you are using within the failover records.
- **Associate With Health Check:** Yes (then select which health check you want Route 53 to perform)

# Geolocation Routing Policy

If you choose a geolocation routing policy, you can decide where users will be directed to based on their location. Users in the United States, for instance, may be routed to the U.S. East region, whereas users in Europe may get routed to a European Union (EU) West region. When you create a record for a geolocation routing policy, configure it as follows:

- **Name:** This field holds the name of the record plus the name of the hosted zone that the record resides in. The hosted zone will be the default value, so you don't need to specify it if you want the record in the hosted zone. An example for a value would be www for the name, and wiley.com would be the hosted zone.
- **Type:** Select the type of DNS record that you want to create. These were covered earlier in this chapter.
- **Alias:** No
- **TTL (Time to Live):** AWS recommends starting with a lower value like 300 seconds (5 minutes) until you are sure that everything is working properly. DNS won't be queried again until the TTL has expired. If you are using health checks, you should drop this down to 60 seconds or less. This reduces downtime if a host becomes unhealthy.
- **Value:** This should hold the value that you want the record to hold. For example, if you are creating an A record, you would enter an IPv4 address.
- **Routing Policy:** Geolocation
- **Location:** This field should contain the names of the countries that you are wanting DNS to respond to. It is also best practice to include an entry that has default for the location. This will apply to countries not explicitly called out in this field.
- **Sublocation:** If the United States was one of the countries that was put in the Location field, you can choose to break out individual states within the Sublocation field if desired.
- **Set ID:** This is a value that identifies the individual records that you are using within the geolocation records.
- **Associate With Health Check:** Yes (then select which health check you want Route 53 to perform)

# Geoproximity Routing Policy

On the surface, the geoproximity routing policy seems similar to the geolocation policy in that it allows you to determine where your users will be directed to based on their location. The difference with a geoproximity routing policy is that you can also set a bias. The bias allows you to route more or less traffic to resources and can be used to grow or reduce the size of the defined region.

## Latency Routing Policy

Latency routing policies direct your end users or customers to the region that can provide the lowest latency. The most important thing to remember about this is that the region with the best latency may not be the region that is closest to the end user or customer. When you create a record for a latency routing policy, configure it as follows:

- **Name:** This field holds the name of the record plus the name of the hosted zone that the record resides in. The hosted zone will be the default value, so you don't need to specify it if you want the record in the hosted zone. An example for a value would be www for the name, and wiley.com would be the hosted zone.

- **Type:** Select the type of DNS record that you want to create. These were covered earlier in this chapter.

- **Alias:** No

- **TTL (Time to Live):** AWS recommends starting with a lower value like 300 seconds (5 minutes) until you are sure that everything is working properly. DNS won't be queried again until the TTL has expired. If you are using health checks, you should drop this down to 60 seconds or less. This reduces downtime if a host becomes unhealthy.

- **Value:** This should hold the value that you want the record to hold. For example, if you are creating an A record, you would enter an IPv4 address.

- **Routing Policy:** Latency

- **Region:** This should be the region where the host exists that you are creating the record for.

- **Set ID:** This is a value that identifies the individual records that you are using within the latency records.

- **Associate With Health Check:** Yes (then select which health check you want Route 53 to perform)

## Multivalue Answer Routing Policy

A multivalue answer routing policy is able to return multiple answers (IP addresses) in response to a DNS query. By using a multivalue answer routing policy, you can be assured that the IP addresses being returned are from healthy hosts, since this routing policy can do health checks if you set it to do so.

NOTE    If there are eight or fewer healthy hosts, the query will respond with all the healthy records.

When you create a record for a multivalue answer routing policy, configure it as follows:

- **Name:** This field holds the name of the record plus the name of the hosted zone that the record resides in. The hosted zone will be the default value, so you don't need to specify it if you want the record in the hosted zone. An example for a value would be www for the name, and wiley.com would be the hosted zone.

- **Type:** Select the type of DNS record that you want to create. These were covered earlier in this chapter.

- **Alias:** No

- **TTL (Time to Live):** AWS recommends starting with a lower value like 300 seconds (5 minutes) until you are sure that everything is working properly. DNS won't be queried again until the TTL has expired. If you are using health checks, you should drop this down to 60 seconds or less. This reduces downtime if a host becomes unhealthy.

- **Value:** This should hold the value that you want the record to hold. For example, if you are creating an A record, you would enter an IPv4 address.

- **Routing Policy:** Multivalue Answer

- **Set ID:** This is a value that identifies the individual records that you are using within the multivalue answer records.

- **Associate With Health Check:** Yes (then select which health check you want Route 53 to perform)

## Weighted Routing Policy

Weighted routing policies have a couple of use cases. One of the most common use cases is when doing *blue/green deployments* (done to test new versions of software). In this use case, you can configure the weights to allow 25 percent of the traffic to go to the hosts running the new version of the software but route the other 75 percent of the traffic to the hosts running the old software. AWS has a formula available that allows you to calculate how the weights will play out using this type of policy:

> Blue/green deployments are used for testing new versions of application code. They are discussed in more depth in Chapter 19, "Elastic Beanstalk."

Weight of an individual record/Sum of the weights of all the records

When you create a record for a weighted routing policy, configure it as follows:

- **Name:** This field holds the name of the record plus the name of the hosted zone that the record resides in. The hosted zone will be the default value, so you don't need to specify it if you want the record in the hosted zone. An example for a value would be www for the name, and wiley.com would be the hosted zone.

- **Type:** Select the type of DNS record that you want to create. These were covered earlier in this chapter.

- **Alias:** No

- **TTL (Time to Live):** AWS recommends starting with a lower value like 300 seconds (5 minutes) until you are sure that everything is working properly. DNS won't be queried again until the TTL has expired. If you are using health checks, you should drop this down to 60 seconds or less. This reduces downtime if a host becomes unhealthy.

- **Value:** This should hold the value that you want the record to hold. For example, if you are creating an A record, you would enter an IPv4 address.

- **Routing Policy:** Weighted

- **Weight:** You can enter a number between 0 and 255 in this field. If the record doesn't work the way you think it should after assigning the weight, check the formula to ensure that you are getting what you expect.

- **Set ID:** This is a value that identifies the individual records that you are using within the weighted records.

- **Associate With Health Check:** Yes (then select which health check you want Route 53 to perform)

You may have noticed that many of these routing policies depend on health checks to ensure that traffic is routed only to healthy hosts. Let's take a deeper dive into performing health checks and configuring failover.

# Health Checks and Failover

The magic of automatic failover in Amazon Route 53 starts with the health check. There are three types of Amazon Route 53 health checks that you can choose to create. Each one works a little differently, so let's look at each one.

- **Monitor an endpoint:** You can create a health check that will monitor the health of an endpoint at specified intervals of time. Health may be evaluated by either response time or failed health checks.

- **Monitor other health checks:** You can create a health check that uses other Route 53 health checks to determine whether endpoints are healthy or unhealthy. This health check requires a certain number of "child" health checks to be healthy for it to consider itself healthy.

- **Monitor CloudWatch alarms:** You can create a health check that can use CloudWatch alarms based on metrics that were specified to determine whether an endpoint is healthy or unhealthy. This health check will show healthy as long as CloudWatch is in an OK state. An OK state is illustrated in Figure 17.2. If CloudWatch changes to an ALARM state. then the health check is considered to be unhealthy.

**FIGURE 17.2**    A good health check will list Status as Healthy and Alarms as 1 of 1 OK.

| Status | | Description | | Alarms |
|---|---|---|---|---|
| an hour ago        now | Healthy | http://34.203.220.177:80/index.html | | ☺ 1 of 1 in OK |

Once a health check is configured, you choose how you want a failover event to occur. Common configurations include active-active and active-passive. Just keep in mind that if you have endpoints configured with health checks and you miss adding a health check to one of the endpoints, that endpoint will always be considered healthy whether it is or not.

When an endpoint is considered unhealthy and failover is set up, Route 53 will stop sending traffic to that endpoint until it becomes healthy again. You can configure notifications to be sent so that you are aware when an endpoint becomes unhealthy.

# Summary

Domain Name Service (DNS) allows you to map hostnames to IP addresses and IP addresses to hostnames. You can query the DNS server with whichever piece of information you have and get the result back. Amazon Route 53 is the DNS service within AWS, though it provides more than simple name resolution. The Amazon Route 53 Resolver is the service that performs recursive lookups in response to queries.

Amazon Traffic Flow allows you to associate policies to your traffic, which can improve performance and latency for your customers and/or users.

AWS Private DNS creates a private hosted zone in Amazon Route 53 that can act like the internal DNS you are accustomed to using. Endpoints must be within a VPC to take advantage of AWS Private DNS.

Routing policies are assigned to records when they are created. These policies tell Amazon Route 53 how it should respond to queries that are made against that record. There are seven routing policy types: simple, failover, geolocation, geoproximity, latency, multivalue answer, and weighted.

Health checks can be created to check endpoints, other health checks, or CloudWatch alarms. Unhealthy health checks can be used to initiate a failover event to ensure that only healthy endpoints are servicing users or customers.

# Resources to Review

Amazon Route 53 FAQs:

    https://aws.amazon.com/route53/faqs/

Choosing a Routing Policy:

    https://docs.aws.amazon.com/Route53/latest/DeveloperGuide/routing-policy.html

Creating Amazon Route 53 Health Checks and Configuring DNS Failover:

    https://docs.aws.amazon.com/Route53/latest/DeveloperGuide/dns-failover.html

# Exam Essentials

**Understand how DNS works.** Domain Name Service (DNS) is used to resolve names and IP addresses. In a forward lookup, a name is resolved to an IP address, and in a reverse lookup an IP address is resolved to a hostname. Your client will query the local DNS server for a record. If your local DNS knows the address, it will respond with it; if it doesn't, it will reach out to the top-level domain (TLD) DNS servers and work its way down the chain until it locates the authoritative DNS server and gets the response for the query.

**Know the various DNS record types.** Know the main DNS record types and when you would want to use them. For the exam in particular, know what A records, PTR records, CNAME records and alias records, MX records, and TXT records are used for.

**Understand what routing policies do in Route 53.** Although you don't need to memorize everything about the routing policies and how to set them up, you should know which routing policies are valid and what they are used for.

**Remember how health checks work.** Remember the three different types of health checks and how they work in relation to failovers.

# Exercises

To complete these exercises, you will need two EC2 instances. We will be using the metadata screen for proof that failover has occurred successfully.

---

**EXERCISE 17.1**

### Create a Hosted Zone

To do the activities in the following exercises, we need a hosted zone to work in. So let's create that first.

1. Log into the AWS Management Console, click Services, and under Networking & Content Delivery select Amazon Route 53.

2. Under DNS Management, click Get Started Now.

3. Click Create Hosted Zone.

4. Type an unused domain name; I'm using **sometestorg.com**. I own this domain name, so it is safe for me to use.

This creates a hosted zone with Name Server (NS) and Start of Authority (SOA) records.

---

**EXERCISE 17.2**

## Create a Health Check

For this exercise to work, you need to have two EC2 instances up and running. If you don't have any currently, you will need to create them to continue. I created two t2.micro servers running Amazon Linux, but you can choose whatever you'd like. They will need to have port 80 open and a web server installed on them. You can use the following script to follow along, I recommend putting it in the User Data field so it happens while the servers are being provisioned. We will use the `index.html` page later on (change the last line to WEB2 for the second server). Note that you must allow the software to install before continuing.

```
#!/bin/bash
yum update -y
yum install -y httpd
service start httpd
chkconfig httpd on
usermod -a -G apache ec2-user
chown -R ec2-user:apache /var/www
chmod 2775 /var/www
find /var/www -type d -exec chmod 2775 {} \;
find /var/www -type f -exec chmod 0664 {} \;
echo "I am WEB1" > /var/www/html/index.html
```

1. Click Services, and under Compute select EC2.

2. Select each of the two instances and take note of their public IP addresses. You will need them for this exercise.

3. Click Services, and then under Networking & Content Delivery select Amazon Route 53.

4. Click Health Checks.

5. Click Create Health Check.

6. For name, enter a name that makes sense to you. I have called mine **Web1-HC**.

7. Leave What To Monitor set to Endpoint.

8. Under Monitor An Endpoint, select IP Address, and then enter the IP address of you first instance. Under Path, type **index.html**.

9. Click Advanced Configuration to expand the options. Choose Fast for the request interval and 2 for the failure threshold.

10. Click Next.

11. On the screen "Get notified when a health check fails," click Yes for Create Alarm.

12. Click New SNS Topic. For the topic name, I chose **Web1-HealthCheck**.

13. Enter your email address under Recipient Email Addresses.

14. Click Create Health Check.

Click Refresh until the instance is listed as healthy before continuing to the next exercise.

---

### Create the A Records for Failover

Last but not least, let's create the records for the web servers as well as a failover routing policy.

1. Click Hosted zones and then click the domain name you created in Exercise 17.1.

2. Click Create Record Set.

3. For Name, type **www**.

4. For Value, type the IP address of the first web instance.

5. For Routing Policy, choose Failover and select Primary.

6. Choose Yes for Associate With Health Check, and then choose the name of the health check you created in Exercise 17.2. Your settings should look similar to Figure 17.3.

**FIGURE 17.3** Your settings should look similar to mine in this image (your IP address in the Value box will be different).

7.   Click Create.

8.   Click Create Record Set.

9.   For Name, type **www**.

10.  For Value, type the IP address of the second web instance.

11.  For Routing Policy, choose Failover and select Secondary.

12.  Choose No for Associate With Health Check.

13.  Click Create.

You have now created a failover set. Based on our test solution, if you went to www.sometestorg.com, you could be directed to the WEB1 server. If the WEB1 server goes down (say you stopped it), then www.sometestorg.com would direct you to the WEB2 server. The only way to test this is to own the domain name in question; you can purchase a domain to play with on AWS for a reasonable cost. The domain I use in these exercises is one that I purchased.

# Review Questions

You can find the answers in the Appendix.

1. What is the reasoning behind the name of Amazon's Route 53 service?

   **A.** There are 53 types of record sets allowed by DNS.

   **B.** Port 53 is the port over which DNS operates.

   **C.** DNS allows up to 53 entries in a single record set.

   **D.** Port 153 is the port over which DNS operates.

2. Which of the following is not a record type supported by Route 53?

   **A.** NAPTR

   **B.** NS

   **C.** SPF

   **D.** TEXT

3. You are setting up a new website for a client and have their website loaded into an S3 bucket. They want to ensure that the site responds to the company name—wisdompetmedicine—both with and without the www part of the address. What types of records do you need to create? (Choose two.)

   **A.** CNAME

   **B.** A

   **C.** MX

   **D.** SRV

4. You are setting up DNS for an application running on an EC2 host in your network. The application exposes its API through an IPv6 address; what type of recordset will you need to create for access to this API?

   **A.** AAAA

   **B.** A

   **C.** ALIAS

   **D.** MX

5. You have a Lambda-based serverless application. You have several Lambda@Edge functions triggered by a CloudFront distribution and need to set up DNS. What type of records would you need to use?

   **A.** CNAME

   **B.** A

   **C.** Alias

   **D.** AAAA

6. You have an application running in a VPC with an existing DNS record. You have a backup of the application running as a warm standby in another VPC in a different region. If traffic stops flowing to the primary application, you want traffic to be routed to the backup. What type of routing policy should you use?

   A. Simple routing

   B. Failover routing

   C. Latency routing

   D. Multivalue answer

7. You have a fleet of EC2 instances serving content through application load balancers in multiple regions. You want to ensure that all available hosts can respond to traffic. Which routing policy should you use?

   A. Simple routing

   B. Failover routing

   C. Latency routing

   D. Multivalue answer

8. You have an application running with copies in three different regions: US East 1, US West 1, and AP East 1. You want to ensure your application's users always receive a response from the copy of the application with the lowest network traffic response time. Which routing policy should you use?

   A. Simple routing

   B. Failover routing

   C. Latency routing

   D. Multivalue answer

9. Which of the following routing policies does not allow you to provide multiple hosts for resolution?

   A. Simple routing

   B. Failover routing

   C. Latency routing

   D. All of these policies allow for multiple hosts.

10. You are responsible for a marketing website running in AWS. You have a requirement from the marketing team to provide an alternate version of the site intended for A/B testing with the current site. However, they only want a small portion of traffic sent to the new version of the site as they evaluate the changes they've made. Which routing policy should you use?

    A. Multivalue answer

    B. Failover routing

    C. Weighted routing

    D. Geolocation routing

**11.** You are examining a weighted routing policy with three destination hosts, with values of 10, 80, and 50. You want to ensure that the first host receives 20 percent of the site traffic, the second host receives 50 percent , and the third host receives all remaining traffic. To what should you change these values?

   **A.** 20, 50, *

   **B.** 5, 15, 80

   **C.** 10, 25, 15

   **D.** 20, 50, 50

**12.** Which of the following is not possible when using AWS Private DNS?

   **A.** Setting up private DNS without using a VPC

   **B.** Exposing records to other AWS VPCs

   **C.** Exposing records to other AWS regions

   **D.** Exposing records to other AWS accounts

**13.** Which of the following can you not do using private DNS? (Choose two.)

   **A.** Block particular domains in a VPC.

   **B.** Configure DNS failover for the privately hosted zone.

   **C.** Expose a private DNS record selectively to the Internet.

   **D.** Create health checks for instances that only have private IP addresses.

**14.** Which of the following must you configure to control how traffic is routed from around the world to your applications using Amazon Route 53 Traffic Flow? (Choose two.)

   **A.** Traffic record

   **B.** Traffic policy

   **C.** Policy record

   **D.** Policy route

**15.** You have taken over a domain that has a working traffic policy and policy record. You now want to point additional DNS names at that domain and ensure that the existing traffic flows are maintained. How would you accomplish this? (Choose two.)

   **A.** Create CNAME records for each new DNS name and point the CNAME at the domain with an existing traffic policy and policy record.

   **B.** Create A records for each new DNS name and point the A at the domain with an existing traffic policy and policy record.

   **C.** Create Alias records for each new DNS name and point the Alias at the domain with an existing traffic policy and policy record.

   **D.** Create AAAA records for each new DNS name and point the AAAA at the domain with an existing traffic policy and policy record.

16. Which of the following is a not a type of health check offered by Amazon Route 53?

    A. Endpoint monitoring

    B. Other health check monitoring

    C. CloudTrail monitoring

    D. CloudWatch monitoring

17. What happens in Amazon Route 53 if an unhealthy response comes back from a health check? (Choose two.)

    A. Responses are no longer sent to the failing host.

    B. When the host comes back online, responses are automatically sent back to the host.

    C. All responses to the failing host are retried until a response is received.

    D. A CloudWatch alarm is automatically triggered and sent out via notification.

18. Which factor is the determinant in deciding where traffic flows when Amazon Route 53 has a latency-based routing policy in place?

    A. The closest region to the requestor

    B. The region with the lowest latency to the requestor

    C. The region with the most available network resources

    D. The weighting set in the routing policy

19. Why might you use a geoproximity routing policy rather than a geolocation routing policy?

    A. You want to increase the size of traffic in a certain region over time.

    B. You want to ensure that all U.S. users are directed to U.S.-based hosts.

    C. You want to route users geographically to ensure compliance issues are met based on requestor location.

    D. You are concerned about network latency more than requestor location.

20. You are seeing intermittent issues with a website you maintain that uses Amazon Route 53, a fleet of EC2 instances, and a redundant MySQL database. Even though the hosts are not always responding, traffic is being sent to those hosts. What could cause traffic to go to these hosts? (Choose two.)

    A. You need to use a failover routing policy to take advantage of health checks on hosts.

    B. You need to turn on health checks in Amazon Route 53.

    C. The hosts are failing a health check but not enough times in a row to be taken out of service by Amazon Route 53.

    D. The hosts should be put behind an application load balancer (ALB).

# Automation and Optimization

# Chapter

## 18

# CloudFormation

---

**THE AWS CERTIFIED SYSOPS ADMINISTRATOR – ASSOCIATE EXAM TOPICS COVERED IN THIS CHAPTER MAY INCLUDE, BUT ARE NOT LIMITED TO, THE FOLLOWING:**

Domain 2.0: High Availability

✓ 2.1  Implement scalability and elasticity based on use case

✓ 2.2  Recognize and differentiate highly available and resilient environments on AWS

Domain 3.0: Deployment and Provisioning

✓ 3.1  Identify and execute steps required to provision cloud resources

✓ 3.2  Identify and remediate deployment issues

Domain 7.0: Automation and Optimization

✓ 7.3  Automate manual or repeatable process to minimize management overhead

As more organizations move to the cloud, the desire to create an automated process to provision new resources has also grown. The key driver is that the process to provision the resources is standardized and repeatable, while also being easy to maintain and adapt to new requirements from the organization.

Infrastructure as a service (IaaS) has become the standard way to accomplish this, and AWS CloudFormation gives you the tools you need to implement it in a scalable and flexible manner.

This chapter includes:

An introduction to infrastructure as a service (IaaS)

Using stacks and templates in AWS CloudFormation

Customizing stacks with parameters and outputs

Improving templates with helpers

# An Introduction to IaaS

If you have never heard of *infrastructure as a service* (IaaS), you've been missing out! Rather than spend hours manually provisioning a server and building off a checklist, you can automatically build servers that are identical, every time, within a matter of minutes. It's easy to see why many organizations have begun to go down this route when you consider the time savings involved.

By using IaaS, you are able to make server provisioning more like software provisioning. For instance, when you make changes to a template that is being used to build IaaS solutions, you can deploy to a Development environment first. After testing the changes to ensure that they meet the needs of your organization, you can push the same template changes to Production. The changes are made exactly the same as they were in Development which results in less downtime and happier customers.

Another great advantage is that the templates you use can act similarly to documentation for your environment. Since the environment is defined in the template, it is always the most up-to-date documentation for how your infrastructure is being built.

Now I'm sure you've read the last few paragraphs and you're thinking that you're going to have to go back to school to learn a new programming or scripting language, but here's the deal. AWS gives you their implementation for IaaS, which is called *AWS CloudFormation*. You don't need to be a developer to work with CloudFormation. In fact, you don't need any programming or scripting background at all. CloudFormation templates are written in *JavaScript Object Notation* (JSON) or YAML Ain't Markup Language (YAML), which is a simple key:value pair representation of what you are trying to build. The examples in this chapter are presented in JSON because it is far more common.

AWS CloudFormation takes advantage of the AWS APIs, and since every part of AWS can be controlled via an API call, this means that CloudFormation can be used to configure the majority of AWS as well. If you aren't familiar with application programming interfaces (APIs), don't worry! CloudFormation is the component you will interact with using your JSON templates. Of course, if you want to play with the API you can do so using either the AWS CLI or the AWS SDK. The CLI is also helpful in running CloudFormation and looking at the outputs of the stack once it's built. A *stack* is an instance of a template that is running in an AWS region. You can have multiple stacks built from one template. A common example might be using the same template to build both a Development and a Production stack.

When you first begin creating templates, one of the most important things to think about are dependencies. An EC2 instance must have a virtual private cloud (VPC) and a subnet to live in, and you'll need to create a security group before the instance so that you can attach it to the instance when it is created. Once the template has been created, you can use it to create, update, and yes, even delete your infrastructure in a predictable and reliable manner.

# CloudFormation Templates

Templates are where the magic happens in CloudFormation. While you can do a ton of things with them, and there are multiple components you can use to customize your template, Resources is the only required component.

## *AWSTemplateFormatVersion*

The `AWSTemplateFormatVersion` section tells CloudFormation what the template will be able to do—basically, what its capabilities will be. There is currently only one valid value for this component and that is `2010-09-09`. Here's an example of what this would look like in JSON:

```
"AWSTemplateFormatVersion" : "2010-09-09"
```

## Description

This section must be located underneath of the format version. It consists of a string of text that describes what the template is for or what it does. This field is optional. If you choose to use it, this is what the component looks like in JSON:

```
"Description" : "This is my awesome template."
```

## Metadata

You can use the metadata section to add more information about your templates. This is typically used if you want to call out information specific to certain parts of your template, as in:

```
"Metadata" : {
  "Instances" : {"Description" : "This template only uses Linux instances"},
  "Databases" : {"Description" : "This template only builds MySQL in Amazon
RDS"}
}
```

## Parameters

Although a static template might be somewhat useful, the real strength in using a template comes with the ability to enter a custom value every time you use the template to create a stack (or update it). A common use case might be where you want to define the instance types that you will allow someone to use in the template. This ensures that no one builds a larger instance type than what you want to allow and gives you the ability to define a default as well. The example I just described follows in JSON. We are allowing a template user to choose t2.nano, t2.micro, or t2.small. If they choose nothing, they will be given the default of t2.micro.

```
"Parameters" : {
  "InstanceTypeParameter" : {
    "Type" : "String",
    "Default" : "t2.micro",
    "AllowedValues" : ["t2.nano", "t2.micro", "t2.small"],
    "Description" : "Type t2.nano, t2.micro, or t2.small. Default is t2.micro."
  }
}
```

## Mappings

Mappings allow you to specify a key and value pair. Although you can't use most functions in a mapping, you can use the Fn::FindInMap function to retrieve values. You are not able to use parameters or pseudo parameters inside a mapping either. This is discussed in more detail in the later section "Improving Your Templates." The following is an example of a mapping that selects AMI IDs for each region. This allows the same template to be used across regions while still being able to choose the same AMI (whose ID number will be different between regions).

```
"Mappings" : {
  "RegionMap" : {
    "us-east-1"        : { "AmazonLinux" : "ami-XXXXXXXXXXXXXXXXX"},
    "us-west-1"        : { "AmazonLinux" : "ami-XXXXXXXXXXXXXXXXX"}
  }
}
```

## Conditions

A condition is used to determine whether a resource should be created or whether a certain property should be assigned. If you want to use conditions, you must not only define your conditions in a Conditions section, you must also set the inputs that you want the conditions to evaluate in the Parameters section and associate the conditions with the resources that you want to create or update. This happens in the Resources and Outputs sections. A great example of this is using a condition to determine whether you are deploying to Production or Development. In this example, we create a condition called CreateProdResources and we specify that this condition will be true if the EnvType parameter is set to prod.

```
"Conditions" : {
    "CreateProdResources" : {"Fn::Equals" : [{"Ref" : "EnvType"}, "prod"]}
  }
```

You can then use this condition in a parameter. In the next example, you can see that we have created a parameter named EnvType, which defaults to Dev. We have said that this parameter can be set to either prod or dev. If prod is entered, then the condition will be true and other actions that specify the condition as a requirement will execute. In this way, you can make your dev instances smaller than your prod instances to reduce cost.

```
"Parameters" : {
    "EnvType" : {
      "Description" : "Environment type.",
      "Default" : "dev",
      "Type" : "String",
      "AllowedValues" : ["prod", "dev"],
      "ConstraintDescription" : "You need to pick prod or dev."
    }
  }
```

## Transform

Transform allows you to choose one or more macros for CloudFormation to use. These macros are run in the order in which they are defined. There are two macros hosted by CloudFormation that you should be familiar with. `AWS::Serverless` specifies which version you should use of the AWS Serverless Application Model. This in turn specifies what syntax you are allowed to use and how CloudFormation will process it. `AWS::Include` uses template snippets that are stored outside of your CloudFormation template.

## Resources

The resources section specifies the actual resources that you want to create, modify, or delete. This includes things like EC2 instances, storage, and security groups. Examples of types of resources are as follows:

- `AWS::EC2::Instance`
- `AWS::EC2::SecurityGroup`
- `AWS::IAM::Role`
- `AWS::EC2::VPC`

To actually create a resource, you name it, and then declare the type of resource and any properties that are necessary. In this example, I use Resources to describe an EC2 instance that I want CloudFormation to build for me. You can see the resource type is `AWS::EC2::Instance` and under Properties, the AMI ID is displayed.

```
"Resources" : {
  "MyNewEC2" : {
    "Type" : "AWS::EC2::Instance",
    "Properties" : {
      "ImageId" : "ami-XXXXXXXXXXXXXXXXX"
    }
  }
}
```

## Outputs

With the Outputs section, you can do a couple of things. You can set the CloudFormation template to output the results of a stack build to the CloudFormation console, return a response if called, or use the output as the input into another stack. You can have up to 60 outputs in a single template. Here's an example of how you would declare an output:

```
"Outputs" : {
  "Logical ID" : {
    "Description" : "Info regarding the output value",
    "Value" : "<value>",
```

```
    "Export" : {
      "Name" : "<value to be exported>"
    }
  }
}
```

# Creating and Customizing Your Stacks

Now that you know all about templates, let's talk stacks. Stacks are where the magic happens! A *stack* is an instance of a template, and you can have multiple stacks created from the same template. For a stack to be successfully created, all the resources within the stack must be successfully created. If any one of the resources fails to be created properly, then CloudFormation will roll the stack back and delete any resources that were successfully created before the failure.

You can work with stacks in CloudFormation from the AWS CloudFormation Console, the AWS API, or the AWS CLI. Remember that while it is free to use CloudFormation, you are charged for the resources that it creates if they are something you would normally be charged for. EC2 instances or Lambda functions are great examples of this.

## Parameters

We covered what you can use parameters for in the previous section on templates, and this is where you get to put them into practice. Parameters are what takes a static template and makes a more dynamic solution. There are four types of parameters that you can use, and their type dictates the input that they are expecting to see:

- String
- Number
- List
- Comma-delimited list

It is important to validate your inputs whenever you are using parameters. After all, one type could cause the entire stack to roll back and that could be very frustrating! Four methods are available in CloudFormation to validate inputs:

- AllowedValues
- AllowedPattern
- MaxLength/MinLength
- MaxValue/MinValue

## Outputs

When you create a stack from a template and there are outputs defined, you will get the output upon completion. Outputs can be used to integrate with other environments—for example, when one stack's output is used as an input to another stack, or you choose to view the output in the CloudFormation Console.

# Improving Your Templates

Once you get your templates created and you have successfully created a stack, the next step is to refine your templates. You can refine them using built-in functions, mappings, and pseudo parameters. Let's dig a little further into each of these and see how you can use them to improve your templates.

## Built-In Functions

Built-in functions allow you to assign values to properties that you can't access until runtime. AWS CloudFormation has several built-in functions that you can use:

- `Fn::Base64`—Converts the string passed to it to Base64. This is needed for passing user data for building EC2 instances.
- `Fn::Cidr`—Used to create an array (a group) of CIDR blocks inside a larger CIDR block
- `Fn::FindInMap`—Used in the Resources section to reference a value in the Mappings section of the template
- `Fn::GetAtt`—Returns an attribute that is used and/or assigned to a resource
- `Fn::GetAZs`—Returns a list of availability zones available in the region specified in the template
- `Fn::ImportValue`—Allows you to import a value from the output of another stack
- `Fn::Join`—Used to append multiple values together using a delimiter that you choose
- `Fn::Select`—Used to return a single value from an array; values are chosen by their index number
- `Fn::Split`—Works the opposite of `Fn::Join`. Used to split multiple values using a delimiter that you specify
- `Fn::Sub`—Can be used to substitute a variable with a string
- `Fn::Transform`—Chooses a macro for CloudFormation to use to process the stack

Here's an example to put it into perspective. When you create an EC2 instance, you can use user data to customize what is installed on the EC2 instance or how certain settings are configured. You can do this with CloudFormation as well, but one of the challenges is that the input must be in Base64. Now, you could manually convert each line of your script to Base64, but you would need to update that whenever something changed. Or you can use the Fn::Base64 function to simply convert your script to Base64 at runtime. This approach makes it much easier to edit the user data script when you need to. The example that follows shows you how to use two functions to input the user data into a CloudFormation template. Fn::Base64, as discussed, converts everything in user data into Base64. Fn::Join joins together two or more strings—in this case, two or more lines (\n is an escape character and is used as the delimiter in this case to represent a new line). The code then installs a web server, changes directories to the root web directory, and then creates a simple HTML page that will display "I am a happy little web server!" when you navigate to it after the web server build has completed.

```
"UserData" : {"Fn::Base64": {"Fn::Join" : ["\n", [
    "#!/bin/bash -ex",
    "yum install -y httpd",
    "cd /var/www/html",
    "echo '<html><body>I am a happy little web server!</body></html>' > index.html",
    "service httpd start"
]]}}
```

## Mapping

Mapping allows you to map keys to values. For each mapping a key must have a unique name, and keys are allowed to contain multiple values. In this example, we have a mapping called RegionAMI. The key in this case is the region name us-east-1 and the values are AmazonLinux and Ubuntu.

```
"RegionAMI" : {
    "us-east-1" : {
        "AmazonLinux" : "ami-XXXXXXXXXXX",
        "Ubuntu" : "ami-XXXXXXXXXXX"
}}
```

A built-in function, Fn::FindInMap, is then used to point to the mapping that you created earlier. This allows you to specify what you want (AmazonLinux) without having to remember the AMI ID for the specific region that you are in. This is demonstrated here:

```
"ImageID" : {"Fn:FindInMap": ["RegionAMI", "Ref":"AWS::Region", "AmazonLinux"]}
```

## Pseudo Parameters

Last, but certainly not least, are pseudo parameters. These are parameters that are created with CloudFormation as opposed to parameters that you create in your templates.

- `AWS::AccountID`—AWS account ID
- `AWS::NotificationARNs`—ARNs for notification topics
- `AWS::NoValue`—Removes attribute
- `AWS::Partition`—Returns partition resource is in
- `AWS::Region`—Region of the current stack
- `AWS::StackId`—ID of current stack
- `AWS::StackName`—Name of current stack
- `AWS::URLSuffix`—Returns domain suffix

To use pseudo parameters, you use the Ref function and then the name of the pseudo parameter of the argument. For example:

```
{"Ref": "AWS::Region"}
```

# Issues with CloudFormation Templates

There are two issues that could cause you problems as you begin working with CloudFormation.

The first issue is that while templates can be used across regions, AMI IDs are unique to the region they are in. I have given you examples in this chapter of how to account for that in your template. If your stack fails to build, make sure that you have the right AMI ID for the region that you are trying to create the stack in.

The second issue I want to call out is JSON syntax. You use commas at the end of each line to tell JSON to expect another line. If the comma is not there, JSON will assume that it has reached the last line. So, if your template is building a stack but things are not looking the way that you expect them to, check your JSON and ensure that you have commas where you need them.

# Summary

IaaS allows you to build infrastructure dynamically with the use of code, which removes error-prone manual processes and replaces them with repeatable processes. CloudFormation is the tool that AWS has made available to customers who want to use IaaS.

Templates define how you want your infrastructure to look, and stacks are instances of a template. You can have multiple stacks created from one template, and you can use parameters, mappings, and pseudo parameters to customize stacks, even when deployed from the same template.

# Resources to Review

What Is AWS CloudFormation?

https://docs.aws.amazon.com/AWSCloudFormation/latest/UserGuide/Welcome.html

Working with Stacks:

https://docs.aws.amazon.com/AWSCloudFormation/latest/UserGuide/stacks.html

Sample Templates:

https://docs.aws.amazon.com/AWSCloudFormation/latest/UserGuide/cfn-sample-templates.html

AWS CloudFormation FAQs:

https://aws.amazon.com/cloudformation/faqs/

# Exam Essentials

**Understand what CloudFormation does.** CloudFormation allows you to build your infrastructure from a template, which ensures that resources are built the same way every time. CloudFormation is AWS' tool that allows you to do infrastructure as a service (IaaS).

**Define the relationship between templates and stacks.** Templates are the definition of your environment, whereas stacks are instances of the template. This means that the stack contains all the resources defined in the template. Stacks are an all-or-nothing deal; if any one resource fails to be built successfully, then the entire stack will fail and be rolled back.

**Remember what the sections in a JSON template are used for.** You need to remember what the various sections in the JSON template are used for. You won't be expected to write your own JSON template on the exam, but you may be shown samples and asked questions based on what you are seeing.

# Exercise

For this chapter, you will create your very first CloudFormation template and stack.

### Create a CloudFormation Stack

1. Log into the AWS Management Console.

2. Click Services; then under Management & Governance select CloudFormation.

3. Select Stacks in the CloudFormation Console menu.

4. Click Create Stack.

5. On the Specify Template screen, choose Use A Sample Template and then select Wordpress Blog from the drop-down under Simple.

6. Click Next.

7. On the Specify Stack Details screen, enter a name for your stack; I used **studyguide102019**.

8. Enter the passwords you want to use for DBPassword and DBRootPassword.

9. Enter a username in the DB Username field.

10. Leave the instance type as t2.small.

11. Under KeyName, select the keypair you will use to authenticate.

12. Click Next.

13. On the Configure Stack Options screen, accept the defaults and click Next.

14. On the Review page, click Create Stack.

Once you click Create Stack, CloudFormation goes to work setting up your stack for you. When the status has changed from CREATE_IN_PROGRESS to CREATE_COMPLETE, you have successfully completed your first CloudFormation deployment. These sample templates are a fantastic way to learn, and you can always view the templates you have created by clicking your stack and selecting the Template tab shown in Figure 18.1.

**FIGURE 18.1**    You can click the Template tab to view the JSON template for the stack that you created.

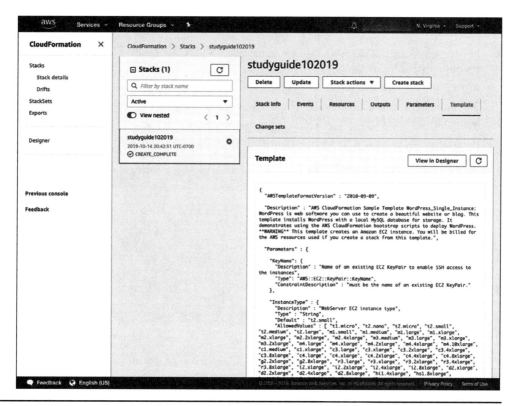

# Review Questions

You can find the answers in the Appendix.

1. In what ways can you use AWS services to automate and minimize overhead in an IaaS environment? (Choose two.)
   - **A.** Ensure deployments to all environments are identical.
   - **B.** Build instances in an identical way across all environments.
   - **C.** Replace manual steps with JavaScript to minimize console usage.
   - **D.** Define environments in XML rather than console-based manual steps.

2. Which of the following AWS tools and services is not closely associated with CloudFormation?
   - **A.** YAML
   - **B.** AWS API
   - **C.** AWS SDK
   - **D.** JSON

3. What does the AWSTemplateFormatVersion section of a CloudFormation template indicate?
   - **A.** The date that the template was originally written
   - **B.** The date that the template was last processed
   - **C.** The capabilities of the template based on the version available at the indicated date
   - **D.** The date that the template was last updated

4. What is the only required component in a template?
   - **A.** Parameters
   - **B.** Metadata
   - **C.** Resources
   - **D.** Outputs

5. In what section of a CloudFormation template would you indicate values that are either dynamic or should be processed at runtime?
   - **A.** Inputs
   - **B.** Parameters
   - **C.** Variables
   - **D.** Metadata

**6.** Which of the following statements about resources and their names are true with regard to CloudFormation? (Choose two.)

   **A.** You can assign actual resource names to a resource when you create it.

   **B.** You can assign logical names to a resource when you create it.

   **C.** You can map a logical name to a specified AWS resource name in a template.

   **D.** You cannot assign actual resource names to AWS resources via CloudFormation.

**7.** You want to create a number of different environments but allow for easy separation of those environments via billing. How can you best accomplish this using CloudFormation?

   **A.** Assign each environment different names.

   **B.** Assign each resource in an environment a set prefix (like dev-[resource name]).

   **C.** Assign tags to each resource in an environment.

   **D.** You cannot differentiate resources created in a single CloudFormation template.

**8.** You are running a complicated CloudFormation stack, and you're encountering errors that don't occur until most of the stack has been executed. You're finding that it takes nearly an hour to clean up all the resources created by the stack before trying it again. How can you reduce this cleanup time?

   **A.** Enable Automatic Rollback On Error.

   **B.** Build a second CloudFormation template to tear down all resources that you can then run as needed.

   **C.** Disable Automatic Rollback On Error.

   **D.** Enable the CleanupResources option within your template.

**9.** You have a stack that creates a number of EC2 instances and then initiates scripts on each instance. However, the next steps in your stack are failing because they depend on resources that those scripts configure, and the stack is executing before the scripts complete. How can you overcome this problem?

   **A.** This is not possible using CloudFormation.

   **B.** You need to use the WaitCondition resource to block further execution until the scripts on the instances complete.

   **C.** You need a separate CloudFormation stack, and you have to set your initial stack to call the second stack.

   **D.** You need a separate CloudFormation stack that you can run manually after the scripts on your instances complete.

**10.** Which of the following can you not create using CloudFormation?

   **A.** VPC

   **B.** NACL

   **C.** Elastic IP

   **D.** You can create all of these using CloudFormation.

11. From which of the following can you not execute a CloudFormation stack?

    A. AWS CLI

    B. AWS API

    C. AWS SDK

    D. You can execute CloudFormation from all of these.

12. What is the difference between an instance and a template with regard to CloudFormation?

    A. A template specifies what should occur, and an instance is a specific run of that template.

    B. An instance specifies what should occur, and a template is a specific run of that instance.

    C. An instance is a function that runs your template.

    D. A template is a function that runs your instance.

13. Which of the following is not allowed as a data type for a parameter?

    A. List

    B. Comma-delimited list

    C. Array

    D. Number

14. You want to accept custom CIDR blocks as inputs to your CloudFormation stack. What validation might you use to ensure the CIDR block is correctly formatted as an input parameter?

    A. AllowedValues

    B. MinLength

    C. ValueMask

    D. AllowedPattern

15. What does AWS refer to the set of resources created by a template instance as?

    A. A stack set

    B. A stack

    C. An instantiation

    D. An instance run

16. You are building a number of CloudFormation templates to be executed by several members of the operations team. However, these templates require a number of sensitive passwords that you don't want to be shown as the template executes. How can you prevent these values from being shown?

    A. Mark the parameter as NoEcho.

    B. Mark the parameter as EchoOff.

    C. Mark the parameter as NoOutput.

    D. Mark the parameter as OutputOff.

**17.** You want to ensure the URL to a web application created by a CloudFormation stack is captured. What element(s) would be used to accomplish this?

   **A.** A template parameter

   **B.** An output value

   **C.** A lookup data table

   **D.** A set of resources' configuration values

**18.** You want to supply a website URL to a stack that an API call will use as part of setting up an EC2 instance. What element(s) would be used to accomplish this?

   **A.** A template parameter

   **B.** An output value

   **C.** A lookup data table

   **D.** A set of resources' configuration values

**19.** You want to create several new EC2 instances using the latest AWS-supported version of an SUSE Linux AMI. What element(s) would be used to accomplish this?

   **A.** A template parameter

   **B.** An output value

   **C.** A lookup data table

   **D.** A set of resources' configuration values

**20.** You want a stack to pop up a dialog for entry of a database username when that database is being created. What element(s) would be used to accomplish this?

   **A.** A template parameter

   **B.** An output value

   **C.** A lookup data table

   **D.** A set of resources' configuration values

# Chapter

# 19

# Elastic Beanstalk

**THE AWS CERTIFIED SYSOPS ADMINISTRATOR – ASSOCIATE EXAM TOPICS COVERED IN THIS CHAPTER MAY INCLUDE, BUT ARE NOT LIMITED TO, THE FOLLOWING:**

**Domain 2.0: High Availability**

✓ 2.1  Implement scalability and elasticity based on use case

✓ 2.2  Recognize and differentiate highly available and resilient environments on AWS

**Domain 3.0: Deployment and Provisioning**

✓ 3.1  Identify and execute steps required to provision cloud resources

✓ 3.2  Identify and remediate deployment issues

**Domain 7.0: Automation and Optimization**

✓ 7.1  Use AWS services and features to manage and assess resource utilization

✓ 7.2  Employ cost-optimization strategies for efficient resource utilization

✓ 7.3  Automate manual or repeatable process to minimize management overhead

For organizations with web applications, a choice must be made as to how to support those web applications. The choice can become even more complex if the application is business critical and needs to be highly available, or if you need to make changes to improve performance.

AWS has simplified the architecting and administering of web applications with the introduction of AWS Elastic Beanstalk. With Elastic Beanstalk, you can focus on your web application rather than focusing on software or hardware. It is simple to build in high availability or account for performance needs—all from a single console.

This chapter includes:

An introduction to Elastic Beanstalk

Deployment options using Elastic Beanstalk

Troubleshooting deployment options

# What Is Elastic Beanstalk?

You may be wondering why we are covering Elastic Beanstalk (arguably a tool meant for developers) in a book meant for the SysOps Administrator – Associate certification. The reasoning is simple: you need to understand how Elastic Beanstalk works because you may be asked to do deployments for your developers, or you may be called in when something isn't working right. If you are in a smaller organization, you may even be the one developing an application. Understanding how Elastic Beanstalk works and what its options are could be critical in being able to successfully deploy applications for your organization.

As a system administrator, you likely understand how to manage your AWS infrastructure. You know how to configure the individual components like the Amazon EC2 instances, the Elastic Load Balancers, the Auto Scaling groups, databases, and so forth. But here's the thing: when you have a web application that is business critical, you just want it to run. Considering that the majority of web applications today use the same basic tiered architecture, that is something that can be accomplished manually or automatically. Any time you can automate something, it is worth looking at how to accomplish that. That brings us back to Elastic Beanstalk.

*Elastic Beanstalk* is a managed service that simplifies the administration and deployment of web applications within AWS. It takes advantage of AWS CloudFormation to provision all the resources that you need to successfully run your web application. You can still customize those resources to a very high degree; you still have full control over the configuration. However, instead of having to architect the network and build the EC2 instances, the subnets, and the Auto Scaling groups, you simply specify the type of web application that you want to run. Elastic Beanstalk takes care of the instance configuration, as well as the operating system installation and configuration. Even better, Elastic Beanstalk is a free service. You pay only for the resources that you are using.

You should be aware of three architectural models when you are deploying infrastructure through Elastic Beanstalk:

**Single-Instance Deployment**   A single EC2 instance and the supporting infrastructure are deployed to support your web app. This is a good solution for a development environment.

**Load Balancer and Auto Scaling Group**   EC2 instances that are not only load balanced, but also set up in an Auto Scaling group. This is a good solution for production or preproduction environments.

**Auto Scaling Group Only**   EC2 instances are put into an Auto Scaling group but are not taking advantage of a load balancer. This model is best for applications that are not web-based in a production environment.

## Platforms and Languages

If you are developing your own applications, or if your developers ask which languages are supported by Elastic Beanstalk, you will find that a very large number of languages and platforms are supported. As of this writing, the list languages and platforms include the following:

- Packer Builder
- Single Container Docker
- Multicontainer Docker
- Preconfigured Docker
- Go
- Java SE
- Java with Tomcat
- .NET on Windows Server running IIS
- Node.js
- PHP
- Python
- Ruby

As I mentioned earlier, Elastic Beanstalk uses CloudFormation to deploy the resources it needs to provision. Just about anything that you can normally provision can be used within Elastic Beanstalk, including EC2 instances, Amazon RDS instances, and more. A high level of customization is available, including the ability to choose instance types, sizes, and Amazon Machine Images (AMIs). This is easy to see when you choose Configure More Options on the Create A Web App screen in Elastic Beanstalk, shown in Figure 19.1.

**FIGURE 19.1** A multitude of configuration options are available in Elastic Beanstalk.

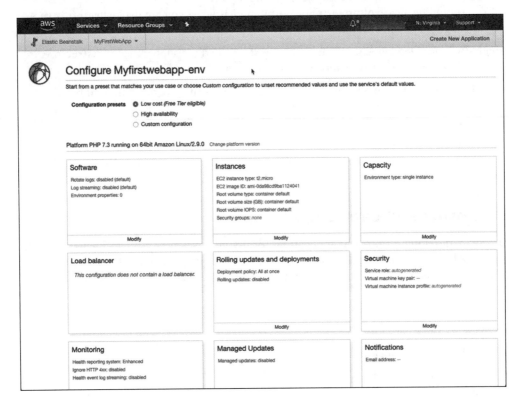

Once you have made your selections, and you choose Create App, Elastic Beanstalk uses CloudFormation to deploy the infrastructure that you need in the way that you set it to be built. The basic flow of things that happen when Elastic Beanstalk deploys an app are:

1.  Elastic Beanstalk builds the EC2 instance with the base AMI that was selected.

2.  Elastic Beanstalk sends the new code for the application to the EC2 instance.

3.  Application dependencies are resolved on the EC2 instance (this process can be long, based on how many dependencies need to be installed).

4.  The application is installed on the EC2 instance and is available for use.

## Creating a Custom Platform

As you saw in the "Platforms and Languages" section earlier, you have a wide range of platforms to choose from. But what happens if you need a platform that is not offered? You create a custom platform, of course! I know I made it sound easy in that last sentence. Creating custom platforms is an advanced topic, but it does allow you to create a whole platform from scratch to support your workloads if Elastic Beanstalk doesn't natively offer support for it. I'm not just talking about custom AMIs. You can use custom AMIs with Elastic Beanstalk with no further modifications necessary, and Elastic Beanstalk will use its scripts and build the platform stack just as it normally would. When creating a custom platform, you are specifying the image and the scripts necessary along with custom configuration settings to build your platform.

To create custom platforms, you use Packer. Packer is a tool put out by HashiCorp that allows you to use scripts to install and configure software on your images. You create a Packer platform in Elastic Beanstalk and from there AWS will manage the Packer platform for you once you upload your *platform archive*. A platform archive is a zip file containing all the configuration files and scripts necessary to build your platform. This process is discussed in detail later.

To create your custom platform, you provide a Packer template to Elastic Beanstalk, along with any scripts or files that the template needs when it builds the AMI. All the configuration components are specified in the *platform definition file*, named platform.yaml, which includes the builder that was used to create the image, which AMI to use, and so on. Here's an example that can be used to provision the latest version of Amazon Linux:

```
version: "1.0"
provisioner:
  type: packer
  template: custom_platform.json
  flavor: amazon
```

 The only required fields in the platform.yaml file are the version number, the provisioner type, and the provisioner template. Everything else is optional.

If you don't want to use the latest version of Amazon Linux, you can specify which version you want to install in the metadata section of the platform.yaml file, along with other information you might deem important:

```
metadata:
  maintainer: John Doe
  description: My Awesome Platform
```

```
operating_system_name: Amazon linux
operating_system_version: 2018.03.0
```

So now that you have your `platform.yaml` file, let's look at the Packer template. In the first code sample, you can see where it says `template: custom_platform.json`. That is what tells Elastic Beanstalk what the name of the Packer template is; you can call it whatever you like, and you just need to reference the appropriate name in the `platform.yaml` file. The first couple of lines in the JSON set up the variables for all the scripts. Elastic Beanstalk creates three environmental variables: `AWS_EB_PLATFORM_NAME`, `AWS_EB_PLATFORM_VERSION`, and `AWS_EB_PLATFORM_ARN`. These variables are mapped to `platform_name`, `platform_version`, and `platform_arn` in the `custom_platform.json` file. The values for `platform_name` and `platform_version` are pulled from the `platform.yaml` file, and `platform_arn` is set by the build script (`builder.sh`), which we'll discuss soon. `env` is needed when you build your template because it tells Elastic Beanstalk that you are referencing an environmental variable.

```
"variables": {
  "platform_name": "{{env `AWS_EB_PLATFORM_NAME`}}",
  "platform_version": "{{env `AWS_EB_PLATFORM_VERSION`}}",
  "platform_arn": "{{env `AWS_EB_PLATFORM_ARN`}}"
},
```

In the `builders` section of the JSON, you give it some basic configuration parameters. If you are using one of the AWS templates, you will need to add the region and the source AMI, as these will be blank in the template.

```
"builders": [
  {
    "type": "amazon-ebs",
    "name": "HVM AMI builder",
    "region": "us-east-1",
    "source_ami": "ami-00eb20669e0990cb4",
    "instance_type": "t2.micro",
    "ssh_username": "ec2-user",
    "ssh_pty": "true",
    "ami_name": "AmazonLinux_Packer (built on {{isotime \"20191028150405\"}})",
    "tags": {
      "eb_platform_name": "{{user `platform_name`}}",
      "eb_platform_version": "{{user `platform_version`}}",
      "eb_platform_arn": "{{user `platform_arn`}}"
    }
  }
],
```

The last part of the custom_platform.json file is the provisioners section. In this section, you define the provisioners that can be used to install and configure the software on the machine image that you have chosen. In this example, you can see that there are two provisioners defined: one for files and one for the shell.

```
"provisioners": [
  {
    "type": "file",
    "source": "builder",
    "destination": "/tmp/"
  },
  {
    "type": "shell",
    "execute_command": "chmod +x {{ .Path }}; {{ .Vars }} sudo {{ .Path }}",
    "scripts": [
      "builder/builder.sh"
    ]
  }
]
```

Those are the basic components of your custom_platform.json file: variables, builders, and provisioners. Once you have saved the file, you are ready to go.

If you have downloaded one of the premade templates, you will already have the structure that follows. I highly recommend using a template for your first custom platform to help you learn about the basic components. When you unzip the template, the uncompressed folder will have these basic components.

- builder: This folder includes all the files that Packer needs to create your custom platform.
- custom_platform.json: This is the template file we discussed earlier.
- platform.yaml: This is the definition file discussed earlier.
- ReadMe.txt: This file is used for documentation and should describe what the platform/template is going to do.

Once you have made your edits, compress the folder once more and then open the AWS Management Console. Select Elastic Beanstalk, and when you build your application, select Elastic Beanstalk Packer Builder. Choose Upload Code and select the zip file you created. Your screen should look similar to Figure 19.2.

**FIGURE 19.2**   You can upload your configuration files to Elastic Beanstalk through the AWS Management Console.

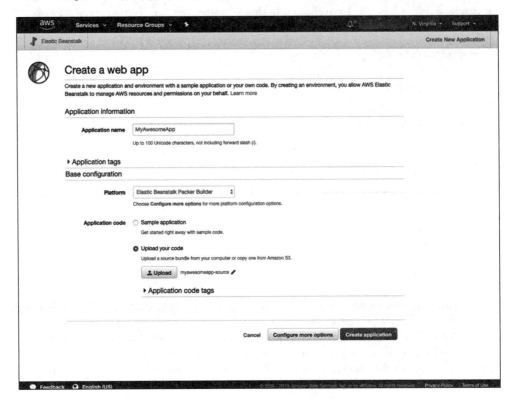

# Updates in Elastic Beanstalk

The previous section covered the basic architectural models and how Elastic Beanstalk deploys an application in steps. What happens when you need to update your code? Four types of deployment options are used when updating your code, and these show up on the exam with great frequency. The four deployment types are:

- All-at-once
- Rolling
- Rolling with additional batches
- Immutable

We'll discuss each model in more detail in this section.

# All-at-Once Deployment

When you are in your development environment, you often want to do a code refresh for your application quickly. Traditionally, development environments don't have the same uptime requirements that production deployments do either, which makes the *all-at-once deployment* a perfect option.

All-at-once stops all the applications, deploys the new application, and then starts it. This is the fastest deployment model by far, and it does not incur any additional cost since you have the same number of instances running before and after the update.

# Rolling Deployment

In a production environment, it isn't likely that you will get approval to bring an application down to update it if there is an alternative. One such alternative that works well for production environments is a rolling deployment. When you use a *rolling deployment*, you select a percentage of your EC2 instances to upgrade at once. This approach does make the application run below the capacity that it normally would, so it is best to do this type of deployment at a time when the application is not being used heavily. Both versions of the application end up running at the same time, and since you are not adding instances, there is no additional cost to using this deployment method.

# Rolling with Additional Batches Deployment

If you like the rolling model but you can't run under capacity, then *rolling with additional batches* is for you. This deployment model launches some new EC2 instances to support your application upgrade before taking the old instances out to update the application. When the application has been completely updated, the batch systems are terminated. This results in a longer deployment period, as well as additional costs given the additional instances that are spun up. However, if this is a business-critical application, it ensures that your application is always running at capacity, rather than under as it would with a plain rolling deployment.

# Immutable Deployment

Of the four deployment types, an *immutable deployment* takes the longest to fully deploy. For production environments, where a little additional cost is acceptable, this can be a fantastic model to use. When you deploy new code, Elastic Beanstalk creates a temporary Auto Scaling group with one new instance. Once that instance reports back healthy, it will build additional instances until it matches the number you have in production. When the application reports back as healthy from all the new instances, Elastic Beanstalk transfers them to the production Auto Scaling group and then terminates the old instances and the temporary Auto Scaling group.

The upside to this deployment is that there is absolutely no downtime, and you can have a much higher confidence level that the deployment was successful. You are also able to roll back to the old version very quickly if there is a failure—in fact, Elastic Beanstalk will terminate the new instances if they are not able to become healthy, before they are ever put into the production Auto Scaling group.

# Testing Your Application with a Blue/Green Deployment

*Blue/green deployments* are not an official Elastic Beanstalk deployment option; however, they should still be discussed in this chapter because they are an important method that can be used to test a new version of an application against production traffic.

A blue/green deployment refers to using your production environment (blue) and your staging environment (green) side-by-side to test your new code with real production traffic. It is a fantastic way to find issues with your code not discovered during testing, and it reduces the impact to your customers if an issue is found.

It's important to understand that blue/green deployments are not a direct feature offered by Elastic Beanstalk. You need to create two environments, and then use Amazon Route 53 to use weighted policies to distribute a certain percentage of the traffic to your blue deployment and the other percentage to your green deployment. This requires two different URLs, which are created automatically by Elastic Beanstalk. Once you validate that everything looks good with the new version, you change the weight in the Route 53 policy to 0 for the old environment or remove it from the routing policy altogether. If something does go wrong with the new deployment, you have the ability to quickly fail back to the working version of your application within seconds by adding it back into the routing policy. Once the application has been validated, you can delete the second (Staging) environment to reduce cost; just ensure that the Route 53 policy has been edited to point only to the new production environment first.

AWS recommends cloning your current environment when doing blue/green deployments to create your second environment and then updating that second environment. The benefit to cloning your production environment is that you are getting an exact copy of Production to work with. This allows you to perform the most accurate and reliable testing of your new application.

# Configuring Elastic Beanstalk

When you create a new environment, even if you select one of the preconfigured applications, chances are that you are going to want to customize your application a bit. You are given the chance to do this when you provision your application. After you choose the platform you want to use, click the Configure More Options button. One of the first things that sticks out is some presets. Low Cost uses free-tier eligible services and keeps the configuration complexity down to a minimum. This is great for development or test lab loads. High Availability, on the other hand, provides an application load balancer with an Auto Scaling group that by default allows one to four instances. If you change any of the settings, the Configuration presets will automatically change to Custom Configuration. I have chosen a Tomcat web application with sample code. As an example, let's assume that I will need an RDS database to support my web application. I can scroll down to Database and click Modify, as shown in Figure 19.3.

**FIGURE 19.3**   Modifying the database settings in Elastic Beanstalk

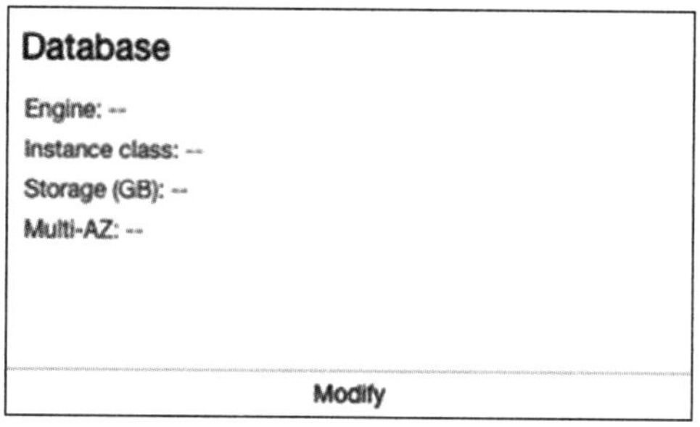

You can customize multiple settings before you even deploy your application. These include:

- Software
- Instance types and sizes
- Capacity
- Load balancers
- Updates and deployment types
- Security
- Monitoring
- Managed Updates
- Notifications
- Networking
- Databases
- Tags

You don't need to memorize these for the exam, but you should know that they exist, how to get to them, and how to configure them. I suggest clicking through the various options and seeing just how much you can do within Elastic Beanstalk. It is incredibly customizable, and you may be asked questions related to customizing a specific setting in Elastic Beanstalk on the exam.

# Securing Elastic Beanstalk

The Shared Responsibility Model that you learned about earlier in this book still very much applies to Elastic Beanstalk, even though it is a managed service. As a reminder, AWS is responsible for security of the cloud, and you are responsible for security in the cloud. There are several components that you need to account for; let's examine each one.

## Data Protection

Although AWS is responsible for security of the cloud, you are still responsible for protecting your data, even when using a managed service like Elastic Beanstalk. The suggestions are the same as if you had stood up the environment manually. They include protecting the root and user accounts by adding multifactor authentication (MFA), using encryption for data at rest and in transit, and using AWS CloudTrail to log all activities taken within the console or via the AWS API.

## Identity and Access Management

Elastic Beanstalk provides two managed policies: one that provides read only access and one that provides full access. These policies can be attached to IAM groups to allow for easier administration of access.

- `AWSElasticBeanstalkFullAccess` is the managed policy that grants full access. It allows you to configure, add, or delete Elastic Beanstalk applications and all their resources.
- `AWSElasticBeanstalkReadOnlyAccess` is the managed policy that grants read access. Users with this policy may view all the resources within Elastic Beanstalk but may not make any changes.

## Logging and Monitoring

The same logging and monitoring services that you use with other AWS infrastructure can be used with Elastic Beanstalk. Amazon CloudWatch, AWS CloudTrail, and even Amazon EC2 instance logs can all be used to aid in troubleshooting, and with CloudTrail you will be able to satisfy the need for audit trails.

## Compliance

Elastic Beanstalk gets checked regularly by auditors outside of AWS for many of the popular compliance frameworks and programs, including HIPAA, PCI-DSS, SOC, and

FedRAMP. You can download these compliance reports at any time via AWS Artifact, which is available here: `https://console.aws.amazon.com/artifact/`. Please note that you will need an AWS login to access these reports. If you don't have a login currently, you can create one for free. You will be asked for a credit card; however, you will not be charged. The card is only used if you incur expenses within AWS.

## Resilience

Elastic Beanstalk makes use of the same global infrastructure as the other services: regions and availability zones. It is up to you to build an infrastructure with Elastic Beanstalk that takes advantage of these features.

## Configuration and Vulnerability Analysis

AWS makes it simple for you to keep your platforms up-to-date with a feature called Managed Updates. This feature will automatically apply patches and minor updates to your platform so that you don't have to worry about it. Tools like Amazon Inspector can be used to assess the environment to make sure that vulnerabilities are reduced, and AWS Trusted Advisor can also offer insights into security best practices.

## Security Best Practices

As you might expect, security best practices for Elastic Beanstalk are similar to what you would have with manually deployed infrastructure. Keeping your platform up-to-date can reduce vulnerabilities, and implementing the concept of least privilege can ensure that only authorized users are able to perform tasks in Elastic Beanstalk. Making sure that you are not only monitoring logs and API calls but also configuration baselines is also important to the overall security of your organization.

## Applying Security Best Practices to Elastic Beanstalk

When you configure Elastic Beanstalk, you can make changes to Security settings before creating your environment. I would like to call attention to a few tiles you get when you choose to configure more options, or when you click Configuration after an environment is built.

- **Security:** Allows you to update IAM settings and set the keypair that you want to use for your Amazon EC2 instances
- **Monitoring:** Allows you to set up basic or detailed Amazon CloudWatch logging
- **Managed Updates:** Allows automated patching of your Amazon EC2 instances

# AWS Elastic Beanstalk CLI

Although you won't need to know a lot about the command-line interface (CLI) used in Elastic Beanstalk, you should know some of the basics so that you won't get a surprise on the exam. You may have used the AWS CLI in the past, and you can still use it with Elastic Beanstalk. However, the length of the commands when using the AWS CLI can become a bit unwieldy, especially for scripting functions. AWS released the EB CLI to resolve that issue.

The *EB CLI* contains many commands specific to Elastic Beanstalk and allows you to easily create, modify, and delete your environments all from the command line. The EB CLI makes it far easier to script application environment builds.

For instance, to check the status of your application environment with the AWS CLI you type the following:

```
aws elasticbeanstalk describe-environment-health --environment-name
<environment_name> --attribute-names All
```

With the EB CLI, however, the command is much simpler:

```
eb status <environment_name>
```

> Installing the EB CLI is not exceptionally complicated; however, it should be noted that it does not work with Python 3.8 as of this writing. You will need to install Python 3.7 to get the installation of the EB CLI to work properly. You may want to check AWS documentation to see if Python 3.7 is still recommended or if you can use a newer version.

There is a link in the resources section to the EB CLI reference guide that gives you an idea of the sheer number of commands that are at your disposal.

# Troubleshooting Elastic Beanstalk

Supporting Elastic Beanstalk may be part of your job duties; if so, this section will be very valuable to you. Understanding how it works is important, and understanding what to do when things are working the way they are expected to work may be equally as important.

One of the most common issues or complaints is that resolving dependencies takes too long. You may even run into timeout issues due to the time needed to resolve the dependencies before the application can be installed. The simplest resolution for this is to create a *golden image* that has all the dependencies installed already. This strategy shortens deployment time considerably, especially if there are a large number of dependencies.

If you find that commands are timing out, you can adjust the deployment timeout to allow for a longer period of time. Although this isn't as common as the dependencies causing an issue, it is certainly possible.

If you need to access an external resource, make sure that the security group in place is correctly configured to allow the necessary traffic in and out.

Last, but not least, if the health of your application is red be sure to check CloudWatch for recent log file entries that may give you a clue as to what happened, and review environment events as well. If you can't figure out why your application is failing health checks, you can always roll back to a previous version of the application that worked properly.

# Summary

Elastic Beanstalk is a managed service that allows you to focus on deploying applications rather than on managing infrastructure services. Multiple languages and platforms are supported with Elastic Beanstalk, as are several architectural models.

Four deployment options are available: all-at-once, rolling, rolling with additional batches, and immutable. All-at-once is great for development deployments, and the other three are well suited for preproduction and production. All-at-once and rolling incur no additional costs, whereas rolling with additional batches and immutable incur additional costs due to the extra instances that must run to support them.

Security in Elastic Beanstalk is similar to security with traditional infrastructure. You can use many of the same tools that you are already familiar with to monitor, assess, and remediate your environment.

If you run into issues with Elastic Beanstalk, the use of a golden image or the modification of timeouts may be beneficial. In addition, traditional tools like security groups and Amazon CloudWatch are available. Security groups must have appropriate permissions, and Amazon CloudWatch logs may assist in finding the root cause of the issue.

# Resources to Review

AWS Elastic Beanstalk FAQs:

> https://aws.amazon.com/elasticbeanstalk/faqs/

Getting Started Using Elastic Beanstalk:

> https://docs.aws.amazon.com/elasticbeanstalk/latest/dg/GettingStarted.html

AWS Elastic Beanstalk Custom Platforms:

> https://docs.aws.amazon.com/elasticbeanstalk/latest/dg/custom-platforms.html

Deployment Policies and Settings:

> https://docs.aws.amazon.com/elasticbeanstalk/latest/dg/using-features
> .rolling-version-deploy.html

AWS Elastic Beanstalk Security:

> https://docs.aws.amazon.com/elasticbeanstalk/latest/dg/security.html

EB CLI Command Reference:

> https://docs.aws.amazon.com/elasticbeanstalk/latest/dg/eb3-cmd-commands.html

Install the EB CLI Using Setup Scripts:

> https://docs.aws.amazon.com/elasticbeanstalk/latest/dg/eb-cli3-install.html

Troubleshooting:

> https://docs.aws.amazon.com/elasticbeanstalk/latest/dg/troubleshooting.html

# Exam Essentials

**Remember that you are responsible for managing the app.**   The great thing about Elastic Beanstalk is that you are responsible for managing your application but that AWS is responsible for maintaining the underlying services since Elastic Beanstalk is a managed service. You still need to ensure that your platform is patched, a task that is made simpler with managed updates.

**Remember the deployment modes for applications.**   Deployment modes are a popular line of questioning on the exam. Remember the differences and use cases between all-at-once, rolling, rolling with additional batches, and immutable.

# Exercise

For this exercise, you need only an AWS account to log in with. The default VPC will work just fine for our purposes.

---

**EXERCISE 19.1**

### Deploy a Sample Application in Elastic Beanstalk

1. Log into the AWS Management Console.

2. Click Services; then click Elastic Beanstalk under Compute.

3. Click Get Started in the Elastic Beanstalk Console, shown in Figure 19.4.

**FIGURE 19.4** The Elastic Beanstalk Console is your starting point for building your application in AWS.

4. For Application Name, type **MyFirstEBApp**.

5. Click the Platform drop-down box and choose PHP.

6. For Application Code, leave Sample Application selected and click Configure More Options.

7. Leave Low Cost selected, scroll down, and click Create App.

   It will take several minutes for the instance to be deployed. If you switch to CloudFormation, which was covered in the previous chapter, you will see the stack being built there.

8. When the build is finished and you see the dashboard for your application, click the URL in the breadcrumb area. The URL will end with <region-name> .elasticbeanstalk.com.

9. When you see the Congratulations screen, you have deployed your first application!

To tear down the application so that you aren't charged for anything further, click the Actions button in the application's dashboard and choose Terminate Environment. You will be asked to type the name of the environment to confirm. Enter the name and click Terminate. Once you are on the application dashboard, and it is gray with the words (Terminated), click the Actions button again and choose Delete Application. Type the name of the application and click Delete.

# Review Questions

You can find the answers in the Appendix.

1.  Which of the following AWS architectural models does Elastic Beanstalk support? (Choose two.)
    A.  Single-instance deployment
    B.  Multi-instance deployment
    C.  Load balancer and Auto Scaling group
    D.  Redundant deployment

2.  Which of the following architectural models is targeted at web-based production environments?
    A.  Single-instance deployment
    B.  Multi-instance deployment
    C.  Load balancer and Auto Scaling group
    D.  Auto Scaling group only

3.  Which of the following architectural models is targeted at database instances running in a production environment?
    A.  Single-instance deployment
    B.  Multi-instance deployment
    C.  Load balancer and Auto Scaling group
    D.  Auto Scaling group only

4.  Which of the following are required in a `platform.yaml` file? (Choose two.)
    A.  A provisioner template
    B.  The number of instances to deploy
    C.  A name for the custom platform being defined
    D.  A version number

5.  What is the purpose of the `custom_platform.json` file required in defining a custom platform? (Choose two.)
    A.  It defines the AMI source, name, and region to use.
    B.  It defines the number of instances to create.
    C.  It defines the variables used by the custom platform.
    D.  It defines the supported languages in the custom platform.

**6.** Which of the following are supported deployment models in Elastic Beanstalk? (Choose two.)

    **A.** Rolling with additional batches deployment

    **B.** Rolling with incremental updates deployment

    **C.** Mutable deployment

    **D.** Immutable deployment

**7.** Why might you choose to use a rolling with additional batches deployment? (Choose two.)

    **A.** You don't want your application to completely stop when updates are made.

    **B.** You want the cheapest possible deployment model.

    **C.** You must always maintain maximum capacity in terms of running instances.

    **D.** You never want two versions of an application running at one time.

**8.** You are responsible for a critical production application that must always be up and running. Cost is not an option, and ensuring that any new instances are healthy before accepting traffic is a requirement. Which deployment model should you use?

    **A.** Rolling with additional batches deployment

    **B.** All-at-once deployment

    **C.** Rolling deployment

    **D.** Immutable deployment

**9.** You are running a production environment that serves thousands of customers. You have a no-downtime requirement for updates but are allowed to perform updates in times of day when usage of the application is minimal. Which is the most cost-effective approach to deployment in this scenario?

    **A.** Rolling with additional batches deployment

    **B.** All-at-once deployment

    **C.** Rolling deployment

    **D.** Immutable deployment

**10.** Which of the following can you *not* customize when using Elastic Beanstalk?

    **A.** Load balancer properties

    **B.** Monitoring policies

    **C.** AMIs used for instances

    **D.** You can configure all of these.

**11.** Which of the following would be required to set up a blue/green deployment? (Choose two.)

    **A.** Amazon Route 53

    **B.** Elastic Beanstalk

    **C.** Multiple application environments

    **D.** Amazon RDS

**12.** How is security in an Elastic Beanstalk environment different from security in a manually managed environment?

   **A.** Elastic Beanstalk manages the security of your environment completely.

   **B.** Elastic Beanstalk automatically protects the root account with MFA.

   **C.** Elastic Beanstalk manages security in the cloud as well as security of the cloud.

   **D.** Security is the same in both environments.

**13.** Which of the following are managed policies provided by Elastic Beanstalk? (Choose two.)

   **A.** `AWSElasticBeanstalkWriteAccess`

   **B.** `AWSElasticBeanstalkReadOnlyAccess`

   **C.** `AWSElasticBeanstalkReadWriteAccess`

   **D.** `AWSElasticBeanstalkFullAccess`

**14.** Which of the following is true about a default Elastic Beanstalk deployment?

   **A.** All instances created are private.

   **B.** A custom private VPC is created.

   **C.** All database instances are private.

   **D.** The created application endpoint is publicly available.

**15.** How should you manage access to your Elastic Beanstalk applications and deployments?

   **A.** Through the Elastic Beanstalk user management console

   **B.** Through the Elastic Beanstalk CLI tool

   **C.** Through the AWS Console using IAM permissions and roles

   **D.** Through the AWS Console using EB permissions and roles

**16.** Which of the following are required to access the Elastic Beanstalk API? (Choose two.)

   **A.** A user's access key

   **B.** A user's Elastic Beanstalk username

   **C.** A user's AWS username

   **D.** A user's secret key

**17.** Which databases are available for use on Elastic Beanstalk?

   **A.** MySQL, PostgreSQL, DynamoDB, and SQL Server

   **B.** Any database available through AWS as long as it supports read replicas

   **C.** Any relational database available through AWS but not any of the NoSQL databases

   **D.** Any database available through AWS

**18.** Who is responsible for updates to the underlying Elastic Beanstalk environment, such as Java or Tomcat updates?

   **A.** AWS

   **B.** You, the user

   **C.** AWS is responsible for major updates, and you are responsible for minor updates.

   **D.** You are responsible for major updates, and AWS is responsible for minor updates.

**19.** Why might you use the Clone An Environment option within Elastic Beanstalk? (Choose two.)

   **A.** You want to perform a minor version update on the Java version in your environment.

   **B.** You want to create a new environment to make changes to without affecting your existing running environment.

   **C.** You want to test a major version update on the Java version before deploying it to your running environment.

   **D.** You want to test a set of IAM permissions before rolling them out.

**20.** Which of the following does Elastic Beanstalk store in S3? (Choose two.)

   **A.** Server log files

   **B.** Database swap files

   **C.** Application files

   **D.** Elastic Beanstalk log files

# Appendix

# Answers to Review Questions

# Chapter 1: Introduction to Systems Operations on AWS

1. B. AWS Organizations is the AWS service for managing and organizing multiple accounts.

2. C. CloudTrail provides an API call tracker for services that interact within AWS. It provides compliance and tracking but is also ideal for simply watching API traffic.

3. B. CloudWatch is the core AWS monitoring tool. While CloudTrail provides API tracking, it's CloudWatch that is ideal for full application monitoring.

4. C. Auto Scaling in AWS is the process by which application resources can be added to or removed from a group, and scale to meet demand.

5. A, C. The obvious answer here is Auto Scaling groups, which are the core of AWS' scalability solutions. In addition to that, an elastic load balancer is key to routing traffic to various instances. While CloudFront and Lambda can be used in scalable applications, neither is really required.

6. A, C. The key here is understanding the acronyms. EBS is elastic block storage, and RDS is the AWS relational database service, both of which are storage services. EC2 is Elastic Compute Cloud and is a compute service, and VPC stands for virtual private cloud and is concerned with networking.

7. B. Option B, Identity and Access Management, is the AWS IAM service, and is usually called simply IAM. It is the approach AWS provides for user management, as well as handling groups, roles, permissions, policies, and the like.

8. A, D. The shared responsibility model makes this distinction: you are responsible for security *in* the cloud, and AWS is responsible for the security *of* the cloud. This means that AWS provides secure resources and infrastructure, and you the customer provide security of the resources and applications you deploy into the cloud.

9. A. It can seem as if the shared responsibility answer is best (option D), but customers actually have no deep access into regions or availability zone infrastructure. As a result, it is wholly up to AWS to secure these constructs.

10. A. AWS VPC, the virtual private cloud, is AWS' basic networking building block. A VPC contains subnets and instances within those subnets.

11. B. CloudFormation is AWS' deployment mechanism. Written in JSON, CloudFormation provides templates that can be used to create standardized application templates for deployment.

12. A. AWS offers four support plans: Basic, Developer, Business, and Enterprise. There is no such thing as a Free plan, although there is a free *tier* of AWS access.

13. A. A network access control list (ACL) behaves somewhat similar to a firewall in an on-premises architecture. Network ACLs (NACLs) aren't replacements for firewalls, because

there is not an exact 1-to-1 mapping between cloud components and on-premises ones. However, NACLs explicitly determine the types and ports of traffic that are allowed into and out of Amazon VPCs, and so are similar in nature to a firewall.

**14.** B. There are two primary resources for real-time administration interaction with AWS: the console and the CLI (command-line interface). The console is web-based, so the CLI is the better answer here.

**15.** A, C. The key to this question is the term "network environment." While you would likely use EC2 instances and databases via RDS in hosting a web application, the question asks specifically how to create the actual hosting environment itself. For that task, you'll need a Virtual Private Cloud (VPC) to construct the actual networking space (including subnets) and CloudFormation for repeatable deployments of that infrastructure.

**16.** D. The AWS Service Level Agreement (SLA) defines how AWS responds to outages and service degradations, and it includes specifics for every service in terms of response and uptime.

**17.** B. The AWS Shared Responsibility Model lays out the roles and responsibilities of both users and AWS itself in relation to the cloud environment.

**18.** B. A region is a separate geographic area in which AWS has availability zones and in which services run.

**19.** D. AWS regions do not have a set number of availability zones. In fact, regions often have AZs added or removed based on usage.

**20.** C. An AWS region is a geographic area within AWS. Within each region there are availability zones, which function as virtual datacenters.

# Chapter 2: Amazon CloudWatch

**1.** C. By default, CloudWatch collects metrics every 5 minutes, although you can modify this frequency to as little as 1 minute.

**2.** D. CloudWatch provides a number of metrics, and their names aren't always easy to recall. Here, it's VolumeThroughputPercentage that you want.

**3.** B. Step one here is to recognize that most CloudWatch metrics report in seconds rather than minutes. This means you can eliminate options A and C. Of options B and D, B is correct: VolumeIdleTime reports on how long the volume was idle with no I/O occurring.

**4.** C. CloudWatch's most basic—and often most useful—metric on compute is CPUUtilization, which reports as a percentage of how much of the instance's CPU is currently in use.

**5.** C. A resource group is primarily used to group resources that need to be viewed, metriced, and reacted to as a single unit, ideally on a single dashboard (option C). Resource groups have nothing to do with multi-region or multi-AZ setups (and CloudWatch is not limited by either), and they do not have anything to do with default versus nondefault metrics (option D).

**6.** B. You do not have to stop or terminate a running instance to enable detailed monitoring. You simply select the instance in the AWS management console and select Enable Detailed Monitoring (under the Actions ➤ CloudWatch Monitoring menu).

**7.** A. Resource groups are organized based on user-defined tags attached to resources.

**8.** A. Memory is not provided as a standard CloudWatch metric, and you'd need to create a custom metric for reporting on it.

**9.** B. CloudWatch can check status as often as 1 minute, either in a custom metric or in detailed monitoring, if that metric is standard. A high-resolution metric can be created as a custom metric and check more frequently.

**10.** B, D. CloudWatch offers two monitoring levels: Basic and Detailed.

**11.** A, D. CloudWatch does not provide memory reporting by default, and throughput is not a metric reported on for EC2, which is compute-related rather than networking-related.

**12.** B. This is pretty esoteric, but it is unfortunately the type of thing AWS might ask on an exam. Auto Scaling groups created via the console use basic monitoring, whereas groups created via the CLI use detailed monitoring by default. Strange, but true.

**13.** C. CloudWatch has limited ability to report on memory usage, which is why memory isn't a default CloudWatch metric. Option C, responding to thread count, isn't something that CloudWatch can monitor—and is related to memory again. You'd need a third-party tool for that sort of metric.

**14.** C. You can eliminate options A and B immediately, as CloudWatch cannot collect metrics more often than once a minute. This leaves options C and D. Option D is out as it would certainly affect the system's overall performance; turning off processes typically is viewed as interruptive. This leaves option C: adding a metric and seeing if the traffic out of the suspect EC2 instance correlates to the traffic into the DynamoDB instances.

**15.** B. When detailed monitoring is enabled, CloudWatch will update every minute. This is the most frequent option; the default option is 5-minute increments.

**16.** C. The key here is that the metric in question is high resolution. High-resolution metrics are custom and are not constrained by the rules of standard CloudWatch metrics. They can publish as often as every second (although not more frequently).

**17.** D. CloudWatch Events are triggered by changes in a resource's state (like an EC2 instance starting up, option B), logins to the console or access of the AWS API (option C), scheduled triggers (option A), or code-based triggers. This leaves option D; API calls to programmatic APIs within your code are best monitored by CloudTrail and are not going to generate CloudWatch Events.

**18.** B. AWS uses (not surprisingly) the AWS prefix to their namespaces: AWS/DynamoDB, AWS/S3, and so forth.

**19.** D. CloudWatch defines alarms in terms of predefined thresholds that are absolute, rather than relative to existing conditions. In other words, while you can monitor a metric hitting a specific high or low value (such as latency over 10 ms or output at 0 bytes), you cannot define a metric that measures usage relative to that same metric at an earlier point in time—and that's exactly what option D describes. You'd need to write custom code to read a metric and compare it with stored values from that same metric at earlier points in time to accomplish option D. That makes it the answer that would require custom programming.

**20.** A. A rule indicates how an event should be routed. It potentially matches an event and, in the case of a match, sends that event on to a target.

# Chapter 3: AWS Organizations

**1.** B, C. AWS Organizations provides management of multiple accounts in one place (option C). It also typically aggregates account costs, and the higher summative costs are eligible for AWS volume discounts (option B).

**2.** B, C. IAM provides users, groups, roles, and permissions. AWS Organizations provides organizational units and service control policies, as well as consolidated billing features. The components of AWS Organizations are not part of IAM (and vice versa).

**3.** B. AWS Organizations groups accounts into organizational units (OUs), allowing for groupings of permissions and roles.

**4.** A. An SCP in AWS Organizations is a service control policy and can be applied to an organizational unit (OU) to affect all users within that OU. It effectively applies permissions at an organizational level, in much the same way that a group applies them at a user level.

**5.** C. Service control policies (SCPs) are applied to OUs (organizational units) in AWS Organizations.

**6.** A. Service control policies (SCPs) are permission documents that can be applied to accounts and organizational units.

**7.** B, C. Organizational units and accounts are AWS Organizations constructs to which SCPs can be applied. Users and groups are IAM constructs to which policies can be applied.

**8.** B. AWS Organizations does not provide for batched or automated account creation, although it does make creating multiple accounts with similar organization and structure simple.

**9.** A. IAM should be used for access management, especially when dealing with a single account, as described in this question.

**10.** C. While this is a permissions question, and therefore related to IAM, whenever you have what amounts to a companywide (or organizationwide) policy, AWS Organizations is likely the best approach. Here, a service control policy could be applied across all accounts restricting access to SSH.

**11.** D. The most significant issue with tagging resources and using those tags to manage billing is that a number of AWS services are difficult to tag, as they are system-level services that are not exposed in the same manner as resources like EC2 instances, containers, and managed services. Additionally, some services are not readily identifiable, creating confusion. AWS Organizations addresses all of these problems.

**12.** C. You do not receive any discounts on standard AWS fees, including those associated with moving data across regions (option C). However, you certainly could receive discounts on those fees based on volume achieved by combining all account usage, rather than treating each account separately (to which option D alludes).

**13.** B. In an AWS Organizations multi-account setup, all reserved instances will use the lowest hourly price from any account in the organization. This means that all accounts effectively benefit from any member account's lowest rate. This is a lesser known advantage of AWS Organizations but can have significant cost impact if a lot of reserved instances are being used.

**14.** A, B. This is a pretty classic use case for AWS Organizations. You could use organizational units to organize accounts and service control policies to standardize resource permissions and access. Consolidated billing is a feature that would provide value here, but it isn't something you set up as much as it is something that you'd take advantage of. Resource tagging would not apply, because you'd be using AWS Organizations for billing management.

**15.** C, D. Consolidated billing and resource tagging are both features that would be useful for centralizing the billing of multiple accounts. Organizational units and service control policies are useful for management from a system administration point of view, but not so much from a billing point of view.

**16.** B. Every organization in AWS Organizations should have a single master account. All other accounts are controlled and organized by this account.

**17.** A. Using organizations is ultimately about multi-account management, and every organization should have a master account and one or more member accounts. While you could potentially create an organization with just a single master account, it wouldn't make much sense and would also go against AWS best practice.

**18.** A. This is a case where the answer might be a bit unintuitive (and unfortunate). A single account can only belong to a single organizational unit. This means that you can't have an account in both a production and an EastCoast OU, for example.

**19.** B. You can nest OUs in AWS Organizations, but that nesting functions similar to account membership in an OU. A single OU can belong to one other OU at any time, but no more than one.

**20.** A, D. AWS Organizations has replaced consolidated billing as the preferred option for managing multiple accounts together. To manage your accounts through one bill, you need to set up AWS Organizations (option A), which will require you to choose or create a master account for your organization (option D).

# Chapter 4: AWS Config

1. **C, D.** AWS Config provides both continuous monitoring and continuous assessment. Continuous deployment and continuous integration are part of the AWS developer toolset.

2. **C.** The best way to notify people in an organization about configuration changes is to connect AWS Config directly to SNS, the Simple Notification Service. This service can then send out texts and other notification types to interested parties. While CloudWatch can receive messages and then send them out, it is a less direct and simple solution than SNS. CloudTrail is for auditing and API logging, and SQS is a queue service.

3. **B.** AWS Config normalizes configurations and stores them in Amazon Simple Storage Service (S3). You'll need to be careful here, as DynamoDB is a useful service for configuration information; it stores key:value pairs. However, AWS Config uses S3 for this purpose.

4. **B, D.** This is a tough question and needs to be read carefully. A configuration item contains basic information about a resource, configuration data for the resource (option C), a map of related resources (option A), AWS CloudTrail event IDs (not CloudWatch IDs, from option B), and metadata about the configuration item itself (not about connected resources). So both B and D are the correct selections, as neither are part of a configuration item.

5. **B, C.** This is another difficult question. The keys when deciphering configuration items are configuration of the resource, intrinsic or identifying information about the resource, and information about the configuration item. In this case, that translates to the instance type of the EC2 instance (which is intrinsic to the resource) and the time that the configuration item was captured (metadata about the configuration item itself). While the user who created the instance and the time that the instance has been running are important, they are not specific to the configuration of the instance, and they do not uniquely identify the instance. Therefore, they're not part of a configuration item. (Note that the time a resource was created is reported, so you could calculate the running time of the instance, but that value is not directly reported.)

6. **B.** Code to evaluate a custom rule should be put into a Lambda function. That function can then be associated with the rule in AWS Config.

7. **A, C.** Rules can be triggered in two ways: by a configuration change or through a periodic frequency, which you set. In both cases, rules are evaluated when triggered.

8. **A, C.** AWS Config provides relevant information to changes made to resources. In this case, that would include a record of who made the change (A) as well as the source IP address from which that change was requested (C). API calls (B) are the domain of AWS CloudTrail, and AWS console logins would be reflected in logs, not AWS Config.

9. **D.** AWS Config doesn't affect how users actually use AWS, including the changes they make to configurations. It can only evaluate configurations after those changes are made. You'd need to use IAM permissions and roles and the AWS Service Catalog to prevent changes from happening at all.

**10.** C. AWS Config is enabled on a per-region basis. However, it can be enabled and then disabled and then re-enabled again. Therefore, option C is correct.

**11.** A. Continuous integration relates to automated testing of new code as its pushed into a version repository, which in this case is option A. In this set of answers, you're looking for references to actual code and then the testing of that code. The other options deal with deployment or configuration and are therefore not correct.

**12.** D. AWS lets you create up to 150 rules per account. You can request that limit be raised if needed.

**13.** A, B. A rule in AWS requires several pieces of information: an indication of whether the rule is change-based or periodic (option A) and a resource ID or type (option B). You can specify a tag key to match (option C), but it is not required, and you do not configure notifications on rules in the rule itself (option D).

**14.** B, C. A periodic rule can be triggered every 1, 3, 6, 12, or 24 hours. Lesser and greater frequencies are disallowed.

**15.** D. AWS Config is itself an AWS resource that provides APIs. This means that you can use AWS CloudTrail to view logs of those API calls, including calls to create new rules.

**16.** C. AWS Config returns a single evaluation for a resource, and that resource is compliant only if it is compliant for all rules that apply to the resource. In this case, since not all rules are compliant, the evaluation would return Noncompliant (option C).

**17.** C. AWS Config is primarily concerned with providing point-in-time information about resources (option A) and to provide a baseline configuration that is considered acceptable (options B and D). CloudTrail would be used to determine the caller to a resource API.

**18.** B, C. AWS Config allows you to work with configurations across accounts and regions using multi-account multi-region data aggregation (option C). While use of AWS Organizations is not required, it is recommended by AWS as a means to provide central account receipt of configuration reporting (option B).

**19.** A, B. Three of these options are valid: you will need an S3 bucket for storing aggregated information (option A), IAM policies to allow writing to that bucket (option B), and you can use an SNS topic to send out notifications (option C). However, the first two are required whereas setting up an SNS topic is optional, making the correct options A and B. There is no such service as AWS Log Aggregator (option C).

**20.** C. AWS Config is itself an AWS resource that provides APIs. This means that you can use AWS CloudTrail to view logs of those API calls, including calls to create new rules.

# Chapter 5: AWS CloudTrail

**1.** A. CloudWatch is the choice for performance metrics. Performance is not the same as an API log. While API logs via CloudTrail might help in troubleshooting performance, they are not themselves measures of performance.

**2.** B. Auditing is a key word for both CloudTrail and AWS Config. For API usage, though, CloudTrail is the correct choice.

**3.** C. Configuration should pretty clearly point you to AWS Config, and that's absolutely the correct answer here.

**4.** B. This is getting a bit meta, but CloudTrail is ideal for logging access to a service—and in this case, the AWS Config service. Remember that audit and log trails apply to all AWS services, including the monitoring services themselves.

**5.** D. The key here is to understand that the default setting for a CloudTrail trail is to function in all regions. Therefore, any new Lambda functions in new regions will automatically be picked up. You don't need to perform any additional configuration.

**6.** B. AWS allows five trails per region before you need to raise any predefined limits.

**7.** D. You can write logs from AWS CloudTrail to any S3 bucket in any region, regardless of where other logs are being written or if the trail writing the logs is in a different region.

**8.** A. EU West 2 already has the maximum number of allowed trails: three cross-region trails and two region-specific trails, adding up to five, the predefined limit.

**9.** D. The problem here is EU West 1. That region has three cross-region trails, and an additional two region-specific trails, for a total of five. You will not be able to add any more trails—cross-region or specific to EU West 1—until one of the existing trails is removed.

**10.** B. This isn't difficult but can trip you up—especially if you're already thinking about AWS CloudTrail. While AWS CloudTrail does log events related to API access, it does *not* send out notifications or alarms. That is the province of SNS.

**11.** A, D. CloudTrail is the obvious portion of the answer, as it logs API access. But you'll want to use something like SNS to actually send out notifications. SWF is for workflow and not appropriate here. CloudWatch does provide monitoring and alarms but is geared at resource usage, not API access.

**12.** A, B. CloudTrail provides API logging and can be used for monitoring, and CloudWatch monitors the underlying AWS resources. Both can be used to detect anomalies or unusual access patterns. SWF is a workflow tool, and Trusted Advisor makes recommendations but does not provide real-time monitoring.

**13.** B. CloudTrail is the AWS service for logging and is particularly helpful for auditing and compliance.

**14.** C. CloudTrail is on by default in AWS accounts. You can simply log in and begin viewing up to 90 days of account activity without any other setup (option C).

**15.** D. AWS CloudTrail supports all of these services and, in fact, almost all available AWS services.

**16.** D. When a trail is applied to all regions, a new trail is created in each region (option D), and all deliver activity to a single S3 bucket. No additional trails are needed.

**17.** D. By default, log files generated by CloudTrail are encrypted using S3 SSE (option A). You can also optionally turn on S3 MFA Delete to further protect files in S3 (option C), and use

SSE-KMS for CloudTrail log files (option B). Using customer-managed keys is not an option for CloudTrail logs (option D) and is the correct answer.

**18.** C. The events logged by CloudTrail include who made the request (option A), the services used, the actions performed, the parameters for the action (option B), and the response returned by the service (option D). This leaves option C as not being reported: the username of the requestor.

**19.** D. Logs are automatically decrypted by Amazon S3 and do not need any special work to be decrypted.

**20.** C, D. All of these services could likely be used in some way to facilitate this monitoring. However, the question specifically asks about alarms and the CLI, which is an API client to Amazon. Therefore, the API calls could be recorded by CloudTrail (option C) and pushed to a CloudWatch Log (option D) for processing or notification. While notification would be used via SNS, the question doesn't specifically ask for a notification mechanism.

# Chapter 6: Amazon Relational Database Service

**1.** A. Amazon RDS primarily offers the ability to increase the size of a database instance without major hassle. This translates into scalability: you can scale up your database instances to handle growing usage (option A). However, this is not elastic; this process cannot be done automatically (option C) or in a brief moment of increased usage (option B). And network access to databases has little to do directly with RDS (option D).

**2.** D. Options A, B, and C are all true of Auto Scaling policies but not of Amazon RDS. While Amazon RDS makes increasing the size of a database instance easy, as well as initial provisioning, it does not offer automatic instance changes or on-the-fly elasticity. Therefore, option D is correct.

**3.** A. The key here is to remember that Amazon RDS does not handle scaling automatically. Therefore, it is quite possible that utilization hits 100 percent (option A) if you do not scale your database instances manually.

**4.** C. Amazon RDS will patch your system automatically, but only when what is deemed a critical security or reliability patch is available (option C). This means that minor patches, or patches that don't affect security or reliability, are deferred (option B).

**5.** A, B. Limiting access to a database instance can come in a few forms. IAM roles (option A) can provide a service-level restriction to Amazon RDS instances, and NACLs (option B) can provide restrictions at the subnet or VPC level. Option C looks correct, but user permissions apply to the database once a user has already accessed the instance and is therefore incorrect. Bastion hosts (option D) are not applicable here.

6. B, C. Amazon RDS offers automated snapshots, which are taken daily (option B). You can also create a snapshot of your database at any time (option C). This is not limited to a maintenance window, either (option D).

7. B. By default, Amazon RDS sets up automated backups with a 7-day retention period.

8. B. Read replicas do not have backups configured by default, as the primary instance is typically the instance backed up.

9. D. In a multi-AZ configuration, the standby instance cannot be in the same availability zone as the primary instance.

10. A. In a multi-AZ configuration, replication is done synchronously, not asynchronously.

11. A, C. In a multi-AZ configuration, a failure triggers a number of events. The standby instance becomes the primary instance, and any DNS requests to the database will be resolved to the standby instance going forward.

12. A. This should be a simple question to correctly answer. Any time you want to increase read performance, a read replica is going to significantly improve performance.

13. D. Read replicas can be in the same availability zone as the primary instance, a different availability zone than the primary instance in the same region, or a different region than the primary instance altogether.

14. C. In a multi-AZ configuration, the standby instance must be in a different availability zone but in the same region as the primary database instance.

15. A, B. Read replicas are ideal for improved performance in high-read situations (option A), but not in high-write situations (option C). They are also great for reading data related to reporting (option B). They are not failover solutions (option D).

16. C. Amazon Aurora volumes can be as large as 64 TB, and this same size limit applies to Aurora tables.

17. C, D. Amazon Aurora can function as a drop-in replacement for both MySQL and PostgreSQL.

18. A, D. AWS will both patch your database instances and take backups of them automatically (options A and D). However, AWS will not optimize queries and has no idea of your organization's compliance requirements.

19. B. All of these options could potentially help the problem, but the question specifically mentions issues with write requests. Both ElastiCache (option A) and read replicas (option C) are aimed specifically at improving read requests. While this might lighten the overall load on the database instance and have an effect on write requests, only option B directly addresses the problem with a heavier-weight instance type.

20. D. Any active connections to a failing instance typically fail or terminate abnormally as the instance to which they are connected cannot serve those requests (option D).

# Chapter 7: Auto Scaling

1. D. EC2 Auto Scaling can scale only instances. With launch templates, you can scale a group with both on-demand (option A) and spot instances (option B), making the correct answer option D.

2. A, B. A launch configuration contains the ID of the AMI to use to launch an instance (option A), any block mappings (option B), a key pair for connecting, the instance type to launch, and one or more security groups for the instance.

3. D. Be wary of any question that asks you to determine how many instances are running in a group at a given time. Even with a desired capacity set to 3, the number of instances in a group will fluctuate based on triggers. For example, this group might have scaled up to 5 and still be in the process of scaling back down to the new desired capacity of 3. Because of this uncertainty, the correct answer is option D.

4. B, C. Launch templates can only be created from scratch or from launch configurations, and not from an EC2 instance, so option A is incorrect. (You can copy parameters from an instance but not create a template directly from an instance.) Templates do allow for versioning and slight variations in copies (option B), as well as for using both on-demand and spot instances (option C). They do not, however, allow multiple versions to be assigned to the same group, as is the case with launch configurations.

5. C. This is the type of question you can only hope for on an exam; it's basic and direct, as well as simple. The only parameter that would change automatically is Desired Capacity. In this case, it would presumably increase if network saturation occurs to provide an additional instance (or more) in times of peak traffic.

6. D. Your launch templates do not provide a means to indicate a target availability zone. You can specify AZs to use in your Auto Scaling group, but the launch template is focused on individual instances to launch within the group. The group then has the ability to place those instances in appropriate AZs.

7. D. All parameters in a launch template are optional. Although it would be unusual and arguably not that helpful to have a launch template with no AMI ID or key pair (for example), it's allowed by AWS.

8. D. As a general principle, the larger an Auto Scaling group, the less effective a static scaling policy turns out to be. Imagine adding a single instance to a fleet of 50 and expecting anything but fairly marginal results! In cases where you have large instance counts, PercentChangeInCapacity is often the most effective approach as it can proportionally scale. In the event that using a percentage isn't an option, the next best option is likely using ChangeInCapacity with a higher number or setting up scaled policies for different tiers of change.

9. C. First, eliminate option D; unless the new instances were launched mere seconds ago, this is not the best answer. The other options all propose a common situation: something has changed related to the new instances as compared to the ones that are working correctly. A keypair (option A) might affect SSH access, but not web access. A different availability zone

should not affect access, as the Auto Scaling group and load balancer should automatically handle this. Option C, however, is valid: a different security group could result in web traffic being disallowed in, causing a lack of connectivity.

10. **A, D.** The recurring scheduled surge of activity makes selecting option A a good first choice. Knowing ahead of time that activity increases at 4 and decreases at 8 means you can adjust the desired capacity of the group accordingly. Option D is also correct, although a bit trickier. Over 4 hours, if the maximum of the group were sufficient to handle the traffic, there would be problems only in the first chunk of access time (perhaps 4 to 4:30). You would then expect enough additional instances to have launched to resolve any problems. That problems persist until demand decreases at 8 suggests that the group never launches enough instances. This is a case where the maximum value should be tweaked to account for this.

11. **B.** By default, an EC2 Auto Scaling group has a cooldown period of 300 seconds, or 5 minutes.

12. **B.** All of these options are possible with both launch templates and launch configurations except for option B. Only a launch template can be versioned.

13. **A, C.** Long cooldown periods (option A) can result in instances not being started quickly enough to meet demand. Additionally, a scaling event might occur but the step size is not large enough (option C), meaning that multiple scaling events—each with instance startup and cooldown periods involved—must occur to quickly scale out.

14. **A, C.** Only launch templates allow you to use spot instances along on-demand instances, whereas launch configurations allow just on-demand instances. Additionally, T2 instances can only be used with launch templates.

15. **D.** Auto Scaling groups do not restart failed instances (option D). Instead, if an instance fails its health check, a new instance is started up (option C).

16. **C.** Health checks begin on a new instance as soon as it enters the InService state. This ensures that the instance is fully capable of responding to the health check prior to that check being executed.

17. **C.** The most likely answer here, given that health checks are passing, is a spot price change that causes a spot instance to terminate. This occurs to a spot instance regardless of whether or not it is in an Auto Scaling group.

18. **A, B.** Whenever an instance is moved into a Standby state, the Auto Scaling group assumes this change was intentional. It therefore stops health checks and reduces desired capacity by 1 until the instance is put back into the InService state.

19. **C.** The first criterion for termination of an instance is the number of instances in an availability zone. Since zone 3 has the most instances, it will be the zone from which an instance is terminated. Then, the regular priority is followed, as listed in option C.

20. **B, D.** Both options B and D reflect termination policies that are specific to certain types of instances. Option B works only if you have instances with launch templates (which is not required), and option D works only if you are using an allocation strategy to mix spot and on-demand instances.

# Chapter 8: Hubs, Spokes, and Bastion Hosts

1. B. VPC peering connections always begin with pcx, then a dash, and then a random string of numbers. The only connection name here that matches this format is option B.

2. A. A bastion host is a host that is outside of a private VPC, and it provides access to the resources within the VPC (option A). It does not assign any IP addresses but does itself have a public IP address (which often is elastic).

3. A, D. Bastion hosts should be as secure as possible. Of the options provided, using multifactor authentication and whitelisting addresses are the only two that are valid. Bastion hosts typically aren't accessed on port 80, so option B does not make sense in this context. Option C is not helpful as more than just administrators would need to access the bastion host.

4. A. VPC peering can save costs by preventing egress (option A). Data that moves between two peered VPCs will not be egressed and will instead flow across the AWS network, reducing overall egress costs.

5. B. VPCs can be peered across regions, whether or not the two VPCs are in the same account (option B).

6. A, C. This is simply a case of rote memorization, unfortunately. Interregion VPC peering doesn't support jumbo frames (option C) or IPv6 traffic (option A).

7. B, D. Bastion hosts must be accessible from the Internet to be useful. This requires that they exist in a public subnet (option B) and have a public IP address (option D). Though it is common for a bastion host to have an elastic IP address (option C), it is not a requirement.

8. C. Peered VPCs cannot have clashes in their IP addresses, which means nonoverlapping CIDR blocks.

9. A, D. Bastion hosts are typically secured using a variety of mechanisms, especially security groups (option A). They should also be in Auto Scaling groups to ensure they are always available when needed (option D).

10. A. AWS does not allow transitive routing, which is traffic flowing from one VPC peered to another VPC, and then from that VPC to a third peered VPC.

11. D. The key here is that this question represents two different transmissions. The first, from VPC B to VPC A, is allowed, and the second from VPC A to VPC C, is also allowed. This would only be disallowed if traffic were directed to flow from VPC B directly to VPC C.

12. D. This is a bit tricky but raises a good test-taking tip: if you are asked about limits and an answer provides a default limit but says that default can be raised, that is likely the correct answer. In this case, that answer is option D.

**13.** D.  VPC peering connections do not require any hardware to set up or run.

**14.** A.  Bastion hosts and NAT devices are quite similar, and the core difference is in the direction that traffic flows. Bastion hosts allows traffic into private resources from the Internet whereas NAT devices allow private resources to access out to the Internet.

**15.** C.  Neither option A nor B helps you secure or otherwise improve the network you've inherited. Of options C and D, both are valuable, but C provides security and should be done before adding logging (another important step).

**16.** A, D.  Bastion hosts are not for web access (options B, C) but instead for direct access, typically through SSH (option A) and/or RDP (option D).

**17.** D.  Edge-to-edge routing is the exact scenario described in this question: there are two peered VPCs and one of those VPCs also connects to an additional network. Routing is not allowed in AWS from one "edge" (the private additional network) through a middle VPC to the peered VPC.

**18.** B.  In a hub-and-spoke model, you have one central VPC that all other VPCs are peered with. This means that for a model with *n* VPCs, you'd have (*n*-1) peering connections. In this case, with five total VPCs, you'd expect four of those to have peering connections with the central VPC.

**19.** B.  This one takes some careful reading and might even be worth diagramming. Only option B provides a working, legal AWS solution, though: logs are moved to VPC A from both B and C, each with their own VPC peering connections, as transitive routing is disallowed. Then VPC D has its own peering to A for loading data. This is actually a classic hub-and-spoke model using a VPC (A in this case) as a shared services VPC for log aggregation.

**20.** A.  This one isn't hard in concept but takes some very careful reading. You want to route anything that has a destination IP address within a peered VPC through the peering connection with that VPC. In this question, the only answer that matches that is option A.

# Chapter 9: AWS Systems Manager

**1.** D.  While AWS Systems Manager does prevent many critical vulnerabilities through patching, it is not itself a service for alerting users to critical vulnerabilities.

**2.** D.  All AMIs that have Windows or Linux from the Amazon marketplace will have the AWS Systems Manager preinstalled. Anything using a different operating system (such as macOS) or from a third party will need AWS Systems Manager installed.

**3.** B.  Any instance running an SSM agent will need to assume an IAM role for connecting to the AWS Systems Manager service (option B). There is no such policy as AWSSystemsManager (option C).

**4.**   A. This requires pure rote memorization. The name of the policy is AmazonEC2RoleforSSM.

**5.**   A, B. Only AWS instances, on-premises instances, or in some cases other cloud provider instances can be managed by AWS Systems Manager. It cannot manage containers or Lambda functions.

**6.**   A, D. You can create resource groups using tags (option A), which in turn implies you can use a tag to indicate environment, application, and so forth (option D). You cannot create resource groups based on IAM roles or account numbers.

**7.**   C. Resource groups can filter resources based on tag or environment, and they can query based on tags as well. However, they cannot span multiple regions.

**8.**   A, C. AWS Systems Manager supports command, policy, and automation documents.

**9.**   A, B. AWS Systems Manager supports documents in JSON and YAML.

**10.**  D. All of these document types can interact with State Manager.

**11.**  A. The only one of these that is an actual command is the Run command (option A), which is what command documents interact with.

**12.**  B. AWS KMS is the only encryption protocol supported by Session Manager.

**13.**  C, D. State Manager is aimed at compliance, which can in turn help provide useful security measures on your instances.

**14.**  B, D. Both AWS CodeBuild and AWS CodeDeploy can work with the Parameter Store.

**15.**  B. A patch baseline stores the patches that will be automatically deployed to your instances. If you want to avoid a certain patch, simply remove it from the baseline.

**16.**  A, B. During a maintenance window, you can update patches, run PowerShell commands, execute Lambda and step functions, and build AMIs. You cannot remove patches or restart an instance.

**17.**  D. AWS Systems Manager documents can be used cross-platform without any changes (option D).

**18.**  D. No action is required here because the AWS Systems Manager is already open source, and its code is available on GitHub. Note that option C is incorrect because the Systems Manager agent comes preinstalled only with Linux and Windows AMIs (not macOS) and only if those AMIs come from the Amazon Marketplace.

**19.**  B. The Run command allows you to execute scripts and other commands on instances. In this case, a Run command could execute the compliance script needed.

**20.**  B, C. You can change the default patching behavior either by writing an automation document or by writing your own AWS Systems Manager command (options B and C).

# Chapter 10: Amazon Simple Storage Service (S3)

1. D. S3 allows file uploads up to 5 TB, so none of the issues are related to file size limits (options B, C). Instead, the Multipart Upload option will upload larger files—AWS recommends anything larger than 100 MB—in multiple parts and will often resolve the issue.

2. A. This is another question that is tricky unless you work through each part of the URL, piece by piece. The first clue is that this is a website hosted on S3, as opposed to directly accessing an S3 bucket. Where website hosting is concerned, the bucket name is part of the fully qualified domain name (FQDN); where direct bucket access is concerned, the bucket name comes after the FQDN. This is an essential distinction. This means that options B and C are invalid. Then, you need to recall that the S3-website portion of the FQDN is always connected to the region; in other words, it is not a subdomain. The only choice where this is the case is option A.

3. C, D. PUTs of new objects have a read after write consistency. DELETEs and overwrite PUTs have eventual consistency across S3.

4. C. First, note that "on standard class S3" is a red herring and irrelevant to the question. Second, objects on S3 can be 0 bytes. This is equivalent to using touch on a file and then uploading that 0-byte file to S3.

5. C. This is a matter of carefully looking at each URL. Bucket names—when not used as a website—always come after the fully qualified domain name (FQDN); in other words, after the forward slash. That eliminates option A. Additionally, the region always comes earlier in the FQDN than amazonaws.com, eliminating option D. This leaves options C and B. Of the two, option C correctly has the complete region, us-east-2.

6. B. The key here is the phrase "usually accessed multiple times." You really want a blending of S3 standard (most accessible but also highest cost) and S3-IA (documents accessed less frequently and cheaper). Intelligent tiering (option B) provides for this; it will move documents into S3-IA when not accessed, but then when accessed, they are moved back to standard (and located there for additional accesses).

7. A. S3 Standard provides 99.99 percent availability.

8. D. All S3 storage classes provide the same durability: eleven 9s, or 99.999999999 percent.

9. C. S3 One Zone-IA provides 99.5 percent availability.

10. D. All S3 storage classes with the exception of S3 One Zone-IA store data in at least three availability zones, and often more (depending on the region and AZ availability).

11. A. When a new S3 bucket is created, only the bucket creator can access that bucket and its resources.

12. A, D. There are four ways to control access: IAM policies (option A), bucket policies, access control lists (option D), and query string authentication.

**13.** B, C.  SSE-IAM (option A) and Amazon Client Encryption Toolkit are not valid Amazon or AWS tools or services. SSE-S3 and SSE-KMS are, and both are available for encryption.

**14.** B.  The Amazon S3 Encryption Client gives you complete control over your keys.

**15.** A, C.  Amazon Glacier Deep Archive is both less expensive than standard Glacier and also provides fewer access options.

**16.** B, C.  S3 Intelligent-Tiering is ideal for unknown or changing access patterns, as it will adjust the location of files based on usage between S3 Standard and S3 Standard-IA.

**17.** A, D.  Remember that all S3 storage classes share the same durability; this means that option A is true. Then, you need to know that availability decreases moving from S3 Standard to S3 Standard-IA to S3 One-Zone IA. This means that options B and C are false and option D is true.

**18.** A.  Although S3 Intelligent-Tiering moves data between S3 Standard and S3 Standard-IA, its performance is identical to S3 Standard.

**19.** B.  S3 Intelligent-Tiering provides 99.9 percent availability.

**20.** B.  This is pretty straightforward. Since you do not want to move the data out of Glacier, turning on Expedited retrieval is the fastest way to access the data.

# Chapter 11: Elastic Block Store (EBS)

**1.** B.  IOPS stands for input/output operations per second.

**2.** B.  Provisioned IOPS SSD supports 32,000 IOPS, far more than any other volume type.

**3.** D.  All EBS volume types can be as large as 16 tebibytes.

**4.** A.  General-purpose SSDs are ideal for general usage, including a system boot volume.

**5.** C.  A throughput-optimized HDD is perfect for data warehouses, since the workload needs to consistently stream and process large data sets.

**6.** B.  A database workload will need to support a lot of IOPS, and a provisioned IOPS SSD is the best choice for these types of workloads.

**7.** C, D.  Neither a throughput-optimized HDD nor a cold HDD can be selected as boot volumes.

**8.** A.  Default volumes created through the console are general-purpose SSDs.

**9.** A.  Only the two SSD types can be bootable (options A and B). Of those two types, the general-purpose SSD is the cheaper option.

**10.** A.  Default volumes created through the console are general-purpose SSDs.

**11.**  A, B.  Snapshots of EBS volumes are both incremental (option A) and stored on S3 (option B). However, they are accessible only through the EC2 API—not the S3 API—and they are taken while the volume is running, not unmounted.

**12.**  B.  You can always create snapshots from encrypted volumes, and those snapshots will also be encrypted.

**13.**  C.  Unencrypted snapshots can be encrypted by copying them in the AWS console and selecting the option to encrypt the copy.

**14.**  C.  The only reason a snapshot would not contain all of the data from an application using the volume would be if the application or the operating system of the application was caching content. All of the other options are incorrect; volumes and instances do not need to be unmounted or stopped, respectively, and option D is completely made up.

**15.**  B.  Encryption keys are always unique 256-bit AES keys.

**16.**  A, C.  You can either copy the unencrypted snapshot to an encrypted snapshot and then launch a new instance from that (option C), or you can select the option to encrypt the instance at creation time (option A).

**17.**  A.  For any EBS volume that is set to persist beyond the lifetime of an EC2 instance, the data on that volume will stay, regardless of the state of the instance.

**18.**  D.  Root volumes by default will delete on termination of the attached instance. However, by setting the Delete on Termination flag to No, you can prevent this behavior and maintain the data on that volume past the life of the instance.

**19.**  D.  You can always change the volume type of a running volume with the console, API, or CLI.

**20.**  C.  Somewhat surprisingly, AWS states that snapshots of any volume size—from 1 TB to 16 TB—should take the same amount of time, on average. There can be minor inconsistencies, but in general, all snapshots are designed to take the same amount of time.

# Chapter 12: Amazon Machine Image (AMI)

**1.**  C.  AMIs can be public, private, or shared. There is no protected accessibility level.

**2.**  C.  AMIs are available only in a single region. However, they can be copied to other regions (option C). In this question, then, the desired AMI simply needs to be copied from US-West-1 to US-East-2, and then it can be used.

**3.**  A, C.  AMIs are available through Amazon via AWS, through the AWS Marketplace (option C), through the AWS community, and by creating one from an instance (option A). There is no such thing as the Global AMI Marketplace (option B), and vendors make their AMIs available through AWS, not an external GitHub repository (option D).

**4.** A, D. AMIs can be either instance-backed or EBS-backed. There is no such thing as a volume-backed AMI or an EMS-backed AMI.

**5.** A. Shared AMIs are available for broad use, but permissions to use the AMI must be granted by the owner of the AMI.

**6.** A, B. Private AMIs cannot be shared across accounts. You would need to convert the AMI to a shared AMI (option B) and then, as the owner of the AMI, grant permissions to your coworker to use that AMI (option A).

**7.** A. If you expect workloads to be short-lived—such as in a volatile Auto Scaling group as described in the question—then an instance-backed AMI is your best choice. EBS-backed AMIs are more suitable for preserving data for longer periods of time, and there is no such thing as a transient-backed AMI.

**8.** B. EBS-backed AMIs are ideal for longer-lived jobs. The only short-lived instance in the list of answers is a container-based application (option B), so that would be a poor candidate for an EBS-backed AMI.

**9.** C. Only accounts in which an AMI is launched are billed (option C), regardless of the creator or owner of the AMI.

**10.** B, D. You can copy an AMI to a new region, but the resulting AMI is both distinct from the source AMI (option B) and has its own unique identifier (option D).

**11.** D. A deregistered AMI cannot be used to start an instance. You can, however, register a new AMI from an EBS snapshot.

**12.** A, C. EBS-backed AMIs can be encrypted using a KMS customer master key or a customer managed key that you specify.

**13.** B. The action to launch an EC2 instance from an AMI is called RunInstances.

**14.** C. This is a bit tricky and must be memorized. New instances are, unless otherwise specified, set to use the encryption state of the AMI's source snapshot. This preserves the encryption from AMI to instance.

**15.** A, B. You can both set encryption by default (option A) and supply encryption instructions at instance launch (option B). Although you can encrypt an instance after launch, that does not satisfy the question's requirement to keep the instance encrypted at all times, and using a different AMI is not a valid option.

**16.** B. Amazon images are easily distinguished because they consistently use amazon as an owner in the account field.

**17.** B. You can easily share an AMI with other AWS accounts by adding the account IDs to the AMI's permissions. You do not need to make the AMI public to accomplish this.

**18.** D. There is no limit to the number of AWS accounts with which an AMI can be shared and used.

**19.** D. AWS actually doesn't copy launch permissions, user-defined tags, or S3 bucket permissions when an AMI is copied from one region to another. All of these must be re-created on the new AMI.

**20.** B. When an AMI is copied to a new account, a duplicate of that AMI is created in the new account. The new AMI is owned by the owner of the new account, which in this case is your coworker.

# Chapter 13: IAM

**1.** C. Users of AWS are responsible for security in the cloud, whereas AWS is responsible for security of the cloud.

**2.** A, D. AWS is responsible for security of the cloud, meaning that they maintain and secure the physical servers and actual networking equipment within AWS. Individual users must handle application security as well as network port configuration (this latter is typically accomplished through network ACLs and security groups).

**3.** A, B. Users of AWS are responsible for security in the cloud, which in this case would include the operating system of any EC2 instances as well as encrypting (or choosing to encrypt) data. AWS manages RDS instance security and operating systems as well as their physical datacenters.

**4.** C. Shared responsibility indicates that both the user and AWS has some significant responsibility. In the case of EC2 instances (option C), AWS patches and maintains the host EC2 instances, whereas users maintain and patch the operating system running on those hosts.

**5.** B. When using AWS-provided encryption options such as SSE-S3 and SSE-KMS, AWS handles the actual encryption process. However, the user must specify what is to be encrypted, resulting in a shared responsibility.

**6.** B, C. The two types of users in an AWS account are the root user and IAM users. There can be only one root user but as many IAM users as desired.

**7.** C. The principle of least privilege means that users have only enough permissions to do their job. Although options A and B are valid principles in a solid AWS IAM setup, they do not define the principle of least privilege.

**8.** A, B. Users can identify themselves through a username (option A) for the web console and through an access key (option B) for the AWS API and SDK.

**9.** D. Key pairs are created primarily for access to AWS resources, specifically an EC2 instance. Access to the web console is through a username and password, and access to the CLI and SDK is through an access key.

**10.** C. For accessing running EC2 instances, you'll need a valid key pair. Using this key pair, you can use SSH or RDP to access and authenticate running instances.

11. C. Unlike with a group, permissions granted through a role are temporary for a user.

12. B. EC2 instances cannot be assigned group membership and can only be assigned policies through IAM roles. An IAM policy can be directly assigned to an instance, though.

13. D. IAM policies can be assigned to user, groups, and roles.

14. A, D. AWS recommends the use of managed policies (option D) rather than inline policies, because managed policies are defined once and can be assigned to multiple users, groups, and/or roles (option A).

15. D. The version of a policy references the language used in the policy (option D), rather than anything related to the specific policy or policy author.

16. A, B. Valid policies have versions, statements, sids (option B), effects (option A), principals, actions, resources, and conditions. They do not have ids or affects.

17. B, D. The principal indicated in a policy should reference an IAM user (option B), role, or federated user (option D), and provide access to resources for that user.

18. A, B. Passwords both expire and are subject to password policies set in the AWS Console or otherwise. Access keys, on the other hand, are long-lived (option A) and are not governed by password policies (option B). This makes them potentially more dangerous if care is not taken to regulate and control them.

19. C, D. The term access key in AWS parlance refers to both an access key ID and a secret access key. The two as a pair provide programmatic access to the AWS CLI and SDK.

20. A, C. You can import your own keys into AWS KMS (option C) or allow AWS KMS to create keys for you (option A).

# Chapter 14: Reporting and Logging

1. D. Monitoring and reporting in AWS provides information that can be used in security, compliance, and performance. All are equally important in specific contexts, so the best answer here is option D.

2. B. For gathering metrics, Amazon CloudWatch (option B) is the best choice. AWS Config gathers information on configuration and compliance, and AWS CloudTrail monitors API calls.

3. C. AWS CloudTrail provides insight into API calls, and a client interacting with a REST API is exactly that.

4. B. The Amazon CloudWatch Logs Agent, when installed on an instance, provides metrics not available in any other manner, including using the basic Amazon CloudWatch capabilities.

5. B. AWS CloudTrail maintains collected data on API calls for 90 days by default, although this setting can be changed.

**6.** D. AWS CloudTrail will collect information on any API call made—even between AWS services, such as in option C—within AWS. The only option that is not an API call is a login to the console (option D). That information is collected, but not by AWS CloudTrail.

**7.** B, D. AWS CloudTrail trails apply to a single region by default (option D) but can be applied to all regions (meaning options A and C are both false). They also collect both management and data events (option B).

**8.** C. Management events in AWS CloudTrail relate to security, registering devices, configuring security rules, routing, and setting up logging. In the options, this would include A, B, and D. Option A is a security event, B is setting up a security rule for routing, and D is a routing data rule. Option C, on the other hand, is related to data and is a data event rather than a management event.

**9.** A, C. Because data events capture the movement, creation, and removal of data, they are typically much higher volume than management events (option A). Data events are also disabled by default (option C), making them different from management events.

**10.** A, C. The RunInstances and TerminateInstances events are considered write events. This is easiest to remember because they are not read events, and AWS provides only two options: read and write. Collecting these events, then, would require a trail be set to Write-Only or All (which collects all events).

**11.** A. AWS CloudTrail will collect the first copy of any management event in a region for free. Any additional copies incur cost, though, as do all copies (including the first) of a data event.

**12.** A. A single Amazon CloudWatch alarm can monitor only a single metric at once.

**13.** D. CloudWatch alarms have three states: OK, ALARM, and INSUFFICIENT_DATA. INVALID_DATA is not a valid alarm state.

**14.** A, C. In this scenario, there would need to be three out-of-threshold data points within the evaluation period of 10 minutes to trigger an alarm. This means that both options A and C would trigger an alarm. Note that it is possible that the scenario in option D would trigger an alarm, depending on when the out-of-threshold metrics occurred (inside 10 minutes), but it is not clear from the answer, so options A and C are better answers.

**15.** A,C. There are four possible settings for handling missing data points: notBreaching (A), breaching, ignore, and missing (C).

**16.** C. A log stream is a collection of events from a single source (option C). Option As and B describe a log group, and there is no CloudWatch analog for option D.

**17.** A. AWS Config does not provide mediation mechanisms. You can write code to remediate situations that cause notifications via AWS Config, but the remediation capability is not a standard part of AWS Config itself.

**18.** A, C. AWS Config will notify you if a bucket has been granted public access (provided you have set that baseline up in AWS Config). You would then need to remediate that access, and that would require AWS Lambda (option C).

**19.** C. Configuration items do not include IAM-related information (option C). They do include event IDs (option A), configuration data about the resource, basic information about the resource such as tags, a map of resource relationships (option B), and metadata about the CI, including the version of the CI itself (option D).

**20.** D. A change-triggered rule will be evaluated every time a resource is changed, meaning that it is the most immediate evaluation available. Periodic rules are evaluated against a specific schedule. Tagged and immediate evaluations are not actual AWS concepts.

# Chapter 15: Additional Security Tools

**1.** B, D. Amazon Inspector offers two types of assessments: network assessments and host assessments.

**2.** C. Assessment templates are used by Amazon Inspector to determine what rules should be used in assessing and evaluating an environment.

**3.** B. Host assessments require an agent to be installed, but network assessments do not.

**4.** D. The Runtime Behavior Analysis package identifies risky behavior, including open and unused ports. Although the Security Best Practices package is also related to this area, it is the Runtime Behavior Analysis package that will identify open ports specifically.

**5.** D. The Network Reachability rules package covers all of these areas, as well as security groups, NACLs, subnets, VPCs, direct connections, and Internet gateways.

**6.** B, C. Amazon GuardDuty looks for reconnaissance, instance compromise, and account compromise.

**7.** A, D. Vulnerability scans typically look for IP addresses, hostnames, open ports, and misconfigured protocols. These are key areas to focus on when securing your system.

**8.** C. Amazon GuardDuty stores security findings in the region in which they apply, so with three regions, you would have three different sets of findings.

**9.** B. In a multi-account setup, findings remain in individual accounts but are aggregated into the master account as well.

**10.** A, B. Amazon GuardDuty analyzes AWS CloudTrail, VPC flow logs, and AWS DNS logs.

**11.** A, C. Security findings are maintained by region. To aggregate findings across regions, you'd need to use AWS CloudWatch events and push findings to a common data store, like Amazon S3. You can then use those findings—now in a single S3 bucket—however you like.

**12.** D. Amazon GuardDuty analyzes AWS CloudTrail, VPC flow logs, and AWS DNS logs. It does not offer analysis of EC2 instance logs directly (although some of that data is available through flow logs).

**13.** C.  Amazon GuardDuty is not a log storage service and does not offer options for retaining logs.

**14.** C.  You can both suspend and disable the GuardDuty service. However, only disabling the service will result in findings and configurations being deleted.

**15.** A, C.  Amazon GuardDuty delivers findings to two places: the GuardDuty console and AWS CloudWatch events. There is no such thing as an Amazon GuardDuty CLI, and Amazon Inspector does not have access to GuardDuty findings.

**16.** A.  Amazon GuardDuty threat intelligence stores IP addresses (as well as domains) that are known to be used by malicious attackers on the Internet.

**17.** B.  You can run network assessments without host access. However, you cannot run host assessments without installing the Amazon Inspector agent on the hosts, which would require host access.

**18.** A.  You can set Amazon CloudWatch Events to monitor scaling events, and then launch an assessment based on that event.

**19.** D.  Amazon Inspector offers four severity levels: High, Medium, Low, and Informational.

**20.** A.  Metrics are published to Amazon CloudWatch via Amazon Inspector.

# Chapter 16: Virtual Private Cloud

**1.** A, D.  AWS does not provide support for IPv6 NAT devices, including NAT instances (option A) and NAT gateways (option D).

**2.** C.  This could be memorized, and /16 turns out to be a common CIDR block mask (along with /24). However, you could also start with /32 (a single IP) and just double the number as you go from /32 to /31 to /30, all the way to /16. So a /24 has 256 IP addresses, /20 has 4096, all the way up to /16 with 65,536 addresses (option C).

**3.** D.  The key here is that you need 16 usable IP addresses. However, AWS will use the first and last address of any given network range. (Technically, AWS reserves the right to use those IPs and doesn't always take advantage of that.) Therefore, /28, which has 16 addresses, only provides 14 usable addresses. The next size up would be /27 (option D), which is correct in this case.

**4.** C.  The number after the slash in CIDR notation provides the number of bits available for the network address; the remaining number of bits for the host address is 32 minus the bits already used. So here, the bits available for the host address would be $32 - 20$ (in /20), so 12 bits (option C).

**5.** A, D.  Any instance responding to IPv6 requests should have an IPv6 address and reside within a VPC with IPv6 addresses available through a CIDR block. So you need a CIDR block assigned with the VPC (option A) and an IPv6 address assigned to the instance (option D).

**6.** C. All IPv6 CIDR blocks in AWS are /56.

**7.** D. You cannot select specific IPv6 addresses when using IPv6 within AWS. Addresses are instead automatically allocated from Amazon's pool of IPv6 addresses.

**8.** D. You cannot select specific IPv6 addresses when using IPv6 within AWS. Addresses are instead automatically allocated from Amazon's pool of IPv6 addresses.

**9.** B. AWS restricts VPCs to using a /16 netmask, resulting in 65,536 IP addresses.

**10.** B. This question provides somewhat limited information, but it does give you everything you need to work this problem. First, there are nine applications, and each has three environments. That means you'll need 27 application environments (since they can't be mixed). But you can share VPCs and subnets, it appears; three applications can exist within each VPC, and there does not appear to be a restriction against sharing space within the same environment. That means the 27 applications can be reduced to nine "logical blocks." But wait—each application needs a private subnet and a public one. This means that you'll need 18 subnets total: nine application subnets with a public and a private component each.

**11.** A, D. Public subnets must have a route to an Internet gateway (option D), and that gateway must be attached to the VPC in which the subnet exists (option A).

**12.** B, D. Egress-only Internet gateways are only required when you have IPv6 addresses (option D) and hosts with those addresses are in private subnets that need to access the Internet (option B). This is because IPv6 addresses are not able to use NAT devices to connect to the Internet.

**13.** B. Traffic from private instances should flow from the private instance to a NAT device, which then routes traffic to an Internet gateway and finally out to the Internet (option B).

**14.** A. In almost every scenario where a private instance needs to access the Internet, a NAT gateway is preferred by AWS as it is managed. However, in situations where you might have extremely high bandwidth requirements—which is the case in this question—a NAT instance is better as it allows for customized sizing and management.

**15.** C. In general, this is a case for a VPC endpoint. Both options B and C are types of VPC endpoints, but S3 requires a gateway endpoint (option C), rather than an interface endpoint, and is therefore correct.

**16.** B. For most services, an interface endpoint is the correct type of VPC endpoint to use. However, for Amazon S3 or Amazon DynamoDB you'd need to use a gateway endpoint. That makes option B correct here.

**17.** C, D. VPN tunnels in AWS require a virtual private gateway (option D) and a customer gateway (option C).

**18.** C. This question is not as hard as it looks, as many of the answers are technically incorrect. If you are allowing resources from another subnet and want to retain the security of those resources, you can chain security groups and simply use another security group as the source for traffic (option C).

**19.** C.  Be careful here! Although AWS typically rearranges NACL rules to order them from low to high in a top-to-bottom visual sense, it is the rule number that matters, not the "position" in the NACL table. NACLs are evaluated from the lowest-numbered rule to the highest.

**20.** D.  The default NACL always has a rule numbered 100 that allows in all inbound traffic. You need to counteract this by either removing it or adding a rule—which the question indicates has been done—but also ensuring that rule is numbered lower than rule 100 to take precedence.

# Chapter 17: Route 53

**1.** B.  DNS operates over port 53 (B), which is actually far more important to know than that it also is the source of the naming of the Route 53 service in AWS.

**2.** D.  Although Route 53 does support text records, the record type is TXT, not TEXT, so D is incorrect. Route53 does support NAPTR, NS, and SPF records.

**3.** A, B.  You will need an A record to map an incoming hostname (like `wisdompetmedicine.com`) to an S3 bucket. You will also need a CNAME record to map a subdomain, like `www .wisdompetmedicine.com`, to the bare domain name.

**4.** A.  You would need an AAAA recordset because this is an IPv6 address. A records point domain names to IPv4 addresses, and AAAA records point domain names to IPv6 addresses.

**5.** C.  Whenever you need to associate a domain name with an AWS service—such as Cloud-Front, S3, or a VPC endpoint—you have to use an Alias record rather than an A or AAAA record. This is because most AWS services do not expose static IP addresses, which an A record expects.

**6.** B.  This is a textbook case for a failover routing policy. If traffic cannot reach a primary instance or service, Route 53 will "fail over" routing to a backup or secondary instance.

**7.** D.  When you have multiple hosts that can respond to traffic and are only concerned about the health of the hosts, you can use a multivalue answer policy. In this case, you'd point the responses at the various Application Load Balancers (ALBs).

**8.** C.  This should be a pretty easy one: latency routing policies return responses to users based on network latency.

**9.** D.  All of the options allow for multiple hosts. It is easy to forget that a simple routing policy allows multiple hosts to be entered; it simply returns responses randomly, without any of the logic applied for most policies.

**10.** C.  This is a good use case for weight routing. You can send (for example) 10 percent of traffic to the new site and the remaining traffic to the existing site using weighting values.

**11.** C. Numbers in a weighted routing policy indicate the percentage of traffic to route to that host, in relation to the sum of all the weight numbers. In this case, option C would add up in total to 50, so you'd double each value to get its percentage of traffic: 20 percent for host 1, 50 percent for host 2, and 30 percent for host 3. This is the requirement in the question, so it is the correct answer.

**12.** A. Route 53 uses VPCs to manage privately hosted zones, so you are required to use VPCs with private DNS. Option A, then, is not possible. Private DNS does support exposing records to other VPCs, regions, and accounts.

**13.** C, D. Private DNS has very few limitations and, in most cases, can do everything a publicly hosted zone can. However, health checks are not possible on instances that expose only private IP addresses, and you cannot expose a private record to the Internet under any circumstances.

**14.** B, C. For Amazon Route 53 Traffic Flow to work, you'll need both a traffic policy (option B) and a policy record (option C). The traffic policy is the rules to define how traffic should flow, and a policy record connects that traffic policy to an application's DNS name.

**15.** A, C. If you want to point one DNS name at another DNS name, you typically use a CNAME (option A). This would only be a problem if the CNAME was intended to receive requests for a zone apex record (like example.com) rather than a subdomain (like www.example.com) and redirect them. You can also use AWS Alias records to point requests to an existing domain with policies already set up (option C).

**16.** C. You can set up health checks in Amazon Route 53 to check an endpoint, other health checks already set up, or alarms in CloudWatch. You cannot directly monitor via Cloud-Trail (option C), although you could monitor an alarm that was triggered by a CloudTrail event.

**17.** A, B. Amazon Route 53 will stop sending requests to failing hosts and will also resend requests when that host responds as healthy again (options A and B). Although retries and alarms in CloudWatch can be set up, they are not by default, so both option C and option D are incorrect.

**18.** B. Latency-based policies are focused on latency (as the name implies). This does not always translate to the closest region to the requestor, as some regions may be closer to the requestor but have longer lag times.

**19.** A. A geoproximity policy, like a geolocation policy, routes users to the closest geographical region. This means that options B and C are incorrect, as they are common to both types of routing policy. Option D would imply the use of latency-based routing, leaving only option A. This is the purpose of a geoproximity policy: you can apply a bias to send more or less traffic to a certain region.

**20.** B, C. Health checks are not always turned on in Amazon Route 53 (and generally are not by default), so that's the first thing to check (option B). All policies can use health checks, so option A is incorrect, and an ALB is not required to use health checks, making D incorrect as well. It takes three successive failures of a health check by default to take a host out of commission, so option C is also a possible answer.

# Chapter 18: CloudFormation

1.  **A, B.** AWS provides services like CloudFormation that allow for capturing environments, although in JSON and YAML rather than XML (so option D is incorrect). This does allow deployments to be identical (option A), though, as well as building identical environments (option B). You can replace manual steps with code, but it's not JavaScript (so option C is incorrect).

2.  **C.** CloudFormation uses JSON and YAML for actual notation, so options A and D are associated (and not correct choices). Of the two remaining options, CloudFormation does often use the AWS API, but not the AWS SDK, for interaction. So option C is the choice that is not associated with CloudFormation.

3.  **C.** AWSTemplateFormatVersion indicates the version of the template—and therefore what its capabilities are—by indicating the date associated with that version.

4.  **C.** CloudFormation templates allow for all the provided answers, but they require only a Resources component to be valid.

5.  **B.** The Parameters section in a template provides for indication of values used throughout the rest of the template.

6.  **B, D.** You can assign a resource a logical name in a CloudFormation template (option B) but not an actual AWS-specific name (so option D is also true). AWS then maps your logical names to the actual AWS resource names.

7.  **C.** While you can separate resources using names or prefixes, the AWS-recommended approach is to use tagging (option C).

8.  **A.** CloudFormation provides an Automatic Rollback On Error option that will cause all AWS resources created to be deleted if the entire stack doesn't complete successfully.

9.  **B.** You can use CloudFormation's WaitCondition resource to act as a block of further action until a signal is received from your application (in this case, when the instance scripts finish running).

10. **D.** CloudFormation allows for creation of all these resource types (and quite a few more).

11. **D.** You can use the AWS CLI, API, SDK, and the console to execute CloudFormation stacks.

12. **A.** You create CloudFormation templates and indicate what should occur. Instances are then specific runs of those templates.

13. **C.** Parameters can be lists, comma-delimited lists, numbers, and strings. They cannot be arrays (option C).

14. **D.** CIDR blocks come in specific patterns, and therefore you should use AllowedPattern to ensure they are properly supplied.

**15.** B. A stack in AWS terminology is the set of AWS resources created and managed by a CloudFormation template.

**16.** A. You can mark parameters as NoEcho to ensure that a certain parameter value is not shown as the template executes.

**17.** B. The URL to a web application created by a stack is an output value. One way to think of this is to see that the value cannot be created until the stack runs.

**18.** A. This would be an input value, as it is something user-supplied and required by the template at runtime.

**19.** C. Here, you really don't want to use a template parameter. Instead, it's better to have CloudFormation look up the AMI name and location through a lookup table that would always hold current values.

**20.** A. Template parameters are the preferred way to allow for user input during stack creation.

# Chapter 19: Elastic Beanstalk

**1.** A, C. While all of these concepts are supported by Elastic Beanstalk, AWS specifically calls out single-instance deployment (A) and load balancer and Auto Scaling group (C) as supported models. Elastic Beanstalk also supports an Auto Scaling group–only model.

**2.** C. The load balancer and Auto Scaling group model is ideal for production (because of the scalability) and for web-based environments, because multiple requests can be distributed across multiple hosts.

**3.** D. It's important to note that AWS considers load-balanced environments as ideal for web-based instances, but not necessarily for databases or backend services. This is because many databases should scale but not necessarily have a load balancer in front of them. For databases, you would want to use an auto-scaling group to allow automatic scaling, but you would not want a load balancer in front of the database servers. This sort of question can come up on the exam and is not always obvious to answer.

**4.** A, D. `platform.yaml` requires three fields: a version number (D), a provisioner type, and a provisioner template (A).

**5.** A, C. `custom_platform.json` is pretty straightforward in defining everything your custom platform needs, such as the AMI details (A) and custom variables (C). However, it does not define items that are nonstatic, such as the number of instances that might be used or the supported languages.

**6.** A, D. Elastic Beanstalk supports a number of deployment models, including rolling with additional batches and immutable (A and D). The other two options are made-up terms.

**7.** A, C. Both the rolling deployment and the rolling deployment with additional batches deployment models allow you to ensure your application is always running (A). But you would then use the additional batches option to ensure you maintain maximum capacity throughout the process (C).

**8.** D. An immutable deployment is often slower and more expensive than the other models but ensures both the health and maximum confidence in a new deployment.

**9.** C. Both versions of a rolling deployment as well as an immutable deployment satisfy the no-downtime requirement. However, the rolling deployment is the least expensive option. Additionally, because you have no requirement to maintain capacity, you can avoid the extra costs of using additional batches or an immutable deployment.

**10.** D. All of these are configurable options for Elastic Beanstalk. In fact, there is very little that you cannot configure when using Elastic Beanstalk.

**11.** A, C. Blue/green deployments require multiple environments (C) that can run side by side as well as Route 53 (or something similar) for weighted routing policies. Although you can use Elastic Beanstalk, it is not required, and Amazon RDS is unrelated.

**12.** D. There is no difference in security between an Elastic Beanstalk environment and a manual one. In both cases, there are recommendations, but you ultimately must manage and set up security in the cloud.

**13.** B, D. The two policies provided by Elastic Beanstalk are AWSElasticBeanstalkReadOnlyAccess and AWSElasticBeanstalkFullAccess.

**14.** D. Elastic Beanstalk automatically creates a publicly available endpoint for your application in a default deployment.

**15.** C. Permissions for Elastic Beanstalk are managed through IAM, just as all permissions in AWS are.

**16.** A, D. Just as you are required to use IAM permissions for accessing Elastic Beanstalk along with the rest of the AWS platform, you use your access key (A) and secret key (D) for accessing the Elastic Beanstalk API in the same way you'd access any other AWS API.

**17.** D. Elastic Beanstalk allows usage of any AWS-supported database.

**18.** D. Elastic Beanstalk will automatically perform minor version updates, but you must perform any major updates to ensure backward compatibility and application functionality is not interrupted.

**19.** B, C. Elastic Beanstalk automatically handles minor updates (A), and IAM permissions apply to all environments (D) and don't get "rolled out." However, you can use a cloned environment to test new features (B) or a major version update (C).

**20.** A, C. Elastic Beanstalk will store application files and server log files in S3.

# Index

**Note to the Reader:** Throughout this index **boldfaced** page numbers indicate primary discussions of a topic. *Italicized* page numbers indicate illustrations.